# FIFTH EDITION

# WRITING THEMES ABOUT LITERATURE

### Edgar V. Roberts

*Herbert H. Lehman College*
*of*
*The City University of New York*

PRENTICE-HALL, INC., Englewood Cliffs, New Jersey 07632

*Library of Congress Cataloging in Publication Data*

ROBERTS, EDGAR V.
    Writing themes about literature

    Includes index.
    1. English language—Rhetoric.   2. Literature—
Study and teaching.   I. Title.
PE1408.R593   1983        808'.0668        82-25027
ISBN 0-13-971655-6

Editorial/production supervision and interior design: Virginia Rubens
Cover design: Diane Saxe
Manufacturing buyer: Harry P. Baisley

ISBN 0-13-971655-6

PRENTICE-HALL INTERNATIONAL, INC., *London*
PRENTICE-HALL OF AUSTRALIA PTY. LIMITED, *Sydney*
EDITORA PRENTICE-HALL DO BRASIL, LTDA., *Rio de Janeiro*
PRENTICE-HALL CANADA INC., *Toronto*
PRENTICE-HALL OF INDIA PRIVATE LIMITED, *New Delhi*
PRENTICE-HALL OF JAPAN, INC., *Tokyo*
PRENTICE-HALL OF SOUTHEAST ASIA PTE. LTD., *Singapore*
WHITEHALL BOOKS LIMITED, *Wellington, New Zealand*

# Contents

# To the Instructor

In offering the fifth edition of *Writing Themes About Literature* I have tried to keep and strengthen those qualities that have occasioned so much support from so many of you over the years. As always, my approach is based not on genres, from which theme assignments are to be somehow determined, but instead, each chapter is designed to produce full-length student themes on any assigned text, regardless of genre. The chapters, naturally, may also be used as the basis of study and classroom discussions about the various approaches. In addition, they may be used for paragraph-length assignments. The result is that the book offers great scope and variety either for a one-semester composition course or for a two-semester or three-quarter sequence, with the possibility of complete or close to complete use.

As in past editions of *Writing Themes About Literature*, the chapters are arranged in order of difficulty, going from simpler to more complex matters as your students progress. With the précis theme in Chapter 1, students may begin with the simplest form of writing about any of the genres. The first three themes become broader in scope, with Chapter 3, on likes or dislikes, being new in this edition. The next three are designed primarily for narrative (both prose and poetry) and drama. Applicable to any of the genres are the next four chapters, including that on imagery, a "literary" subject that is essential to the study of just about all writing. (On the advice of a number of readers, I have placed this chapter earlier in the sequence of chapters than in past editions.) These chapters provide a number of reading and writing techniques that build to the comparison–contrast theme. This theme could suitably employ any analytic technique that students have acquired up to that point in the course. The theme of extended comparison could be an assignment that might be made as the long theme for the one-semester course.

From the eleventh to the eighteenth chapters, the topics are more technical and sophisticated. The later chapters (i.e., evaluation, review, and research) may be considered as approaches which combine and build upon any and all of the various techniques of analysis that students have been developing in the earlier chapters. As in the past, I have kept the chapter on film because of the possibilities that it affords for analyzing the films that are now being introduced as a regular feature of many courses as a complement to written literature.

Although you might wish to assign the chapters in sequence throughout your course, you are at liberty to assign them as you choose, in any order you wish. One instructor, for example, might decide to omit the first two chapters and repeat assignments such as those on character and setting. Another might prefer not to use the longer comparison-contrast theme, but might repeat the shorter one for a number of separate assignments such as comparative studies of imagery, structure, character, personal likes, or point of view. Still another might wish to use just a few of the chapters, assigning them two or more times until it seems clear that the students have overcome all problems with the materials. The book offers the possibility for such uses according to the instructor's needs.

As in each past edition of *Writing Themes About Literature,* the chapters are composed of two parts. The first is a discussion of the problems raised by a particular literary approach, and the second is a sample theme (or two, or in one case, three) showing how the problems may be treated in a theme.

I have designed all changes in the descriptive sections to emphasize the process of writing itself. Most of these sections are extensively revised; some are almost entirely rewritten. I had always planned these sections as instruction in the process of understanding literary concepts, preparing materials for a theme, and writing the theme. My changes bring this process into even stronger focus. All discussions of analytical concepts have the thrust of enabling students to know what to look for and what to do in the invention–prewriting stages of their themes.

Keeping with the plan to develop the book in an ascending order of difficulty, and also to emphasize the in-course, practical nature of the writing assignments, in revising and rewriting the first half of this book I have tried to minimize references to critical problems that are of interest mainly to the student of literature. Generally, I have cut discussions of exceptions, qualifications, and "pitfalls" in favor of including these at the appropriate places in the Instructor's Manual.

In the latter half of the book, however, I have assumed that your students will have become more sophisticated and increasingly more expert, and I have made revisions accordingly. Users of past editions will recognize great changes in the chapter on prosody (13). I have divided the subject into three parts—rhythm, segments, and rhyme—each one of which may produce a separate theme. Many responses to earlier editions have shown that, although prosody is shunned in some one-semester introductory classes, it is nevertheless expected in many programs and in many advanced placement and graduate record examinations. Therefore I hope that my revised treatment of the topic in the fifth edition of *Writing Themes About Literature* will prove helpful for both themes and detailed study.

The fourteenth chapter is also extensively modified and changed from earlier editions. It has been divided into two parts, one a general theme on close reading techniques (Chapter 8 in the fourth edition) and the other a specific close reading for style. My rationale in this change is that instructors might wish to use either part, depending on the level of students and the goals and interests of the course.

The remaining chapters through seventeen are retained from earlier editions, with a notable change being the inclusion of three sample themes rather than one in Chapter 15 to show the three different types of reviews described in that chapter. This alteration does not simply represent a change, I believe, but an innovation. In Chapter 17 there are a number of excisions and other changes. Chapter 18, on the research theme, has been taken from its old position in the Appendix and expanded. With all these changes, it may be said that the fifth edition of *Writing Themes About Literature* is truly comprehensive for courses of composition in which literature is introduced, and also for literature courses at any level.

The sample themes are presented in the belief that the word *imitation* does not have to be preceded by adjectives like *slavish* or *mere*. The purpose is to give students a concrete visualization of what might be done on particular assignments. Such examples, I believe, help them in their own composing and writing. With the sample in mind, they have a construction that gives them something to aim for. Without such an example, they must add the task of creating their own form of expression to the already formidable need for understanding new concepts and interpreting a new work of literature. Although some students will follow the samples closely, others will wish to adapt the discussions and samples to their own needs or wishes. The samples thus encourage students to write at a more advanced level than they otherwise might be able to do.

Because the sample themes are guides, they represent a full treatment of each of the various topics. Nevertheless, in this edition they have been kept within the approximate lengths of most assignments in freshman classes. If students are writing outside of class, they can readily create themes as full as the samples. Even though the samples treat an average of three aspects of particular topics (making for the traditional five-para-graph theme), there is nothing to prevent assigning only one aspect, either for an impromptu or for an outside-class theme. For example, using the chapter on setting, you might assign a paragraph about the use of setting in only the first scene of a story, or you might require a paragraph about interior settings, or about references to a particular color, or about the use of light and darkness. With such variations, not only the entire sample theme, but separate parts, may be used as a guide.

To make the sample themes more accessible to students, where possible I have based them on the pieces included in Appendix C (many of the discussions are also based on these). This practice (except for longer works) was adopted in the second edition of *Writing Themes About Literature*, but reader response did not warrant its continuance in the third and fourth editions. Now, because of renewed recommendations, it is adopted sys-tematically here, with the exception of several of the later chapters, where my assumption has been that at more advanced levels instructors would be basing assignments on longer works (e.g., *Hamlet, Black Elk Speaks*), or on full-length films (e.g., *Virgin Spring*). Thus the student studying point of view can compare the sample theme on that topic with the complete text of Frank O'Connor's "First Confession" which is printed in Appendix C. This story is also used in the two comparison–contrast themes in Chapter 10, in the sample theme on character developed extensively in the intro-ductory section on the writing process, and in the first part of Chapter 14. It is my hope that my reliance on these anthologized works will give the fifth edition a unity and coherence that will help students in understanding the nature of their own assignments.

Following each sample theme is a commentary—a feature new in the fourth edition and continued in the fifth—presented to help students make the connection between the precepts in the first part of the chapter and the example in the second.

My hope is that all revisions and changes will be readable and clear. Throughout, I have tried to use an easy, "plain" style, to borrow a de-scription from classical rhetoricians. This has meant a general shortening of sentences and paragraphs, and a preference for concrete words of the least number of syllables that correctness will allow. The success of my attempts will have to await the responses of students as expressed in their themes.

The fifth edition brings into focus something that has always been true of *Writing Themes About Literature*. The book is to be used in the classroom as a practical guide for writing. It is also a guide to a number of literary approaches which are clarified for students through the reinforcement of writing. The chapters are writing assignments and the goal is to improve student writing. The reading of literary works is introduced as the means of developing support for ideas during the early stages of planning, drafting, and actual writing of themes. In short, the stress throughout the book is on the process of writing.

This method, which has been constant in my book since its first edition appeared in 1964, is designed to equip students to face the situations encountered in college. There they are required to write about problems in other subjects like psychology, economics, sociology, biology, and political science. Instructors in these departments present texts or ask their students to develop raw data, and they assign writing on this basis. Writing is on external, written materials, not on descriptions of the student's own experiences or on opinions. Writing is about reading.

Yet we instructors of composition face the problem we have always faced. On the one hand the needs of other departments have caused a wide diversification of subject matter, creating both a strain on the general knowledge of the staff and also a certain thematic disunity. On the other, in programs where personal experiences or offhand topic materials are the subject matter, the course has little bearing on writing for other courses. As an institutional matter, recent emphasis on writing-across-the-curriculum has created a greater awareness of the disciplinary writing needs of other departments. But coordinators and instructors of composition still face the problem of content in the basic writing courses. With a background in literature, the English faculty has the task of meeting the service needs of the institution without compromising their own disciplinary commitment.

The approach in this book is suited to deal with this problem. Teachers can work with their own discipline—literature—while also fulfilling their primary responsibility of teaching writing. Thus the book is designed to keep all these problems in perspective:

- The requirement of the institution for composition.

- The need of students to develop writing skills based on written texts.

- The responsibility of English faculty to teach writing while still working within their own area of expertise.

It is therefore gratifying to claim that the approach in *Writing Themes About Literature* has been tested for many years. It is no longer new, but it is still novel. It works. It gives coherence to the sometimes fragmented composition course. It also provides for adaptation and, as I have stressed, variety. Using the book, you can develop a virtually endless number of new topics for themes. One obvious benefit is the possibility of entirely eliminating not only the traditional "theme barrels" of infamous memory in fraternity and sorority houses, but also the newer interference from business "enterprises" that provide themes to order.

While *Writing Themes About Literature* is designed, as I have said in the past, as a rhetoric of practical criticism for students, it is based on profoundly held convictions. I believe that true liberation in a liberal arts curriculum is achieved only through clearly defined goals. Just to make assignments and to let students do with them what they can is to encourage them to continue in a state of frustration and mental enslavement. But if students can develop a deep knowledge of specific approaches to subject material, they can begin to develop some of that expertness which is essential to freedom. As Pope said:

> True ease in writing comes from art, not chance,
> As those move easiest who have learned to dance.

It is almost axiomatic that the development of writing skill in one area—in this instance the interpretation of literature—can have an enabling effect on the development of skill in other areas. The search for information with a particular goal in mind, the asking of pointed questions, the testing, rephrasing, and developing of ideas—all these and more are transferable skills on which students can build throughout their college years and beyond.

I have one concluding article of faith. Those of us whose careers have been established in the study of literature have made commitments to our belief in its value. The study of literature is valid in and for itself. But literature as an art form employs techniques and creates problems for readers that can be dealt with only through analysis, and analysis means work. Thus, the immediate aim of *Writing Themes About Literature* is to help students to do their work and to write about it. But the ultimate objective (in the past I wrote *"primary* objective") is to promote the pleasurable study and, finally, the love of literature.

# Acknowledgments

As I complete my preparation of the fifth edition of *Writing Themes About Literature* I once again express my thanks to those who have been so loyal to the earlier editions. In seeking for words of gratitude I am truly teased out of thought. My feelings on this occasion far exceed my ability to express them.

The changes in this new edition—far more extensive than I thought possible when I began my revisions—are based again, first of all, on my own experiences and thought and also on my continued work with my students at Herbert H. Lehman College. But as I think about the far-reaching changes I am particularly impressed with how much my book has been influenced by the collective wisdom of many, many other people. Conversations and discussions with others have influenced my changes in innumerable and sometimes immeasurable ways. I have especially bene-fited from the ideas and suggestions of Carol MacKay, Michael Shugrue, and George F. Hayhoe, who read a first version of the fifth edition in manuscript, and whose influence on the present text was profound. Additional thanks are due to Douglas Buttress, Peter DeBlois, Kathleen Dubs, Henry Jacobs, and John Ramsey, all of whom offered detailed suggestions for improvement. I should particularly like to acknowledge my indebtedness to William Oliver, Phil Miller, Bruce Kennan, and Bud Therien, all of Prentice-Hall, for their firm, strong, and supportive force. Their knowledge and insights have been genuinely creative. My special thanks go to Virginia Rubens, the production editor of the fifth edition, and to Ilene McGrath, who copyedited the manuscript.

*Edgar V. Roberts*

## *preliminary*

# *The Process of Writing Themes About Literature*

The chapters that follow are theme assignments based on a number of analytical approaches important to the study of literature. The assignments are designed to fulfill two goals of composition and English courses: (1) to write good themes, and (2) to assimilate great works of literature into the imagination. On the negative side, the chapters aim to help you avoid writing themes that are no more than retellings of a story, vague statements of like or dislike, or biographies of an author. On the positive side, the book aims to help you improve your writing skills through the use of literature as subject matter. Integral to your writing is your standard of literary judgment and the knowledge you need to distinguish good literature from bad. The book aims to encourage the development of these abilities by requiring you to apply, in well-prepared themes, specific approaches to good reading.

No educational process is complete until you have applied what you have studied. That is, you have not really learned something until you can talk or write about it or until you can apply it to some question or problem. The need for application requires you to recognize where your learning is incomplete, so that you may strengthen your knowledge. Thus, it is easy for you to read the chapter on *point of view* (the position from which details are seen, described, and considered), and it is presumably easy to read, say, Frank O'Connor's story "First Confession." But your grasp of point

1

of view as a concept will not be complete—nor will your appreciation of at least one aspect of the technical artistry of O'Connor's story be complete—until you have written about point of view in the story. (Please see Chapter 5.) As you write, you may discover that you need to go back to the work, to study your notes on it, and to compare them with what you understand about the problem itself. In writing, you must check facts, grasp their relationship to your topic, develop insights into the value and artistry of the work, and express your understanding in a well-organized and well-developed theme. After you have finished a number of such themes, you should be able to approach other literary works with more certainty and skill. The more you know and the more you can apply, the more expert and demanding you will be.

## General Reading Habits

The need to write themes on specific topics of literary analysis should help you improve your general reading and study habits. The principle of being a good reader is to derive a factual basis for emotional responses and intelligent interpretation. Obviously, everyone goes about reading in his or her own way, but it stands to reason that casual readers may often read so superficially that their responses are uncertain and unreliable. Preparing and writing a number of separate analytical themes should enable you to develop habits that you can use long after you have left your writing class. Here are some of the general habits that you should have as a long-range goal:

1. Study each word carefully. Look up all words you do not know.
2. Consider your thoughts and responses as you read. Did you laugh, smile, worry, get scared, feel a thrill, learn a great deal, feel proud, find a lot to think about? Try to describe how the various parts of the work caused your reactions.
3. Make notes on interesting characterizations, events, techniques, and ideas. If you like a character, try to describe what you like. If you dislike an idea, try to describe what you dislike.
4. Try to see patterns developing. Make an outline or scheme for the story or main idea. What are the conflicts in the story? How are these resolved? Is one force, idea, or side the winner? Why? How do you respond to the winner, or the loser?
5. Is there anything you do not understand? Make a note of the difficulty and ask your instructor about it in class.
6. For further study, underline what seem to be key passages. Write some of these on cards, and carry the cards with you. When you are riding or walking to class, or at other times, try to memorize phrases, sentences, or lines of poetry.

## What Is Literature?

Technically, anything spoken or written is literature. This includes everything from a grocery list to Shakespeare's sonnets. It seems clear, however, that a grocery list, though written, should be excluded as "literature" because it does not do those things that we expect from literature. That is, it does not interest, entertain, stimulate, broaden, or ennoble the reader. Even though the list may be structured according to the places in a supermarket (dairy areas, frozen food areas, produce areas, and so on) it is not designed to engage the reader's imagination. A grocery list, in short, is simply useful. It is not literature. Rather, it is to works that invite emotional and intellectual engagement that we confine our definition of literature.

The literature that is studied in introductory college courses is most often in a written form. This form offers certain advantages, although they may not seem immediately clear. Written literature gives great flexibility. You can choose to read a work according to your mood at any time you wish. Compared with a television show, for example, which you can see only when it is scheduled, literature offers freedom. When you read, you depend only on your own effort and imagination. There are no actors, no settings, no photographic or musical techniques to supersede your own reconstruction of the author's ideas. If you wish, you may reread a passage once or many times. You may stop reading and think for a while about what you have just read. Or you may get up to do something else if you need to. When you return you may pick up your book and continue it just where you left it. The book will always wait for you and will not change during the time you are gone. By contrast, any such interruptions with a film or television show are virtually permanent losses; you must wait for the repeats or else see the picture again to pick up where you left off, unless, that is, you invest in an expensive reproducing machine. In short, with a book you gain freedom and adaptability, whereas with a television show or movie you must force yourself to conform to demands of other people.

This is not to denigrate the "warmer" media of television and film, but only to contrast them with written forms of literature. All literature, in whatever form, has many things to offer you. The study of literature should help you develop what William Hazlitt, in a work entitled "Advice to a Patriot," called "long views." This term is idealistic and somewhat broad in meaning, yet it describes the value of literary study and humanistic study generally. The idea is that none of us can learn a great deal about the world if we rely only on our own limited experiences in the small areas around us. However, if we read extensively, we can build up our thoughts and our insights. Reading satisfies curiosity and stimulates imagination. It provides knowledge about our own times, and it also teaches us about the lives and concerns of people at other times and in other cultures. Writers of imaginative literature do not write works of psychology, politics, morality, philosophy, and religion, yet we learn about these topics as we read. Literature accelerates growth and transforms our perceptions of life in ways that we can never predict, or ever even know for sure. It makes us human. William Wordsworth, in his "Tintern Abbey" poem, described such an effect:

> . . . thy mind
> Shall be a mansion for all lovely forms,
> Thy memory be as a dwelling-place
> For all sweet sounds and harmonies;

It is from a base such as this that you can see your own life and the obligations that you face as a human being living in the 1980s. Without such a base you can be a follower. With such a base, however, with "long views" like those that literature can encourage, you may develop those capacities that can help you become a leader.

## Types of Literature: The Four Genres

In practice, works of literature fall into four categories or *genres:* (1) narrative, (2) drama, (3) poetry, and (4) nonfiction prose. All these forms have many common characteristics. While the major purpose of nonfiction prose, for example, is to inform, the other genres also provide information (although informing is incidental to the others). All the genres are art forms, each with its own internal requirements of structure and style. In varying degrees, all the forms are dramatic and imaginative. Even a work of nonfiction prose designed to instruct will be unsuccessful unless it makes at least some appeal to the imagination.

### NARRATIVE FICTION

A narrative is an account of a series of events, usually fictional, although sometimes fictional events may be tied to events that are genuinely historical. The two kinds of narrative fiction you will read most often are *short stories* and *novels. Myths, parables, romances,* and *epics* are also part of the genre. A short story is usually about one or two characters undergoing some sort of difficulty or facing some sort of problem. The characters may go uphill or downhill, but they almost never remain the same, for even staying the same may usually be interpreted as either downhill or uphill. Although the characters will interact with other characters and with the circumstances surrounding them, usually these relationships are described fairly briefly, for the shortened form of the story does not permit a great deal of development about how human character changes in response to human beings and environment. The novel, on the other hand, permits a full development of these interactions, and its length is caused by this fullness of development. Like the short story, the novel usually focuses on a small number of characters, although the cast of secondary characters is often large and the number of incidents is multiplied.

## DRAMA

A drama or play is designed to be performed on a stage by live actors. It therefore consists of dialogue together with directions for action. Like narrative fiction, it focuses on a single character or a small number of characters. Drama does not rely on narration, however, but presents you with speech and action which actually *render* the interactions that cause change in the characters and that resolve the conflicts in which the characters are engaged. Drama shows you people talking and doing, whereas narrative tells you about these activities. (To the degree that short stories and novels actually include dialogue, they use the technique of drama.) A *film script* is like drama although films often require much unspoken action, therefore verging on *pantomime*. It is often difficult to read a dramatic text because you miss a good deal of what real actors could bring to their parts by way of interpretation. Reading a play therefore requires a good deal of imaginative reconstruction on your part.

The dramatic types are *tragedy, comedy,* and *farce.* In the face of human disasters, tragedy attempts to elevate human values. Comedy treats people as they are, laughing at them or sympathizing with them, but showing them to be successful nevertheless. Farce exaggerates human foolishness, gets the characters into improbable and lunatic situations, and laughs at everyone in sight.

## POETRY

Poetry is a broad term that includes many subtypes, such as *sonnet, lyric, pastoral, ballad, song, ode, drama* (which may be in either prose or poetry), *epic, mock epic,* and *dramatic monologue.* Essentially, poetry is a compressed and often highly emotional form of expression. Each word counts for more than in prose, and the basic arrangement is separate lines rather than paragraphs, although *stanzas* correspond to paragraphs, and *cantos* sometimes correspond to chapters. Poetry relies more heavily than prose on *imagery,* that is, on a comparative, allusive, suggestive form of expression that is applicable to a wide number of human situations. It is this compactness of expression, combined with the broadness of application, that makes poetry unique. Because poetry is so compact, the *rhythms* of poetic speech become as vital as the emotions and ideas. Sometimes these rhythms are called the *music* of poetry. Some poetic forms are fairly free, particularly poetry written since the time of the American poet Walt Whitman. Other forms are carefully arranged and measured into definite, countable units, and often employ *rhymes* to affect the minds of the readers and listeners.

The topic material of poetry can be just about anything. Love, personal meditations, psychological studies, reviews of folklore, attacks on conspicuous consumption, religious worship, friendship, funerary occasions, celebrations of the seasons, observations on life in the streets or in the home—these are just a few of the topics found. While writers of narrative and drama confine themselves exclusively to their respective forms, the poet is free to select any form he or she wishes. Thus some of the best poetry is dramatic (for example, Shakespeare's plays) and narrative (Milton's epic poem *Paradise Lost*).

NONFICTION PROSE

This is a broad term referring to short forms like *essays* and *articles* and to longer nonfictional and nondramatic works. The essay or article is a form designed primarily to express ideas, interpretations, and descriptions. The topics of essays are unlimited; they may be on social, political, artistic, scientific, and other subjects. In an essay an author focuses on one topic such as the influence of diet on health or the contrast between envy and ambition. The writer usually develops a single topic fully but not exhaustively. When exhaustiveness is the aim, the writer expands the essay into the form of an entire book, which retains the same centralized focus as the essay but permits a wide examination and application of the entire subject.

The *article* is a form closely related to the essay. It is designed to explore and draw conclusions from facts and sometimes is exclusively factual. Therefore the article is used in all scholarly areas, such as economics, chemistry, physics, geology, anthropology, and history. When an article is used exclusively for the reporting of research findings, it is distant from the essay in style, but when a writer combines factual material with conclusions and interpretations, the article comes close to the essay. When the scope of the article is enlarged, it grows into a complete book.

## What Is Literary Analysis?

Literary analysis is no different from any other kind of analysis: it attempts to find truth. The process of analysis begins with dividing a problem into parts. Once the parts are separated and considered singly, it is easier to study their natures, functions, and interrelationships. For example, if you have a problem in chemical qualitative analysis of finding the elements in a solution, you can make only one test at a time. If you tried to make all your tests at once, you would not be able to control or distinguish your results.

In very much the same way, you cannot talk about everything in a literary work at once, even though the work is an entirety. It is better to narrow the scope of your discussion by dealing with separate topics like point of view, character, or imagery. (These are a few of the chapter assignments in this book.) Your topics will then be small enough so that you can go deeply into them.

As you develop materials for your themes, please remember that literary analysis is a way of deepening your understanding and appreciation of the work. To this end, there are four broad areas of analysis: (1) meaning, (2) form, (3) technique, and (4) background. These are not distinct classes, but overlap. For example, if you write about point of view, you will need to stress its connection to ideas (meaning). Similarly, a discussion of ideas (meaning) often extends to the origin of the ideas (background). It is always wise, in fact, to emphasize the connection of your topic to other elements in the work. In this way you are really demonstrating the relationship of literary analysis to literary appreciation, which is the aim, though sometimes unacknowledged, of all intelligent discourse about literature.

## THE USE OF IMAGINATION IN WRITING ABOUT LITERATURE

One of the major problems in literary analysis is that you will somehow remain *outside* the work and only with difficulty see the work as the author saw it. The goal is to try to recreate to some degree the way in which the author looked at the work, to see the blank page the author originally saw and to try to reconstruct the choices and ideas the author had. Thus you should exert a good deal of imagination when you read a work. If you had an idea about rendering a personality that is insecure and fearful, as Franz Kafka did in his story-fantasy "A Country Doctor," you might try to create such a story yourself. A clinician, for example, might give a straightforward report of a character suffering from a deep-rooted sense of inadequacy. But Kafka chose to represent this story from the point of view of the country doctor himself, describing his fears in the form of a fantasy, a dream in which mysterious horses appear to carry him off to a sickroom where a young man is ill of a disease that cannot be diagnosed. In considering this story you would serve yourself well if you tried to visualize in what other ways this story could be told, what other organization could be used. In short, you should face the story as an open situation which offers innumerable possibilities.

If you can develop a capacity to look at works in this way, you can then understand better what the author has actually done. You will be in a position both of looking at the work as a finished product and determining what the work is actually like, and of seeing it as a developing product that comes into being as a result of many artistic, conscious choices. The questions to ask as you prepare your themes are: How else could this be done? What would be the possible effects of some other method? In what way or ways is the method the author chose superior to these other ways? In answering these questions you are developing the objectivity necessary to evaluate works, while preserving your sense of the work that is actually there. You may never need to include the answers to these questions, but the fact that you raised them will sharpen your own observations and interpretations.

## Writing Themes About Literature

### THE NEED FOR A POINT

Writing is not like classroom discussion and ordinary conversation, because writing must stick with great determination to a specific point. Classroom discussion is a form of organized talk, but there may be digressions that are sometimes not relevant. Thus classroom discussion, while formal, is free and spontaneous. Ordinary conversation is usually random and disorganized. It shifts frequently—sometimes without clear cause—from topic to topic, and it is sometimes needlessly repetitive. Writing, by contrast, is the most concise and highly organized form of expression that will ever be required of you.

### WHAT IS A THEME?

It needs to be emphasized again and again that writing demands tight organization and control. The first requirement of the finished theme— although it is *not* the first requirement in the writing process—is that it have a *central idea*. The word *theme* is defined by the presence of this idea, for to be a theme, a piece of writing must have the central idea as its core. Everything in the theme should be directly related to this idea or should contribute to the reader's understanding of the idea.

Let us consider this thought as it relates to themes about literature. Such a theme should be a brief "mind's full," not an exhaustive treatment, on a particular subject; it might be a character study, an analysis of point of view, or a comparison-contrast, for example. This "mind's full" is achieved by the consistent reference to the central idea throughout the theme. That is, typical central ideas might be (1) that a character is strong and tenacious,

(2) that the point of view makes the action seem personalized, or (3) that one work is better than the other. Everything in the themes written with these central ideas is to be related to these ideas. Thus (1) the fact that the character works like a slave for ten years shows her strength and tenacity, (2) the fact that details such as a brother-sister conversation are reported is a sign of the personal quality, and (3) the fact that one work tells more about its characters than the other is a sign of superiority.

In the finished theme, all these principles should hold. When planning and writing your theme, you should have them as your goal. Here they are again:

1. The theme should cover the assigned topic (for example, character, point of view, etc.).
2. The theme should have a central idea that governs its development.
3. The theme should be organized so that every part contributes something to the reader's understanding of the central idea.

### "WRITER'S BLOCK"

This is not the same as saying that themes just organize themselves magically as they are being written. When students look at a finished, polished, well-formed essay written by someone else, they may at first believe that it was perfect as it flowed from the writer's pen or typewriter. Realizing that their own beginning work does not come out so well, they often despair and go into "writer's block." That is, they may sit for hours facing their blank sheets of paper, waiting for the perfect, polished theme to "arrive." Because it does not appear, they are able to write nothing at all; they are blocked.

This cause of writer's block—the belief that the theme must be perfect the first time it is written—is false. The fact is that everyone has to work hard to produce a good piece of writing. If you could see the early drafts of some of the writing you admire, you would be surprised—and encouraged—to see how tentative they are. In final drafts, early ideas are discarded and others added; new facts are introduced: early paragraphs are cut in half and assembled elsewhere with parts of other early paragraphs; words are changed (and misspellings sometimes corrected); sentences are revised or completely written over; and new writing is added to flesh out the reassembled materials.

All of this is a normal process. In fact, for your own purposes, you should use finished themes as goals at which you should aim. How you reach the goal is up to you, because everyone has unique work habits. But you should emphasize for yourself that writing is a process in which you have to overcome not only the difficulties of reading and interpreting the literary work, but also the obstacles offered by your own mind. While they are trying to write, many people find that their minds wander. They think about something else, look out the window, turn on the radio or television set, go to sleep, get something to eat, go out to find a little action, or do anything else to delay the moment of composition.

Many of these difficulties can be overcome by the realization that things do not need to be perfect the first time. It is important just to start writing, no matter how bad the first products seem, to create a beginning. You are not committed to anything you do. You may throw it out and write something else that you believe is better. But if you keep it locked in your mind you will have nothing to work with, and then your frustration will be justified.

## The Process of Writing a Theme

Despite what has just been said, there are a number of things you can do systematically in the process of writing a theme about literature. These have been entitled *invention* and *prewriting*. Invention is the process by which you discover or create the things you want to say. Prewriting is that process by which you study, think, raise and answer questions, plan, develop tentative ideas and first drafts, cross out, erase, change, rearrange, and add. In a way, prewriting and invention are merely different words for the same processes of planning and thinking. They both acknowledge the sometimes uncertain way in which the mind works and also the fact that ideas are often not known until they get written down. Writing, at any stage, should always be thought of as a process of discovery and creation. There is always something more to develop.

The following description of the writing process is presented as an approximation of what you should be doing in planning and writing your themes. You may change the order or omit some steps. In the entire process, however, you will probably not vary the steps widely.

Not every single step in the writing process can be detailed here. There is not enough space to illustrate the development of separate drafts before the final draft. If you compare the original notes with early drafts of observations and paragraphs, however, you can see that many changes take place and that one step really merges with another.

1. *Read the work through at least once for general understanding.* It is important that you have a general knowledge of the work before you try to start developing materials for your theme. Be sure, in this reading, to follow all the general principles outlined above (p. 2).

2. *Take notes with your specific assignment in mind.* If you are to write about a character, for example, take notes on things done, said, and thought about by that character. The same applies if your assignment is on imagery, or ideas, and so on. By concentrating your notes in this way, and by excluding other elements of the work, you are already focusing on your writing assignment.

3. *Use a pen or a pencil as an extension of your mind.* Writing, together with actually *seeing* the things written, is for most people a vital part of thinking. Therefore you must get any thoughts down on paper so that you have a concrete form of your thoughts. Your hand is a psychological necessity in this process. Let your ideas flow through your hand so that you will have something visible to work with later.

In addition, at some advanced part of the composing process, prepare a complete draft of what you have written. A clean, readable draft gives you the chance to see everything together and to make even more improvements. Sight is vital.

4. *Use the questions provided in the chapter on which the assignment is based.* Your answers to these questions, together with your notes and ideas, will be the basis of your theme.

5. *For all your preliminary materials, use cards or only one side of the paper.* In this way, you may spread out everything and get an overview as you plan and write your theme. Do not write on both sides of the paper, for ideas that are out of sight are often "out of mind."

6. *Once you have put everything together in this way, try to develop a central idea.* This will serve as the focus of your planning and writing.

## FINDING A CENTRAL IDEA

You cannot find a central idea in a hat. It comes about as a result of the steps just described. In a way, you might think of discovering a central idea as the climax of your initial note-taking and invention. Once you have the idea, you have a guide for accepting some of your materials, rejecting others, rearranging, changing, and rewording. It is therefore necessary to see how the central idea may be developed and how it may be used.

Let us assume that your assignment is a theme about the character Jackie, in Frank O'Connor's story "First Confession." (For the complete story, please see Appendix C, pp. 333–339). The following is a collection of notes and observations that you might write when reading the story for this assignment (Chapter 4: Character Analysis). Notice that page numbers are noted, so that you can easily go back to the story at any time to refresh your memory on any details.

> Jackie the narrator blames others, mainly his grandmother, for his troubles. He hates her bare feet and her eating and drinking habits. He dislikes his sister, Nora, for "sucking up" to the grandmother. Also, Nora tells on him. He is ashamed to bring a friend home to play because of grandmother. (p. 334)

> He likes money rather than Mrs. Ryan's talk of hell.
> He is shocked by the story about the "fellow" who "made a bad confession." (p. 335)

After learning to examine his conscience, he believes that he has broken all ten commandments because of the grandmother.
He lies about a toothache to avoid confession. A kid's lie. (p. 335)


He believes his sister is a "raging malicious devil." He remembers her "throwing" him through the church door. (p. 335)
Very imaginative. Believes that he will make a "bad confession and then die in the night and be continually coming back and burning people's furniture." This is funny, and also childish. He thinks women are hypocrites. (p. 336)
He is frightened by the dark confessional. (p. 336)


Curious and adventurous. He gets up on the shelf and kneels.
He is also frightened by the tone of the priest's voice. He falls out on the church floor and gets whacked by his sister. (p. 337)


Note: All the things about Jackie as a child are told by Jackie as an older person. The man is sort of telling a joke on himself.


Jackie is smart, can think about himself as a sinner once the priest gives him a clue. He likes the kind words of the priest, is impressed with him. He begins reacting against the words of Mrs. Ryan and Nora, calling them "cackling." (p. 337)


He has sympathy for his mother. Calls her "poor soul." Seems to fear his father, who has given him the "flaking." (p. 334)


Note: Jackie is a child, and easily swayed. He says some things that are particularly childish and cute, such as coming back to burn furniture. His fears show that he is childish and naive. He is gullible. His memory of his anger against his sister shows a typical attitude of brother and sister.

## Writing Observations from Your Notes: "Brainstorming"

Once you have a set of notes like these, your job is to make something out of them. They are by no means a theme, but you can begin working them into one by studying them closely and making observations about them. For the assignment we are considering here, you should try to establish traits of character. If you were studying a comparable set of notes on, say, a main idea in the work, you would try to concentrate on thoughts or ideas. The same technique would apply if you were discussing likes, point of view, imagery, and so on.

With this in mind, you can write a set of single-sentence observations. The following are all based on the previous set of notes, and they are all on character traits rather than actions. As you will see, some of them are phrased not as positive statements, but as questions to be explored further.

> Jackie likes thinking about money (the half crown) rather than hell. Is he irreligious, or does this show his childish nature?

> He has a dislike for his sister that seems to be normal brother-and-sister rivalry.

> He tells a fib about the toothache, but he tells everything else to the priest. He is not a liar.

> He blames his gran for his troubles. Is he irresponsible? No, he is just behaving like a child.

> He is curious and adventurous, as much as a seven-year-old can be.

> He is easily scared and impressed (see his response to the bad confession story, and his first response to the priest).

> He says cute things, the sort of things a child would say (the old man in the pew, coming back to burn the furniture). He seems real as a child.

These are all observations that might or might not turn out to be worth much in your theme. It is not possible to tell until you do some further thinking about them. These basic ideas, however, are worth working up further, along with some more substantiating details.

## Developing Your Observations as Paragraphs

That, then, is the next step. As you develop these ideas, you should be consulting the original set of notes and also looking at the text to make sure that all your facts are correct. As you write, you should bring in any new details that seem relevant. Here are some paragraphs written in expansion of the observations presented above. You might consider this paragraph-writing phase a "second step" in the brainstorming needed for the theme:

1. Jackie comes to life. He seems real. His experiences are those that a child might have, and his reactions are lifelike. All brothers and sisters fight. All kids are "heart scalded" when they get a "flaking."

2. Jackie shows a great amount of anger. He kicks his grandmother on the shin and won't eat her cooking. He is mad at Nora for the penny that she gets from grandmother, and he "lashes out" at Nora with the bread knife. He blames his troubles on his grandmother. He talks about the "hyprocrisy of women." He thinks that the stories of Mrs. Ryan and the religion of his sister are the "cackle of old women and girls" (p. 337)

3. Everything about Jackie as a child that we get in the story is told by Jackie when he is older, probably a grown man. The story is comic, and part of the comedy comes because the man is telling a joke-like story about himself.

4. Jackie's main characteristic is that he is a child and does many childish things. He remembers his anger with his sister. He also remembers being shocked by Mrs. Ryan's stories about hell. He crawls onto the ledge in the confessional. He is so impressed with the bad confession story that he says twice that he fears burning furniture. Some of these things are charming and cute, such as the observation about the old man having a grandmother and his thinking about the money when Mrs. Ryan offers the coin to the first boy who holds his finger in the candle flame.

## Determining Your Central Idea

Once you have reached this stage in your thinking, you are ready to assemble all your materials and see how well they might fit a theme. You should now be searching hard for a central idea, for once you have that, you can shape your thoughts into a form for development as a theme.

If we study the notes, brainstorming observations, and paragraphs, we can find an idea that is common to them all: Jackie has many childlike characteristics. The anger, the sibling rivalry, the attraction to the coin, the fear of burning someone's furniture, the fib about the toothache—all these can be seen as childlike. Once we have found this common bond (and it could easily have been some other point, such as Jackie's anger, or his attitude toward the females around him), we can use it as the central idea for our developing theme.

Because the central idea is so vital in shaping the theme, it should be written as a complete sentence. Just the word "childishness" would not give us as much as any of the following sentences:

1. The main trait of Jackie is his childishness.
2. Jackie is bright and sensitive, but above all childlike.
3. Jackie is no more than a typical child.
4. Jackie is above all a child, with all the beauties of childhood.

Each one of these ideas would make a different kind of theme. The first would promote a theme showing that Jackie's actions and thoughts are childlike. The third would do much the same thing, but would also stress Jackie's limitations as a child. The second would try to show Jackie's better qualities, and would show how they are limited by his age. The fourth might try to emphasize the charm and "cuteness" that were pointed out in some of the notes and observations.

The point here is this: Because the central idea is so important in shaping materials for the theme, it should be phrased carefully as a sentence. You should try out as many different ways of phrasing as you can. You may ultimately decide on the first sentence you write, but in trying different shapes for your central idea, you may get new thoughts about where you want your theme to go.

Once you have the central idea (let us use the first one), you will be able to bring materials into focus with it. Let's take paragraph two in the brainstorming phase, the one about Jackie's anger. With childishness as our central idea, we can use the topic of anger as a way of illustrating Jackie's childlike character. Is his anger adult or childish? Is it normal or psychotic? Is it sudden or deliberate? In the light of these questions, we may conclude that all the examples of angry action and thought can be seen as normal childlike responses or reflections. With the material thus "arranged" in this way, we can reshape the second paragraph as follows:

| Original Paragraph | Reshaped Paragraph |
|---|---|
| Jackie shows a great amount of anger. He kicks his grandmother on the shin and won't eat her cooking. He is mad at Nora for the penny that she gets from grandmother, and he "lashes out" at Nora with the bread knife. He blames his troubles on his grandmother. He talks about the "hypocrisy of women." He thinks the stories of Mrs. Ryan and the religion of his sister are the "cackle of old women and girls" (p. 337) | Jackie's great amount of anger is child-like. Kicking his grandmother, refusing to eat her cooking, and lashing out at Nora with the bread knife are the re-flexive actions of childish anger. His jealousy of Nora and his distrust of women (as hypocrites) are the results of thought, but immature, childish thought. His religious anger, still child-like, is his claim that the fears of Mrs. Ryan and Nora are the "cackle of old women and girls" (p. 337) |

Notice here that the materials in each paragraph are substantially the same but that the central idea has shaped the right-hand paragraph. The left-hand column describes Jackie's anger, while the one on the right makes the claim that all the examples of angry action and thought are childlike and immature. Once our paragraph has been shaped in this way, it is almost ready for placement into the developing theme.

## THE THESIS SENTENCE

Using the central idea as a guide, we can now go back to the earlier materials for arrangement. The goal is to establish a number of points to be developed as paragraphs in support of the central idea. The paragraphs written during the brainstorming will serve us well. Paragraph two, the one we have just "shaped," discusses childish anger. Paragraph three has material that could be used in an introduction (since it does not directly discuss any precise characteristics, but instead describes how the reader gets the information about Jackie). Paragraph one has material that might be good in a conclusion. Paragraph four has two topics (it is not a unified paragraph), which may be labeled "responses" and "outlook." We may put these points into a list:

1. Responses
2. Outlook
3. Anger

Once we have established this list, we may use it as the basic order for the development of our theme.

For the benefit of the reader, however, we should also use this ordering for the writing of our *thesis sentence*. This sentence is the operative sentence in the first part of the following general plan for most themes:

Tell what you are going to say.

Say it.

Tell what you've said.

The thesis sentence tells your reader what to expect. It is a plan for your theme: it connects the central idea and the list of topics in the order you plan to present them. Thus, if we put the central idea at the left and our list of topics at the right, we have the shape of a thesis sentence:

| Central idea | Topics |
|---|---|
| The main trait of Jackie is his childishness. | 1. Responses<br>2. Outlook<br>3. Anger |

From this arrangement we can write the following thesis sentence, which should usually be the concluding sentence before the body of the theme (that section in which you "say it," that is, in which you develop your central idea):

> The childishness is emphasized in his responses, outlook, and anger.

With any changes made necessary by the context of your final theme, this thesis sentence and your central idea can go directly into your introduction. The central idea, as we have seen, is the glue of the theme. The thesis sentence shows the parts that are to be fastened together, that is, the topics in which the central idea will be demonstrated.

## THE BODY OF THE THEME:
## TOPIC SENTENCES

The term regularly used in this book for the development of the central idea is *body*. The body is the section where you present the materials you have been working up in your planning. You may rearrange or even reject some of what you have developed, as you wish, as long as you change your thesis sentence to account for the changes. Since in our thesis sentence we have three topics, we will use these. Most of your themes will require that you write from 400 to 600 words. If we allow about 100 words for each of the points, that means you will most often write three 100-word paragraphs in the body of your theme. There may be more or fewer, and they may be longer or shorter, depending on how much supporting detail you are able to bring to your points.

Just as the organization of the entire theme is based on the thesis sentence, the organization of each paragraph is based on its *topic sentence*. The topic sentence is made up of one of the topics listed in the thesis sentence, combined with some assertion about how the topic will support the central idea. The first topic in our example is Jackie's responses, and the topic sentence should show how these responses illustrate a phase of Jackie's childishness. Suppose we choose the phase of the child's gullibility or impressionability. We can put together the topic and the phase, to get the following topic sentence:

> Jackie's responses show childish impressionability.

The details that will be used to develop the paragraph will then show how Jackie's responses exactly illustrate the impressionability and gullibility associated with children.

You should follow the same process in forming your other topic sentences, so that when you finish them you can use them in writing your theme.

## THE OUTLINE

All along we have actually been developing an *outline* to give our finished theme an easily followed plan. Some writers never use a formal outline at all, whereas others find the outline to be quite helpful to them as they write. Still other writers insist that they cannot produce an outline until they have finished their themes. All of these views can be reconciled if you realize that finished themes should have a tight structure. At some point, therefore, you should create an outline as a guide. It may be early in your prewriting, or it may be late. What is important is that your final theme follows an outline form.

The kind of outline we have been developing here is the "analytical sentence outline." This type is easier to create than it sounds, for it is nothing more than a graphic form, a skeleton, of your theme. It consists of the following:

1. Title
2. Introduction
    a. Central idea
    b. Thesis sentence
3. Body
    a. ⎫
    b. ⎬ points predicted in the thesis sentence
    c. etc. ⎭
4. Conclusion

The conclusion is optional in this scheme. Because the topic of the conclusion is a separate item, it is technically independent of the body, but it is part of the thematic organization and hence should be closely tied to the central idea. It may be a summary of the main points in the theme ("tell what you've said"). It may also be an evaluation or criticism of the ideas, or it may suggest further points of analysis that you did not write about in the body. In each of the following chapters, suggestions will help you in developing materials for your conclusions.

Remember that your outline should be a guide for organizing many thoughts and already completed paragraphs. Throughout our discussion of the process of writing the theme, we have seen that writing is discovery. At the right point, your outline can help you in this discovery. That is, the need to make your theme conform to the plan of the outline may help you to reshape, reposition, and reword some of your ideas.

When completed, the outline should have the following appearance (using the character study of Jackie in "First Confession"):

1. Title:   "Jackie's Childish Character in O'Connor's 'First Confession' "
2. Introduction. Paragraph 1
    a. Central idea:   The main trait of Jackie is his childishness.
    b. Thesis sentence:   This childishness is emphasized in his responses, out-
        look, and anger.
3. Body:   Topic sentences for paragraphs 2–4
    a. Jackie's responses show childish impressionability.
    b. His outlook reflects the simplicity of a child.
    c. His anger is also that of a child.
4. Conclusion. Paragraph 5
    Topic sentence: Jackie seems real as a child.

By the time you have created an outline like this one, you will have been planning and drafting your theme for quite some time. The outline will thus be a guide for *finishing* and *polishing* your theme, not for actually developing it. Usually you will have completed the main parts of the body and will use the outline for the introduction and conclusion.

Briefly, here is the way to use the outline:

1. Include both the central idea and the thesis sentence in your introduction. (Some instructors require a fusion of the two in the final draft of the theme. Therefore, make sure you know what your instructor expects.) Use the suggestions in the chapter assignment to determine what else might be included in the introduction.

2. Include the various topic sentences at the beginning of your paragraphs, changing them as necessary to provide transitions or qualifications. Throughout this book the various topics are confined to separate paragraphs. However, it is also acceptable to divide the topic into two or more paragraphs, particularly if the topic is difficult or highly detailed. Should you make this division, your topic then is really a *section*, and your second and third paragraphs should each have their own topic sentences.

Usually, in paragraphs of demonstration your topic sentence should go first in the paragraph. The details then "illustrate" or "show" the truth of the assertion in the topic sentence. (Details about the use of evidence will follow below, pp. 23–25.) It is also acceptable to have the topic sentence elsewhere in the paragraph, particularly if your paragraph is a "thought paragraph," in which you use details to lead up to your topic idea.

Throughout this book, for illustrative purposes, all the central ideas, thesis sentences, and topic sentences are underlined so that you may distinguish them clearly as guides for your own writing.

## The Sample Theme

The following theme is a sample of the finished product of the process we have been illustrating. You will recognize the various organizing sentences because they are underlined. These are the sentences from the outline, with changes made to incorporate them into the theme. You will also see that some of the paragraphs and thoughts have been taken from the prewriting stages, with necessary changes to bring them into tune with the central idea. (Please see the illustration of this change on p. 15.)

In each of the chapters in this book there are one or two similar sample themes. It would be impossible to show the complete writing process for each of these themes, but you may assume that each one was completed more or less as the one that has been described and illustrated here. There were many good starts, and many false ones. Much was changed and rearranged, and much was redone once the outline for the theme was established. The materials for each theme were developed in the light of the issues introduced and exemplified in the first parts of each of the chapters. The plan for each theme corresponds to an outline, and its length is within the limits of most of the themes you will be assigned to write.

## Jackie's Childish Character in O'Connor's "First Confession"

[1] Jackie, the main character in O'Connor's "First Confession," is a child at the time of the action. All the things we learn about him, however, are told by him as a man, or at least as an older person. The story is funny, and part of the comedy comes because the narrator is telling what amounts to a joke on himself. For this reason he brings out his own childhood childishness. That is, if Jackie were mature, the joke would not work because so much depends on his being young, powerless, and gullible. The main thing about Jackie, then, is his childishness.* This quality is emphasized in his responses, outlook, and anger.†

[2] Jackie's responses show the ease with which a child may be impressed. His grandmother embarrasses him with her drinking, eating, and unpleasant habits. He is so "shocked" by the story about the bad confession that twice he states his fear of saying a bad confession and coming back to burn furniture. He is quickly impressed by the priest and is able to change his mind about his sins (to his own favor) after no more than a few words with this man.

[3] His outlook above all reflects the limitations and the simplicity of a child. He is not old enough to know anything about the outside world, and therefore he supposes that the old man next to him at confession has also had problems with a grandmother. This same limited view causes him to think only about the half crown when Mrs. Ryan talks about punishment. It is just like a child to see everything in personal terms, without the detached, broad views of an experienced adult.

[4] His anger is also that of a child, although an intelligent one. Kicking his grandmother and lashing out against Nora with the bread knife are the reflexive actions of childish anger. He also has anger that he thinks about. His jealousy of Nora and his claim that women are hypocrites are the results of thought, even though it is immature and childish. His thinking about religion after first speaking to the priest makes him claim that the fears of Mrs. Ryan and Nora are the "cackle of old women and girls" (p. 337). He is intelligent, but he is also childish.

Jackie therefore seems real as a child. His reactions are the right ones for

*Central idea
†Thesis sentence
For the text of this story, please see Appendix C, pp. 333–339.

[5]
a child to have. All brothers and sisters fight, and all children are "heart scalded" when they get a "flaking." The end of life and eternal punishment are remote for a child, whose first concern is the pleasure that money can buy. Therefore, Jackie's thoughts about the half crown are truly those of a child, as are all his thoughts and actions. The strength of "First Confession" is the reality of Jackie's childlike nature.

## Theme Commentaries

Throughout this book, short commentaries follow each of the sample themes. Each discussion points out how the assignment is handled and how the instruction provided in the first part of the chapter is incorporated into the theme. For themes in which several approaches are suggested, the commentary points out which one is employed. When a sample theme uses two or more approaches, the commentary makes this fact clear. It is hoped that the commentaries will help you develop the insight necessary to use the sample themes as aids in your own writing.

## Some Common Problems in Writing Themes About Literature

The fact that you understand the writing process and can apply the principles of developing a central idea and organizing with an outline and thesis sentence does not mean that you will have no problems in writing well. It is not hard to recognize good writing when you see it, but it is usually harder to explain why it is superior.

The most difficult and perplexing questions you will ask as you write are: (1) "How can I improve my writing?" (2) "If I got a C on my last theme, why wasn't the grade a B or an A? How can I get higher grades?" These are really the same question, but each has a different emphasis. Another way to ask this question is: "When I first read a work, I have a hard time following it. Yet when my instructor explains it, my understanding is greatly increased. I would like to develop the ability to understand the work and write about it well without my instructor's help. How can I succeed in this aim? How can I become an independent, confident reader and writer?"

The theme assignments in this book are designed to help you do just that. One of the major flaws in many themes about literature is that, despite the writer's best intentions and plans, they do no more than retell a story or describe an idea. Retelling the story shows only that you have read the work, not that you have thought about it. Writing a good theme, however, shows that you have digested the material and have been able to put it into a pattern of thought. In only one of the following chapters are you asked to retell a story or rephrase factual material. This is the *précis theme* (Chapter 1), and even here a major purpose is to help you make the distinction between retelling a story and making an analysis for a theme. All other chapters require and illustrate analytical processes that show your thought and understanding.

### ESTABLISHING AN ORDER
### IN MAKING REFERENCES

There are a number of ways in which you may set up patterns of development to show your understanding. One is to refer to events or passages in your own order. You may reverse things, or even mix them around, as long as they fit into your own thematic plans. Rarely, if ever, should you begin your theme by describing the opening of the work; it is better to talk about the conclusion or the middle of the work first. Beginning the body of your theme by referring to later parts of the work will almost force you to discuss your own central idea rather than to retell events. If you look back at paragraph three of the sample theme on "First Confession," you will see that this technique has been used. The two references there are presented in reverse order from the story. This reversal shows the theme writer's own organization, not the organization of the work being analyzed.

### YOUR MYTHICAL READER:
### A STUDENT WHO HAS READ
### BUT NOT THOUGHT

Another important idea is to consider the "mythical reader" for whom you are writing your theme. Imagine that you are writing to other students like yourself. They have read the assigned work, just as you have, but they have not thought about it. You can immediately see what you would write for such mythical readers. They know the events or have followed the thread of the argument. They know who says what and when it is said. As a result, you do not need to tell these readers about everything in the work, but should think of your role as that of an *explainer* or *interpreter*. Tell them what things mean in relationship to your central idea. *Do not, however, tell them the things that happen.*

To look at the situation in still another way, you may have read stories about Sherlock Holmes and Dr. Watson. Holmes always points out to Watson that all the facts are available to both of them, but that, though Watson *sees*, he does not *observe*. Your role is like that of Holmes, explaining and interpreting facts, and drawing conclusions that Dr. Watson has been unable to draw for himself. Once again, if you look back at the sample theme on "First Confession," you will notice that everywhere *the assumption has been made that the reader has read the story already.* References to the story are thus made primarily to remind the reader of something he or she already knows, but *the principal emphasis of the theme is to draw conclusions and develop arguments.*

## USING LITERARY MATERIAL
## AS EVIDENCE

The analogy with Sherlock Holmes should remind you that whenever you write on any topic, your position is much like that of a detective using clues as evidence for building a case, or of a lawyer using evidence as support for arguments. If you argued in favor of securing a greater voice for students in college government, for example, you would introduce such evidence as past successes with student government, increased maturity of modern-day students, the constitutional amendment granting 18-year-olds the right to vote, and so on.

Writing about literature requires evidence as well. *For practical purposes only,* when you are writing a theme, you may conveniently regard the work assigned as evidence for your arguments. You should make references to the work only as a part of the logical development of your discourse. Your objective is to convince your reader of your own knowledge and reasonableness, just as lawyers attempt to convince a jury of the reasonableness of their arguments.

The whole question of the use of evidence is a far-reaching one. Students of law spend years studying proper uses of evidence. Logicians have devised the system of syllogisms and inductive reasoning to regulate the use of evidence. It would not be logical, for example, to conclude from Shakespeare's play *Macbeth* that Macbeth behaves like a true friend and great king. His murders, his rages, and his pangs of guilty conscience form evidence that makes this conclusion absurd.

To see how material from the work may become supporting evidence in a theme, let us refer again to the sample theme on "First Confession." The fourth paragraph is about Jackie's anger being an aspect of his childlike nature. Four separate details from the story are introduced in support. If you will also look again at how this paragraph was first developed in the light of the central idea (p. 15), you will see that the details are not introduced to tell the story. Two of them specifically show the reflexive nature of childhood anger, and the other two show Jackie's immature, childish thought, despite his obvious intelligence. Use this way of introducing detail as a model for your own themes.

It is vital to use evidence correctly in order for your reader to follow your idea. Let us look briefly at two examples to see how writing may be made better by the evidential use of details. These are from themes analyzing Thomas Hardy's story "The Three Strangers."

1

After a short lapse of time, the second stranger enters to seek shelter from the rain. He is a rather full-fleshed man dressed in gray, with signs on his face of drinking too much. He tells the guests that he is en route to Caster-bridge. He likes to drink, exhausting the large mug full of mead that is offered to him, and quickly demanding more, which makes Shepherd Fennel's wife extremely angry. With the mead going to his head and making him drunk, he relates his occupation by singing a song in the form of a riddle. This second stranger is a hangman who is sup-posed to hang a man in Casterbridge for stealing a sheep. As he reveals his occupation, stanza by stanza, an in-creasing air of dismay is cast over the guests. They are horrified by the hang-man's description of his job, but he makes a big joke about all the grim details, such as making a mark on the necks of his "customers" and sending them to a "far countree."

2

Hardy uses the second stranger—the hangman—to produce sympathy for the shepherds and distrust of the law. By giving the hangman a selfish thirst for mead, which drains some of the Fennels' meager supply, Hardy justifies Mrs. Fennel's anger and anxiety. An even greater cause for anxiety than this personal arrogance is the harsh legal oppression that the hangman repre-sents to the shepherds. Indeed, the shepherds were already sympathetic to the plight of Summers, the first stranger (whose crime seems reward-able, not punishable), but the domi-neering manner of the hangman clearly makes them go beyond just sympathy. They silently decide to oppose the law by hiding Summers. Hardy thus makes their obstructionism during the later manhunt seem right and reasonable. Perhaps he has stacked the deck against the law here, but he does so to make the reader admire the shepherd folk. In this plan, the hangman's ob-noxiousness is essential.

Although the first example has more words than the second (174 words in column 1, 151 in column 2), it is not adequate, for it shows that the writer felt only the obligation to retell the story. The paragraph is cluttered with details and it contains no conclusions and no observations. If you had read the story, the paragraph would not provide you with a single piece of new information, and absolutely no help at all in understanding the story. The writer did not have to think much in order to write the para-graph. On the other hand, the second column is responsive to the reader's needs, and it required a good deal of thought to write. Phrases like "Hardy thus makes" and "In this plan" show that the writer of the second theme has assumed that the reader knows the details of the story and now wants help in interpretation. Column 2 therefore leads readers into a pattern of thought that may not have occurred to them when they were reading the story. In effect, column 2 brings evidence to bear on a point and excludes all irrelevant details; column 1 provides nothing more than raw, undirected evidence.

The answer to that difficult question about how to turn *C* writing into *A* writing is to be found in the comparison of the two columns. Besides using English correctly, superior writers always allow their minds to play upon the materials. They always try to give readers the results of their thoughts. They dare to trust their responses and are not afraid to make judgments about the literary work they are considering. Their principal aim in referring to events in a work is to develop their own thematic pattern. Observe this quality again by comparing two sentences which deal with the same details from the story:

|  1  |  2  |
|---|---|
| He likes to drink, exhausting the large mug full of mead that is offered to him, and quickly demanding more, which makes Shepherd Fennel's wife extremely angry. | By giving the hangman a selfish thirst for mead, which drains some of the Fennels' meager supply, Hardy justifies Mrs. Fennel's anger and anxiety. |

Sentence 1 is detailed but no more. Sentence 2 links the details as a pattern of cause and effect within the author's artistic purpose. Notice the words "By giving" and "Hardy justifies." These indicate the writer's *use* of the facts. There are many qualities in good writing, but perhaps the most important is the way in which the writer uses known facts as evidence in a pattern of thought that is original. Always try to achieve this quality in all your writing about literature.

KEEPING TO YOUR POINT

Whenever you write a theme about literature, then, you must pay great attention to the proper organization and to the proper use of references to the work assigned. As you write, you should try constantly to keep your material unified, for should you go off on a tangent, you are following the material rather than leading it. It is all too easy to start with your point but then wander off into a retelling of events or ideas. Once again, resist the tendency to be a narrator rather than an interpreter.

Let us look at another example. The following paragraph is taken from a theme on the "Idea of Personal Responsibility in Homer's *The Odyssey*." This is the third paragraph; the writer has stated the thematic purposes in the first paragraph, and in the second has shown that various characters in *The Odyssey* believe that human beings are responsible for their actions and must bear the consequences.

More forcefully significant than these statements of the idea is the way it is demonstrated in the actions of the characters in the epic. Odysseus, the hero, is the prime example. Entrapped by Polyphemus (the son of Poseidon the Earth-Shaker by the nymph Thoosa) and threatened with death, Odysseus in desperation puts out the eye of his captor, who then begs his father Poseidon for vengeance. Answering his son's anguished curse, Poseidon frustrates Odysseus at every turn in the voyage back to Ithaca, and forces him to wander for ten years before reaching home.

This paragraph shows how easily writers may be diverted from their objective in writing. The first sentence rightly states that the idea is to be demonstrated in the actions of the epic. That the remainder of the paragraph concentrates on Odysseus is no flaw, because the writer concentrates on other characters in following paragraphs. The flaw is that the material about Odysseus does not go beyond the story itself; it does not come to grips with the topic of personal responsibility; it does not indicate understanding. The material may be relevant to the topic, but the writer does not point out its relevance. Remember always that in expository writing you should not rely on making your meaning clear simply by implication; you must make all relationships *explicitly* clear.

Let us see how this problem can be solved. If the ideal paragraph could be schematized with line drawings, we might say that the paragraph's topic should be a straight line, moving toward and reaching a specific goal (explicit meaning), with an exemplifying line moving away from the straight line briefly in order to bring in evidence, but returning to the line after each new fact in order to demonstrate the relevance of this fact. Thus, the ideal scheme would look like this:

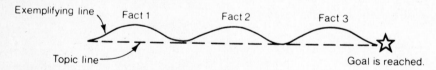

Notice that the exemplifying line, or the example or the documenting line, always returns to the topic line. A scheme for the above paragraph on *The Odyssey*, however, would look like this:

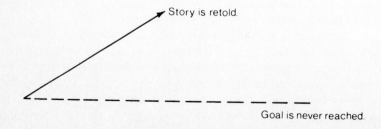

How might this paragraph be improved? The best way is to reintroduce the topic again and again throughout the paragraph to keep reminding the reader of the relevance of the exemplifying material. Each time you mention the topic you are bringing yourself back to the line, and this practice should prevail no matter what the topic. If you are analyzing point of view, for example, you should keep pointing out the relevance of your material to the point of view of the work, and the same applies to *character* or whatever aspect of literature you are studying. According to this principle, we might revise the paragraph on *The Odyssey* as follows, keeping as much of the original wording as we can. (Parts of sentences stressing the relationship of the examples to the topic of the paragraph are underlined.)

> More forcefully significant than these statements of the idea is the way it is demonstrated in the actions of the characters in the epic. Odysseus, the hero, is the prime example. When he is entrapped and threatened with death by Polyphemus (the son of Poseidon the Earth-Shaker by the nymph Thoosa), Odysseus in desperation puts out the eye of his captor. Though his action is justifiable on grounds of self-preservation, he must, according to the main idea, suffer the consequences. Polyphemus begs his father Poseidon for vengeance. Poseidon hears, and accordingly this god becomes the means of enforcing Odysseus' punishment, since Odysseus, in injuring the god's son, has insulted the god. The Ithacan king's ten years of frustration and exile are therefore not caused by whimsy; they are punishment for his own action. Here the idea of personal responsibility is shown with a vengeance; despite the extenuating circumstances, the epic makes clear that characters must answer for their acts.

The paragraph has been lengthened and improved. You might object that if all your paragraphs were lengthened in this way your theme would grow too long. The answer to this objection is that *it is better to develop a few topics fully than many scantily.* Such revision might require you to throw away some of your topics or else to incorporate them as subpoints in the topics you keep. This process can only improve your theme. But the result of greater length here is that the exemplifying detail points toward the topic, and the paragraph reaches its goal.

The same need for sticking to your point is true of your entire theme, for you will not be successful unless you have thoroughly convinced your reader that your central idea is valid. The two following themes should illustrate this truth. The theme on the left is only rudimentary. The writer begins by indicating a concern for the harm the parents cause their children in the two plays being compared. Although occasionally the theme gets back to this point, it rarely gets above the level of a précis. The theme in the right-hand column is superior because the writer announces a central idea and pursues it throughout. As in the earlier paragraph, those parts of the following themes that emphasize the central idea will be underlined.

The type of theme is *comparison-contrast* (Chapter 10), and the assignment was made specifically on Arthur Miller's *All My Sons* and Tennessee Williams's *The Glass Menagerie*.

### Theme 1
### A Comparison of
### Two Plays

Miller's *All My Sons* and Williams's *The Glass Menagerie* are the two plays being compared. Both plays have the family as the center around which the characters revolve. In both families, the parents hurt the children. Miller writes of a well-off, factory-owning family; Williams of a low-class family.

The comparison of the families may start with the fathers. Joe Keller of *All My Sons* is an ambitious, conniving, and good businessman. He allows a defective shipment to go through because, as he says, he could not let forty years' work go down the drain. He also says to Chris that he did what he did because he wanted Chris to have something for his future, a business. Not much is mentioned of the father in *The Glass Menagerie*, but from what is given the reader, we picture him as a worthless drunkard. He had no purpose in life and consequently was a poor provider for his family. One should not condone Keller for what he did, but at least Keller had some initiative and

### Theme 2
### The Destruction of
### Children by Parents
### in Two Plays

In both Miller's *All My Sons* and Williams's *The Glass Menagerie,* the family is the center of the action. Miller's family is well off; Williams's is lower class. This difference is not material in view of the fact that both dramatists demonstrate the destructive effects of parents upon children, regardless of class. It is true that these parents were once children themselves, and that presumably they were recipients of equally destructive effects from their parents. This element gives both plays direct, universal appeal: that is, both plays dramatize the process by which our society is generally hurt by what, to the dramatists, are outmoded economic and social values, transmitted by parents to children. The fathers, mothers, and children will be discussed in that order.

The fathers in both plays seem to be the ones first to do hurt. Both are irresponsible. Joe's unscrupulousness causes the death of twenty-one boys who flew in airplanes made defective by his deliberate negligence. The Wingfield father simply abandons his family. Joe's defense of his action makes good sense. His motives are not bad from a short-term point of view. He really did not want to let forty years of work go down the drain, and he really did want to give Chris (and Larry) a thriving business. His means, however, were selfish and hurtful—primarily economic rather than human and loving— just as the Wingfield father causes his family untold damage by abandoning foresight whereas the Wingfield father had nothing. <u>Both fathers hurt their children.</u>

Next we can compare the mothers in the two works. In Miller's play the mother is a sensitive, unyielding, and loving person. It is she who stands firm in her belief that Larry is still living. By doing this she prevents her other son, Chris, from marrying Ann. In a sense, she is looking out for her son's interest because if Larry was ever to return, chaos would result. Amanda, the mother of *The Glass Menagerie,* is a very sociable person. Her daughter is unbelievably shy. The mother attempts to help her daughter. She does, also, what she thinks will be in the interests of her daughter. Therefore she concludes that marriage is the answer to Laura's problems. We can see how two different mothers with the same goals—happiness for their children—<u>achieve the opposite results because they fail to attend to the needs and desires of their children.</u>

Lastly, the children will be compared. Chris is both an idealistic as well as realistic person. He tries to think the best of people, as he does with his father. When he finds out otherwise, he <u>is terribly shocked and disappointed.</u> Much the same thing happens when Laura finds out that Jim is going to get married; her reaction is one of <u>disappointment and withdrawal.</u> Just when she has finally gotten socially involved with someone, he leaves. So we see how both children have to put up with <u>disappointments;</u> one finds out his father is a murderer, while the other loses the first person she ever loved.

them for a life that to many might seem very pleasant.

While less <u>creators of hurt</u> than <u>agents of it,</u> the mothers in both families also <u>cause much damage.</u> Kate Keller, while sensitive and unyielding, is nevertheless loving. Her firm belief that her son Larry is still alive is caused by a defense against her awareness of <u>Joe's great crime,</u> but <u>the end result is the unhappiness of her son Chris.</u> Her love is mixed with a <u>deliberately unreal outlook.</u> While superficially different from Kate, <u>Amanda is similarly destructive.</u> Attempting to look out for the interests of her daughter, she tries to make a carbon copy of herself, even though her background is dead, as far as her daughter is concerned. Her failure is that she does not see her daughter as an individual with distinct needs. Laura's reaction to her mother's manipulation is <u>withdrawal,</u> but Amanda cannot see any <u>harmful effect.</u> Both mothers, desiring to make their children happy, <u>produce the same unhappy results.</u>

The full effects of <u>these destructive parents are felt by the children.</u> Larry, we learn, <u>has killed himself because of shame for his father's deed.</u> Chris, we see demonstrated, <u>is shocked, angered, and embittered by it.</u> Laura is <u>disappointed,</u> ostensibly by hearing that Jim is going to marry another, but ultimately by having been brought up <u>without a father and with her mentally disjointed mother.</u> Tom simply leaves, but he remembers his mother objectively and his father condescendingly. Thus the effects of the parents on the children, and beyond that, of the society on its members, are the same—<u>destruction and decay.</u>

Through comparing and contrasting the members of each family we have been able to see how these families are different and how they are similar. In both families, however, the children are hurt by well-intentioned but foolish parents.

Comparing and contrasting the two families in this way brings out their similarities. The parents in both families are interesting and not abnormal. They have values which hurt their children. In the Kellers it is money against humanity. In the Wingfields it is social position against individuality. In both families everyone loses, because neither family is committed to the idea of humanity and individuality. Though the relevance of this theme to society at large has been only mentioned, the implication in both plays is that society must make a commitment to human and individual values if it is to survive. If people do not make this commitment, the destructive patterns in the Keller and Wingfield families will continue.

## GROWTH: DEVELOPMENT

There is another reason why the theme on the right is superior. In addition to sticking to the point, the writer in a number of spots suggests that the harmful influences of the parents are related to impractical or unjust economic values. At the end, the writer interprets the central idea by stating that society at large needs to commit itself to human values. In short, the writer has made the idea *grow*, not simply by exemplifying it, but by considering a number of its implications.

The idea of growth or development deserves special treatment. Let us take another example, the eighteenth-century novel *Tom Jones* (1749) by Henry Fielding. This novel is about the childhood and early manhood of Tom Jones, who is apparently a bastard (a shocking topic at the time), but who is eventually recognized as the son of Bridget Allworthy and therefore as a legitimate heir of his uncle, the wealthy Squire Allworthy. Tom is raised and educated with his half-brother Blifil, and during most of the novel Blifil, a hypocritical sort, is seemingly in great favor while Tom is not. Tom experiences many difficulties as he moves toward gaining his birthright and marrying his lifelong sweetheart, Sophia Western. In the end, however, everything turns out well for him, and Blifil is discredited.

Let us assume that a student with an assignment on *Tom Jones* decides on this central idea: "Fielding's exposure of hypocrisy in *Tom Jones* is made most evident in the person of Blifil." This much is good, but the problem is that many students will do no more with this idea than cite a number of instances in the novel which illustrate Blifil's hypocrisy. Such a line of development gets some of the point across, but it does not lead readers toward any new understanding of Fielding's artistic or moral purposes in *Tom Jones*. Something more needs to be done; the writer needs to exert an imaginative effort to interest and arouse potential readers.

As an analogy, let us suppose that we see a pencil and a knife on a table and are asked to describe them. Many people might do no more than simply describe these things, but an imaginative person will write something more. For example, one writer might say that people can use a pencil to create ideas that might change the world or ideas that might strengthen human thought for centuries to come. The first drafts of the Declaration of Independence were probably made with a pencil. Another imaginative writer might say that a knife is a basic tool that has unlocked the previously closed doors of technology and enabled human beings to hunt, to carve, to create, and to make civilization. Before there was modern technology, there was the primitive and useful knife. Both developments of such common subjects promise something interesting; they lead readers imaginatively into new and previously unconsidered areas of perception.

The developing of an idea is hence vital in good writing. The writer should make the subject grow from the initial statement of the central idea. In the case of Blifil's hypocrisy, it is not enough simply to establish that Blifil is a hypocrite, but one must show that this hypocrisy leads to important areas in *Tom Jones* and also to important ideas that Fielding was considering about human nature. In considering the development of the hypocrisy of Blifil, a writer might include the following thoughts:

> Blifil's hypocrisy leads both to serious problems for Tom and Sophia and to the destruction of Blifil himself.
>
> For example, by refusing to tell Allworthy that Bridget, before her death, had acknowledged Tom as her son, Blifil makes it possible for Tom to be disowned by Allworthy and to be cast adrift in the countryside. In despair because of being disowned, Tom has no concern for what happens to him, and in this mood he is self-destructive, as any person might naturally be in such circumstances. He thus commits the sexual indiscretions that give him trouble with Sophia but that also give him pangs of conscience. It is the development of conscience and his concern to raise himself in the esteem of Sophia and Allworthy that make Tom a

developing character worthy of being the center of interest in the novel. Thus, in one respect Tom is hurt by Blifil, but in another, Blifil becomes the cause of Tom's moral growth.

Also, because of his own hypocrisy, Blifil is finally unable to detect his own faults, and to this degree he cuts himself away from common human morality. His fear of Allworthy's anger at the end of the novel does not result from introspective pangs of conscience, but rather from the fear of Allworthy's disfavor and the consequent loss of money that this disfavor will bring. At the end of the work Blifil is nothing more than a money-grubbing hypocrite, to be contrasted with Tom.

As you can see from these examples, the writer has gone from a basic, central idea—that Blifil is a hypocrite—toward a development of that idea in terms of how the hypocrisy is important in the novel *Tom Jones*. Details from the book are naturally included, but they are not mere illustration. Instead, they are used as parts of a process of reasoning or argumentation. In other words, the central idea has been developed; growth has taken place. Without such growth, there is no totally successful writing, just as there is no successful thinking.

It should be clear that whenever you write, an important goal should be the development of your central idea. You should try to go somewhere with your idea, to give your readers insights about the literary materials that they did not have before they started reading. To the degree that you can learn to develop your ideas, you will receive recognition for increasingly superior writing achievements.

Admittedly, in a short theme you will be able to move only a short distance with an idea, but you should never be satisfied to leave the idea exactly where you found it. Nurture it and make it grow. Constantly adhere to your topic and constantly develop it.

## USING ACCURATE AND FORCEFUL LANGUAGE

The best writing has a quality of accuracy, force, and insight. Quite often the first products of our minds are rather weak, and they need to be rethought, recast, and reworded. Sometimes this process cannot be carried out immediately, for it may take days or even weeks for us to gain objectivity about what we say. As a student you usually do not have that kind of time, and thus you must acquire the habit of challenging your own statements almost as soon as you write them. Ask yourself whether they really mean what you want, or if you can make a stronger statement than you have.

As an example, consider the following statement, a central idea about E. M. Forster's short story "The Machine Stops," an allegory about a future world in which people are completely dependent on machinery but perish when the machinery breaks down.

> The central idea of this story is that because of the machine and its marvelous powers, the people place their total dependence on it.

This central idea could not carry you very far if you were writing a theme based on it. But try to restate and strengthen the essential material in the sentence. Two possibilities are as follows:

> 1. Forster shows that human beings, by accepting the machine and by becoming hostile to Nature, have alienated themselves from their environment and are therefore responsible for their own destruction.
> 2. Forster shows that the pursuit of ideas and technology to the exclusion of Nature has led human beings to destroy themselves.

Either of these two sentences would be more helpful as a statement of a central idea than the first example.

Sometimes, in seeking to say something, we wind up saying nothing. Here are two sentences from themes about Robert Frost's "Stopping by Woods on a Snowy Evening."

> 1. It seems as though the author's anticipation of meeting with death causes him to respond as he does in the poem.
> 2. This incident, although it may seem trivial or unimportant, has substantial significance in the creation of his poem; by this I mean the incident which occurred is essentially what the poem is all about.

The vagueness of sentences like these must be resisted. A sentence should not end up in limbo the way these do. The first sentence is satisfactory enough up to the verb "causes," but then it falls apart. If Frost has created a response for the speaker in the poem, it is best to describe *what* that response is rather than to state simply that there *is* a response. A more forceful restatement of the first sentence may thus be, "It seems as though the author's anticipation of meeting with death causes him to think about the need to meet his present responsibilities." With this revision, the writer could go on to a consideration of the meaning of Frost's final stanza and could relate the ideas there to the events and ideas described in the first part of the poem. Without the revision, it is not clear where the writer would go.

The second sentence is so vague that it confuses rather than informs. Essentially, such sentences hint at an idea and claim importance for it, but they never directly define what that idea is. If we adopt the principle that it is always better to name the specific things we are talking about, perhaps the second sentence could be revised as follows:

> Although stopping by the woods to watch the snow fall may seem trivial or insignificant, the incident causes the poet to meditate on beauty and

responsibility; the important thoughts in the poem thus grow from the simplest of events.

When you write your own sentences, you might test them in a similar way. Are you referring to an idea? State the idea directly. Are you mentioning a response or impression? Do not say simply, "The poem left me with a definite impression," but describe the impression: "The poem left me with an impression of sympathy," or "of understanding the hard lot of the migrant farmer." Similarly, do not rest with a statement such as "I found this story interesting," but try to describe what was interesting and why it was interesting. If you always confront your impressions and responses by trying to name them and to pin them down, your sentences should take on exactness and force. Naturally, your instructor will probably tell you whatever you have accomplished or failed to accomplish. Good writing habits that you develop from these criticisms of your work, and from discussions with your instructor, will help you to write more forcefully and accurately.

Whenever you write a theme, then, keep these ideas in mind. Keep returning to the point you wish to make; regard the material of the work you have read as evidence to substantiate your arguments, not as material to be described. Keep demonstrating that all exemplifying detail is relevant to your main point. Keep trying to develop your topic; make it bigger than it was when you began writing. Constantly keep trying to make your statements accurate and forceful. If you observe these precepts, you should be well on the way toward handling any of the following theme assignments successfully.

# chapter 1

# The Précis Theme,
# or Abstract

A précis is a shortening, in your own words, of the text of a written work. In writing a précis you describe, as accurately as possible, what happens in a story or play, or you briefly restate, abridge, digest, or encapsulate the substance or main ideas in an essay, article, or poem. Other words that describe the précis or abstract are *paraphrase, condensation,* and *epitome.* All these words suggest a shortening or a highlighting of only the most significant details and sections of a work.

The length of your précis depends on the extent of the original work and the approximate length of your assignment. Thus, a 3,000-word story might be condensed into 100 or 1,000 words. The amount of detail to include naturally depends on the desired length of the précis. The 1,000-word précis would contain much detail, whereas the 100-word précis would not have much more than the main headings.

## Uses of the Précis

The précis is important in the service of study, research, and speaking and writing. One of the best ways to study any work is to write a précis of it, for by so doing you force yourself to grasp each of the parts. Also, referring later to your précis helps to bring the entire work back to your memory. There are few better ways to begin careful study.

When you do research, you must take notes on the material you find. Here the ability to shorten and paraphrase is essential, for it is impossible to reproduce everything in your notes. The better you are able to write a précis, the better will be your research.

In discussions, you will improve your arguments if you refer briefly but accurately to sections of the work being discussed. When you are writing a theme, particularly a longer one, it is often necessary to remind your reader of the events or facts in the work. Here the need is not to tell *everything*, but just enough so that your conclusions will be self-sustaining. In an argumentative or persuasive speech or theme, when you are trying to convince your listener or reader, it is necessary to get the facts straight in order to eliminate objections that may arise about your use of detail.

For all these occasions you will profit from being able to paraphrase or abstract. Although you will sometimes need to condense an entire story or epitomize an entire argument, most often you will need to refer only to parts of works, because your arguments will depend on a number of separate interpretations. No matter what your future needs are, however, your ability to write a précis will be helpful to you.

## Problems in Writing a Précis

1. ACCURACY.   Just as the précis is important in establishing a "handle" on the facts, one of the first problems in writing a précis is to be sure that you get the facts straight. You should make no unsupported statements. Let us suppose that you are writing about so simple and well-remembered a story as "Hansel and Gretel." Suppose you write that "the children eventually overcome the witch by thrusting her into the oven." This statement is only partially true. It is not *both* children who defeat the witch, but Gretel alone, for Hansel is locked up in a cage at the time the witch and Gretel are preparing the oven. If you think only casually about what to write, however, it would be natural to say that "the children" are both agents of victory. It is important to go over your précis carefully to make sure that all you say is factually correct.

2. USING YOUR OWN WORDS.   Another problem is the difficulty you may find in using *your own* words in your précis to replace the words and ideas in the original. The best way is to read the work carefully at least three times. Then put the work away, out of sight, and do your writing. In this way you force yourself to use your own words, without the temptation of borrowing directly from the original.

If you find, however, that you have used some words and phrases from your source, be careful to underline, star, or otherwise mark these borrowed words, and then try to use your own words when you revise. If it seems impossible to make changes of some words, you may preserve a small number of the originals, but be sure to include them within quotation marks in your final draft.

3. SELECTING DETAILS. A third problem is deciding what details to select. Try to pick out only those that are of greatest significance. A writer may tell about two people who, in a restaurant, order a wide variety of dishes and engage in lengthy conversation. Obviously, in a précis you do not want to mention each item of food and drink. If one of the characters gets drunk, however, it might be important to state that the character drank too much. Similarly, you would not need to report all the conversation, but only that part which contained the important details, such as that a character was happy or unhappy. The reporting of detail is critical in the way your précis will be judged. Some things are more important than others, and you must choose details according to this scale of importance.

4. AVOIDING CONCLUSIONS. Surprisingly, a major problem in a précis is to avoid making conclusions. It is true that your understanding of the work determines those details which you think are important and that a précis thus represents the factual basis for most of your conclusions. But in the précis itself you should avoid these conclusions and concentrate only on facts. Report them accurately and impartially. The following columns show the difference between good and bad methods:

| Theme A<br>*with* conclusions:<br>wrong | Theme B<br>*without* conclusions:<br>right |
| --- | --- |
| Gretel fulfills her plan to overcome the witch by pretending ignorance. Thus she confesses her inability to open the door, in this way leading the witch to doom. Angered by Gretel, the witch demonstrates the proper way to open the door. Gretel, having seen the success of her plan, quickly pushes the witch into the fire and rescues Hansel. | Because Gretel states that she is unable to manage the oven, the witch angrily goes to the door and demonstrates the proper way to open it. Gretel then quickly pushes the witch into the fire and rescues Hansel. |

Often, of course, it is necesssary to generalize about parts of the work. Let us suppose that a story contains many details showing that a character is cheerful. It is *proper* to state generally that the character is cheerful, for you may make that statement fairly and it is important to make your theme as brief and as comprehensive as possible. However, it is *improper* here to add your own conclusions, such as "this cheerfulness shows the character's courage in the face of danger." The conclusion may be the right one, but you should not offer interpretations of this type in a précis. Stick to the details.

5. **AVOIDING CHOPPY SENTENCES.** Although you concentrate on essentials in your précis, you should avoid short, choppy sentences. Here is an example:

> It is December, just before Christmas. Phoenix Jackson is beginning to walk to Natchez. She is a black woman. She is old but cheerful. She walks with a cane. She has walked this way many times.

Here there are six sentences, all very short and beginning with the subject followed immediately by the verb. Sentences like these are almost impossible to read for an entire paper. A revision should reduce the number of sentences but keep the same details, as in the following:

> Just before Christmas, Phoenix Jackson begins her familiar walk through the country from her home to Natchez. She is a poor and old black woman, who needs a cane for support, but she is cheerful.

## Your Theme

Your task is to make a reduction of the original with the least possible distortion. Thus you should select things only as they come in the work. In her story "A Worn Path," for example, Eudora Welty reveals in the last page that the main character has gone into town to get medicine for her infirm grandchild. It would be helpful to introduce that detail at the start of the précis, but because the author has included it only at the end of the story, it is proper to bring it in only at the comparable stage of the précis.

If your précis is to be very short, 100 to 150 words, for example, you might confine everything to only one paragraph. If you have a longer word limit, like 200 to 500 words, it is good to arrange your paragraphs according to the natural divisions in the original work. Thus, if the work has parts or sections, you might devote a paragraph to each of these divisions. If an undivided story moves from place to place, as in the sample theme below, you might provide a paragraph for events occurring at each place. Or if the story takes place in only one location, you might use paragraphs to describe (1) the events leading up to the main action, (2) the action itself, and (3) the consequences of the action. If you are writing a précis of an essay or article, you might organize according to the author's main divisions, such as the background of the problem, possible solutions, and consequences. Whether you are writing about fiction, drama, poetry, essay, or article, however, follow the general principle of letting the work itself be your guide about paragraphing.

## Sample Theme

### *A Précis of Eudora Welty's "A Worn Path"*

[1] Just before Christmas, Phoenix Jackson begins her familiar walk through the country from her home to Natchez. She is a poor and old black woman, who needs a cane for support, but she is cheerful. She releases herself from a thorny bush, climbs a high hill, and finds her way through areas with no marked path. She is attacked by a large dog and falls into a ditch, but soon is assisted by a young white hunter, who frightens off the dog. Phoenix sees the man drop a nickel before he chases the dog; she recovers it and hides it. Though the man advises her to go back home, Phoenix resolutely continues on her way toward Natchez.

[2] As she enters town, she is successful in getting a white lady on the street to tie her shoes, for she states that neatly tied shoes are essential for going to an important building. Almost without thinking about where she is going, she climbs many stairs to find the medical office in the building, and then she sits down there, blankly.

[3] While an attendant asks her about her business, a nurse enters and reveals to the attendant that Phoenix has come to get medicine for her grandson, who two or three years earlier had drunk lye and is now totally disabled. Phoenix receives the free medicine, and the attendant gives her a nickel. With these, together with the nickel she had recovered earlier, Phoenix states that she will buy a little paper windmill for her grandson. She then leaves the office.

## Commentary on the Theme

Though many details from the story must necessarily be eliminated, each paragraph concentrates on the major actions that occur in each of the main locations in the story. The sample theme is about 250 words long, and therefore it is possible to include some of the details about Phoenix when she first reaches Natchez. With a shorter word limit it would be necessary to eliminate these details and instead concentrate on the events in the medical office, for these concluding details are more important than what happens to Phoenix on the Natchez streets.

The précis is successful as a précis for the foregoing reasons and also because it includes most of the details that in the story itself are the basis

For the text of this story, please see Appendix C, pp. 340–346.

for Eudora Welty's portrait of Phoenix. She is cheerful even though she has suffered great sorrow and poverty, and her lot in life will not change. She is dependent, forgetful, kind, and trusting, with a harmless trace of larceny. She is both strong and simple. Eudora Welty uses the events in the story to bring out all these traits, and the précis, by the presentation of the same events, could be used as the basis for such conclusions about the character of Phoenix.

# chapter 2

# The Summary Theme

The summary theme is a step beyond the précis. Like the précis, it concentrates on the details in a work, but unlike the précis, it requires the thematic structure of a central idea, a thesis sentence, and topic sentences. Because of these requirements, the summary theme demands that you make judgments. To this degree, you are beginning to write criticism.

This criticism is not just "literary," however; it is characteristic of the mental processes that you must employ in any of your college courses. For example, in a history course you will rarely be requested simply to present a list of facts and dates; you will be required to show how the facts are related to a dominating idea or "tendency" in history. Here is a short paragraph showing how historical details can be placed in the context of an idea; the technique is that of the summary theme:

> The major fault of the British government—and one of the major causes of the Revolutionary War—was not that it imposed taxes, but that it did so without consulting the Colonials. This was true of the Stamp Act, which the British withdrew in 1766 after fierce riots in the colonies. It was also true of the commodities taxes, like those on glass, paint, and tea, which were imposed late in the 1760's. There was a need for these taxes, but the Colonials did not share in making the laws which imposed them, and it was resentment over this, rather than taxation itself, which led to the Boston Tea Party in 1773.

Notice here that the major idea—that there was no consultation—controls the presentation of the facts. This idea is stressed throughout the paragraph. The need for relating facts to a main thought is important in good writing. Writing a summary theme thus should provide you with a basic technique you can apply in your other college courses where extensive writing is required.

## What Do You Summarize?

The summary theme assumes that you are able to write a précis of the work assigned, whether it is a story, a play, a longer poem, an essay, or an article. Once you have reached this level, you will be faced with the major problem of organization; that is, of relating your materials to a main idea. This main idea is your description of the plot or idea of the work.

### PLOT

If your work is a drama or a narrative, you should try to discover the plot. There is a difference between a plot and a story. The story is the set of events, details, or speeches in the work as they appear in chronological or act-by-act order. It is the story that you condense as you write a précis. The plot is something more. It is the reasons or the logic underlying the story and causing it to take the form in which it appears. The essence of plot is the existence of a *conflict* between opposing forces—human beings against themselves, against other human beings, or against some natural or supernatural force. The conflict produces those actions and interactions that are resolved in a *climax*, in which one person, force, or idea wins out.

There is little question, of course, about what happens in the story, since all the events are before you. But there is room for interpretation of the plot, because the reasons why characters do things are not always clear.

If you can make a brief description of the plot, you can use it as the central idea of your theme. In a summary theme about Eudora Welty's "A Worn Path," for example, you might find two possible main thoughts. One is that the life of the rural poor is miserable; the other is that the main character, Phoenix, has strength that rises above this misery. A glance ahead at the first paragraph in the sample theme shows how this second idea can be used as a central idea:

> Welty shows that Phoenix has great personal strength and cheerfulness despite the grimness of her life.

There could be other central ideas, for good plays and stories, like most literary works, are as complex as life itself. There will always be a chance for endless debate about any interpretation, no matter how good or complete it seems. Do not worry about the "rightness" of your interpretation, therefore; just use it to unify your theme.

IDEA

If you have been assigned a nonnarrative work such as a poem, essay, or article, you may look for the same sort of help in the work itself. You have, first, the details in the work—similar to the events in a story—and second, the author's main idea, such as "My love for you goes beyond time" (Shakespeare's Sonnet No. 18) or "Death cruelly cuts short the best and leaves the world to the worst" (Milton's "Lycidas"). The author's ideas here are like the plot in a story or play, and you may use them as your own central idea in a summary theme.

## Planning the Theme

The first thing to do is to study your notes. Try to determine how the events or details fit into a pattern that you can describe as a central idea. In the famous ancient Greek play *Oedipus the King* by Sophocles, for example, it is possible to determine that the events occur as illustrations of the *pride* of Oedipus. That is, the events are caused by his belief that he was superior to his fate. Thus, he killed a stranger on the road when he knew that he was foredoomed to kill his own father, and he married a widowed queen when he knew that he was fated to marry his own mother. Somehow he believed that he was above these deeds and could avoid them. But he could not, and the ancient play shows how Oedipus learns that he, like everyone else, cannot change his fate. In a theme on this play it would be necessary to show how during most of the action Oedipus tries to avoid this realization, thus preserving for a time, at least, his sense of his own importance—his pride. In this manner, for any work, look at the details carefully and try to find a common denominator that will help you launch your theme.

## Choosing and Limiting Details

You need include only enough detail to bring out your central idea. Let us suppose that you are writing about Mark Twain's novel *Huckleberry Finn*, and you establish a central idea that the book is about "the growth of the individual to maturity." You develop the following thesis sentence: "This growth is shown by Huck's experiences under the care of the Widow Douglas and by his trip on a raft with the runaway slave Jim." In developing a theme from this thesis sentence, you would not have to include all the details from the early part of the book, but only those that seem to have an influence on Huck's judgment and developing maturity, such as being told by Tom that a Sunday-school picnic was really a meeting of Arabs. Similarly, you would need to include only those incidents on the river which helped Huck grow; thus you would emphasize details that show his increasing sense of obligation to Jim. You might claim that there is a great deal in the novel that you would be leaving out. *That is exactly the point.* You should include in a summary theme only enough detail to make clear your central idea, and no more. Your job is to write a well-organized theme to give your readers a sense of what to notice on their own reading of the work.

## Organizing Your Theme

Usually there will be two parts in a summary theme, the introduction and the summary itself.

### PART I: INTRODUCTION

The introduction identifies the work, the most significant character or characters, and the general situation; it is the place for your central idea and thesis sentence. In the introduction you should also describe the most noticeable physical characteristics of the work—that it is a play, story, poem, essay, article, or novel; that the work is mainly in dialogue, or narration; that the narration of events is accompanied by descriptions of the hero's thoughts; that the story is told by the hero himself or herself; that the description of present events is augmented by reminiscences of past events; that the reader must infer the relationships among the characters; that much of the story is in dialect; that the author relies on the research of others, and so on.

### PART II: THE SUMMARY

The summary itself grows out of your thesis sentence. The development of your theme should follow the form of the work that you are summarizing. That is, you should present the main events as they occur in the story, even if much of the story is related by a flashback method; you should try to recreate the actual movement of the story itself. Remember, however, that what characterizes your theme *as a theme* is your central idea—your general interpretation of the work—and your guiding topic sentences that give unity to each of your paragraphs. Remind yourself as you write that (1) you should closely follow the work you summarize, (2) you should write accurately, precisely, and vividly, and (3) you should use an occasional word, phrase, or passage from the work to give your reader a taste of the original.

# Sample Theme

## *A Summary of Eudora Welty's "A Worn Path"*

[1]     In "A Worn Path," a story of about 3,500 words, Eudora Welty describes a brief incident in the life of an old but almost timeless black woman, Phoenix Jackson. <u>Welty shows that Phoenix possesses great personal strength and cheerfulness despite the grimness of her life.</u>* The story is mostly narrative, with dialogue when characters other than Phoenix appear, and with monologue as Phoenix herself addresses animals, a thornbush, birds, a scarecrow, and herself. <u>Her spiritual strength and optimism are shown in her walk through the countryside, her experience on the streets, and her meeting with the medical personnel.</u>†

[2]     <u>Her walk to Natchez, by far the longest section of the story, demonstrates Phoenix's strong determination.</u> Just before Christmas she is walking on a way through the countryside that she obviously knows well. This is the "worn path." She conquers a long hill, gets loose from a prickly thornbush, balances on a log across a creek, and crawls through a barbed wire fence. Having no one to speak to, she carries on a cheerful monologue with the creatures and objects around her, thus overcoming her loneliness. When she is attacked by a large black dog she falls in a ditch, from which she is pulled by a young white hunter. He is impressed with her single-mindedness and bravery, although he advises her to go back home. A trace of minor larceny is shown by Phoenix when she steals a nickel the young man had dropped as he left her to scare away the dog, but she is honest enough with herself to realize that this "theft" is a violation of her integrity.

[3]     <u>Once Phoenix reaches Natchez, she has left the danger of the countryside and expects only friendliness on the streets.</u> She sees a white woman carrying Christmas bundles, and persuades this woman to tie her shoelaces, a task which the woman obligingly performs. Phoenix's confidence in this instance is rewarded.

[4]     <u>After Phoenix finds the building that marks her destination, the perspective of the story changes to make plain the grim facts of her daily life.</u> This section is mainly dialogue between the attendant and the nurse. The nurse has known Phoenix for a long time and reveals to the attendant that Phoenix's grandson had drunk lye two or three years before and is now an invalid in the sole care of Phoenix. Phoenix has come for a soothing syrup, which the nurse gives her, while the attendant gives her a nickel. Phoenix decides to buy a paper windmill and take it to her grandson. On this note of confidence and resolution the story ends.

---

*Central idea
†Thesis sentence
**For the text of this story, please see Appendix C, pp. 340–346.**

# Commentary on the Theme

To clarify the distinction between a summary theme and a précis, this summary theme is about the same story that is discussed in the sample theme in Chapter 1. The summary theme contains a paragraph of introduction, in which details about the physical appearance of the story are included. The first paragraph also contains a central idea and a thesis sentence. A précis contains none of this material.

The second paragraph begins with a topic sentence about Phoenix's determination, and all the details in the paragraph are related to her character. The paragraph thus shows that she *conquers* a hill, that she *overcomes* loneliness by speaking to her surroundings, that she is *single-minded* in her discussion with the hunter, and even after stealing the nickel that she is aware of a breach in her *integrity*.

In each of the remaining paragraphs the details are similarly related to positive aspects of Phoenix's character. The theme is therefore unified by means not expected of a précis. A summary theme, like any fully developed theme, will be unsuccessful unless the central idea is emphasized throughout.

# chapter 3

# *The Theme*
# *About Likes or Dislikes*

Generally, you will like a literary work for one or more of the following reasons:

> You like and admire the characters and approve of what they do and
> stand for.
> You learn more about topics very important to you.
> You learn something you had never known or thought before.
> You gain new or fresh insights into things you had already known.
> You learn about characters from different ways of life.
> You are involved and interested in the outcome of the action or ideas,
> and you do not want to put the work down until you have finished it.
> You feel happy because of reading the work.
> You are amused and laugh often as you read.
> You like the author's presentation.
> You find that some of the ideas and expressions are beautiful and worth
> remembering.

Obviously, if you find none of these things in the work, or find something that is distasteful, you will not like the work.

## Keep a Notebook for Your
## First Responses

No one can tell you what you should or should not like. Liking is your own concern. For this reason, in preparing a theme about your likes you should build on your own responses. The best way to do this is to keep a notebook in which you record your thoughts immediately after finishing a work, or even while you are reading it. Be absolutely frank in your opinion. Write about what you like and what you do not like. Try to explain the reasons for your response, even if these reasons are brief. If, on later thought, you change or modify your first impression, record that too. Here is such a notebook entry, about Guy de Maupassant's story "The Necklace" (this story is included in Appendix C, pp. 318–323):

> I liked "The Necklace" because of the surprise ending. It isn't that I liked Mathilde's bad luck, but I liked the way De Maupassant hid the most important fact in the story until the end. Mathilde thus did all that work and sacrifice for no real reason, and the surprise ending makes this point strongly.

This paragraph could easily be developed for a theme. The virtue of it is that it is a clear statement of the writer's liking, followed by an explanation of the major reasons for this response. This pattern, which can best be phrased as "I like [dislike] this because . . . ," is necessary in your notebook entries.

The challenge in writing a theme about likes or dislikes is that, to create a full thematic development, you must explore some of the "because" areas. For this reason it is important to try to pinpoint some of the specific things you liked or disliked while your first impressions of the work are fresh in your mind. If at first you cannot write your reasons fully, at least list the particular things that you liked or disliked. Once you start drafting your theme, you can fill in details and try to phrase your reasons fully and more clearly. If you allow yourself to lose your responses, however, your later task will be that much more difficult.

## What Do You Do with Dislikes?

It is important to know that disliking a work is acceptable and that you do not need to hide this response. Here are two short notebook responses expressing dislike for "The Necklace":

> 1. I didn't like "The Necklace" because Mathilde seems spoiled, and I didn't think she was worth reading about.
> 2. "The Necklace" is not an adventure story, and I like reading only adventure stories.

These are both legitimate responses. The first is based on a distaste for the major character, the second on a preference for stories with rapid action which evoke interest in the dangers faced and overcome by the main characters.

Here is a paragraph expanded from the first response. What is important here is that the reasons for dislike are explained; they would need only slightly more development for an entire theme:

I did not like "The Necklace" because Mathilde seems spoiled and I didn't think she was worth reading about. She is a phony. She nags her husband because he is not rich. She never tells the truth. I especially dislike her hurrying away from the party because she is afraid of being seen in her shabby coat. It is foolish and dishonest of her not to tell Jeanne Forrestier about losing the necklace. It is true that she works hard to pay the debt, but she also puts her husband through ten years of misery that are unnecessary. If Mathilde had faced facts, she might have had a better life. I do not like her and cannot like the story because of her.

As long as your reasons for dislike are clearly stated, as they are in this paragraph, you can confidently base your theme on a dislike. It is better to write directly about your own response than to force yourself into a positive central idea which you do not really believe.

## Putting Dislikes into a Larger Context

If one can give an honest opinion, however, it is also necessary to expand one's taste. For example, the dislike based on a preference for only adventure stories, if it is applied generally, would cause a person to dislike most great works of literature. This seems unnecessarily self-limiting.

If a person can put negative responses into a larger context, it is possible to expand his or her likes in line with very personal responses. A young woman might be deeply involved in personal concerns and therefore be uninterested in seemingly remote literary figures. However, if by reading about literary characters she can gain insight into general problems of life, and therefore her own concerns, she can like just about any work of literature. A young man might like sports events and therefore not care for reading anything but sports magazines. But what interests him in sports is the competition. If he can find competition, or conflict, in a work of literature, he can like that work. The principle here is that already established reasons for liking something may be stimulated by works which at first did not seem to bring them out.

As an example, let us consider the dislike based on a preference for adventure stories again, and see if this preference can be analyzed. Here are some reasons for liking adventure:

1. Adventure has fast action.
2. Adventure has danger.
3. Adventure has daring, active characters.
4. Adventure has obstacles which the characters work hard to overcome.

Not much can be done for "The Necklace" with the first three points, but the last point is promising. In looking at Mathilde Loisel, we can see that she works hard to overcome an obstacle—paying off a large debt. If our student likes adventure because the characters try to gain a worthy goal, perhaps he or she can also like "The Necklace" because of Mathilde's efforts. A comparison like this one can become the basis for a thoughtful favorable response.

The following paragraph shows how the comparison may be expanded to form the basis for an entire theme on liking. (The sample theme is also developed along these lines.)

> I like only adventure stories, and therefore I disliked "The Necklace" because it is not adventure. But I see that one reason for liking adventure is that the characters work hard to overcome difficult obstacles like finding buried treasure or exploring new places. Mathilde also works hard to overcome an obstacle—helping to pay back the money, with interest, borrowed to buy the replacement necklace. I like adventure characters because they stick to things and win out. I see the same toughness in Mathilde. Her problems therefore become interesting as the story moves on after a slow beginning. I can truthfully say that I came to like the story.

This example shows the ability to apply an accepted principle of liking to another work where it also applies. A person who applies principles in this open-minded way can, no matter how slowly, redefine dislikes and expand the ability to like and appreciate many kinds of literature.

Another, equally open-minded way to develop understanding and appreciation is to try to put dislikes in the following light: An author's creation of an unlikable character or repulsive event may be deliberate; your dislike results from the author's *intentions*. A first task of writing therefore becomes the attempt to explain the intention or plan. As you put the plan into your own words, you may find that you can like a work with unlikable things in it. Here is a paragraph showing this pattern:

> De Maupassant apparently wanted the reader to dislike Mathilde, and I do. He shows her as unrealistic and spoiled. She lies to everyone and nags her husband. Her rushing away from the party so that no one can see her shabby coat is a form of lying. But I can like the story itself because De Maupassant makes another kind of point. He does not hide her bad qualities, but makes me see that she herself is the cause of her trouble. If people like Mathilde never face the truth, they will get into bad situations. This is a good point, and I like the way De Maupassant makes it. The entire story is therefore worth liking even though I still do not like Mathilde.

Please observe that neither of the two ways shown of broadening the contexts of dislike is dishonest to the original expressions of dislike. In the first paragraph, the writer applies one of his principles of liking to include "The Necklace." In the second the writer considers her initial dislike in the context of the work, and discovers a basis for liking the story as a whole while still disliking the main character. The main concern is to keep an open mind despite initial dislike, and then to see if this response can be modified.

However, if, after consideration, you decide that your dislike overbalances any reasons you can find for liking, then you should go ahead to write about your dislike of the work. The central idea of such a theme would be the expression of dislike, and the body would develop the major reasons for this response. Thus, a theme on "The Necklace" in line with the earlier paragraph (p. 49), might develop Mathilde's "spoiled" character and her untruthfulness.

## Organizing Your Theme

### INTRODUCTION

You should open by describing briefly the conditions that influenced your response. Your central idea should be whether you liked or disliked the work. The thesis sentence should list the major causes of your response, to be developed in the body of your theme.

### BODY

1. One approach is to consider the thing or things about the work that you liked or disliked (for a list of possible reasons for liking a work, see the beginning of this chapter, p. 47). You may like a particular character, or maybe you got so interested in the story that you could not put it down. Also, it may be that a major idea, a new or fresh insight, or a particular outcome is the major point that you wish to develop. A sample paragraph earlier in this chapter (p. 48) shows how a "surprise ending" can be the cause of a favorable response.

2. Another approach is to give details about how your responses developed in your reading of the work. This approach requires that you pinpoint, in order, the various good parts of the work (or the bad) and how you responded to them. Your aim here should not be to retell the story, but to discuss those details which caused your like or dislike.

3. Two additional types of response are described in some detail above (pp. 49–51). The first is attempting to show how a principle for liking one type of literature may be applied to the assigned work. The second is beginning with an initial dislike but finding a larger context which may permit a favorable response.

### CONCLUSION

Here you might briefly summarize the reasons for your major response. You might also try to face any issues brought up by a change in your responses. That is, if you have always held certain assumptions about your taste but liked the work despite these assumptions, you may wish to talk about your own change or development. This topic is personal, but in a theme about likes or dislikes, discovery about yourself is not undesirable.

---

## Sample Theme

### Some Reasons for Liking Guy de Maupassant's "The Necklace"

---

[1] To me, the most likable kind of reading or entertainment is adventure. Although there are many reasons for my preference, an important one is that adventure characters work hard to overcome obstacles. Because "The Necklace" is not adventure, I did not like it at first. But in one respect the story is like adventure. Mathilde, with her husband, works hard for ten years to overcome a difficult obstacle. Thus, because Mathilde does what adventure characters also do, the story is likable.* Mathilde's appeal results from her hard work, strong character, and sad fate.†

[2] Mathilde's hard work makes her seem good. Once she and her husband are faced with the huge debt of 36,000 francs with interest, she works like a slave to pay it back. She gives up her servant and moves to a cheaper place. She does the household drudgery, wears cheap clothes, and bargains with shopkeepers for low prices. Just like the characters in adventure stories, who sometimes must do hard and unpleasant things, she does what she has to, and this makes her admirable.

[3] Her strong character makes her endure, a likable trait. To do the bad jobs, she needs toughness. At first she is a nagging, spoiled person, always dreaming about wealth and telling lies, but she changes for the better. She sees her responsibility for losing the necklace, and she has enough sense of self-sacrifice to pay for restoring it. She sacrifices "heroically" (de Maupassant's word) not only her position, but also her youth and beauty. Her jobs are not the exotic and glamorous ones of adventure stories, but her force of character makes her as likable as an adventure heroine.

[4] Her sad fate also makes her likable. In adventure stories the characters often suffer as they do their jobs. Mathilde also suffers, but in a different way, because her suffering is permanent while the hardships of adventure characters are temporary. This fact makes her pitiable, and even more so because all her sacrifices are really not necessary. Thus there is a sense of injustice about her which makes the reader take her side.

Obviously "The Necklace" is not an adventure story, but some of the good

---

*Central idea
†Thesis sentence
For the text of this story, please see Appendix C, pp. 318–323.

[5]    qualities of adventure characters can also be seen in Mathilde. Also, the surprise revelation that the lost necklace was false is an unforgettable twist which makes her more deserving than she seems at first. De Maupassant has arranged the story so that the reader finally admires Mathilde. "The Necklace" is a skillful and likable story.

---

## Commentary on the Theme

The argument in this theme is that "The Necklace," which at first was not liked, can be liked because Mathilde, the major character, has qualities that evoke liking for characters in works of adventure. Each of the reasons brought out for liking Mathilde is also a reason for liking adventure characters. Although the liking for adventure is thus a bridge which the writer crosses on the way to liking "The Necklace," some other reasons are brought out in the conclusion.

In the introduction the connection is made between adventure characters and Mathilde. The thesis sentence lists three topics for development in the body of the theme.

Paragraph two gives instances of Mathilde's hard work as a cause for liking, and concludes by comparing Mathilde and adventure characters as workers. The third paragraph gives examples of Mathilde's toughness of character and also compares her strength with that of adventure characters. In paragraph four a comparison on the basis of suffering and hardship is made, and the pity and sympathy felt for Mathilde are claimed as causes for liking her. The conclusion restates the comparison, and also lists the surprise ending and the development of the story as reasons for liking "The Necklace."

# chapter 4

# The Theme
# of Character Analysis

Character in literature is an extended verbal representation of a human being, specifically the inner self that determines thought, speech, and behavior. Through dialogue, action, and commentary, literature captures some of the interactions of character and circumstance. Literature makes these interactions interesting by portraying characters who are worth caring about, rooting for, and even loving, although there are also characters at whom you may laugh or whom you may dislike or even hate.

## Choice and Character

The choices that people make indicate their characters, if we assume that they have freedom of choice. We always make silent comparisons with the choices made or rejected. Thus, if you know that John works twelve hours a day, while Tom puts in five, and Jim sleeps under a tree, you have a number of separate facts, but you do not conclude anything about their characters unless you have a basis for comparison. This basis is easy: The usual, average number of working hours is eight. With no more than this knowledge for comparison, you might conclude that John is a workaholic, Tom lazy, and Jim either unwell or a dropout. To be fair, you would need to know much more about the lives and financial circumstances of each character before your conclusions would be final.

## Character and Completeness

In literature you may expect such completeness of context. You may think of each action or speech, no matter how small or seemingly unusual, as an accumulating part of a total portrait. Whereas in life things may "just happen," in literature the actions, interactions, speeches, and observations are all arranged to give you the details you need for conclusions about character. Thus you read about important events like a first confession (O'Connor's "First Confession"), a long period of work and sacrifice (De Maupassant's "The Necklace"), the taking of a regular journey of mercy (Welty's "A Worn Path"), or a sudden change from anger to love (Chekhov's *The Bear*). From these happenings in their contexts you make inferences about the characters involved. In effect, you determine the "character" of the various characters.

## Major Character Traits

In writing about a literary character, you should try to describe the character's major trait or traits. As in life, characters may be lazy or ambitious, anxious or serene, aggressive or fearful, assertive or bashful, confident or self-doubting, adventurous or timid, noisy or quiet, visionary or practical, reasonable or hotheaded, careful or careless, fair or partial, straightforward or underhanded, "winners" or "losers," and so on.

With this sort of list, to which you may add at will, you can analyze and write about character. For example, in studying Mathilde Loisel, the main character in De Maupassant's "The Necklace" (and the subject of the sample theme, pp. 60–61), you would note that she spends much time at the start in daydreaming about wealth she cannot have. She might be considered a dreamer. This is not unusual, but she is so swept up in her visions of ease that she is unhappy with the life that she has. It is fair to conclude that this conflict indicates a weakness or flaw, because her dream life hurts her real life. It is out of conflicts such as this that you can get a "handle" on characters for your theme.

## Appearance, Action, and Character

When you study character, be sure to consider physical descriptions, but also be sure to relate the physical to the mental. Suppose your author stresses the neatness of one character and the sloppiness of another. Most likely, these descriptions can be related to your character study. The same also applies to your treatment of what a character *does*. Go beyond the actions themselves and try to indicate what they show *about* the character. Always try to get from the outside to the inside, for it is on the inside that character resides.

## Change and Development

There is a great deal of interaction between character and the outcome of any story or drama. In some types of literature certain character traits are essential. In cowboy or detective stories, for example, it is essential that the main characters be strong, tough, steadfast, and clever so that they may overcome the obstacles before them or solve the crime. In Greek tragedy a fatal flaw of character is the cause of the hero's downfall. In these cases there are consequences that proceed logically and inevitably from character; the characters stay the same throughout the work and therefore cause their own success or failure.

In many works, however, you will see a change or growth of character, and therefore an outcome that might have seemed inevitable will alter. You may decide for yourself whether human character is capable of radical change, or whether change is really to be described as growth or development. If a person who as a child was very combative becomes successful and peaceful as an adult lawyer, he or she may simply have transferred youthful aggression into the acceptable arena of legal wrangles and tangles. Was there a change or was there development? Similarly, Shakespeare's Juliet is a young, impressionable girl at the start of *Romeo and Juliet*, but by the end of the play she is a determined, resolute woman. Does her character change, or does it develop? It is more important to observe and discuss such character modifications accurately than to take an arbitrary position on whether you have change or development. Of course some authors arrange their characterizations as an embodiment of either change or development. If the position of the author is clear to you, you must take this view into account in your analysis of the character.

## How Is Character Disclosed in Literature?

In preparing your theme, you should look for the following four specific ways in which writers may give you information about character. Always remember that authors rely on you for the knowledge of ordinary behavior to make the comparisons spoken of earlier.

1. *What the characters themselves say (and think, if the author expresses their thoughts).* On the whole, speeches may be accepted at face value to indicate

the character of the speaker. Sometimes, however, a speech may be made offhand, or it may reflect a momentary emotional or intellectual state. Thus, if characters in deep despair say that life is worthless, you must balance this speech with what the same characters say when they are happy. You must also consider the situation or total context of a statement. Macbeth's despair at the end of *Macbeth* is voiced after he has been guilty of ruthless political suppression and assassination. His speech therefore reflects his own guilt and self-hatred. You should also consider whether speeches show change or development. A despairing character might say depressing things at the start but happy things at the end. Your analysis of such speeches should indicate how they show change in your character.

2. *What the characters do.* You have heard that "actions speak louder than words," and you should interpret actions freely as signs of character. Thus you might consider Phoenix's trip through the woods (Welty's "A Worn Path") as a sign of a loving, responsible character, even though Phoenix nowhere says that she is loving and responsible. The difficulty and hardship she goes through on the walk, however, justify such a conclusion.

Sometimes you may find that action is inconsistent with words. Here you might have hypocrisy, weakness, or an approaching change. Smirnov, in Chekhov's *The Bear*, would be crazy to teach Mrs. Popov how to use the dueling pistol properly, because she has threatened to kill him with it. But he is about ready to declare love for her, and this cooperative if potentially self-destructive act shows that his loving nature is even stronger than his sense of self-preservation.

3. *What other characters say about them.* In literature, as in life, people always talk about other people. If the speakers are shown as honest, you may usually accept their opinions as accurate descriptions of character. But sometimes a person's prejudices and interests distort what that person says. You know, for example, that the word of a person's enemy is usually slanted, unfair, or even untrue. Therefore an author may give you a good impression of characters by having a bad character say bad things about them. Similarly, the word of a close friend or political manager may be biased in favor of a particular character. You must always consider the context and source of all dramatic remarks before you use them in your analysis.

4. *What the author says about them, speaking as storyteller or observer.* What the author says about a character is usually to be accepted as truth. Naturally, authors must be accepted on matters of fact. But when they *interpret* the actions and characteristics of their characters, they themselves assume the critic's role, and their opinions may be either right or wrong. For this reason authors frequently avoid interpretations and devote their skill instead to arranging events and speeches so that their conclusions are obvious to the reader.

## Reality and Probability

You are entitled to expect that characters in literature will be true to life. That is, their actions, statements, and thoughts must all be what human beings are *likely* to do, say, and think under given conditions. This is the standard of *probability*.

Probability does not rule out surprise or even exaggeration. Thus, in Chekhov's *The Bear*, the main characters, who are strangers when the short play opens, fall in love. This change might at first seem improbable, but it is only sudden. Chekhov shows that both Mrs. Popov and Smirnov have deeply loving and emotional natures, and that they are given to suddenness or whim. Under the emotional crisis of their threatened duel, it is therefore probable that they would turn directly to loving each other. The action, though surprising and exaggerated, meets the standard of probability.

There are, of course, many ways of rendering the probable in literature. Fiction attempting to mirror life—the realistic, naturalistic, or "slice of life" types of fiction—sets up conditions and raises expectations about the characters that are different from those of fiction attempting to portray a romantic, fanciful world. A character's behavior and speech in the "realistic" setting would be out of place in the romantic setting.

But the situation is more complex than this, for within the romantic setting a character might reasonably be *expected* to behave and speak in a fanciful, dreamlike way. Speech and action under both conditions are therefore *probable* as we understand the word, although different aspects of human character are presented in these two different types of works.

It is also possible that within the same work you might find some characters who are realistic but others who are not. In such works you have contrasting systems of reality. Shakespeare creates such a contrast in *Richard II*. Richard is a person with unrealistic expectations of himself and those around him; he lives in a dream world and is so out of touch with his surroundings that ultimately he is destroyed. You might also encounter works where there are mythical or supernatural figures who contrast with the realism of the other characters. In judging characters in works of this type, your only guide is that of probability.[1]

---

[1]You may reasonably wonder about how you should judge the character of gods, or devils, for that matter. Usually gods embody the qualities of the best, most moral human beings, although the ancient Greeks sometimes attributed to the gods some of the same follies and faults that beset humanity. To judge a devil, try thinking of the worst human qualities, but remember that the devil is often imagined as a character with many engaging traits, the easier to deceive poor sinners and lead them into hell.

# Does the Character Come to Life?

With all these considerations in mind, you can see that literary characters should be true to life, under given circumstances and within certain literary specifications. The key to your study of character should always be to discover if the character—whether intended by the author to be a lifelike person or a romantic hero—does and says what you believe human beings might do and say under the exact conditions presented by the author. Do the characters ring true? Do they come to life? Do they illustrate many qualities that add up to accurate representations of human beings? Or do they seem to be one-dimensional or flat? The degree to which an author can make a character come alive is a mark of skill, and if you think that your author is successful in this regard, you should say so in your theme.

# Organizing Your Theme

## INTRODUCTION

Your theme should have a clearly stated central idea that runs throughout the entire character analysis. Your central idea will be whatever general statement you make to describe the character. The thesis sentence must be a brief statement of the main sections of your theme.

## BODY

The organization is designed to illustrate and prove your central idea. You have much freedom in organizing your main points. Some possible methods are the following:

1. Organization around a central characteristic, like "kindness, gentleness, generosity, firmness," or "resoluteness of will frustrated by inopportune moments for action, resulting in despondency, doubt, and melancholy." A body containing this sort of material would demonstrate how the literary work brings out each of these qualities.

2. Organization around a development or change of character. Here you would attempt to show the character traits that a character possesses at the start of the work, and then describe the changes or developments that occur. Try to determine the author's view on such changes; that is, is the change genuine, or does the author establish hidden traits in the character which are brought out as the story progresses?

3. Organization around central incidents that reveal primary characteristics. Certain key incidents will stand out in a work, and you might create

an effective body by using three or four of these as guides for your discussion, taking care to show in your topic sentences that your purpose is to illuminate the character you have selected, not the incidents. In other words, you would regard the incidents only as they bring out truths about character. Naturally, with this arrangement, you would have to show how the incidents bring out the characteristics and also how they serve to explain other things the character might do.

## CONCLUSION

The conclusion should contain your statements about how the characteristics you have brought out are related to the work as a whole. If the person was good but came to a bad end, does this discrepancy elevate him or her to tragic stature? If the person was a nobody and came to a bad end, does this fact cause you to draw any conclusion about the class or type of which he or she was a part? Or does it illustrate the author's view of human life? Or both? Do the characteristics explain why the person helps or hinders other characters? Does your analysis help you to clear up any misunderstanding that your first reading of the work produced? Questions such as these should be raised and answered in your conclusion.

---

### Sample Theme

*The Character of Mathilde Loisel
in Guy de Maupassant's "The Necklace"*

---

[1]    Guy de Maupassant's character Mathilde Loisel, in "The Necklace," is above all a dreamer. Her dreams make her both weak and strong.* Her weakness is that her dream is not to have high ideals, but rather to have a life of ease and wealth. Her strength is her willingness to work to keep her dreams of honor. De Maupassant shows her qualities in the introduction, the cover-up, and the poverty she endures.†

[2]    In the early part of the story Mathilde is a young housewife dreaming about wealth. She thinks money is everything, and her highest aim is ease and luxury, which she thinks that she was somehow born to have. Her husband, a lower-rank clerk, can afford only a small household. Mathilde gets angry at this gap between her dream and the reality of her life. The result is that she is not able

*Central idea
†Thesis sentence
For the text of this story, please see Appendix C, pp. 318–323.

to like anything that she has. She does not treat her husband with love and respect, but whines at him instead about their condition. Her borrowing of the necklace for the big party is, in a way, her attempt to escape her drab life and live out her dream, if only for a night.

[3] The cover-up of the loss of the necklace brings out the worst in Mathilde. She believes more strongly in the real value of the jewels than in her friendship with Jeanne Forrestier. If she had told the truth to Jeanne, she would never have had the trouble she faced. But her character is too weak to permit her to endure the embarrassment that the truth would bring. Thus, by covering up, she loses friendship, truth, and financial future all at the same time.

[4] But her life of poverty and sacrifice to pay back the money lenders brings out her strengths. She pitches in to work. She gives up her servant, her good address, and everything else connected with her dreams of good living. Although her character is excellent in this respect, her hard work makes her loud and coarse, just the opposite of the wealthy, refined person she dreamed of becoming.

[5] Thus Mathilde is a character whose dream life keeps her from seeing the truth until the truth hits her with a vengeance. It is this weakness, not her bad luck, that gives her all her pain. It is this same weakness that brings out her best quality of sharing the work to preserve her honor and good name. She may be dreamy, unlucky, and foolish, but she is not bad. On balance, she comes out looking good, getting a life that is much worse than she deserves.

---

## Commentary on the Theme

This theme is representative of the first type of organization described above, organization around a central characteristic (p. 59). The central characteristic described is Mathilde's dreaminess. The introduction asserts that this quality produces a character of both weakness and strength. The second paragraph develops her weakness inasmuch as Mathilde's dreams make her too unhappy to adjust to the life she has with her husband. This paragraph relies for its data on the author's descriptions of Mathilde's dreams and on her own complaints when her husband announces the party. The judgment on Mathilde is based on the theme writer's apparent belief that dream life should not have a negative effect on real life.

Paragraph three continues with the weak side of Mathilde, showing the disastrous effects of her false values. The data for this paragraph are taken from the description of the activities to hide the loss, together with a comparison of how a frank admission of the loss might have avoided the large debt.

The fourth paragraph emphasizes Mathilde's strengths, which result, like her weakness, from her character as a dreamer. The judgment is clearly based on the idea that hard work and cooperation are virtues.

The concluding paragraph attempts to weigh Mathilde's character (one might wish to dispute the assertion that the bad luck is not the major cause of her trouble), and states that her willingness to endure her hardship makes her seem worthy of a better fate than she received.

# chapter 5

# The Theme About Point of View

Point of view is the position from which details in a literary work are perceived, described, and interpreted. It is a method of rendering, a means by which authors create a centralizing intelligence, a narrative personality, an intellectual filter through which you receive the narration or argument. Other terms describing point of view are *viewpoint, unifying voice, perspective, persona, mask, center of attention,* and *focus.*

In practice, you can think of point of view as the character or speaker who does the talking. To write about point of view is to describe the effect of the speaker—his or her circumstances, traits, motives, and limitations—on the literary work.

You might respond that our definition means that authors do not use their own "voices" when they write, but somehow change themselves into another character, who may be a totally separate creation. This response is right. It is true that authors, as writers of their own works, are always in control of what gets written, but it does not follow that they always use their own voices. It is not easy to determine exactly what one's "own voice" is. Test yourself: When you speak to your instructor, to your friend, to a child, to a person you love, or to a distant relative, your voice always sounds the same. But the personality—or persona—that you employ changes according to the person you are talking to. Your point of view changes.

When writing about point of view, therefore, you should try to determine the nature of the speaker. It is not helpful to deal vaguely with "the author's point of view," as though you were talking about opinions. What you need is to analyze and describe the character and circumstances of the speaker.

## Point of View and "Throwing the Voice"

A helpful way to think of point of view is that the speaker is a ventriloquist's dummy and the author is the ventriloquist. The author "throws" the voice into the dummy, whose words you actually read. Although the dummy or speaker is the one who is talking, the author is the one who makes the speaker believable and consistent. Often, of course, the speaker is the author in person, as nearly as that identity can be determined. But just as often the voice is separate and totally independent, a character who is completely imagined and consistently maintained by the author.

In short, the author creates not only stories and ideas, but also the speaker. To discuss point of view is to discuss the speaker.

It is most important to understand this fact. As an exercise, suppose for a moment that you are an author and are planning a set of stories. Try to imagine the speakers you would create for the following situations:

A happy niece who has just inherited $25 million from an uncle recalls a childhood experience with the uncle years ago.

A disappointed nephew who was cut off without a cent describes a childhood experience with the same uncle.

A ship's captain who is filled with ideas of personal honor, integrity, and responsibility describes the life of a sailor who has committed a cowardly act.

A person who has survived a youth of poverty and degradation describes a brother who has succumbed to drugs and crime.

An economist looks at problems of unemployment.

A person who has just lost a job looks at problems of unemployment.

In trying to create voices and stories for the various situations, you will recognize the importance of your *imagination* in the selection of point of view. You are always yourself, but your imagination can enable you to speak like someone else totally distinct from yourself. Point of view is hence an imaginative creation, just as much a part of the author's work as the events narrated or the ideas discussed.

## Point of View as a
## Physical Position

Thus far we have considered point of view as an interaction of personality and circumstance. There are also purely physical aspects, specifically (1) the actual place or position from which speakers or narrators see and hear the action, and (2) the capacities of the speakers as receivers of information from others. If narrators have been at the "scene" of an action, this position gives them credibility because they are reporting events they actually saw or heard. Some speakers may have been direct participants in the action; others may have been bystanders. It is possible that a speaker may have overheard a conversation, or may have witnessed a scene through a keyhole. If the speakers were not "on the spot," they must have gained their "facts" in a believable way. They could get them from someone else who was a witness or participant. They could receive letters, read newspaper articles, go through old papers in an attic or library, or hear things on a radio or television program. Sometimes the unidentified voice of the author comes from a person who seems to be hovering somehow right above the characters as they move and speak. Such a speaker, being present everywhere without being noticed, is a reliable source of all information presented in the narrative.

## Kinds of Points of View

The kinds of points of view may be classified fairly easily. You may detect the point of view in any work by determining the grammatical voice of the speaker. Then, of course, you should go on to all the other considerations thus far discussed.

### FIRST PERSON

If the story is told by an "I," the author is using the *first-person* point of view, usually a fictional narrator and not the author. First-person speakers report everything they see, hear, and think, and as they do so, they convey not only the action of the work, but also some of their own background, thinking, attitudes, and even prejudices. The speaker's particular type of speech will have a great effect on the language of the work itself. A sailor will use many nautical terms, and a sixteen-year-old boy may use much slang. For these reasons, the first-person speaker is often as much a subject of interest as the story itself. Nick Carraway in F. Scott Fitzgerald's *The Great Gatsby* is such a speaker. Nick is ostensibly a minor character in the action who tells what is happening in the lives of Gatsby and the Bu-chanans. Sometimes the "I" narrator is the major character in the book, like Mark Twain's Huckleberry Finn or Swift's Gulliver.

## THIRD PERSON

If the narrator is not introduced as a character, and if everything in the work is described in the third person (that is, *he, she, it, they*), the author is using the *third-person* point of view. There are variants here.

The third-person point of view is called *omniscient* (all-knowing) when the speaker not only describes the action and dialogue of the work, but also seems to know everything that goes on in the minds of the characters. In the third-person omniscient point of view authors take great responsi-bility: by delving into the minds of their characters, they assume a stance that exceeds our ordinary experience with other persons. Like God, the omniscient speaker attempts to show the inner workings of a character's mind. If you encounter the omniscient point of view, you may be sure that the writer is displaying concern with psychological patterns and motiva-tions. The omniscient point of view is characterized by phrases like "He thought . . ." and "As she approached the scene, she considered that . . ." and so on.

If an author uses the third person but confines the narration mainly to what one single character does, says, and sometimes thinks, then you have the third-person *limited* point of view. While the omniscient point of view takes in the thoughts of most of the characters, the limited focuses on only one. The limited viewpoint is thus midway between the first- and third-person points of view. In Guy de Maupassant's story "The Necklace," for example (see Appendix C, pp. 318–323), the character Mathilde Loisel is the major focus of the narration. Everything in the story is there because she would have experienced it, heard about it, or thought about it.

## DRAMATIC

Writers using the *dramatic* point of view confine the work mainly to quotations and descriptions of actions. They avoid telling you that certain characters thought this or felt that, but instead allow the characters them-selves to voice their thoughts and feelings. Often, too, an author using the dramatic point of view will allow certain characters to interpret the thoughts and feelings of other characters, but then attitudes and possible prejudices of these speakers enter into your evaluation of their interpretations. The key to the dramatic point of view is that the writer presents the reader with action and speech but does not overtly guide the reader toward any conclusions. Naturally, however, the conclusions may be readily drawn from the details presented. Guy de Maupassant is famous for creating stories rendered in the dramatic point of view, as are Hemingway and Sherwood Anderson.

It goes without saying that many novels, being long works, often have an intermingling of viewpoints. In a largely omniscient narrative, the writer may present a chapter consisting only of action and dialogue—the dramatic point of view—and another chapter that focuses entirely on one person— the limited. Writers of short stories, on the other hand, usually maintain a consistent and uniform point of view.

## Point of View and "Evidence"

When you write a theme about point of view, you should try to consider all aspects that bear on the presentation of the material in the work you have read. You may imagine yourself somewhat like a member of a jury. Jury members cannot accept testimony uncritically, for some witnesses may have much to gain by misstatements, distortions, or outright lies. Before rendering a verdict, jury members must consider all these possibilities. Speakers in literary works are usually to be accepted as reliable witnesses, but it is true that their characters, interests, capacities, personal involvements, and positions to view action may have a bearing on the material they present. A classic example is the Japanese film, *Rashomon*, in which four separate persons tell a story as evidence in a court, and each presents a version that makes that person seem more honorable than he or she actually was. While most stories are not as complex as this, you should always consider the character of the speaker before you render your verdict on what the story is about.

## Organizing Your Theme

In a theme on point of view, the areas of concern are language, selection of detail, characterization, interpretive commentaries, and narrative development. Your theme might be organized to include analysis of one, a few, or all of these elements. Generally you should determine how the point of view has contributed toward making the story uniquely as it is, and also toward your interpretation of the story. In what way has the author's voice entered into your response to the story? Are there any special qualities in the work that could not have been achieved if the author had used another point of view?

## INTRODUCTION

In your introduction you should get at the matters that you plan to develop. Which point of view is used in the work? What is the major influence of this point of view on the work (for example—"The omniscient point of view causes full, leisurely insights into many shades of character," or "The first-person point of view enables the work to resemble an exposé of back-room political deals.")? To what extent does the selection of point of view make the work particularly interesting and effective, or uninteresting and ineffective? What particular aspects of the work (action, dialogue, characters, description, narration, analysis) do you wish to analyze in support of your central idea?

## BODY

The questions you raise here will of course depend on the work you have studied. It would be impossible to answer all of the following questions in your analysis, but going through them should make you aware of the sorts of things you can include in the body of your theme.

If you have read a work with the first-person point of view, your analysis will necessarily involve the speaker. Who is she (if a woman)? Is she a major or a minor character? What is her background? What is her relationship to the person listening to her (if there is a listener)? Does she speak directly to you, the reader, in such a way that you are a listener or an eavesdropper? How does the speaker describe the various situations? Is her method uniquely a function of her character? Or (if a man), how reliable is he as an observer? How did he acquire the information he is presenting? How much does he disclose? How much does he hide? Does he ever rely on the information of others for his material? How reliable are these other witnesses? Does the speaker undergo any changes in the course of the work that have any bearing on the ways he presents the material? Does he notice one kind of thing (e.g., discussion) but miss others (e.g., natural scenery)? What might have escaped him, if anything? Does the author put the speaker into situations that he can describe but not understand? Why? Is the speaker ever confused? Is he close to the action, or distant from it? Does he show emotional involvement in any situations? Are you sympathetic to his concerns or are you put off by them? If the speaker makes any commentary, are his thoughts valid? To what extent, if any, is the speaker of as much interest as the material he presents?

If you encounter any of the third-person points of view, try to determine the characteristics of the voice employed by the author. Does it seem that the author is speaking in his or her own voice, or that the narrator has a special voice? You can approach this problem by answering many of the questions that are relevant to the first-person point of view. Also try to determine the distance of the narrator to the action. How is the action described? How is the dialogue recorded? Is there any background information given? Do the descriptions reveal any bias toward any of the characters? Are the descriptions full or bare? Does the author include descriptions or analyses of a character's thoughts? What are these like? Do you see evidence of the author's own philosophy? Does the choice of words direct you toward any particular interpretations? What limitations or freedoms devolve upon the story as a result of the point of view?

CONCLUSION

In your conclusion you should evaluate the success of the author's point of view: Was it consistent, effective, truthful? What did the writer gain (if anything) by the selection of point of view? What was lost (if anything)? How might a less skillful writer have handled similar material? After answering questions like these, you may end your theme.

## Problems in Writing Your Theme

1. In considering point of view, you will encounter the problem of whether to discuss the author or the speaker as the originator of attitudes and ideas. If the author is employing the first-person point of view, there is no problem. Use the speaker's name, if he or she is given one (e.g., Nick Carraway, Huck Finn, Holden Caulfield), or else talk about the "speaker" or "persona" if there is no name. You face a greater problem with the third-person points of view, but even here it is safe for you to discuss the "speaker" rather than the "author," remembering always that the author is manipulating the narrative voice. Sometimes authors emphasize a certain phase of their own personalities through their speakers. There are naturally many ideas common to both the author and the speaker, but your statements about these must be inferential, not absolute.

2. You may have a tendency to wander away from point of view into retelling the story or discussing the ideas. Emphasize the presentation of the events and ideas, and the causes for this presentation. Do not emphasize the subject material itself, but use it only as it bears on your consideration of point of view. Your object is not just to interpret the work, but also to show how the point of view enables you to interpret the work.

Obviously you must talk about the material in the work, but use it only to illustrate your assertions about point of view. Avoid the following pattern of statement, which will always lead you astray: "The speaker says this, which means this." Instead, adhere to the following pattern, which will keep your emphasis always on your central idea: "The speaker says this, which shows this about her and her attitudes." If a particular idea is difficult, you might need to explain it, but do not do so unless it illustrates your central idea.

3. Remember that you are dealing with point of view in the *entire* work and not simply in single narrations and conversations. For example, an individual character has her own way of seeing things when she states something, but in relation to the entire work her speech is a function of the dramatic point of view. Thus, you should not talk about Character *A*'s point of view, and Character *B*'s, but instead should state that "Using the dramatic point of view, Author *Z* allows the various characters to argue their cases, in their own words and with their own limitations."

4. Be particularly careful to distinguish between point of view and opinions or beliefs. Point of view refers to the total position from which things are seen, heard, and reported, whereas an opinion is a thought about something. In this theme, you are to describe not the ideas, but the method of narration of an author.

## Sample Theme

*Frank O'Connor's First-Person Point of View in "First Confession"*

[1]
In Frank O'Connor's "First Confession," a story based in early twentieth-century Ireland, the point of view is first person. The speaker is an adult named Jackie, who recalls the events leading up to and including his first confession as a boy of seven. <u>Jackie has good recall and organizing ability, but has limited adult perspective.</u>* <u>These qualities make the story detailed, dramatic, and objective.</u>†

[2]
<u>The detail of the story seems vivid and real because O'Connor presents Jackie as a person with strong recall.</u> Events such as the knife scene, the drinking and eating by the barefoot grandmother, and the stories of Mrs. Ryan are colorful. They seem like high points of childhood that an adult would truly remember. The entire confession is presented as if it just happened, not as if it were an almost forgotten event of the past. Such vivid details, which give the story great interest, depend on their being still alive in the narrator's memory.

<u>Beyond simple recall, O'Connor's drama rests on the organizing skills of the narrator.</u> The story is made up of scenes that are unified and connected.

*Central idea
†Thesis sentence
For the text of this story, please see Appendix C, pp. 333–339.

[3] Thus the first part of the confession, ending with Jackie's falling out of the confessional and being whacked by Nora, is a short but complete farce. The burning handprints of the man of the bad confession become a theme in Jackie's mind as he waits for the priest. In the confession itself Jackie mentions even the dramatic pause before the priest responds to the confessed plan to kill the grandmother. The drama in all these scenes results from a good story-telling narrator.

[4] The objective quality of "First Confession," accounting for O'Connor's humor, is related to a flaw in the narrator. Jackie makes remarks about the action, but these are childish and not adult. A more mature narrator might comment about the fear the boy gains through his religious instruction, the difficulties of his family life, or the beauty of his first confession. But from the adult Jackie's point of view we get no such comments. O'Connor makes Jackie stick to the events, and therefore he keeps the story objective, simple, and funny.

[5] Thus O'Connor's selection of the first-person point of view gives the story strength and humor. Jackie the adult is faithful to his childhood feelings. We get everything from his side, and only his side. He never gives his father or his sister any credit. It is the consistent point of view that makes "First Confession" both comic and excellent. If Jackie showed more adult understanding, O'Connor's humor would be gone, and the story would not be such good entertainment.

---

## Commentary on the Theme

This theme emphasizes both the abilities and the flaw of the narrator and attempts to relate these qualities to the nature of "First Confession." The introduction provides a brief background of the story, but gets right to the point of view. The qualification of Jackie as a first-person observer is mentioned, followed by the central idea and thesis sentence. The second paragraph states that the vivid detail of the story results from Jackie's powerful recall. The third paragraph connects the dramatic quality of the various scenes with his skill as a storyteller. In the fourth paragraph a flaw in Jackie's adult character—a lack of adult perceptiveness—is shown as the cause of the objectivity and humor in the story. The conclusion states that the point of view is consistent, even if it is immature. The last sentence goes back to paragraph four: The humor depends on the narrator's having a lack of sympathy for and understanding of childhood antagonists. Throughout the theme, therefore, certain qualities of the story are connected directly to the character, ability, and limited perspective of the point of view or centralizing mind.

# chapter 6

# The Theme About Setting

Setting refers to the natural and artificial scenery or environment in which characters in literature live and move. Things such as the time of day and the amount of light, the trees and animals, the sounds described, the smells, and the weather are part of the setting. Paint brushes, apples, pitchforks, rafts, six-shooters, watches, automobiles, horses and buggies, and many other items belong to the setting. References to clothing, descriptions of physical appearance, and spatial relationships among the characters are also part of setting. In short, the setting of a work is the sum total of references to physical and temporal objects and artifacts.

The setting of a story or novel is much like the sets and properties of the stage or the location for a motion picture. The dramatist writing for the stage is physically limited by what can be constructed and moved. Writers of nondramatic works, however, are limited only by their imaginations. It is possible for them to include details of many places without the slightest external restraint. For our purposes, the references to setting will be to literary works that establish a setting either in nature or in manufactured things.

The action of a story may occur in more than one place. In a novel, the locale may shift constantly. Although there may be several settings in a work, the term *setting* refers to all the places mentioned. If a story is short, all the scenes may be in one city or countryside, and so a theme about setting could include a discussion of all the locations within the story. If the story is longer, it is best to focus on the setting of only one major scene; otherwise you would be forced beyond the limits of a single theme.

## Types of Settings

### NATURAL

The setting for a great deal of literature is the out-of-doors, and, naturally enough, Nature herself is seen as a force that shapes character and action. A deep woods may make walking difficult or dangerous, or it may be a place where lovers meet at night. Long distances may keep characters apart and make them different; when they meet, they may have problems that were made by their separation. A barren desert at night may make travelers seek a shelter that turns out to be unsafe. The ocean may produce storms that threaten lives, or it may be so calm that sailing ships cannot move on it. Other natural places may be the location of a quest for identity or of a meditation about the vastness of God and the smallness of human beings.

### MANUFACTURED

Manufactured things always reflect the people who made them. A building or a room tells about the people who build it and live in it, and ultimately about the social and political orders that maintain the conditions. A rich house shows the expensive tastes and resources of the characters owning it. A few cracks in the plaster and some chips in the paint may show the same persons declining in fortune and power. Ugly and impoverished surroundings may contribute to the weariness, insensitivity, negligence, or even hostility of the characters living in them.

## Studying the Uses of Setting

In preparing to write about the setting of any work, your first concern should be to discover all the details that conceivably form a part of setting, and then to determine how the author has used these details. For example, as writers stress character, plot, or action, they may emphasize or minimize setting. At times a setting will be no more than a roughly sketched place where events occur. In other stories, the setting may be used as an active participant in the action. An instance of such "participation" is Eudora Welty's "A Worn Path," where the woods and roadway provide obstacles that are almost active antagonists against Phoenix as she pushes her way to Natchez.

You might also observe that setting may be a kind of pictorial language, a means by which the author makes statements. In the concluding scene of E. M. Forster's *A Passage to India*, a large rock divides the pathway along which the two major characters are riding. This rock is a direct barrier between them, but it is more than that. It is a visual way of asserting that there are profound cultural and political differences separating England and India and that these two cultures must go their separate ways.

Authors might also use setting as a means of organizing their works. It is often comic, for example, to move a character from one setting to another (provided that no harm is done in the process). Thus, Stephen Crane provokes smiles in the first part of "The Bride Comes to Yellow Sky" by shifting a backwoods town marshal into the plush setting of a Pullman railroad car. Crane's descriptions of the awkwardness of the marshal and the patronizing airs of the other characters are humorous.

Another organizational use of setting is the framing or enclosing method: An author frames a story by opening with a description of the setting, and then returns to the description at the end. Like a picture frame, the setting constantly influences the reader's response to the story. An example of this method is Hemingway's story "In Another Country," which is set in Milan, Italy, in World War I. The opening picture is one of windy, autumnal chill, with dusky light illuminating dead animals hanging in a butcher's shop. The twilight casts a pall over a hospital courtyard. At the story's end, one of the main characters gets the news that his wife has died. He has been wounded and is in the hospital, and the news of his wife's death leaves him despondently looking out the windows. What he sees is the same gloomy scene described at the opening of the story. By concluding in this way, Hemingway has enclosed the events in a setting of dusk, depression, and death.

## Setting and Atmosphere

Setting also affects the *atmosphere* or *mood* of stories and poems. You might note that the description of an action requires no more than a functional description of setting. Thus, an action in a forest needs just the statement that the forest is there. However, if you read descriptions of the trees, the shapes, the light and shadows, the animals, the wind, and the sounds, you may be sure that the author is working to create an atmosphere or mood for the action. There are many ways of creating moods. Descriptions of "warm" colors (red, orange, yellow) may contribute to a mood of happiness. "Cooler" colors may suggest gloom. References to smells and sounds bring the setting even more to life by asking additional sensory responses from the reader. The setting of a story on a farm or in a city apartment may evoke a response to these habitats that may contribute to a story's atmosphere.

## Organizing Your Theme

### INTRODUCTION

In a theme on setting it is tempting to do no more than describe scenes and objects. You can correct this tendency by emphasizing the connection between setting and whatever aspect you choose. A central idea would thus be, "The setting is inseparable from the action." Throughout your theme, as long as you show how the setting is related to the action, you will be sticking to your central idea. Your thesis sentence should be a plan of the major paragraphs or sections of the theme (e.g., "This connection is made in the actions taking place in late afternoon, night, and morning," or "The closeness of setting and action is shown in details about the cabin and the ocean," and so on).

### BODY

Following are four possible approaches to themes about setting. The one you choose is your decision, but you may find that some works almost invite you to pick one approach over the others. While each approach outlines a major emphasis in your theme, you may wish to bring in details from one of the others if they seem important at any point in your theme.

1. **SETTING AND ACTION.** Here you explore the use of setting in the various actions of the work. Among the questions to be answered are these: How detailed and extensive are the descriptions of the setting? Are the scenes related to the action? (Are they essential or incidental?) Does the setting serve as part of the action (places of flight or concealment; public places where people meet openly, out-of-the-way places where they meet privately; natural or environmental obstacles; sociological obstacles; seasonal conditions such as searing heat or numbing cold, etc.)? Do details of setting get used regularly, or are they mentioned only when they become necessary to an action? Do any physical objects figure into the story as causes of aspiration or conflict (e.g., a diamond necklace, a saddle, a doll, a revolver, a canary, a meal)?

2. **SETTING AND ORGANIZATION.** A closely related way of writing about setting is to connect it to the organization of the work. Some questions to help you get started with this approach are these: Is the setting a frame, an enclosure? Is it mentioned at various parts, or at shifts in the action? Does the setting undergo any expected or unexpected changes as the action changes? Do any parts of the setting have greater involvement in the action than other parts? Do any objects, such as money or property, figure into the developing or changing motivation of the characters? Do descriptions made at the start become important in the action later on? If so, in what order?

**3. SETTING AND CHARACTER.** Your aim here is to pick those details that seem to have a bearing on character and to write about their effects. The major question is the degree to which the setting seems to interact with or influence character. You might get at this topic through additional questions: Are the characters happy or unhappy where they live? Do they express their feelings, or get into discussions or arguments about them? Do they seem adjusted? Do they want to stay or leave? Does the economic, cultural, or ethnic level of the setting make the characters think in any unique ways? What jobs do the characters perform because of their ways of life? What freedoms or restraints do these jobs cause? How does the setting influence their decisions, transportation, speech habits, eating habits, attitudes about love and honor, and general folkways?

**4. SETTING AND ATMOSPHERE.** Here you should write about those aspects of setting that seem designed to evoke a mood. Some questions are: Does the detail of setting go beyond the minimum needed for action or character? Are the details clear or vague? Are words used essentially to "paint" verbal pictures? Does the author make references to colors, shapes, sounds, smells, or tastes? Does the setting seem to be used to comment on the story (e.g., a carnival scene in daylight as a complement to love, or at night as an ironic backdrop for murder; a scene among computers to reflect on numbered, unfolded, unspindled, computerized people)?

## CONCLUSION

You always have the option of summarizing your major points as your conclusion, but you might also want to write about anything you neglected in the body of your theme. Thus, you might have been treating the relationship of the setting to the action and may wish to mention something about any ties the setting has with character or atmosphere. You might also wish to point out whether your central idea about the setting also applies to other major aspects of the work.

---

## Sample Theme

*De Maupassant's Use of Setting in "The Necklace"*
*to Show the Character of Mathilde*

---

In "The Necklace" De Maupassant does not give much detail about the setting. He does not describe even the necklace, which is the central object in the plot, but he says only that it is "superb." Rather he uses setting to reflect

[1] the character of the major figure, Mathilde Loisel.* He gives no more detail than is needed to explain her feelings. This carefully directed setting may be considered as the first apartment, the dream-life mansion rooms, and the attic flat.†

[2] Details about the first walkup apartment on the Street of Martyrs are presented to explain Mathilde's unhappiness. The walls are "drab," the furniture "threadbare," and the curtains "ugly." There is only a country girl to do housework. The tablecloth is not cleaned, and the best dinner dish is beef stew boiled in a kettle. Mathilde has no pretty dresses, but only a theatre dress which she does not like. These details show her dissatisfaction about life with her low-salaried husband.

[3] The dream-life, mansion-like setting is like the apartment, because it too makes her unhappy. In Mathilde's daydreams, the rooms are large, filled with expensive furniture and bric-a-brac, and draped in silk. She imagines private rooms for intimate talks, and big dinners with delicacies like trout and quail. With dreams of such a rich home, she feels even more despair about her modest apartment.

[4] Finally, the attic flat indicates the coarsening of her character. There is little detail about this flat except that it is cheap and that Mathilde must carry water up many stairs to reach it. De Maupassant emphasizes the drudgery that she must bear to keep up the flat, such as washing the floor using large pails of water. He indicates her loss of refinement by writing that she gives up caring for her hair and hands, wears cheap dresses, speaks loudly, and swears. In this setting, she no longer has her dreams of the mansion-like rooms. Thus the flat in the attic goes along with the loss of her youth and beauty.

[5] In summary, De Maupassant focuses everything, including the setting, on Mathilde. Anything extra is not needed, and he does not include it. Thus he says little about the big party scene, but emphasizes the necessary detail that Mathilde was a great "success." In "The Necklace," De Maupassant uses setting as a means to his end—the story of Mathilde and her needless misfortune.

## Commentary on the Theme

This theme illustrates the approach of relating setting to character. The introduction makes the point that De Maupassant uses only as much detail as he needs, and no more. There is nothing to excess. The central idea is that the details of setting may be directly related to Mathilde's character and feelings. The thesis sentence does not indicate a plan to deal with all the aspects of setting in the story, but only two real ones and one imaginary one.

*Central idea
†Thesis sentence
For the text of this story, please see Appendix C, pp. 318–323.

Paragraphs two and three show how Mathilde's real-life apartment and dream-life mansion fill her with despair about her life. The fourth paragraph relates her flat in the attic in a cheaper neighborhood to the dulling and coarsening of her character. The idea here is that while better surroundings at the start fill her with despair, the ugly attic flat does not seem to affect her at all. At least, De Maupassant says nothing about her unhappiness with the poorer conditions.

The conclusion makes the assertion that, in the light of the general concentration in the story on the character of Mathilde, the setting is typical of De Maupassant's technique in "The Necklace."

# chapter 7

# *The Theme
About a Major Idea*

An idea, narrowly defined, is a concept, belief, thought, proposition, principle, or assertion, but broadly speaking it is the product of any thinking process. In writing about an idea in a literary work, you may equate the word with *meaning*. In answering the question, "What does this, or that, mean?" your response will usually be in the form of a principle about human nature, conduct, or motivation. This is an idea.

Thus, you may state the following idea in writing about Phoenix Jackson from Welty's "A Worn Path": "She shows that human beings who are commited to care and nurture will suffer for this commitment." In discussing Mrs. Popov in Chekhov's *The Bear*, you might write that she "illustrates the idea that, even if a commitment to the dead is strong, the commitment to life is stronger."

## How Do You Express Ideas?

Although an idea may be expressed in a phrase or single word, you will not give your reader much help unless you state ideas in complete sentences. Thus, "parental love" may be an idea in itself, but it is not specific as an idea for a theme. However, if you write, "Parental love is stronger than the love of country," that sentence could be used as the central idea for a theme about Luigi Pirandello's story "War." In this story, a major character, at the end, breaks down over grief for the loss of his dead son, despite his early claims that parents should be proud and glad to sacrifice children for the glory of their country. Similarly, the extension of parental commitment to one's grandchild could be shown as the idea underlying Phoenix's strength in enduring her hardships and disappointment. Whenever you select an idea for your theme, be sure to write it as a complete sentence.

Also be sure to phrase your sentence as an idea, not as a short description of the story. Thus, you might write, "O'Connor's 'First Confession' is a story about the family troubles a boy has before his first confession." This sentence describes the story fairly well, but it does not state an idea, and it would not be helpful for a theme. It would likely cause you to retell the story rather than discuss certain characters and events as they relate to an idea. A better sentence for an idea would be, "O'Connor's 'First Confession' shows the limitation of trying to instill religion through fear and punishment." This sentence would help you to concentrate on the behavior and advice of the sister, father, and Mrs. Ryan, and to show how their making Jackie confused illustrates the weakness of their threats of punishment. The end result would be a theme about an idea, not a retelling of the story.

## Ideas and Values

As you write about an idea, you should know that ideas are tied closely to the values, or "value system," of your author. Unless an idea is abstract, say the idea of a geometric form, it usually carries with it some value judgment. Thus, an author may write a poem about the idea that warfare feeds on gullibility and destroys life. Here is a fragment from such a poem, Stephen Crane's "War Is Kind":

> Do not weep, maiden, for war is kind.
> Because your lover threw wild hands toward the sky
> And the affrighted steed ran on alone,
> Do not weep.
> War is kind.
>
> —lines 1–5

Implicit in the poem are the values that life is a gift that should be treasured and not destroyed, and also that the power of persuasion—particularly the political persuasion in times of war that requires people to fight and be killed—is destructive and therefore bad. In talking about Crane's ideas in this poem, you would also discuss these values.

## How Do You Find Ideas?

This is a key question. You read the work, consider the main characters and action, study the work some more, think, and express your judgment about the meaning in terms of an idea. As you study, you should know that there is latitude about the exact phrasing but that there should be agreement on the general outlines and extent of the idea. Thus, you might discover that Shakespeare's *Macbeth* illustrates a number of ideas, such as: (1) achieving ambition by ruthless means destroys innocent and guilty alike, (2) trusting the advice of the wrong person is self-destructive, and (3) using force to keep political control only causes rebellion. Although any one of these choices could be an idea for a theme about *Macbeth,* together with others that you might pick, they all have in common the danger or destructiveness of the means to which Macbeth resorts to gain and keep power. In other words, you have wide choice in deciding which idea you write about, but most of the ideas on a particular topic will have general similarities.

With this in mind, you may study your work for ideas. As you look, and think, you should realize that authors may express ideas in any or all of the following ways. You should also realize that the following classifications are for your convenience, because in a literary work all the methods may be occurring at the same time.

DIRECT STATEMENTS BY THE AUTHOR. Often an author states ideas directly, by way of commentary, to guide you or deepen your understanding. In the second paragraph of "The Necklace," for example, De Maupassant states the idea that women without strong family connections must rely on their charm and beauty to get on in the world. You might find this idea patronizing today, but it is nevertheless a true version of what De Maupassant says. In using it, and using other ideas directly from an author, you would likely wish to adapt it somewhat in line with your understanding of the story. Thus, a good idea for a theme would be this: " 'The Necklace' shows the idea that women, with no power except their charm and beauty, are helpless against chance or bad luck."

DIRECT STATEMENTS BY THE PERSONA. (Please see Chapter 5, about point of view, pp. 63–71.) Often personae state their own ideas. These may be the same as those of the author, or they may be totally the reverse. In addition, the author may cause the persona to make statements indicating a limited character. Thus the adult Jackie, in O'Connor's "First Confession," says things that show some of his ideas to be immature. You must be careful and use your ingenuity in deciding how closely the persona's ideas correspond with the author's.

DRAMATIC STATEMENTS MADE BY CHARACTERS. In many works, different characters state ideas that are in conflict. Authors may thus present thirteen ways of looking at a blackbird and leave the choice up to you. They may provide you with guides for your choice, however. For instance, they may create an admirable character whose ideas may be the same as their own. The reverse would be true for a bad character.

IMAGERY. Authors often use figurative language for their ideas. As an example, here is a comparison from Chaucer's long poem *Troilus and Criseyde*, where Criseyde thinks about the harm that her love with Troilus will bring about:

> How that an eagle, feathered white as bone,
> Under her breast his long claws set
> And out her heart he rent [tore].
> —lines 926–28

This comparison suggests the idea that, granted the conditions of male supremacy, the act of falling in love for a woman without the power to protect herself may be self-destructive. Chaucer's story bears out this idea.

CHARACTERS WHO STAND FOR IDEAS. Although characters are busy in the action of their respective works, they may also be shown to stand for ideas or values. Mathilde Loisel in "The Necklace" may be thought of as an embodiment of the idea that women of the nineteenth-century middle class, without the possibility of a career, are hurt by unrealizable dreams of wealth.

When you have two different characters, their ideas may be compared or contrasted. Mrs. Ryan and the priest in O'Connor's "First Confession," although they never meet and discuss things, represent totally opposing ideas about the true nature and function of religion.

In effect, characters who stand for ideas may be considered as symbols. Thus, in the stories of J. D. Salinger, the introduction of a bright, intuitive child is symbolic, for the child represents Salinger's idea that the insights of children, who are close to God in time, are evidence for the existence and nature of God. For this reason, children in Salinger's stories give an emotional and spiritual lift to jaded adults because they transmit traces of residual divine glory.

THE WORK ITSELF AS IT REPRESENTS IDEAS. One of the most important ways in which authors express ideas is to render them as an inseparable part of the total impression of the work. All the events and characters may add up to an idea that is made effective by the impact of the story itself. Thus, although an idea may not be directly stated, it will be clear after you have finished reading. For example, in the novel *A Passage to India*, E. M. Forster dramatizes the idea that political, racial, and national barriers keep human beings apart when their greater interest is to unite. He does not use these words, but this idea is clearly rendered in the novel. Similarly, Shakespeare's *Hamlet* embodies the idea that a person doing an evil act sets strong forces in motion that cannot be stopped until everything in their path is destroyed.

When you write your theme, you should explore all these modes and use as many as you think will best provide you with the information you need. It may be that you rely most heavily on the author's direct statements, or on a combination of these and your interpretation of characters and actions. Or you might focus exclusively on a persona and use his or her ideas as a means of describing the author's.

As you write, you should make a point of stating the various sources of your facts. Thus, you might be writing sentences like these:

> Wordsworth describes a childhood theft of a boat to illustrate his idea that Nature is a corrective, moral force [author's statement].

> In one of his last speeches, Macbeth presents the idea that life is without purpose [dramatic statement by a character]. It would appear that Shakespeare creates this speech to support the idea that the use of illegal force leads to a moral dead end.

> Gulliver expresses the idea that religious controversy should be resolved by high authority [statement by a persona]. Because religion deals with mysteries and is potentially divisive, Gulliver's idea here seems close to Swift's.

> The priest's thoughtful, good-humored treatment of Jackie, contrasted with the harsh, punishing treatment by the others, shows the idea that religious incentive is best implanted by kindness and understanding, not by fear [idea embodied in the work as a whole].

Recognizing sources in this way keeps the lines of your conclusions clear. Thereby you will help your reader in following your arguments.

## Organizing Your Theme

In developing and planning your theme, you can help yourself by answering questions like these: What is the best wording of the idea that you can make? What has the author done with the idea? How can the actions be related to the idea? Might any characters be measured according to whether they do or do not live up to the idea? What values does the idea seem to suggest? Does the author seem to be proposing a particular cause? Is this cause personal, social, economic, political, scientific, ethical, esthetic, or religious? Can the idea be shown to affect the organization of the work? How? Does imagery or symbolism develop or illustrate the idea?

### INTRODUCTION

In your introduction you might state any special circumstances in the work that affect ideas generally or your idea specifically. Your statement of the idea will serve as the central idea for your theme. Your thesis sentence should indicate the particular parts or aspects of the work that you will examine.

BODY

The exact form of your theme will be controlled by your objective, which is (1) to define the idea, and (2) show its importance in the work. Each work will invite its own approach, but here are a number of areas that you might wish to include for your discussion:

1. **THE FORM OF THE WORK AS A PLAN, SCHEME, OR LOGICAL FORMAT.**
   *Example:* "The idea makes for a two-part work, the first showing religion as punishment, and the second showing religion as kindness and reward."
   *Example:* "Marvell's idea of the need to experience life in light of approaching death prompts the sequence of a condition, a negation of that condition, and a logical conclusion."

2. **A SPEECH OR SPEECHES.**
   *Example:* "The priest's conversation and responses to Jackie show in operation the idea that kindness and understanding are the best means to encourage religious commitment."

3. **A CHARACTER OR CHARACTERS.**
   *Example:* "Eliot's Prufrock is an embodiment of the idea that human beings in the twentieth century have been deprived of their identity and importance."

4. **AN ACTION OR ACTIONS.**
   *Example:* "The pursuit by the outlaws and the rescue by the rural police indicate Crane's optimistic idea that, on balance, the world furnishes protection and justice despite great danger."

5. **VARIOUS SHADES OR VARIATIONS OF THE IDEA.**
   *Example:* "The idea of punishment as a corrective is shown simply in the father, with spite in Nora, and with sadistic physical pain and cosmic torture in Mrs. Ryan."

6. **A COMBINATION OF THESE TOGETHER WITH ANY OTHER ASPECT RELEVANT TO THE WORK.**
   *Example:* "The idea that life is filled with ironies is shown in Hamlet's 'To be or not to be' soliloquy, his decision not to kill Claudius during the prayer scene, and his killing of Claudius after the death of his mother." [Here the idea would be applied to speech, character, and action.]

CONCLUSION

In your conclusion you might add your own thoughts. Here you would be considering the validity or force of the idea. If you are convinced, you might wish to say that the author has expressed the idea forcefully and convincingly, or else you might wish to show how the idea applies to current conditions. If you are not convinced, it is never enough just to say you disagree; you should try to show the reasons for your disagreement. If you would like to mention an idea related to the one you have discussed, you might introduce that here, being sure to stress the connection.

## Sample Theme

*The Idea of the Strength of Love in Chekhov's* **The Bear**

[1]
In the one-act farce *The Bear,* Anton Chekhov shows a man and woman, who have never met before, falling suddenly and helplessly in love. With such an unlikely main action, ideas may seem unimportant, but one can find a number of ideas in the play. A very important one is that love and desire are powerful enough to overcome the strongest obstacles.* This idea is shown as love conquers commitment to the dead, renunciation of womankind, and anger.†

[2]
Commitment to her dead husband is the obstacle to love shown in Mrs. Popov.She states that she has made a vow never to see daylight because of her mourning, and she spends her time staring at her husband's picture and comforting herself with her faithfulness. Her devotion to the dead is so intense that she claims at the start that she is already in her grave. In her, Chekhov has created a strong obstacle to love so that he might illustrate his idea that love conquers all. By the play's end, Mrs. Popov is embracing Smirnov.

[3]
Renunciation of women is the obstacle for Smirnov.He tells Mrs. Popov that his experience with women has made him bitter and that he no longer gives "a good goddamn" about women. His disillusioned words seem to make him an impossible candidate for love. But, in keeping with Chekhov's idea, Smirnov is the one who is soon confessing to the audience that he has fallen headlong for Mrs. Popov. For him, the force of love is so strong that he would even claim happiness at being shot by "those little velvet hands."

[4]
Anger and the threat of violence make the greatest obstacle.The two characters become so mad over Smirnov's demand for payment that Smirnov challenges Mrs. Popov to a duel! Because of their individual obstacles, it would seem that the threat of the duel, even if poor Luka could forestall it, would cause the beginning of lifelong hatred between the two. And yet love knocks down all these obstacles, in line with Chekhov's idea that love's power is absolutely irresistible.

The idea, of course, is not new or surprising. It has been the cause of life

---

*Central idea
†Thesis sentence
**For the text of this story, please see Appendix C, pp. 324–332.**

[5] for all of us. What is surprising about Chekhov's use of the idea is that love in *The Bear* wins out suddenly against such bad conditions. These conditions bring up an interesting and closely related idea. Chekhov may be suggesting that the obstacles themselves, together with the intense involvement produced by anger, cause love. In the speeches of Smirnov and Mrs. Popov, one can see hurt, disappointment, regret, frustration, annoyance, anger, and rage. Yet at the high point of these negative feelings, the characters fall in love. Could Chekhov be saying that it is a mixture of such feelings that brings out love, in the way the Universe was created by God out of Chaos? <u>Though *The Bear* is a farce, and a good one, Chekhov's use of the idea of love's power is anything but farcical.</u>

---

## Commentary on the Theme

This theme is based on the dialogue, soliloquies, and actions of the two major characters in Chekhov's play. Throughout, these sources are mentioned as the authority for the various conclusions. The idea about love's power is treated as it affects the organization of the play. There are thus three large structural units (which in fact are interwoven): the obstacles to love in (1) Mrs. Popov, (2) Smirnov, and (3) their anger.

The introduction notes the farcical action of the play but claims that a major serious idea, the theme's central idea, may be found in it nevertheless. The thesis sentence lists the three structural units just mentioned.

As an operative part of Chekhov's idea, paragraphs two through four detail the nature of the obstacles to be overcome by love. Note that in paragraph two the obstacle is characterized as "strong," in paragraph three as "impossible," and in paragraph four as "lifelong hatred." The concluding paragraph deals with a modest personal admission of the truth of the main idea and the surprise in Chekhov's use of it. The related idea about the closeness of love to all the other strong emotions is concluded with a tribute to Chekhov's use of the idea in the play.

# *chapter 8*

# *The Theme on a Problem*

A problem is any question that you cannot answer easily and correctly about a body of material that you know. The question, "Who is the major character in *Hamlet?*" is not a problem, because the obvious answer is Hamlet.

Let us, however, ask another question: "Why is it correct to say that Hamlet is the major character?" This question is not as easy as the first, and for this reason it is a problem. It requires that we think about our answer, even though we do not need to search very far. Hamlet is the title character. He is involved in most of the actions of the play. He is so much the center of our liking and concern that his death causes sadness and regret. To "solve" this problem has required a set of responses, all of which provide answers to the question "why?" With variations, most readers of Shakespeare's play would likely be satisfied with the answers.

More complex, however, and more typical of most problems, are questions like these: "Why does Hamlet talk of suicide in his first soliloquy?" "Why does he treat Ophelia so coarsely in the 'nunnery' scene?" "Why does he delay in avenging his father's death?" It is with questions like these that themes on a problem will normally be concerned. Simple factual responses do not answer such questions. A good deal of thought, together with a number of interpretations knitted together into a whole theme, is required.

## The Usefulness of Problem Solving

The techniques of problem solving should be useful to you in most of your courses. In art, for example, you might need to write on the problem of representationalism as opposed to impressionism. In philosophy you may encounter the problem of whether reality is to be found in particulars or universals. You should know what to do with problems of this sort.

Without question, you have already had a good deal of experience in problem solving. The classroom method of questions and answers has caused you to put facts and conclusions together just as you need to do in a theme on a problem.

The process of solving problems is one of the most important experiences in the development of people's abilities as good readers and thinkers. Uncritical readers do not think about what they read. When they are questioned, they are embarrassed by what they do not remember or understand. However, if they try to answer their own questions as they read, they will have to search the material deeply and try to command it. In dealing with their questions, they must test a number of provisional solutions and organize and develop their responses. As they do these tasks, they become skilled as good, critical readers. In short, if they ask and answer their own questions as a matter of habit, they cannot lose.

## Strategies for Your Theme About a Problem

The first purpose in a theme on a problem is to convince your reader that your solution is a good one. This you do by making sound conclusions from supporting evidence. In nonscientific subjects like literature you rarely will find absolute proofs, so your conclusions will not be *proved* in the way you can prove triangles congruent. But your organization, your use of facts from the text, your interpretations, and your application of general or specific knowledge should all be designed to make your conclusions *convincing.* Your basic strategy is thus persuasion.

Because problems and solutions change with the work being studied, each theme on a problem will be different from any other. Despite these differences, however, a number of common strategies might be adapted to whatever problem you face. You might wish to use one or more of these strategies throughout your theme. Always, you should be trying to solve the problem—to answer the question—and you should achieve this goal in the most direct, convenient way.

**STRATEGY 1: THE DEMONSTRATION THAT CONDITIONS FOR A SOLUTION ARE FULFILLED.** In effect, this development is the most basic in writing, namely, illustration. In your theme, you first explain that certain conditions need to exist for your solution to be plausible. Your central idea—really a brief answer to the question—will be that the conditions do indeed exist. Your development will be to show how the conditions may be found in the work.

Let us suppose that you are writing on the problem of why Hamlet delays revenge against his uncle, Claudius (who before the play opens has murdered Hamlet's father, King Hamlet, and has become the new king of Denmark). Suppose that, in your introduction, you make the point that Hamlet delays because he is never completely sure that Claudius is guilty. This will be your "solution" to the problem. In the body of your theme you would support your answer by showing the flimsiness of the information Hamlet receives about the crime (i.e., the two visits from the Ghost and Claudius' distress at the play within the play). Once you have "attacked" these sources of data on the grounds that they are unreliable, you will have succeeded. You will have proposed a fair solution to the problem and will have shown that this solution is consistent with the facts of the play.

STRATEGY 2: THE ANALYSIS OF WORDS IN THE PHRASING OF THE PROB-LEM. Another good approach is to explore the meaning and limits of important words or phrases in the question as it has been put to you. Your object should be to clarify the words and show how applicable they are. You may wish to define the words and to show whether they have any special meaning.

You will find that attention to words in this way might give you enough material for all or part of your theme. Thus the sample theme in this chapter briefly considers the meaning of the word "effective" when applied to Robert Frost's poem "Desert Places." Similarly, a theme on the problem of Hamlet's delay would benefit from a treatment of the word *delay:* What, really, does *delay* mean? What is the difference in Hamlet's case between reasonable and unreasonable delay? Does Hamlet in fact delay unreasonably? Is his delay the result of a psychological fault? Would speedy revenge be more or less reasonable than the delay? By the time you had devoted such attention to the word, you would have written a goodly amount of material that could be arranged into a full theme on the problem. Also, of course, you could use just a part of this material.

STRATEGY 3: THE REFERENCE TO LITERARY CONVENTIONS. Sometimes your best argument may be to establish that the problem can be solved by reference to the literary conventions of the work. Like people, literary works are not all the same; they reflect differences in stance and convention. Thus, the Greek tragedy *Oedipus the King* is different from Shakespeare's *Hamlet*, and Welty's "A Worn Path" is unlike O'Connor's "First Confession." What might appear to be a problem can often be treated as a normal characteristic, given the particular work you are studying. For example, a problem about the "artificiality" of the choruses in *Oedipus* may be resolved by reference to the fact that the choruses were normal features of Greek drama.

Similarly, you may find a problem about an "unreal" occurrence in a work. But if you can show that the work is laid out as a fantasy or as a dream, and not as a faithful representation of everyday reality, then you can also show that the "unreal" occurrence is normal *for that work*. A problem about the unnatural overreaction and bitterness of Goodman Brown in Hawthorne's "Young Goodman Brown" might be handled in this way. Suppose that the problem is the following: "Is Brown's bitterness unnaturally excessive inasmuch as it is caused by nothing more than a dream?" An answer to this question can be found in the demonstration that the entire story is dreamlike and symbolic and that Brown's reaction is made in what Hawthorne took to be an unreal, dehumanized system. Brown's entire existence, in other words, is unnatural, and his bitterness and suspicion are necessary consequences of this state. Here, the strategy is to resolve an apparent difficulty by trying to establish the context in which the difficulty vanishes. With variations, this method can work for many similar problems.

**STRATEGY 4: THE ARGUMENT AGAINST POSSIBLE OBJECTIONS: PROCATALEPSIS.** With this strategy, you raise an objection to your solution and then argue against this objection. This strategy, called *procatalepsis* or *anticipation*, is useful because it helps you to sharpen your own arguments. That is, the need to answer objections forces you to make analyses and use facts that you might ordinarily overlook. Although procatalepsis may be used point by point throughout your theme, you may find it most useful at the end. (Please see the last paragraph of the sample theme.) The situation you visualize is that someone might object to your arguments even after you have made your major points. If you can raise the objections first, before they are made by someone else, and then answer them, your theme will be that much more powerful and convincing.

Your aim with the strategy of procatalepsis should be to show that, compared with your solution, the objection (1) is not accurate or valid, (2) is not strong or convincing, or (3) is an exception, not a rule. Here are some examples of these approaches. The objections raised are underlined, so that you can easily distinguish them from the answers.

a. *The objection is not accurate or valid.* Here you reject the objection by showing that either the interpretation or the conclusions are wrong and also by emphasizing that the evidence supports your solution.

> Although Hamlet's delay is reasonable, the claim might be made that his greater duty is to kill Claudius in revenge as soon as the Ghost accuses Claudius of his murder. This claim is not persuasive because

it assumes that Hamlet knows everything the audience knows. The audience accepts the Ghost's word, right from the start, that Claudius is guilty, but from Hamlet's position there is every reason to doubt the Ghost and not to act. Would it not seem foolish and insane for Hamlet to kill Claudius, who is king legally, and then to claim that he did it because the Ghost told him to do so? The argument for speedy revenge is not good, because it is based on an incorrect view of the situation actually faced by Hamlet.

b. *The objection is not strong or convincing.* Here you *concede* that the objection has some truth or validity, but you then try to show that it is weak and that your own solution is stronger.

One might claim that Claudius' distress at the play within the play is evidence for his guilt and that therefore Hamlet should carry out his revenge right away. This argument has merit, and Hamlet's speech after Claudius has fled the scene ("I'll take the Ghost's word for a thousand pound") shows that the King's conscience has been caught. But this behavior is not a strong enough cause for killing him. One could justify a full investigation of Hamlet's father's death on these grounds, yes, but not killing for revenge. Claudius could not be convicted in any court on the strength of testimony that he was disturbed at seeing the Murder of Gonzago on stage. Even after the play within the play, the reasons for delay are stronger than those for action.

c. *The objection is an exception, not a rule.* Here you reject the objection on the grounds that it could be valid only if normal conditions were suspended. The objection depends on an exception, not a rule.

The case for quick action is simple: Hamlet should kill Claudius right after seeing the Ghost (I.3), or else after seeing the King's reaction to the stage murder of Gonzago (III.2) or the Ghost again (III.4). This argument wrongly assumes that due process does not exist in the Denmark of Hamlet and Claudius. Redress under these circumstances, goes the argument, must be both personal and extra-legal. The fact is, however, that the world of Hamlet is civilized, a place where legality and the rules of evidence are precious. Thus Hamlet cannot rush out to kill Claudius, because he knows that the King has not had anything close to due process. The argument for quick action is poor because it rests on an exemption being made from civilized law.

## Organizing Your Theme

Writing a theme on a problem requires you to argue a position: Either there is a solution or there is not. To develop this position requires that you show the steps that have led you to your conclusion. The general form of your theme will thus be (1) a description of the conditions that need to be met for the solution you propose, and then (2) a demonstration that these conditions exist. If your position is that there is no solution, then your form would be the same for the first part, but your second part—the development—would show that these conditions have *not* been met.

As with most themes, you may assume that your reader is familiar with the work you have read. Your job is to arrange your materials convincingly around your main point. You should not use anything from the work that is not relevant to your central idea. You do not need to discuss things in their order of appearance in the work. You are in control and must make your decisions about order so that your solution to the problem may be brought out most effectively.

## INTRODUCTION

Begin right away with a statement of the problem, and refer to the conditions that must be established for the problem to be solved. It is unnecessary to say anything about the author or the general nature of the work unless you plan to use this material as a part of your development. Your central idea will be your answer to the question, and your thesis sentence will indicate the main heads of your development.

## BODY

The body should contain the main points of argument, arranged to convince your reader that your solution to the problem is sound. In each paragraph, the topic sentence will be an assertion that you believe is a major aspect of your answer, and this should be followed with enough detail to support the topic. Your goal should be to cause your reader to agree with you.

You might wish to use one or more of the strategies described in this chapter. These are, again, (1) the demonstration that conditions for a solution are fulfilled, (2) the analysis of words in the phrasing of the problem, (3) the reference to literary conventions, and (4) the argument against possible objections. You might combine these if a combination would help your argument. Thus, if we assume that you are writing to explain that Hamlet's delay is reasonable and not the result of a character flaw, you might begin by considering the word *delay* (strategy 2). Then you might use strategy 1 to explain the reasons for which Hamlet does delay. Finally, in order to answer objections to your argument, you might show that he is capable of action when he feels justified in acting (strategy 4). Whatever your topic, the important thing is to use the method or methods that best help you to make a good case for your solution to the problem.

CONCLUSION

In your conclusion you should affirm your belief in the validity of your solution in view of the supporting evidence. You might do this by reemphasizing those points that you believe are strongest. You might also summarize each of your main points. Or you might think of your argument as still continuing and thus might use the strategy of procatalepsis to raise and answer objections that could be made against your solution, as in the last paragraph of the sample theme.

---

## Sample Theme

*The Problem of Frost's Use of the Term "desert places"*
*in the Poem "Desert Places"*

---

[1]
In the last line of "Desert Places," the phrase "desert places" undergoes a shift of meaning. At the beginning it refers to the snowy scene of the first stanza, but at the last line it refers to a negative state of soul. The problem is this: Does the change happen too late to be effective? That is, does the new meaning come out of nowhere, or does it really work as a good closing thought? To solve this problem, one must say that the change cannot be effective if there is no preparation for it before the last line of the poem. But if there is preparation—that is, if Frost does show that the desert places of the natural world are like those within the speaker himself—then the shift is effective even though it comes at the very end. It is clear that Frost makes the preparation and therefore that the change is effective.* The preparation may be traced in Frost's references, word choices, and concluding sentences.†

[2]
In the first two stanzas Frost includes the speaker in his references to living things being overcome. The scene described in line 4 is "weeds and stubble showing last." Then come the hibernating animals "smothered in their lairs" in line 6. Finally the speaker includes himself. He states that he is "too absent-spirited to count," and that the "loneliness" of the scene "includes" him "unawares" (7, 8). This movement—from vegetable, to animal, to human—shows that everything alive is changed by the snow. Obviously the speaker will not die like the grass or hibernate like the animals, but he indicates that the "loneliness" overcomes him. Thus, these first eight lines connect the natural bleakness with the speaker.

Word choices in the third stanza have human connotations and are therefore preparatory. The words *lonely* and *loneliness* (line 9), *more lonely* (10), *blanker*

---

*Central idea
†Thesis sentence
For the text of this story, please see Appendix C, p. 333.

[3] and *benighted* (11), and *no expression, nothing to express* (12) all refer to human as well as natural conditions. The word *benighted* is most important, because it refers not only to night, but also to intellectual or moral ignorance. These words invite the reader to think of negative mental and emotional states. They provide a context in which the concluding shift of meaning will come naturally.

[4] Frost's concluding sentences form the climax of the preparation for the last two words. All along, the poet suggests that the speaker's soul is as bleak as the snowy field. This idea is focused in the last stanza, where in two sentences the speaker talks about himself:

> They cannot scare me with their empty spaces
> Between stars—on stars where no human race is.
> I have it in me so much nearer home
> To scare myself with my own desert places.

[5] In the context of the poem, therefore, the last words do not create a difficult problem of interpretation. They rather pull together the two parts of the comparison that Frost has been building from the very first line. Just as "desert places" refers to the snowy field, it also suggests human coldness, blankness, unconcern, insensitivity, and maybe even cruelty. The phrase does not spring out of nowhere, but is effective as the climax of the major idea of the poem.

[6] Although the conclusion is effective, a critic might still claim that it is weak because Frost does not develop the thought about the negative soul. He simply mentions "desert places" and stops. But the poem is not a long psychological study. To ask for more than Frost gives would be to expect more than sixteen lines can provide. A better claim against the effectiveness of the concluding phrase would be that "desert places" is trite and vague. If the phrase were taken away from the poem, this criticism might be acceptable. But in the poem it takes on the suggestions of the previous fifteen lines, and does so with freshness and surprise. Thus the shift of meaning is a major reason for Frost's success in "Desert Places."

---

## Commentary on the Theme

The introductory paragraph states the problem about whether or not the shift of meaning at the end of Frost's poem is effective. Emphasis is on the condition that the poem must prepare the reader for this shift if effectiveness is to be claimed for it. The central idea indicates that the poem satisfies this requirement and that the shift is effective. The thesis sentence indicates three subjects for development.

The first half of paragraph two draws attention to three references to the snow's bleakness. These are considered in the second half, and thus the paragraph shows that there is preparation early in the poem for the shift. Paragraph three continues this line of development, illustrating the relationship of certain words in the third stanza to the human state, and thus to a shift in the poem from the vegetable to the human world. The fourth paragraph asserts that the concluding sentences build toward a climax of Frost's pattern of development.

Paragraphs five and six are a two-part conclusion. The fifth paragraph summarizes the arguments and offers an interpretation of the phrase. The last paragraph deals with two objections against the effectiveness of the phrase. The theme thus shows that a careful reading of the poem eliminates the grounds for claiming that there is any problem about the last line.

The general development of this theme illustrates strategy 1 described in this chapter (pp. 88–89). The attention to the word *effective* briefly illustrates the second strategy (p. 89). The concluding paragraph shows two approaches to the fourth strategy (pp. 90–91), using the arguments that the objections are not good because they are based on (1) an exception, and (2) an incorrect assumption.

## chapter 9

# Themes
# on (I) Imagery, and
# (II) Symbolism and Allegory

Imagery, on the one hand, and symbolism and allegory, on the other, are closely related because both use elements of literary works to deepen meaning or to stand for something else. Because of their similarities, they are included here together, but because of their differences, two separate kinds of themes are described.

## I. Imagery

Imagery is a broad term referring to the comparison of something known— a description of an object or action—with something to be communicated— a situation or emotional state. It is the means by which authors reach directly into the experience and imagination of their readers to create a desired response.

Imagery works by means of *analogy*, i.e., "This is like that." At the heart of an author's use of imagery is this assumption:

> Not only do I want you to understand my descriptions of this character's attitudes or of that scene or object, but I want you to come close to *feeling* them too. Therefore I will make an analogy—an image—which, by its similarity to your own experience or by its ability to touch your imagination, will intensify your perceptions and heighten your emotions.

For example, to communicate a character's joy and excitement, the sentence "She was happy" is not effective. A writer can get at these feelings better by using an image like this one: "She felt as if she had just inherited five million tax-free dollars." Because readers can easily *imagine* the combination of excitement, disbelief, and joy that such a happening would bring, they can deepen their awareness of these emotions. It is the *image* that evokes this perception—something that no simple description can quite accomplish.

As a literary parallel, let us use John Keats' poem "On First Looking into Chapman's Homer." Keats wrote the poem after he first read Chapman's translation of Homer, the ancient Greek epic poet. His main idea is that Chapman not only translated Homer's words but also transmitted his greatness. A paraphrase of the poem is this:

> I have read much literature and have been told that Homer is the best writer of all, but not knowing Greek, I could not appreciate his works until I discovered them in Chapman's translation. To me, this experience was exciting and awe-inspiring.

This paraphrase also destroys Keats' poetry. Contrast the second sentence of the paraphrase with the last six lines of the sonnet as Keats wrote them:

> Then felt I like some watcher of the skies
> When a new planet swims into his ken;
> Or like stout Cortez when with eagle eyes
> He stared at the Pacific—and all his men
> Looked at each other with a wild surmise—
> Silent, upon a peak in Darien.

If Keats had written only the sentence in the paraphrase, we would probably not read him with interest because we would find no descriptions of objects from which we could derive his emotion. But we can readily respond to the imagery of the last six lines; namely, we can *imagine* how we would have felt if we had been the first astronomers to discover a new planet, or the first explorers to see the Pacific.

## SOME DEFINITIONS

**IMAGE, IMAGERY.** The word *image* refers to single comparisons. Keats' reference to the "watcher of the skies" is an image. *Imagery* is a broader term referring to all the images within a passage ("the imagery of line 5, or of stanza 6"), an entire work ("the imagery of Eliot's 'Prufrock' "), a group of works ("the imagery of Shakespeare's Roman plays"), or an entire body of works ("the development of Shakespeare's imagery").

**VEHICLE, TENOR.** To describe the relationship between a writer's ideas and the images chosen to objectify them, two useful terms have been coined by I. A. Richards (in *The Philosophy of Rhetoric*). First is the *tenor*, which is the total of ideas and attitudes not only of the literary speaker but also of the author. Second is the *vehicle*, or the details that carry the tenor. The vehicle of the five million dollar image is the description of the inheritance. Similarly, the tenor of the last six lines of Keats' sonnet is awe and wonder; the vehicle is the reference to astronomical and geographical discovery.

## Characteristics of Literary Imagery

It would be difficult to find any good piece of writing that does not employ imagery to at least some extent. Imagery is most vital, however, in imaginative writing, where it promotes understanding and shapes the reader's responses.

Usually, imagery is embodied in words or descriptions denoting sense experience that leads to many associations. A single word naming a flower, say *rose*, evokes a positive response. A person might think of the color of a rose, recall its smell, associate it with the summer sun and pleasant days, and recall the love and respect that a bouquet of roses means as a gift. But *rose* is not an image until its associations are used as an analogy, as in these lines by Robert Burns:

> O, my luve's like a red, red rose
> That's newly sprung in June.

Once Burns has made this comparison, he evokes pleasant thoughts and feelings about roses. These become the tenor of the image. That a rose may have unpleasant associations, perhaps because of its thorns, should not be considered. Such an extension of meaning, although truthful, would likely be a misreading of the image.

It would, that is, unless the writer deliberately calls some of these less happy ideas to mind. In one of the most famous poems about a rose, by Edmund Waller ("Go Lovely Rose," in which the speaker addresses a rose that he is about to send to his sweetheart), the speaker observes that roses, when cut, die:

> Then die—that she
> The common fate of all things rare
> May read in thee:
> How small a part of time they share
> That are so wondrous sweet and fair.

Here the poet is directing the reader's responses to the original comparison of the rose with the sweetheart. The structure of the poem is the full development of the image. In this poem, the tenor is an awareness that life is both lovely and fragile.

Imagery is most vivid when it appeals directly to sense experience. References to senses like sight and touch will produce an immediate imaginative response. More complex and intellectualized images require greater effort to reconstruct. Matthew Arnold stated in "Dover Beach" that the world seemed "to lie before us like a land of dreams," a figurative image that has caused much speculation. Shakespeare's line, "And summer's lease hath all too short a date," from Sonnet 18, makes the reader think about the renting and leasing of property. Despite such variety, the common element in imagery is the attempt by writers to convey ideas by referring to sense impressions, objects, and situations that readers can imaginatively reconstruct and to which they can emotionally and intellectually respond.

## Imagery and Rhetorical Devices

The vehicles of imagery have been classified rhetorically. The two most important types are the *simile* and the *metaphor*.

SIMILE. In a simile the vehicle is introduced by *like* or *as*. The second of these two lines is a simile:

> It glows and glitters in my cloudy breast
> Like stars upon some gloomy grove.

In the six lines from the Keats sonnet on Chapman's Homer, quoted on p. 97, there are two similes, each conveying the tenor of the excitement of discovery.

METAPHOR. In a metaphor the comparison is made in the form of a direct equation, without the use of *like* or *as*. The tenor is implied in the vehicle. A metaphor may consist of a single word, as in the word *choirs* in Shakespeare's sonnet "That Time of Year":

> Bare ruined choirs where late the sweet birds sang

Here the word *choirs* refers to a section of a church which has been destroyed. This word in turn affects the meaning of "sweet birds," for on the one hand they are real birds, but on the other they are human singers who sang in the choirs before the destruction.

A metaphor may also be more extensive, as in Shakespeare's sonnet "Poor Soul, the Center of My Sinful Earth," when the speaker equates his body with a house ("mansion") and his soul with a tenant renting the house:

> Why so large cost, having so short a lease,
> Dost thou upon thy fading mansion spend?

Less common forms of imagery are *synecdoche, metonymy, personification,* and *controlling image.*

SYNECDOCHE. In a synecdoche, which is a special kind of metaphor, a small part stands for a large part, usually as a way of stressing a particular aspect of something. The following expression illustrates a synecdoche: "Each day they had the task of attending to four hungry mouths." This is a means of emphasizing that the parents in question were having difficulty in caring for all the needs of four very dependent children.

METONYMY. A metonym, also a metaphor, is a term that stands for something with which it is closely associated. The President, for example, is closely associated with the White House, so that "news from the White House" is news of actions and policies of the President. Similar to this are "the Pentagon," "Broadway," "Haight Ashbury," and so on.

PERSONIFICATION. In personification, something abstract is given human attributes, as in this example from Keats' ode "To Autumn," where the season is personified as a woman:

> Who hath not seen thee oft amid thy store?
>   Sometimes whoever seeks abroad may find
> Thee sitting careless on a granary floor
>   Thy hair soft-lifted by the winnowing wind;

CONTROLLING IMAGE. A controlling image is one that is so thoroughly developed in a work, or is so vital and pervasive, that one may interpret the work in the light of this image. At the beginning of John of Gaunt's speech in Shakespeare's *Richard II*, for example (II.i.33–70), there is a controlling image when Gaunt compares himself to a "prophet." The entire speech is colored by the idea that the speaker giving it, being close to death and therefore close to God and the riddles of the universe, is presenting an accurate forecast of the future, just as the Old Testament prophets did.

# II. Symbolism and Allegory

Symbolism and allegory are closely related to metaphor. A metaphor indicates an analogy by momentarily equating the two things being compared. Symbols and allegories actually *stand* for something else.

## Symbolism

A symbol may be a thing, place, action, person, or concept. In a literary work it has its own objective reality—if it did not have such validity, it would be artificial and therefore weak—but it is used to carry greater meaning than its simple presence might indicate. When a symbol is introduced, it is understood to signify the very specific things intended by the writer. Once it is established in a work, it is often reintroduced like a theme with variations.

To judge whether something is symbolic, you should try to determine if it serves as the vehicle for a significant idea or emotion. Thus, the character Sisyphus, in the ancient myth of Sisyphus, is a symbol. Sisyphus is doomed in the afterlife to roll a large rock up a high hill. Just as he gets it to the top it rolls down, and he then must roll it back up again, and again, and again, for the rock always rolls down as he gets it to the top. His plight has been taken as a symbol for the human condition: A person rarely if ever completes anything. Work must always be done over and over, and the same problems recur without any final solution. But at least people, like Sisyphus, are involved and active and hence can gain satisfaction from their activity.

Some symbols, like the myth of Sisyphus, are generally or universally recognized. Authors referring to them rely on this recognition and understanding. Thus water used in the sacrament of baptism is recognized as a symbol of life. When it spouts up as a fountain, water may symbolize optimism (as upwelling, bubbling life). In a brackish pool, it may symbolize life being polluted or diminished. With the trend toward psychological interpretations of symbols, water may be construed as a reference to sexuality. Thus, lovers may meet by a quiet lake, a cascading waterfall, a purling stream, a wide river, or a stormy sea. The condition of the water in each instance could be interpreted as a symbol of their romantic relationships. Another generally recognized symbol is the serpent, which represents Satan. In "Young Goodman Brown," Nathaniel Hawthorne refers to a walking-stick that resembles a serpent, in this way instantly evoking the image of Satanic evil. But because the stick only "seems" to "wriggle like a serpent," it may also symbolize human tendencies to see evil where it does not exist. (Please see the second sample theme, on Hawthorne's use of this symbol.)

Many more objects and descriptions do not have this generally established rank as symbols. They can be symbols only within their works. For example, the jug of beer (porter) carried by Jackie's grandmother in "First Confession" is one of the things that symbolize for Jackie the grandmother's peasant-like and boorish habits. The porter is symbolic only within the work; a reference to it elsewhere would not carry the symbolic meaning that O'Connor gives it in the story.

In determining whether references like these are symbols, you need to make decisions based on your judgment of the total importance of the references. If they seem of great significance, you can justify claiming them as symbols as long as you can demonstrate their scope. Thus, at the end of "A Worn Path" Phoenix buys a toy windmill for her sick grandson. It is slight, and she pays for it with all the money she has. It will break soon, like her life and that of her grandson, but it is an attempt to give him some small pleasure despite her poverty and the hopelessness of her life. For all these reasons it is correct to interpret the windmill as a symbol of her strong character, generous nature, and pathetic existence.

# Allegory

An allegory is to a symbol as a motion picture is to a still picture. The allegory puts symbols into action. In form the allegory is a complete and self-sufficient narrative, but it also signifies another series of events or conditions of life as expressed in a religion or philosophy. While some works are allegories from beginning to end, many works that are not allegories contain sections or episodes that may be considered allegorically.

If you write about allegory or an allegorical reading, you are to show how the entire story, or an extensive and self-contained episode, may be applied. Thus, John Bunyan's *The Pilgrim's Progress* is a story about Christian's difficult journey from his home in the City of Destruction to his new home in the Heavenly City. The specific application of this allegory is to the rigors and trials of Christian life as Bunyan understood them. The story may also be applied in a secular context, and to make such an application you would need to show that it is relevant to the growth and problems of most people working toward a goal. Bunyan probably intended his episode of the "Slough of Despond," to name only one section in *The Pilgrim's Progress*, to allegorize the doubt and depression that even the firmest Christian believers sometimes have about their faith. In applying the episode generally it would be proper to take the Slough as meaning those moments of doubt, discouragement, and depression that sometimes plague people seeking an education, a work goal, the good life, or whatever. As long as your parallels are close, as this one is, your allegorical reading will have validity.

## FABLE, PARABLE, AND MYTH

Three forms that you might encounter that are close to allegory are *fable*, *parable*, and *myth:*

FABLE. A fable is a short story, often featuring animals with human traits, to which writers and editors attach "morals" or explanations. The fable of "The Fox and the Grapes," for example, signifies the tendency to demean those things we cannot have.

PARABLE. Parables are most often associated with Jesus Christ, who used them in his teaching. They are extremely short narratives which exemplify religious truths and insights. Parables like those of the Good Samaritan and the Prodigal Son are interpreted to show God's active love, concern, understanding, and forgiveness for human beings.

MYTH. Myths are stories, either short or long, that are often associated with religion and philosophy, and also, in anthropological or psychological terms, with various races or cultures. Myths embody scientific truths for pre-scientific societies, and codify the social and cultural values of the civilization in which they were written. In the past the word *mythical* was a way of saying that something was untrue. Today, however, it is proper to be more sympathetic to myths, for the truths are to be found not literally in the stories themselves, but figuratively in the interpretations.

## Allusiveness in Imagery, Symbolism, and Allegory

These modes are often complicated by the *allusion* to other things, such as the classics, the Bible, or contemporary politics. The original source then becomes a vital part of the writer's image. In John Donne's sonnet "I Am a Little World Made Cunningly," for example, the concluding lines are:

> . . . burn me, O Lord, with a fiery zeal
> Of Thee and Thy house, which doth in eating heal.

Reading the last line is made possible if you realize that the metaphor is an allusion to *Psalms* 69.9: "For the zeal of thine house hath eaten me up." Until the Biblical reference is known, however, the line is difficult if not impossible to understand.

This example brings up the problem of how much background you need for understanding imagery or symbols. For the most part your attempt to imagine the experience described or suggested will be enough. But an allusive image, like the Biblical one in Donne's poem, or an archaic symbol, may require a dictionary or other reference work. The scope of your Collegiate Dictionary will surprise you. If you cannot find an entry in your dictionary, however, try an encyclopedia, or ask your reference librarian about standard reference guides such as *The Oxford Companion to English Literature, The Oxford Companion to Classical Literature,* or William Rose Benet's *The Reader's Encyclopaedia.* If you continue to have trouble after using sources like these, see your instructor.

## Preparing for Your Theme

You will need to be alert and to employ all facilities that can aid your understanding and appreciation. Study the poem or passage word by word. Try to discover individual images and patterns of imagery. Take careful notes, and write your reactions as they occur to you. A good thing to do is to make visual aids, trying to bring images to life by drawing diagrams or sketches. In Shakespeare's Sonnet 146, for example, line 13 offers a challenge to the imagination that might be aided by a sketch:

So shalt thou [the speaker's Soul] feed on Death that feeds on
men.

Just how far does this metaphor invite visualization? Do *feed* and *feeds*
suggest an eater who, while eating, is being eaten, or should the words
be read without the attempt to imagine specific feeders? In the age of *Jaws*
and *Jaws II*, one student made the following drawing for these lines:

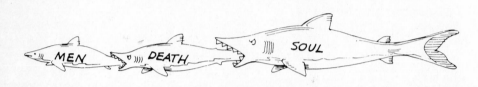

This drawing vividly shows the relationships involved, though it tends to
demean Soul, Death, and Men (perhaps the student was thinking that
human beings, in this case, are "poor fish"). Whether or not you carry
your visualization this far, it is clear that Shakespeare's speaker is calling
Death voracious because it seizes human beings for prey. But he is also
claiming that the Soul can be equally voracious and stronger than Death,
even though it is also dependent on Death in this graphic food chain.

A particularly helpful aid for symbolism is a list. The idea is to show
how qualities of the symbol may be paralleled with qualities of a character
or action. Such a list can give you the substance for much in your theme,
and it can also help you in thinking more deeply about the effectiveness
of the symbol. Here is such a list, for the symbol of the toy windmill in
Welty's "A Worn Path":

| Qualities in the Windmill | Comparable Qualities in Phoenix and her Life |
|---|---|
| 1. Cheap | 1. Poor, but she gives all she has for the windmill |
| 2. Breakable | 2. Old, and not far from death |
| 3. A gift | 3. Generous |
| 4. Not practical | 4. Needs some relief from reality and practicality |
| 5. Colorful | 5. Same as 4 |

An aid for figuring out an allegory or allegorical passage can work well
with a diagram of parallel lines. Along these lines you can place corresponding events, as follows:

| PILGRIM'S PROGRESS | Christian's Burden | Slough of Despond | Valley of the Shadow of Death |
|---|---|---|---|
| CHRISTIAN APPLICATION | Original Sin | Doubt and Despair | Danger of the Loss of the Soul |
| GENERAL APPLICATION | Problems, Shortcomings, Poverty, etc. | Depression, Despondency | General risks and dangers of living |

Some persons might object to making such sketches or diagrams because they might limit your responses too narrowly. But if these aids genuinely help you, go right ahead and use them. You might wish to modify your aids, as you make progress with them, by crossing some things out and by putting others in. As long as what you do can be supported in your work, you will stay on the right track and can even improve the accuracy and forcefulness of your theme.

## Organizing Your Theme

### INTRODUCTION

Whether you are discussing imagery or symbolism and allegory, you should try to relate your topic to the general nature of the work. Thus, images or symbols of suffering might be appropriate to a religious, redemptive work, while those of sunshine and cheer might be right for a romantic one. You should also try to justify any claims that you make about images or symbols. In Swift's *A Modest Proposal*, for example, the eating of infants is proposed: How can this action be viewed as a symbol? Your introduction is the place to establish ideas and justifications of this sort. Your central idea and thesis sentence should be here, too, to guide your reader for the remainder of your theme.

### BODY

**A. IMAGERY.**   There are a number of approaches for discussing imagery. They are not mutually exclusive, and you may combine them as you wish.

1. *The meaning and effect of the imagery.* Here you explain your interpretation of the various images. In Eve Merriam's poem "Robin Hood," for example, Robin Hood comes back to Sherwood Forest to establish the forest

as a preserve next to the "Hood enterprises / for Sherwood Homesights." In explaining this action as metaphor, you would say that modern commercialism has preempted the sense of adventure, romance, and justice that we associate with earlier times. In determining the effect of the metaphor, you would probably draw attention to its combination of cynicism, derision, and amusement.

2. *The frames of reference of the imagery, and the appropriateness of the imagery to the subject matter.* Here you might show the locations from which the images are derived. Does the writer favor images from Nature, science, warfare, politics, business, reading? Are these images appropriate to the subject matter? If the subject is the dreariness of a 9-to-5 office routine, for example, would an image of paper clips and commas be appropriate (see Theodore Roethke's poem "Dolor")? Similarly, in a tragedy, would it be appropriate to refer to images drawn from joyous springtime rituals?

3. *The frequency and the types of images.* Does the writer characteristically express himself or herself in imagery? How many images are there? How often do they occur? Does the writer use images appealing to one sense (sight, hearing, smell, taste, touch) rather than to another? Does he or she record colors, sounds, shapes? Do the images function integrally in the ideas of the work, or in the type of work? How fully does the author rely on the associations of sensuous imagery? (Do references to green plants and trees, for example, suggest that life may be rich and full, or do references to touch suggest amorous warmth?) What conclusions can you draw about the author's—or the speaker's—taste or sensibility as a result of your study?

4. *The effect of one image, or series of images, on the other images and ideas in the work.* Usually you will pick an image that occurs early in the work and determine whether this image acts as a controlling image over the ideas or mood of the work. Thus, the first paragraph of Jonathan Swift's *Battle of the Books* contains a demeaning image about the behavior of sexually aroused dogs. In this way, Swift conveys the impression that the claims to superiority of modern writers and thinkers has a physiological origin that is anything but flattering. In an analysis of this sort, you would try to show the importance of the controlling image throughout the work.

### B. SYMBOLS, SYMBOLISM

1. *The meaning of a major symbol.* Here you interpret the symbol and try to show what it stands for both inside and outside the work. A few of the questions you might pursue are these: How do you determine that the symbol is really a symbol? How do you derive from the work the exact meaning of the symbol? What is the extent of the meaning? Does the symbol undergo any modification if it reappears in the work? How? Does the author create any ironies by using the symbol? Does the symbol give any special strength to the work?

2. *The meaning and relationship of a number of symbols.* What are the symbols? Do they have any specific connection or common bond? Do they suggest a unified reading or a contradictory one? Are the symbols of general significance, or do they operate only in the context of the work? Do the symbols control the form of the work? How? Do they fit naturally into the narrative, or do they seem to be drawn in artificially? Does their use make for any unique qualities or excellences in the work?

#### C. ALLEGORY (FABLE, PARABLE, MYTH)

1. *The application of the allegory.* Does the allegory (fable, parable, myth) refer to anything or anyone specific? Does it refer to an action or particular period of history? Or does the allegory refer to human tendencies or ideas? Does it illustrate, point by point, particular philosophies or religions? If so, what are these? If the original meaning of the allegory seems outdated, how much can be salvaged for people living today?

2. *The consistency of the allegory.* Is the allegory maintained consistently throughout the work, or is it intermittently used and dropped? Explain and detail this use. Would it be correct to call your work *allegorical* rather than *an allegory*? Are there any unnatural or arbitrary events that are introduced because of the allegory (such as the albatross' being hung around the neck of Coleridge's Ancient Mariner to show that he must carry the burden of his crime)?

## CONCLUSION

In your conclusion you might summarize your main points, describe your general impressions, try to describe the impact of the images or symbolic methods, indicate your personal responses, or show what might further be done along the lines you have been developing in the body. You might also try to assess the quality of the images and to make a statement about their appropriateness.

---

## First Sample Theme
## (Imagery in a Poem)

### *A Study of Shakespeare's Imagery in Sonnet 30*

---

| | |
|---|---|
| When to the sessions of sweet silent thought, | 1 |
| I summon up remembrance of things past, | 2 |
| I sigh the lack of many a thing I sought, | 3 |
| And with old woes new wail my dear time's waste: | 4 |
| Then can I drown an eye (un-used to flow) | 5 |

| For precious friends hid in death's dateless night, | 6 |
| And weep afresh love's long since cancelled woe, | 7 |
| And moan th'expense of many a vanished sight. | 8 |
| Then can I grieve at grievances foregone, | 9 |
| And heavily from woe to woe tell o'er | 10 |
| The sad account of fore-bemoaned moan, | 11 |
| Which I new pay, as if not paid before. | 12 |
| But if the while I think on thee (dear friend) | 13 |
| All losses are restored, and sorrows end. | 14 |

[1]  In this sonnet Shakespeare, the speaker, stresses the sadness and regret of remembered experience, but he states that a person with these feelings may be cheered by the thought of a friend. His imagery, cleverly used, creates new and fresh ways of seeing personal life in this perspective.* He presents images drawn from the public and business world of the courtroom, money, and banking or money-handling.†

[2]  The courtroom image of the first four lines shows that the past is alive in the present. Like a justice at a hearing, Shakespeare "summons" his memory of "things past" to appear on trial before him. This image suggests that people are their own judges and that their ideals and morals are like laws by which they measure themselves. Shakespeare finds himself guilty of wasting his time in the past. Removing himself, however, from the strict punishment that the image would require, he does not condemn himself for his "dear time's waste," but instead laments it (line 4).

[3]  With the closely related image of money, Shakespeare shows that living is a lifelong investment and is valuable for this reason. It is not money that is spent, but emotions and commitment. Thus, his dead friends are "precious" because he invested time and love in them, and the "sights" that have "vanished" from his eyes make him "moan" because he went to great "expense" for them (8).

[4]  Like the money image, the reference to banking or money-handling emphasizes the fact that life's experiences are on deposit in the mind. They are recorded there, and may be withdrawn in moments of "sweet silent thought" just as money may be withdrawn. Thus Shakespeare states that he counts out his woes just as a teller counts money. He pays with new woe the accounts that he had already paid with old woe in the past. The imagery suggests that the past is so much a part of the present that a person never finishes paying both the principal and interest of past emotional investments. Because of this combination of banking and legal imagery, Shakespeare indicates that his memory puts him in double jeopardy, for the thoughts of his losses overwhelm him in the present just as much as they did in the past.

[5]  The legal, financial, and money-handling images combine in the last two lines to show how a healthy present life may overcome past regrets. The "dear friend" being addressed in these lines has the resources (financial) to settle all the emotional judgments that the speaker makes against himself (legal). It is as though the friend is a rich patron who rescues him from emotional bank-

*Central idea
†Thesis sentence

ruptcy (legal and financial) and the possible sentence of emotional misery (legal).

[6]

Shakespeare's images are drawn from everyday public and business actions, but his use of them is creative, unusual, and excellent. In particular, the tenor of line 8 ("And moan th'expense of many a vanished sight") stresses that people spend much emotional energy on others. Without emotional commitment, one cannot have precious friends and loved ones. In keeping with this image of money and investment, one could measure life not in months or years, but in the spending of emotion and involvement in personal relationships. Shakespeare, by inviting readers to explore the values brought out by his images, gives a new sense of the value of life itself.

## Commentary on the Theme

This theme treats the three classes of images that Shakespeare introduces in Sonnet 30. It thus illustrates the second approach (p. 106). But the aim of the discussion is not to explore the extent and nature of the comparison between the images and the personal situations spoken about in the poem. Instead the goal is to explain how the images develop Shakespeare's meaning. This method therefore illustrates the first approach (pp. 105–106).

The introduction provides a brief description of the sonnet, the central idea, and the thesis sentence. Paragraph two deals with the meaning of Shakespeare's courtroom image. His money image is explained in paragraph three. Paragraph four considers the banking, or money-handling image. The fifth paragraph shows how Shakespeare's last two lines bring together the three separate strands, or classes of images.

The conclusion comments generally on the creativity of Shakespeare's images. It also amplifies the way in which the money image creates an increased understanding and valuation of life.

## Second Sample Theme (Allegory and Symbolism in a Story)

### *Allegory and Symbolism in Hawthorne's "Young Goodman Brown"*

It is hard to read beyond the third paragraph of "Young Goodman Brown" without finding allegory and symbolism. The opening seems realistic—Goodman Brown, a young Puritan, leaves his home in colonial Salem to take an overnight trip—but his wife's name, "Faith," immediately suggests a symbolic reading. Before long, Brown's walk into the dreamlike forest seems like an allegorical trip into evil. The idea that Hawthorne shows by this trip is that rigid belief destroys the best human qualities, such as understanding and love.* He develops this thought in the allegory and in many symbols, particularly the sunset, the walking-stick, and the path.†

[1]

The allegory is about how people develop destructive ideas. Most of the story seems dreamlike and unreal, and therefore the ideas that Brown gains seem unreal. After the weird night he thinks of his wife and neighbors not with love, but with hatred for their sins during the "witch meeting" deep in the dream forest. For this wrong cause, really no cause at all, he condemns everyone around him, and he lives out his life in unforgiving harshness. This story may be applied allegorically to the pursuit of any ideal or system beyond human love and forgiveness. No matter what *ism* people follow, to the degree that for that *ism* they condemn human beings, take hostages, accept political repression of others, and destroy people and land, they are like Goodman Brown. With his bitterness and distrust, he has destroyed the best in himself—his ability to love and forgive.

[2]

The attack on such dehumanizing belief is found not just in the allegory, but also in Hawthorne's many symbols. The seventh word in the story, *sunset*, may be seen as a symbol. Sunset indicates the end of the day. Coming at the beginning of the story, however, it suggests that Goodman Brown is beginning the long night of his hatred, his spiritual death. For him the night will never end because his final days are shrouded in "gloom" (p. 301). Hawthorne indicates that Brown, like anyone else who gives up on human beings, is cut off, locked in an inner prison of bitterness.

[3]

The next symbol, the walking-stick, suggests the ambiguous and arbitrary standard by which Brown judges his neighbors. The stick is carried by the guide who looks like Brown's father, but it is more. Hawthorne writes that it "might almost be seen to twist and wriggle itself like a living serpent" (p. 293) The serpent is a clear symbol for Satan, who tempted Adam and Eve. The stick is also still a walking-stick, however, and in this respect it is innocent. Hawthorne seems to be using it to symbolize human tendencies to see evil where evil does not really exist. This double meaning squares with his statement about "the instinct that guides mortal man to evil" (p. 297). This instinct is not just the temptation to do bad things, but also the invention of wrongs for arbitrary reasons, and, more dangerously, the condemnation of those who have "done" these wrongs even though they have done nothing more than lead their own quiet lives.

[4]

In the same vein, the path through the forest is a major symbol of the evil of the mental confusion to which Brown is subject. As he walks, the path before him grows "wilder and drearier, and more faintly traced," and "at length" it vanishes (p. 297). This is like the description of the "broad" Biblical way that leads "to Destruction" (Matthew, VII.13). As a symbol, the path shows that most human acts are bad, while a small number, like the "narrow" way to life

[5]

*Central idea
†Thesis sentence
For the text of this story, please see Appendix C, pp. 292–301.

(Matthew, VII.14), are good. Goodman Brown's path is at first clear, as though sin is at first unique and unusual, but soon it is so indistinct that he can see only sin wherever he turns. The symbol thus suggests that, as people follow evil, their moral vision becomes blurred and they cannot choose the right way even if it is in front of them. With such vision, they can hardly be anything other than destructive of their best instincts.

[6]     Through Hawthorne's allegory and symbols, then, the story presents a paradox: How can a seemingly good system lead to bad results? How can noble beliefs backfire so destructively? Goodman Brown dies in gloom because he believes strongly that his wrong vision is real. This form of evil is the hardest to stop, no matter what outward set of beliefs it takes, because wrongdoers who are convinced of their own goodness are beyond reach. Such a blend of evil and self-righteousness causes Hawthorne to write that "the fiend in his own shape is less hideous than when he rages in the breast of man" (p. 298). <u>Young Goodman Brown thus becomes Hawthorne's main symbol.</u> He is one of those who walk in darkness but have forever barred themselves from the light.

---

## Commentary on the Theme

The introduction justifies the treatment of allegory and symbolism because of the way in which Hawthorne early in the story invites a symbolic reading. The central idea relates Hawthorne's method to the idea that rigid belief destroys the best human qualities. The thesis sentence outlines two major areas of discussion: (1) allegory, and (2) symbolism.

Paragraph two considers the allegory not just as Hawthorne intended it—as a criticism of rigid Puritan morality—but as a general criticism of *isms* pursued to the point of dehumanization. Paragraphs three, four, and five deal with three major symbols: the sunset, the walking-stick, and the path. The aim of this discussion is to show the meaning and application of these symbols for Hawthorne's attack on rigidity of belief. Throughout these three paragraphs the central idea—the relationship of rigidity to destructiveness—is stressed. The concluding paragraph raises questions that lead to the idea that Brown himself is a symbol of Hawthorne's idea that the primary cause of evil is the inability to separate reality from unreality.

# chapter 10

# The Themes
# of Comparison-Contrast
# and Extended Comparison-
# Contrast

The comparison theme may be used to compare and contrast different authors, two or more works by the same author, different drafts of the same work, or characters, incidents, and ideas within the same work or in different works. Not only is comparison-contrast popular in literature courses, but it is one of the commonest approaches you will find in other disciplines. The ideas of two philosophers may be compared, or the approaches of two schools of psychology, or two conflicting economic theories. The possibilities for using comparison-contrast are extensive.

## Comparison-Contrast
## as a Way to Knowledge

Comparison and contrast are important means to gaining understanding. For example, suppose that you are having trouble understanding separately the poems "War is Kind" by Stephen Crane and "The Fury of Aerial Bombardment" by Richard Eberhart. When you start comparing the two poems, however, you will immediately notice things that you may not have noticed at first. Both of them treat the horrors of war, but they do so differently. Crane is ironic, whereas Eberhart is quietly bitter. Though Eberhart's topic is the "fury" of bombardment, he does not describe explosions and anguished death, but rather draws attention to human stupidity and to the regrettable deaths of persons with great potential. Crane, on the other hand, achieves his ironic effect by speaking of "slaughter" and "corpses" while at the same time he also speaks of war being "kind." Both poems ultimately agree on the irrationality of war. Making a comparison and contrast in this way enables you to see each poem in perspective, and therefore more clearly. The comparison-contrast method is similarly rewarding whenever you apply it, for perhaps the quickest way to get at the essence of an artistic work is to compare it with another work. Similarities are brought out by comparison, and differences are shown by contrast.

The comparison-contrast method is closely related to the study of *definition*, because definition aims at the description of a particular thing by identifying its properties while also isolating it from everything else. Comparison-contrast is also closely allied with Plato's idea that we learn a thing best by reference to its opposite; that is, one way of finding out what a thing *is* is to find out what it is *not*.

## Clarify Your Intention

Your first problem in this theme is to decide on a goal, for you may use the comparison-contrast method in a number of ways. One objective can be the equal and mutual illumination of both (or more) works. Thus, a theme comparing O'Connor's "First Confession" and Hawthorne's "Young Goodman Brown" might be designed (1) to compare ideas, characters, or methods in these stories equally, without stressing or favoring either. But you might also wish (2) to emphasize "Young Goodman Brown," and therefore you would use "First Confession" as material for highlighting Hawthorne's work. You might also use the comparison-contrast method (3) to show your liking of one work (at the expense of another), or (4) to emphasize a method or idea that you think is especially noteworthy or appropriate.

Your first task is therefore to decide where to place your emphasis. The first sample theme reflects a decision to give "equal time" to both works being considered, without any claims for the superiority of either. Unless you wish to pursue a different rhetorical goal, you will find this theme a suitable model for most comparisons.

## Find Common Grounds
## for Comparison

Your second problem is to select the proper material—the grounds of your discussion. It is useless to try to compare dissimilar things, for then your conclusions will be of limited value. You need to put the works or writers you are comparing onto common ground. Compare like with like: idea with idea, characterization with characterization, imagery with imagery, point of view with point of view, problem with problem. Nothing can be learned from a comparison of "Welty's view of courage and Shakespeare's view of love," but a comparison of "The relationship of love to stability and courage in Shakespeare and Welty" suggests common ground, with points of both likeness and difference. (Please see the second sample theme for the use of this basis for comparison in an extended theme of comparison-contrast.)

In searching for common ground, you may have to use your ingenuity a bit. But just as adding 3/4 and 2/3 may be done by changing these fractions to 9/12 and 8/12 to get 1 5/12, you can usually find a basis for your comparison. Thus De Maupassant's "The Necklace" and Chekhov's *The Bear* at first may seem to be as different as they can be. Yet common grounds do exist for these works, such as "The Treatment of Self-Deceit," "The Effects of Chance on Human Affairs," or "The View of Women." As you can see, apparently unlike works can be put into a frame of reference that permits analytical comparison and contrast. Much of your success in this theme will depend on your ingenuity in finding a workable basis—a "common denominator"—for comparison.

## Methods of Comparison

Let us assume that you have decided on your rhetorical purpose and on the basis or bases of your comparison: you have done your reading, taken your notes, and know what you want to say. The remaining problem is the treatment of your material. Here are two acceptable ways.

A common, but inferior, way is to make your points first about one work and then do the same for the other. This method makes your paper seem like two big lumps, and it also involves much repetition because you must repeat the same points as you treat your second subject. This first method is only satisfactory.

The superior method is to treat your main idea in its major aspects and to make references to the two (or more) writers as the reference illustrates and illuminates your main idea. Thus you would be constantly referring to both writers, sometimes within the same sentence, and would be reminding your reader of the point of your discussion. There are reasons for the superiority of the second method: (1) you do not repeat your points needlessly, for you document them as you raise them; (2) by constantly referring to the two works in relation to your common ground of comparison, you make your points without requiring a reader with a poor memory to reread previous sections. Frequently such readers do not bother to reread, and as a result they are never clear about what you have said.

As a good example, here is a paragraph from a student theme on "Nature as a basis of comparison in William Wordsworth's 'The World Is Too Much with Us' and Gerard Manley Hopkins' 'God's Grandeur.' " The virtue of the paragraph is that it uses material from both poets as a means of development; the material is synthesized by the student (sentence numbers in brackets) as follows:

[1] Hopkins' ideas are Christian, though not genuinely other-worldly. [2] God is a God of the world for Hopkins, and "broods with warm breast and with ah! bright wings" (line 14); Hopkins is convinced that God is here and everywhere, for his first line triumphantly proclaims this. [3] Wordsworth, by contrast, is able to perceive the beauty of Nature, but feels that God in the Christian sense has deserted him. [4] Wordsworth is to be defended here, though, because his wish to see Proteus or to hear Triton is not pagan. [5] He wants, instead, to have faith, to have the conviction that Hopkins so confidently claims. [6] Even if the faith is pagan, Wordsworth would like it just so he could have firm, unshakable faith. [7] As a matter of fact, however, Wordsworth's perception of Nature contradicts the lack of faith he claims. [8] His God is really Nature itself. [9] Hopkins' more abstract views of Nature make me feel that the Catholic believes that Nature is only a means to the worship of God. [10] For Hopkins, God is supreme; for Wordsworth, Nature is.

Letting *H* stand for ideas about Hopkins, and *W* for ideas about Wordsworth, the paragraph may be schematized as follows (numbers refer to sentences):

$$1 = H. \quad 2 = H. \quad 3 = W. \quad 4 = W. \quad 5 = W.H. \quad 6 = W.$$
$$7 = W. \quad 8 = W. \quad 9 = H. \quad 10 = H.W.$$

The interweaving of subject material gives the impression that the student has learned both poems well enough to think of them at the same time. Mental "digestion" has taken place. Thus Wordsworth's ideas of Nature are linked with ideas on the same topic by Hopkins, sometimes within the same sentence. You can learn from this example: If you develop your theme by putting your two subjects constantly together, you will write more economically and clearly than you would by the first method (this statement is true of tests as well as themes). Beyond that, if you have actually digested the material as successfully as this method would show, you will be demonstrating that you have fulfilled one of the primary goals of education— the assimilation and *use* of material. Too often education as presented in a course-by-course and writer-by-writer approach seems to be compartmentalized. You should always be trying to synthesize the materials you acquire, to put them together through comparison and contrast so that you can accustom yourself to seeing things not as *fragments* but as parts of *wholes*.

## Avoid the "Tennis-Ball" Method

As you make your comparison, do not confuse an interlocking method with a "tennis-ball" method, in which you bounce your subject back and forth constantly and repetitively. The tennis-ball method is shown in the following example from a comparison of A. E. Housman's "On Wenlock Edge" and Theodore Roethke's "Dolor":

> Housman talks about the eternal nature of human troubles whereas Roethke talks about the "dolor" of modern business life. Housman uses details of woods, gales, snow, leaves, and hills, whereas Roethke selects details of pencils, boxes, paper-weights, mucilage, and lavatories. Housman's focus is therefore on the torments of people close to Nature; Roethke's on civilized, ordered, duplicated, gray-flanneled humanity. Housman states that the significance of human problems fades in the perspective of eternity; Roethke does not mention eternity but makes human problems seem even smaller by showing that business life has virtually erased human emotion.

Imagine the effect of reading an entire theme presented in this fashion. Aside from its power to bore, the tennis-ball method does not give you the chance to develop your points. You should not feel so cramped that you cannot take several sentences to develop a point about one writer or subject before you bring in comparison with another. If you remember to interlock the two points of comparison, however, as in the example comparing Hopkins and Wordsworth, your method will be satisfactory.

## The Extended
## Comparison-Contrast

For a longer theme, such as a limited research paper or the sort of extended theme required at the end of the semester, the technique of comparison-contrast may be used for many works. The extended theme may also be adapted for tests that deal with general, comprehensive questions. Such questions require that you treat ideas or methods in a number of works.

For themes of this larger scope, you will still need to develop common grounds for comparison, although with more works to discuss you will need to modify the method.

Let us assume that you have been assigned not just two works but five or six. You need first to find a common ground among them which you will use as your central, unifying idea. This is the same as for a comparison of just two works. When you take your notes, sketch out your ideas, make your early drafts, and rearrange and shape your developing materials, try to bring all the works together on your major points. Thus in the second sample theme, all the works are treated on the common basis that they speak about the nature of love and devoted service.

When you contrast the works, you should try to make groups based on variations or differences. Let us assume that three or four works treat a topic in one way while one or two do it in another. Here you treat the topic itself in a straightforward contrast method but may wish to use details from the groups on either side of the issue to support your points. Again, it is desirable to use the analysis of a particular point based on one work so that you can make your theme concrete and vivid. But once you have exemplified your point, there is no need to go into any more detail from the other works than seems necessary to get your point across. In this way, you can keep your theme within limits; if you group your works on points of similarity, you do not need to go into excessive and unproductive detail.

As an example of how works may be grouped in this way, please see the second sample theme. There, four works are grouped into a general category of how love and service may offer guidance and stability for living. This group is contrasted with another group of three works (including two characters from one of the works in the first group), in which love is shown as an escape or retreat.

## Documentation and the Extended Comparison-Contrast Theme

For the longer comparison-contrast theme you may find a problem in documentation. Generally you will not need to locate page numbers for references to major traits, ideas, or actions. For example, if you refer to the end of "First Confession," where the priest gives Jackie some candy, you may assume that your reader also knows this action. You do not need to do any more than make the reference.

But if you are quoting lines or passages, or if you are making any special or unusual reference, you may need to use footnotes or parenthetical references. For page numbers, the second sample theme uses the parenthetical abbreviation system described in Appendix B. For lines of poetry, or parts of lines, the theme uses parenthetical line numbers. Be guided by this principle: If you make a specific reference that you think your reader might want to examine in more detail, provide the line or page number. If you are referring to minor details that might easily be forgotten or not noticed, supply the line or page number. Otherwise, if you are referring to major ideas, actions, or characterizations, be sure that your reference within your theme is sufficiently clear that your reader can easily recall it from his or her own memory of the work. Then you will not need to provide line or page numbers.

## Organizing Your Theme

First you must narrow your subject into a topic you can handle conveniently within the limits of the assignment. For example, if you have been assigned a comparison of Wordsworth and Hopkins, pick out one or two poems of each poet and write your theme about them. You must be wary, however, of the limitations of this selection: generalizations made from one or two works may not apply to the broad subject originally proposed.

INTRODUCTION

State what works, authors, characters, and ideas are under considera-tion, then show how you have narrowed the basis of your comparison. Your central idea will be a brief statement of what can be learned from your paper: the general similarities and differences that you have observed from your comparison and/or the superiority of one work or author over another. Your thesis sentence should anticipate the body of your theme.

BODY

The body of your theme depends on the points you have chosen for comparison. You might be comparing two works on the basis of *point of view* or *imagery*, two authors on *ideas*, or two characters on *character traits*. In your discussion you would necessarily use the same methods that you would use in writing about a single work, except that here (1) you are exemplifying your points by reference to more subjects than one, and (2) your main purpose is to shed light on the subjects on which your com-parison is based. In this sense, the methods you use in talking about point of view or imagery are not "pure" but are instead subordinate to your aims of comparison-contrast. Let us say that you are comparing the ideas in two different works. The first part of your theme might be devoted to analyzing and describing the similarities and dissimilarities of the ideas *as* ideas. Your interest here is not so much to explain the ideas of either work separately as to explain the ideas of both works in order to show points of agreement and disagreement. A second part might be given over to the influences of the ideas on the point of view of the particular works; that is, you might discuss how the ideas help make the works similar or dissimilar. If you are comparing characters, your points might be to show similarities and dis-similarities of mental and spiritual qualities and of activities in which the characters engage.

CONCLUSION

Here you are comparatively free to reflect on other ideas in the works you have compared, to make observations on comparative qualities, or to summarize briefly the basic grounds of your comparison. The conclusion of an extended comparison-contrast theme should represent a final bringing together of the materials. In the body of the theme you may not have referred to all the works in each paragraph; however, in the conclusion you should try to refer to them all, if possible.

If your writers belonged to any "period" or "school," you also might wish to show in your conclusion how they relate to these larger movements. References of this sort provide a natural common ground for comparison.

---

### First Sample Theme
### (Two Works)

*The Treatment of the Need for Understanding in "Young Goodman Brown" by Nathaniel Hawthorne and "First Confession" by Frank O'Connor*

---

[1]     The major difference between "Young Goodman Brown" and "First Confession" is that O'Connor's story is comic, farcical, and pleasant, while Hawthorne's is serious, demonic, and grim. Yet there are many similarities. Both deal with religious materials. Both have episodes that are vivid and dramatic. Both have journeys, one to a forest and the other to a church. And both have major figures who are being initiated into life—one a child and the other a newly married man. A most important agreement is that both works stress that understanding, tolerating, and forgiving people is better than condemning them.* This point is made in the sinful actions, the attitudes, and the conclusions of both works.†

[2]     Sinfulness, or what passes for sinfulness, emphasizes the need for understanding. Things are much worse in "Young Goodman Brown" than in "First Confession." Real sins and punishable crimes (such as infant murder, political corruption, and poisoning) are mentioned by the "sable form" in Hawthorne's demonic forest ritual (p. 299). Above these is Goodman Brown's condemnation of his wife and neighbors. By contrast, Jackie's "sins" of kicking his grandmother and waving the bread knife at Nora are no more than the actions of a confused child. Yet both sets of actions show that there is a need for trying to understand the motives of the sinner. Without understanding, there can be nothing but outright condemnation, which for Hawthorne and O'Connor seems to be a greater sin than any the devil can mention.

[3]     Just like the treatment of sinful actions, the attitudes of the major characters in both works underscore the need for sympathy and understanding. By the end of the story, Goodman Brown shows a complete intolerance of others because he believes that everyone is lost in sin. Where things seem good, he sees only hypocrisy, and he views everyone with mistrust and hatred. Mrs.

*Central idea
†Thesis sentence
For the texts of these stories, please see Appendix C, pp. 292–301 and 333–339 respectively.

Ryan and Nora are very much like Goodman Brown. Nora is suspicious of everything Jackie does and tries to get him punished regularly. In a way, Mrs. Ryan is slightly worse than Goodman Brown, because she teaches children her philosophy of fear and punishment, while Goodman Brown hurts only himself. The negative views of all three, however, show the need for something human and compassionate, the attempt to understand and correct rather than to condemn.

[4]
The conclusions of the stories may be read as both positive and negative illustrations of the advantages of compassion and understanding. In "First Confession" the priest gives Jackie a complete audience, hears his worst secrets, makes sympathetic comments, and gives the boy candy with only three Hail Marys as penance. What could be a more positive model than this for showing the practical benefits of understanding? In contrast, Goodman Brown's vision of evil is obsessive and destructive. He listens to no one sympathetically, as the priest does, and he tries to speak to no one about his troubles, as Jackie finally does. While Jackie confesses his anger and fear, and thus will no longer need to brood about them, Goodman Brown is left alone, in the gloom of his own mind. He goes to his grave convinced that everyone around him is evil, and he never even gives his friends and neighbors a chance. He gets the worst that his religion has to offer, with none of the better parts that Jackie receives.

[5]
There are many other points of comparison that are related to the issue of tolerance and understanding. A major one is the point of view. O'Connor could not get as serious as Hawthorne without disturbing his comedy. Thus his first-person point of view, by which Jackie as an adult tells about his first confession as a seven-year-old, keeps things close to the surface, on a child's level. This outlook makes understanding and forgiveness seem not just possible, but absolutely necessary. Hawthorne, by contrast, writes in the third-person point of view but never enters his character. Brown therefore remains distant, never as close and friendly and as easy to forgive as Jackie is. Although both stories make similar points about the need for human understanding and toleration, they are different and unique.

## Commentary on the Theme

Although this theme points out a number of possible subjects on which the two works could be compared (religion, dramatic scenes, journeys, and characters undergoing initiation), the point chosen for comparison (the central idea) is the need for understanding and forgiveness. The effect of pointing out these subjects in the introduction is to give the reader the impression that the two works have been studied thoroughly and that the subject chosen for comparison has been selected because of its major importance. In other words, there is rhetorical value in this approach to the introduction. The thesis sentence defines three areas in which the central idea is to be examined.

Paragraph two compares the sinful actions in the two stories, stressing the point of agreement and demonstrating that the actions in "Young Goodman Brown" are worse than those in "First Confession." The third paragraph carries the comparison to Goodman Brown, on the one hand, and Nora and Mrs. Ryan, on the other, showing how their negative attitudes fit into the claim about the need for understanding. The fourth paragraph compares the happy ending of "First Confession" with the bleak one in "Young Goodman Brown."

The conclusion does not summarize the major headings of the theme, but stresses instead how the points of view in the two stories can be related to the central idea.

In each of the paragraphs, this theme shows how the two works may be connected by the topic idea. Paragraph three, for example, contains seven sentences. Three show points of similarity and one shows a point of difference. While the remaining three are on single works (two on Hawthorne, one on O'Connor), they are designed to emphasize points of comparison. All the sentences, therefore, carry out the goal of comparison and contrast.

---

## Second Sample Theme
## (Extended Comparison-Contrast)

### *The Complexity of Love and Devoted Service as Shown in Six Works*

---

[1]

On the surface, at least, love and devotion are simple, and their results should be good. A person loves someone, or serves someone or something. This love may be romantic or familial, and the service may be religious or national. But love is not simple. <u>It is complex, and its results are not uniformly good.</u>* Love and devotion should be ways of saying "yes," but ironically they sometimes become ways of saying "no," too. This idea can be traced in a comparison of six works: Shakespeare's Sonnet 116, Arnold's "Dover Beach," Hardy's "Channel Firing," Chekhov's *The Bear*, O'Connor's "First Confession," and Welty's "A Worn Path." The complexity in these works is that love and devotion do not operate in a vacuum but rather in the context of personal, philosophical, economic, and national difficulties. <u>The works show that love and devotion may be forces for stability and refuge, but also for harm.</u>†

<u>Ideal and stabilizing love, along with service performed out of love, is shown by Shakespeare in Sonnet 116 and by O'Connor in "First Confession."</u> Shake-

---

*Central idea
†Thesis sentence
**For the texts of these works, please see Appendix C.**

speare states that love gives lovers strength and stability in a complex world of opposition and difficulty. Such love is like a "star" that guides wandering ships (line 7), and like a "fixed mark" that stands against the shaking of life's tempests (lines 5 and 6). A character who is similarly aware of human tempests and conflicts is the "young priest" who hears Jackie's confession in "First Confession." He is clearly committed to service, and is "intelligent above the ordinary" (p. 337). With service to God as his "star," to use Shakespeare's image, he is able to talk sympathetically with Jackie and to send the boy home with a clear and happy mind.

[2]

For both Shakespeare and O'Connor, love and service grow out of a great human need for stability and guidance. To this degree love is a simplifying force, but it simplifies primarily because the "tempests" complicating life are so strong. Such love is one of the best things that happen to human beings, because it fulfills them and prepares them to face life.

[3]

The desire for love of this kind is so strong that it can also be the cause for people to do strange and funny things. The two major characters in Chekhov's short comedy-farce The Bear are examples. At the play's start, Chekhov shows that Mrs. Popov and Smirnov are following some of the crack-brained and negative guides that people often confuse for truth. She is devoted to the memory of her dead husband, while he is disillusioned and cynical about women. But Chekhov makes them go through hoops for love. As the two argue, insult each other, and reach the point of dueling with real pistols, their need for love overcomes all their other impulses. It is as though love happens despite everything going against it, because the need for the stabilizing base is so strong. Certainly love here is not without at least some complexity.

[4]

Either seriously or comically, then, love is shown as a rudder, guiding people in powerful and conflicting currents. The three works studied so far show that love shapes lives and makes for sudden and unexpected changes.

[5]

This thought is somewhat like the view presented by Eudora Welty in "A Worn Path." Unlike Chekhov and Shakespeare, and more like O'Connor, Welty tells a story of service performed out of love. A poor grandmother, Phoenix Jackson, has a hard life in caring for her incurably ill grandson. The walk she takes along the "worn path" to Natchez symbolizes the hardships she endures because of her single-minded love. Her service is the closest thing to pure simplicity that may be found in all the works examined, with the possible exception of the love in Chekhov's play.

[6]

But even her love is not without its complexity. Hardy in "Channel Firing" and Arnold in "Dover Beach" describe a joyless, loveless, insecure world overrun by war. Phoenix's life is just as grim. She is poor and ignorant, and her grandson has nowhere to go but down. If she would only stop to think deeply about her condition, she might be as despairing as Arnold and Hardy. But her strength may be her ability either to accept her difficult life or to ignore the grimness of it. With her service as her "star" and "ever-fixed mark," she is able to keep cheerful and to live in friendship with the animals and the woods. Her life has meaning and dignity.

[7]

Arnold's view of love and devotion under such bad conditions is different from the views of Shakespeare, Chekhov, O'Connor, and Welty. For Arnold, the public world seems to be so far gone that there is nothing left but personal relationships. Thus love is not so much a guide as a refuge, a place of sanity

[8]

and safety. After describing what he considers the worldwide shrinking of the "Sea of Faith," he states:

> Ah, love, let us be true
> To one another! for the world, which seems
> To lie before us like a land of dreams,
> So various, so beautiful, so new,
> Hath really neither joy, nor love, nor light,
> Nor certitude, nor peace, nor help for pain;
> And we are here as on a darkling plain
> Swept with confused alarms of struggle and flight
> Where ignorant armies clash by night.
>
> —lines 29–37

Here the word *true* should be underlined, as Shakespeare emphasizes "true minds" and as O'Connor's priest is a true servant of God. "True" to Arnold seems to involve a pledge to create a small area of certainty in the mad world like that of "Channel Firing," where there is no certainty. Love is not so much a guide as a last place of hope, a retreat where truth can still have meaning.

[9]   In practice, perhaps, Arnold's idea of love as a refuge is not very different from the view that love is a guide. Once the truthful pledge is made, it is a force for goodness, at least for the lovers making the pledge, just as love works for goodness in Shakespeare, O'Connor, Chekhov, and Welty. Yet Arnold's view is weaker. It does not result from an inner need or conviction, but rather from a conscious decision to let everything else go and to look out only for the small relationship. In an extreme form, this could lead to total withdrawal. Such a passive relationship to other affairs could be harmful by omission.

[10]   The idea that love and devotion as a refuge could be actively harmful is explored by O'Connor in other characters in "First Confession." Nora and Mrs. Ryan seem to think only of sinfulness and punishment. They seek the love of God out of a desire for protection. Their devotion is therefore a means to an end, not the pure goal which operates in Shakespeare, Welty, and O'Connor's own priest. As Jackie says of Mrs. Ryan:

> She . . . wore a black cloak and bonnet, and came every day to school at three o'clock when we should have been going home, and talked to us of hell. She may have mentioned the other place as well, but that could only have been by accident, for hell had the first place in her heart (p. 334).

[11]   Love and devotion for her and for Nora take the form of observing ritual and following rules, such as being sure that all confessions are "good" (that is, complete, with no sins held back). If this obedience were only personal, it would be a force for security, as it is on the personal level for Arnold. But from the safety of their refuge, Mrs. Ryan confuses children like Jackie by describing devilish, sadistic tortures, while Nora tells her father about the bread knife and thus brings down punishment (the "flaking") and a "scalded" heart on Jackie. Even though Mrs. Ryan is not a bad soul, and Nora is no more than a young girl, their use of religion is negative. Fortunately, their influence is counterbalanced by the priest.

Mrs. Ryan and Nora are minor compared with those unseen, unnamed, and distant persons firing the big guns during the "gunnery practice out at sea" in Hardy's "Channel Firing" (line 10). Hardy does not treat the gunners as individuals but as an evil collective force made up of persons who, under the sheltering claim oı devotion to country and obedience of orders, are "striving strong to make / Red war yet redder" (lines 13, 14). For them, love of country is a refuge, just like the love of God for Mrs. Ryan and Nora and the true pledge to love for Arnold's speaker. As members of the military they obey orders and, as Hardy's God says, they are not much better than the dead because they do nothing "for Christés sake" (line 15). They operate the ships and fill the columns of Arnold's "ignorant armies," for Hardy makes clear that their target practice takes place at night (line 1).

[12]

In summary, love and devotion as seen in these various works may be compared with a continuous line formed out of the human need for love and for the stability and guidance that love offers. At one end love is totally good and ideal; at the other it is totally bad. Shakespeare, Welty, Chekhov, and O'Connor (in the priest) show the end that is good. Still at the good end, but moving toward the center, is Arnold's use of love as a refuge. On the other side of the line are Mrs. Ryan and Nora of "First Confession," while all the way at the bad end are the insensible and invisible gunners in "Channel Firing."

[13]

The difficulty noted in all the works, and a major problem in life, is to devote oneself to the right, stabilizing, constructive part of the line. Although in his farce Chekhov makes love win against almost impossible odds, he shows the problem most vividly of all the authors studied. Under normal conditions, people like Mrs. Popov and Smirnov would not find love. Instead, they would continue following their destructive and false guides. They would be unhappy and disillusioned, or else they might become more like Mrs. Ryan and spread talk about their own confused ideas (as Smirnov actually does almost right up to his conversion to love). Like the military and naval forces of Arnold and Hardy, they would then wind up at the destructive end of the line.

[14]

Change, opposition, confusion, anger, resignation, economic difficulty—these are only some of the forces that attack people as they try to find the benefits of love. If they are lucky they find meaning and stability in love and service, as in Sonnet 116, "First Confession," *The Bear*, "A Worn Path," and, to a small degree, "Dover Beach." If confusion wins, they are locked into harmful positions, like the gunners in "Channel Firing" and Mrs. Ryan and Nora in "First Confession." Thus love is complicated by circumstances, and it is not the simple force for good that it should ideally be. The six works compared and contrasted here have shown these difficulties and complexities.

[15]

## Commentary on the Theme

This theme compares and contrasts six works—three poems, two stories, and a play—on the common ground or central idea of the complexity of love and service. The complexity is caused by life's difficulties ("tempests," as Shakespeare calls them) and by bad results. The theme develops the central idea in terms of love as an ideal and guide (paragraphs two–seven) and love as a refuge or escape (eight–twelve), with a sub-category of love as a cause of harm (ten–twelve).

The various works are introduced as they are grouped according to these sections. For example, Sonnet 116, "First Confession" (because of the priest), *The Bear*, and "A Worn Path" are together in the first group—love as an ideal and guide. Because "Dover Beach" and "Channel Firing" are in the second group, these works are brought in earlier, during the discussion of the first group. For this reason, both poems are used regularly for comparison and contrast throughout the theme.

The use of the various works within groups may be seen in paragraph eight. There, the principal topic is the use of love as a refuge or retreat, and the central work of the paragraph is "Dover Beach." However, the first sentence contrasts Arnold's view with the four works in the first group; the fifth sentence shows how Arnold is similar in one respect to Shakespeare and O'Connor; and the sixth sentence shows a similarity of Arnold and Hardy. The paragraph thus brings together all the works being studied in the theme.

The technique of comparison-contrast used in this way shows how the various works may be defined and distinguished in relation to the common idea. Paragraph thirteen, the first in the conclusion, attempts to summarize these distinctions by suggesting a continuous line along which each of the works may be placed. Paragraphs fourteen and fifteen continue the summary by showing the prominence of complicating difficulties, and, by implication, the importance of love. Thus, the effect of the comparison of all the works collectively is the enhanced understanding of each of the works separately.

# chapter 11

# *The Theme*
# *Analyzing Structure*

Structure in literary study may be defined as the organization of a literary work as influenced by its plot (in fictional works) or main idea (in expository works). The word is also sometimes defined as the pattern of emotions in the literary work. Although these two definitions are distinct, they are closely connected and under most circumstances are virtually inseparable. The word *structure* is in fact a metaphor implying that a work of literature, both topically and emotionally, is as connected and unified as a building—a structure.

In imaginative works, structure refers to the chronological position of parts, scenes, episodes, chapters, and acts; it also refers to the logical or associational relationships among stanzas, ideas, images, or other divisions. In expository works, the word necessarily refers to the arrangement and development of ideas. Structure is a matter of the relationships among parts that are often described in terms of cause and effect, position in time, association, symmetry, and balance and proportion.

## The Importance of Structure

In a very real sense, all studies of literature are either directly or indirectly concerned with structure. If you talk about the happy or unhappy ending of a short story, for example, you in fact consider the conclusion in relation to what went before it; inevitably you mention whether the earlier parts of the story demonstrated that the characters earned or deserved what happened to them. This consideration must touch on the logic of the story's action, and hence it is a subject of structure. Similarly, in considering Shakespeare's Sonnet No. 73, you may observe that the first quatrain compares the speaker to dead trees, the second to twilight, and the third to a dying and self-extinguishing fire. When you determine that there is a logical or topical relationship among these quatrains, you are discussing structure.

Since structure is so closely tied to all phases of literary study, you might ask in what way structure is unique. How, for example, does a theme about ideas, or a summary theme, differ from a theme about structure? The difference is one of emphasis: in studying structure you emphasize the logic, or the causes, underlying the major divisions in the work being analyzed; in a summary theme you emphasize the events or ideas that you have cast in a reasonable plan of organization; in a theme about ideas you emphasize the ideas and their importance as they are made apparent in the work. In fact, no matter what topic you are writing about, your finished theme is usually related to the structure of the work, for the major parts of your theme can be conveniently dictated by the organization of the work and the causes for it are your primary concern. Ideas, events, and other things such as point of view and imagery are relevant only as substance for your discussion of structure.

## Types of Structures

1. LOGIC. In a good work of literature, the parts are not introduced accidentally. One part demands another. As a result, quite often a logical pattern of premises and arguments can be found. Andrew Marvell's poem "To His Coy Mistress," for example, could be laid out almost as a logical syllogism:

> If we lived forever, we could delay our love affair.
>
> But we do not live forever.
>
> Therefore, let us begin to love each other.

Most works, of course, will not give such a clear pattern, but it is possible nevertheless to analyze works in terms of (a) the establishment of certain conditions, and (b) the results of these conditions. Swift's "A Modest Proposal"* yields to logical analysis: Swift's speaker makes an outrageous proposal as a result of the conditions he has described in the first part of the work.

---

*See Appendix C, pp. 287–292, for the text of "A Modest Proposal."

The sample theme shows how the method may be applied to a story. Thomas Hardy establishes certain characteristics of his country folk in the first part of "The Three Strangers" and then brings these characteristics into action in the latter part of the story.

2. CHRONOLOGY.   It is never enough simply to assert that events happen in time; time is important only as it permits human reactions to occur, and hence chronology in literature is primarily a convenient classification for the logic of human motivation. For example, in Robert Frost's poem "The Road Not Taken," the first three stanzas describe Frost's taking one road at a fork in the road he was already traveling. As the stanzas progress, it becomes clear that the road taken was actually the way of life he chose. In the final, fourth stanza, he observes that his choice was a major landmark in his life, affecting his present and future and making him different from what he would have been had he taken the other road. The structure of the poem is such that the stanzas move naturally from a brief account of events to their human effects and implications. The last stanza stems inevitably from the first three; it could not be transposed and still make the same sense.

3. CONFLICTS.   The structure of a work may be seen in terms of oppositions or conflicts that continue throughout a work until the final resolution. Conflicts may be seen in all literary works. In the broadest forms, there may be a conflict between life and death, *yes* and *no*, or love and hate. The conflict may be of human beings against other human beings or against the forces of Nature. If the hero of the work is a young person, the major conflict may be between success and failure; such a conflict may involve a series of lesser conflicts within the work, such as learning in school as against ignoring school, making friends or alienating people, escaping one's surroundings or being overwhelmed by them, meeting a person of the opposite sex or being lonely, and so on. It would be difficult to discover a literary work that does not create a conflict or set of oppositions as a basic element in its structure.

4. VARIATIONS ON SITUATIONS AND TYPES OF LITERARY WORKS.   The structure of a work might also be seen in terms of how the author varies a particular situation or type of work. In a male-female relationship, for example, there are a number of actions which might develop, such as (a) lifelong success, (b) temporary success, (c) intermittent success and failure, (d) progressive indifference, (e) mutual toleration, and (f) complete failure. One could study the structure of Shakespeare's *Much Ado About Nothing* by following the developing relationship between Beatrice and Benedick. The relationship begins in toleration or even failure, for the two constantly express hostility toward each other, but as the play goes on the insults change to concern and ultimately to love. One could argue that the two really love each other at the start and that the incidents in the play pro-

gressively make them realize their love. Either way, the discussion would make a successful study of the structure of the play.

Many other human situations may similarly enter into your consideration. Suppose a character is old, or is a child. What would one generally expect of such people, and how does the author bring out and vary the expected situations? Or suppose a character is a criminal. Does this person continue criminal activities throughout the work or does he or she discontinue them? What other sorts of variations could be presumed for such a character?

The category of work you are writing about may be shown to govern its structure. In an adventure story, for example, one should consider the expected ingredients of adventure and compare these with the actual events in the story you have read. If the subject is a love poem, one should list the elements present and then show how the poet either does or does not include these elements and in what order. Your concern here should be to establish the characteristics of the type, or a set of ideal expectations, and then to show the specific elements of the type that are present in the work, being careful to show how these elements determine the form of the work.

Let us take an example of a work that tells about an act of revenge. It is not difficult to determine a set of ideal expectations for such a work. First, the characters must follow a code or idea of justice that places personal revenge above police action. Then there must be an affront and a clear recognition of the affront. Then a decision must be made to carry out revenge, and any obstacles that stand in the way of revenge must be overcome. Finally, if revenge is to be successful, the avenger must arrange an escape, but if the affront has been severe enough, there may be less concern with escaping than with inflicting the fatal blow. In studying the structure of Shakespeare's *Hamlet* you would find that the play follows this pattern of revenge fairly closely, except that the original affront—the murder of Hamlet's father by his uncle—has taken place before the play opens, and that Hamlet has a difficult time in determining the fact that he has indeed been affronted. Much of the play therefore is preoccupied with Hamlet's attempting to discover the truth about his father's death and the uncle's guilt. All the other elements are present in the play in approximately the order listed.

5. EMOTIONS.   Each work of literature may justly be regarded as a pattern capable of producing a complex set of emotions in a reader. The emotions that you feel while reading are the result of an interaction of involvement, time, and the structure of the work. To see that each of these elements is essential, let us regard an experience common to many readers. Often one may read the conclusion of a story or novel before beginning to read seriously at the start. If you have ever "peeked" in this way, you may recall that you knew the facts of the ending but had little if any feeling about

them. When you read that same conclusion in proper sequence, however, you probably had an emotional response to it, even though you had seen it before. The difference in the two readings was that the entire structure of the work itself had no influence on your response the first time but strongly influenced you the second time. Involvement, time, structure—all these make up the basis of emotional response.

Each work of literature may thus be seen as a complex emotional structure. Emotional responses to even a relatively simple literary form like detective fiction, for example, are complex. Such fiction creates suspense by introducing inquisitiveness, doubt, and anxiety, with related emotions of various shades of horror, fear, and sympathy. Detective stories also create both properly and improperly directed hostility (at the true criminal and at the "red herring"), and finally produce satisfaction when the solution of the mystery ends all doubt and anxiety. It is not at all uncommon for such stories to end according to the age-old advice of the theater to "leave them laughing." A joke or a comic description thus may produce a smile that ensures the final defeat of anxiety—at least as far as that story was concerned.

The creation of a certain degree of anxiety is perhaps the principal means by which authors maintain interest. The author of a story about a pioneering trip across the American plains, for example, creates anxiety about whether the forces of Nature will permit the journey to be concluded successfully. If human agents such as outlaws are introduced as antagonists, then this anxiety can be related to hostility and fear, and if the principal characters are virtuous, they usually become objects of admiration.

Such emotions are also interlinked with the structure of drama. In the nineteenth century the German writer Gustav Freytag suggested that the rising and falling actions in a typical five-act play resemble a pyramid. Emotions are brought out by the introduction of the various persons and conflicts, and they are heightened as complications develop and reach a *climax* (the Greek word *ladder;* a climax is a high point or turning point after which a particular outcome is certain) in the third act. After the climax, the falling action begins and the final *dénouement* ("unraveling" of all the threads of the plot) is eventually reached.

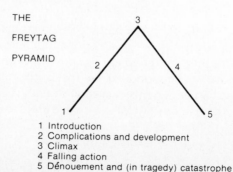

THE FREYTAG PYRAMID

1 Introduction
2 Complications and development
3 Climax
4 Falling action
5 Dénouement and (in tragedy) catastrophe

According to Freytag's model, the emotions before the climax stem out of uncertainty; those after, of inevitability.

The Freytag pyramid can be used to help explain Aristotle's description of tragedy. Aristotle noted that tragedy brings about a purgation—catharsis—of pity and fear. Looking at the pyramid, we can see that fear would be touched most heavily during the tension and uncertainty leading up to the climax, and pity would become the major emotion after it. The point here is that Aristotle's description of the aims of tragedy presupposes a proper arrangement of incidents and that this concern, like his other commentaries on plot in *The Poetics* (VI–XIV), was structural.

If a literary work is an emotional structure, it should reach a satisfactory emotional conclusion—a relaxation of tension. In Greek tragedy, the concluding action, the *exodos,* consists of choral speeches that ponder the meaning of the action. This relatively intellectual section provides the opportunity to relax after the emotional peak of the play.

## Aids in Studying Structure

In studying structure, be sure to take whatever assistance the authors have given you. Have they made divisions in the work, such as stanzas, parts, chapters, cantos, or spaces between groups of paragraphs? Try to relate the subjects of these various divisions, and develop a rationale for the divisions. Is there a geographical location that lends its own mood and color to the various parts of the story? How can these be related to the events? Does the time of the day or time of year shift as the work progresses? Can the events be shown to have a relationship to these various times? Does one event grow inevitably out of another; that is, do the events have logical as well as chronological causation? Is a new topic introduced because it is similar to another topic? Such questions should assist you in your study.

You might also help yourself by following a suggestion made by Aristotle in his *Poetics:*

> . . . the plot [of any work], being an imitation of an action, must imitate one action and that a whole, the structural union of the parts being such that, if any one of them is displaced or removed, the whole will be disjointed and disturbed. For a thing whose presence or absence make no visible difference, is not an organic part of the whole.[1]

As an exercise in applying Aristotle's ideas to the structure of a work, you might imagine that a certain part of the work has been taken away. You might then ask what is wrong with the work remaining. Does it make sense? Does it seen truncated? Why should the missing part be returned?

---

[1]Ch. VIII. 4, in S. H. Butcher, *Aristotle's Theory of Poetry and Fine Art,* 4th ed. (New York: Dover Publications, Inc., 1951), p. 35.

As you answer these questions, you are really dealing with the logical necessity of structural wholeness. For example, let us suppose that the second stanza of Frost's "The Road Not Taken" is missing. The poem immediately becomes illogical because it omits the chronological event leading to the conclusion, and it also omits the logic of Frost's choice of the road he selected. If you attempt similar imaginative exercises with other works, you can help yourself determine whether these works are organic wholes.

You might also aid yourself by drawing a scheme or plan to explain, graphically, the structure of the work. Not everyone can benefit from drawings, but if you are visually oriented, then making a drawing might help you to organize your thoughts and improve your final theme. The story "Miss Brill," by Katherine Mansfield, for example, may be conveniently compared with a person running happily along a narrow path deep within a dark forest and making a turn only to plunge suddenly and unexpectedly off a steep cliff. You might graph this comparison like this:

In writing a theme about the story, you could employ this scheme as a guide for your discussion. This is not to say that the structure of the story could not be profitably analyzed in another way but rather that the scheme would help to give your own study penetration, meaning, and form.

An effective illustration is one that encourages you to see the relationships of the various parts of the work. You might use line drawings like the one for "Miss Brill," or you might use circles, lines, planes, or other geometric forms. One student effectively compared the structure of Donne's poem "The Canonization" to a person entering a building and going upstairs to the top floors. This comparison was effectively augmented with an explanatory drawing. Such a comparison might not readily occur to everyone, but if the scheme is effectively carried out and if the parts of the work are adequately accounted for, the purpose of structural analysis can be effectively served with visual aids of this sort.

## Problems

It is important to develop a central idea that is comprehensive enough to prevent any errors in your assessment of the work's structure. If your first judgment is that a part is not integral to the work, for example, be sure that you have not missed some essential idea that would make it relevant. Ernest Hemingway stated that the last section of *Huckleberry Finn* is "just cheating." It seems apparent that his judgment resulted from an inadequate idea about the meaning of the novel. If he had considered that the work contrasts common sense (Huck's idea of freeing Jim) with quixotism or faulty judgment (Tom's idea of freeing Jim with "style"), he might have modified his statement.

You also have the usual problem of selectivity. Your choice of what to discuss will be made on the basis of your initial analysis and the approach you wish to make. A mere description of what happens in the work and where it happens is not much more than a précis. Your instructors are of course interested in your ability to describe the organization of the work, but they are much more interested in what you *make* out of your description. As always, your point is of primary importance and should be kept foremost.

## Organizing Your Theme

### INTRODUCTION

You should first describe the approach to structure that you plan to take in your theme. You might be studying Marvell's "To His Coy Mistress" as a logical structure (see p. 84). Or you might be considering Milton's "Lycidas" as a funerary meditation. Your central idea should be about the structure, as in the sample theme, where the conflict in Thomas Hardy's story "The Three Strangers" is related to the contrast between the spirit and the letter of the law. If your aim is to show how your work is related to a general type, the introduction is the place to develop your description of the type. Conclude your introduction with your thesis sentence.

### BODY

Work from your introduction into a discussion of the way in which the idea influences the form of the work. If the work is arranged according to stanzas, cantos, books, scenes, acts, chapters, or sections, try to determine the logic of this arrangement. Your emphasis should be on the way in which each of the parts bears on the idea or statement you have accepted as the governing idea or plan of the work, and upon the relationship of part to part. You might talk about *movement* from one part to the next. Does one part end on a note of expectation? Does the next part present material that satisfies that expectation? Does the logic of one part require that other events follow? Does the author provide these events? Does the movement of the work depend on the mental functioning and consequent action of a certain character? Does the author demonstrate that such functioning and actions are truly a part of this character? If you have made any graph or drawing that helps to explain the structure, you could use that as an aid in discussing the relationship of part to part.

If you are showing the structure of your work as it is related to a general type, you should use the technique of comparison-contrast in the body of your paper (see Chapter 10). Obviously your major problem will be to determine an ideal form for your type. This is not difficult to do if you concentrate on your topic. Begin where the story begins, or where the character is at a particular stage in life, and then go on from there. Thus, if your story begins with a young couple meeting, you could imagine a series of typical incidents which would include (1) early acquaintance, (2) growing love, (3) complications (that is, misunderstandings, parental objections, racial or religious differences, money troubles, etc.), (4) the resolution of the complications, and (5) marriage. If the couple is married when the story begins, you might consider whether your couple moves toward success or failure in the work. If success is achieved, then you might establish a form of (1) difficulties (financial, medical, personal, marital, etc.) leading to (2) a successful resolution. If failure is at the end of the road for the couple, then the pattern might be (1) difficulties, leading to (2) defeat. In either case, you would need to establish a form also for the particular nature of the difficulty. Thus, personal difficulties can take the form of conflicts with others, unfair treatment, psychological disturbances, and so on. Your concern would be to show where the author places emphasis.

CONCLUSION

You might conclude your theme with an evaluation of the author's success as far as structure is concerned. Are all the parts of the work equally necessary? Do they occur in the best order? Would the work be damaged if any parts were left out or transposed? Often a work has smaller internal structures that are related to the major one. Thus the story may have been about a person going through a typical day on the way to success, but the story might also contain shorter accounts of other characters either succeeding or failing. Also, major characters may be engaged in an important meeting while minor characters may be meeting on a matter of lesser importance. If you can show how these minor events are related to the major ones, as in the concluding paragraph of the sample theme, you will be stressing your central idea and strengthening your theme.

## Sample Theme

*Conflict and Suspense in the Structure of Thomas Hardy's "The Three Strangers"*

[1] "The Three Strangers" is an intricately woven story of suspense and conflict. The suspense is essential to the conflict, which is an opposition of right and wrong when applied to criminal justice. Hardy's contrasting idea is in keeping with the Apostle Paul's idea that "the letter killeth, but the spirit giveth life" (2 *Corinthians* 3:6).* Legality in Hardy's story is wrong, while illegality is shown to be right. As specific material for this idea, Hardy creates a major incident which presents a conflict for his Wessex shepherds between (1) duty toward law, and (2) duty toward a human being who has been legally condemned but whose crime has in their eyes been extenuated. Hardy develops his conflict and brings out his idea by showing the lives of his natives positively, by portraying his hangman negatively, and by creating suspense about his first stranger, who is the legally condemned "criminal."†

[2] Although readers may not be aware of it during the early part of the story, they are being emotionally manipulated to accept Hardy's view of right and wrong. The first one-sixth of the story is pure description of the way of life of the natives of Higher Crowstairs, who are shown to be warm and human. But in the service of his idea, Hardy is really building up one "side" of the conflict by demonstrating that his natives are such nice, ordinary peasant folk that their judgment on matters of life and death is to be trusted. This is the positive side of Hardy's conflict.

[3] When Hardy does engage both sides of the conflict, at about midpoint in the story, by introducing the second stranger (the hangman), he has already won his case, but he makes sure by negatively presenting this grisly figure as brash, selfish, and obnoxious. When the natives learn of the second stranger's identity as the hangman, they are startled "with suppressed exclamations" (p. 310). The exclamations apparently take the form that if men like the hangman are associated with the letter of the law, the natives—along with the reader—will prefer the spirit even though the spirit may at times be branded as illegal. This reaction could of course not be sustained if the crime of the escaped criminal had been one of violence, but the "crime" was really the theft of a sheep to feed his starving family (p. 310). One may grant that Hardy is rigging the case here, but the conflict is not between right when it is right and wrong

*Central idea
†Thesis sentence
For the text of this story, please see Appendix C, pp. 302–316 (parenthetical page numbers refer to this text).

when it is wrong, but, rather between *legality* when it is *wrong* and *illegality* when it is *right*. It is therefore impossible to disagree with the judgment of the natives at the end that the intended hanging of the sheep thief "was cruelly disproportioned to the transgression" (p. 316), for even if a person were inclined to disagree on abstract legal principles, the emotional thrust of the story is toward extenuation.

[4]
Critical to this extenuation is Hardy's creation of suspense about the identity of the first stranger as Timothy Summers, the escaped thief. In winning the assent of his readers to the values of right and wrong in the story, Hardy avoids a purely legalist reaction against Summers by keeping his identity hidden until the end. In this way, Hardy puts Summers before the eyes of the readers, though unidentified, and develops him as a brave and witty human being. The revelation at the end therefore causes the reader to take a second view of Summers. In retrospect, readers must admire, with the natives, his "marvellous coolness and daring in hob-and-nobbing with the hangman" (p. 316), and they would be outraged if such a person were to be hanged. It is perhaps difficult for readers to take any law seriously that proposes to hang a person for petty theft, but if the issue is seen as one between the letter and the spirit of the law, then Hardy's values are still relevant and his story still possesses great vitality.

[5]
Related to the major conflict are a number of lesser conflicts which are constantly appearing in the story. There is an undertone of fear of the law, for example, among the natives, who live marginally in the "country about Higher Crowstairs" (p. 316) and who therefore perceive the conviction of a person like Summers as a threat to themselves also. There is also a contrast between the law itself, which as an abstract force should be admirable, and the conceited, obnoxious hangman who carries out sentences of the law. In a comic vein, Hardy creates a contrast between the law and the ineptness of the shepherds who are called upon to enforce it; when they make an arrest they use words more appropriate to criminals or to priests. Also, the shepherds are diligent in searching for Summers everywhere but where they know he can be found, to good comic effect.

[6]
In addition there are other little but human contrasts in the story. The Fennels are giving a party for twenty people, but Mrs. Fennel is alarmed about giving away too much food and drink to her guests, and she is disturbed by the self-indulgence of the hangman. There is a small family conflict on this score. Another small conflict occurs on the issue of the musicians whom Mrs. Fennel asks to stop playing but who continue because they have been bribed by an amorous shepherd, Oliver Giles. There are also some noticeable contrasts in age among couples. Oliver is seventeen but is in love with a woman of thirty-three (p. 304), and a young woman is engaged to a man of fifty (p. 310). Beyond all these contrasts or opposites which make up the texture of the story, the technique of suspense is a contrast in itself, for it forces a reconsideration of events already considered, and it creates the need to redefine these events. These are all conflicts which Hardy employs in developing his major conflict between the right of the spirit and the wrong of the letter in "The Three Strangers."

## Commentary on the Theme

The major aspect of structure discussed in the sample theme is conflict. The conflict is between the natives and a positive view of the spirit of the law, on the one hand, and the hangman and a negative view of the law, on the other.

A second aspect of the structure is the use of suspense, which is shown to be related to the positive feature of the conflict. The emotional side of the structure is emphasized throughout the theme, but particularly in paragraph two, where the positive view of the spirit of the law is shown to be connected to the reader's emotional assent to the natives. The concluding two paragraphs show that a number of lesser conflicts are related to the major conflict of the story.

# chapter 12

# The Theme Analyzing Tone

Tone refers to the means by which a writer conveys attitudes. Although it is a technical subject, in practice the discussion of tone sometimes becomes focused on the attitudes themselves. For this reason, the terms *tone* and *attitude* are often confused. You should remember, however, that tone refers not to attitudes but to that quality of a writer's style that reveals or creates these attitudes. It is important to preserve this distinction.

Studying and describing tone require great alertness, because your understanding will depend largely on your ability to make inferences from the work you are reading (sometimes this process is called "reading between the lines"). Your analysis of tone is, in effect, your analysis of the author's mind at work, and through this analysis you can become aware of the vitality of literature—the creativity of the author's mind as seen in his or her words. Reading a work of literature without perceiving its tone is like watching a speaker on television with the sound turned off; without tone you can guess at meaning but cannot understand it fully.

## Tone in Operation

*Tone* in literature has been borrowed from the phrase *tone of voice* in speech. Tone of voice is a reflection of your attitude toward the person or persons whom you are addressing and also toward the subject matter of your

138

discussion. It is made up of many elements: the speed with which you speak, the enthusiasm—or lack of it—that you project into what you say, the pitch and loudness of your speech, your facial expressions, the way you hold your body, and your distance from the person to whom you are speaking.

As a literary example, let us look briefly at this passage from Jonathan Swift's *Gulliver's Travels*.

> Imagine with thy self, courteous reader, how often I then wished for the tongue of Demosthenes or Cicero, that might have enabled me to celebrate the praise of my own dear native country in a style equal to its merits and felicity.[1]

Here is a passage in which Gulliver, Swift's narrator, is perfectly sincere about praising England, whereas Swift the satirist, behind the scenes, is just about to deliver a satiric condemnation. The control of tone makes these contrasting attitudes evident and makes this passage comic. Swift controls the tone by causing Gulliver to refer to the two most famous ancient orators who were known for their ability to speak well but who were also known for their powers to condemn. He also makes Gulliver use the ambiguous phrase "equal to its merits and felicity" and the possibly sarcastic word "celebrate." In conversing with people, you can perceive their tone by all the spoken and "body language" signs; however, in a literary passage like this one you are not aided by anything except what you see on the page. To interpret it properly you have only a dictionary, other reference works, and above all your intelligence.

Tone, of course, may be described in as many ways as there are human moods. Here is a partial list of words that might distinguish tone in particular passages:

admiring, worshiping, approving

strident, subdued, harsh

disliking, abhorring

simple, straightforward, direct, unambiguous

complicated, complex, difficult

forceful, powerful

ironic, sardonic, sarcastic

indirect, understated, evasive

bitter, grim

sympathetic, interested

indifferent, unconcerned, apathetic

[1]*Gulliver's Travels and Other Writings,* ed. Louis A. Landa (Boston: Houghton Mifflin, 1960), p. 102.

antagonistic, hostile

violent, outraged, indignant, angry

elevated, grand, lofty

serious, solemn, sepulchral, ghoulish

comic, jovial, easy, friendly

A thesaurus can supply you with many more words, and it is conceivable that there are, somewhere, literary works to which all the words you discover might be applied.

## Problems in Describing Tone

The study of tone is the study of the ways in which attitudes are manifested in a particular literary work. Therefore, when you write a theme about tone, you must attempt to name and describe these attitudes and analyze the means by which they are expressed. Your statements will be based on inferences that you make from the text.

You must also attempt to describe the *intensity*, the force with which the attitudes are expressed. This task is difficult but necessary, and it is one of the ways by which you can amplify your statements about the nature of the attitudes. The force of the tone depends on the intrinsic seriousness of the situation, the speaker's degree of involvement in it, and his or her control over what is said. You would recognize the differences in intensity between the statements in these two columns:

| 1 | 2 |
|---|---|
| "This report is not what we expected." "Mr. Student, your paper shows promise, but it is not, as yet, up to passing standards." | "This report is terrible." "Mr. Student, your paper is a slovenly disgrace." |

In describing the difference, you would necessarily concentrate on the differing intensities in the quotations. Compare the intensities of the following:

1. Written on a wall in Teheran: "Yankee, go home."
2. Written on a wall in Paris: "Yankee, go home—via Air France."

These last quotations bring up another, closely related, element in the consideration of tone—namely, *control*. Writers may feel deeply about a subject, but if they give vent to their feelings completely, they are likely to create not a literary work but only an emotional display. They must always control the expression of sentiment, because their appeal must be not only to their readers' sympathies but also to their understanding. A fine example of the control of attitude is *Antony and Cleopatra* (V.ii, 241–281).

Cleopatra is about to commit suicide. Just before she does, Shakespeare introduces a country bumpkin to bring her a poisonous snake, which will be the cause of her death. The resulting interchange between Cleopatra, serious and about to die, and the stupid but concerned clown is clearly designed to arouse laughter.

*Enter Guardsman and Clown (with Basket).*

| | |
|---|---|
| GUARD | This is the man. |
| CLEOPATRA | Avoid, and leave him. |

*Exit Guardsman.*

Hast thou the pretty worm of Nilus there
That kills and pains not?

CLOWN    Truly I have him. But I would not be the party that should desire you to touch him, for his biting is immortal. Those that do die of it do seldom or never recover.

CLEOPATRA    Remember'st thou any that have died on't?

CLOWN    Very many, men and women too. I heard of one of them no longer than yesterday; a very honest woman, but something given to lie, as a woman should not do but in the way of honesty—how she died of the biting of it, what pain she felt. Truly, she makes a very good report o' the worm; but he that will believe all that they say shall never be saved by half that they do. But this is most falliable, the worm's an odd worm.

CLEOPATRA    Get thee hence; farewell.

CLOWN    I wish you all joy of the worm.

*(Sets down his basket).*

CLEOPATRA    Farewell. . . .

The problem in interpreting this scene involves Shakespeare's attitude toward Cleopatra and toward his audience. It is likely that Shakespeare introduced the comic scene in order to keep his treatment of Cleopatra from becoming purely sentimental. He knew that one way to produce laughter is to heap misfortune upon misfortune, so that an audience will ultimately respond to additional misfortunes with laughter, not with sympathy. Cleopatra's suicide is the final misfortune, and lest his audience not respond with sorrow, Shakespeare provides the clown to siphon off, as it were, his audience's tension by giving it a legitimate release in laughter. In this way he directs a proper amount of sympathy toward Cleopatra and deepens our concern for her. The situation is complex, but Shakespeare's handling of it is masterly.

## Laughter, Comedy, and Farce

A major aspect of tone is laughter and the comic and farcical modes. No two critics agree on what exactly makes people laugh but all agree that laughter is essential in a person's psychological well-being. Laughter is an *ad hoc*, unpredictable action; what a person finds amusing today will not move him or her tomorrow. The causes of laughter are complicated and difficult to analyze and isolate. However, the major elements in laughter seem to be these:

1. AN OBJECT OF LAUGHTER.   There must be something to laugh at, whether a person, thing, situation, custom, habit of speech or dialect, or arrangement of words.

2. INCONGRUITY.   Human beings have a sense of what to expect under given conditions, and anything that violates these expectations may be a cause of laughter. On a day when the temperature is 100° F., for example, you would reasonably expect people to dress lightly. But if you saw a person dressed in a heavy overcoat, a warm hat, a muffler, and large gloves, who was shivering, waving his arms, and stamping his feet as though to keep them warm, you would likely laugh because this person would have violated your expectation of what a sane person would do under the conditions. His response to the weather is inappropriate or *incongruous*. The standup comedian's story that, "Yesterday afternoon I was walking down the street and turned into a drugstore," is funny because "turned into" can have two incompatible meanings. Here the language itself has furnished its own incongruity. A student once wrote that in high school she had enjoyed singing in the "archipelago choir." This is an inadvertent verbal mistake called a *malapropism,* after Mrs. Malaprop, a character in Richard Brinsley Sheridan's play *The Rivals.* In the student's report about the choir, you expect to see *a capella*—or at least a recognizable misspelling of the word—and when you see *archipelago,* a word that makes sense elsewhere and sounds something like *a capella,* you laugh, or at least smile. Incongruity is the quality common to all these instances of laughter.

3. SAFETY AND/OR GOODWILL.   Seeing a person who has just slipped on a banana peel hurtling through the air and about to crack his or her skull

may cause laughter as long as we ourselves are not that person, for our laughter depends on our being insulated from danger and pain. In farce, where a great deal of physical abuse takes place, such as falling through trapdoors or being hit in the face by cream pies, the abuse never harms the participants. The incongruity of such situations causes laughter, and one's safety from personal consequences—together with the insulation from pain of the participants—prevents the interference of more grave or even horrified responses. The element of goodwill enters into laughter in romantic comedy or in works where you are drawn into general sympathy with the major figures. Here the infectiousness of laughter and happiness influences your responses. As the characters make their way toward success, your involvement with them will produce a general sense of happiness which may cause you to smile and also may cause you to laugh sympathetically.

4. UNFAMILIARITY, NEWNESS, UNIQUENESS, SPONTANEITY. Laughter depends on seeing something new or unique, or on experiencing a known thing freshly. Laughter usually occurs in a flash of insight or revelation, and the situation producing laughter must always possess spontaneity. Perhaps you have had a joke or funny situation explained to you and found that the explanation dampened the spontaneity that would have enabled you to laugh. Although spontaneity is most often a quality of the unfamiliar, it is not lost just because a thing becomes familiar. A good joke, comic incident, or story may retain the power to provoke laughter because of its uniqueness or because of the merit of its views of life. Jokes of this type assume the status of "standing jokes." Novels like *Huckleberry Finn* and Henry Fielding's *Joseph Andrews* retain their wit and spontaneity and thus are always comic. The quality of writing and structuring in works of this type is an element of tone and would provide a suitable topic for study in a theme.

## Irony

One of the most human traits is the capacity to have two or more attitudes toward something. You might love someone but on occasion express your affection by insults rather than praise. A large number of contemporary greeting cards feature witty insults, because many people cannot stand the sentimentality of the "straight" cards and send the insulting card in the expectation that the person receiving it will be amused and will recognize genuine fondness on the sender's part. Expressions in which one attitude is conveyed by its opposite are *ironic*. *Irony* is a mode of ambiguous or indirect expression; it is natural to human beings who are aware of the possibilities and complexities in life. Irony is a function of the realization that life does not always measure up to promise, that friends and loved ones may sometimes be angry and bitter toward each other, that the universe offers mysteries that human beings cannot comprehend, that doubt exists even in the face of certainty, and that character is built through chagrin, regret, and pain as much as through emulation and praise. In expressing an idea ironically, writers pay the greatest compliment to their readers, for they assume sufficient skill and understanding to see through the surface statement into the seriousness or levity beneath.

The major types of irony are *verbal, situational,* and *dramatic.* Verbal irony is a statement in which one thing is said, and another thing is meant. For example, one of the American astronauts was once asked how he would feel if all his reëntry safety equipment failed as he was coming back to earth. He answered, "A thing like that could ruin your whole day." His words would have been appropriate for day-to-day minor mishaps, but since failed safety equipment would cause his death, his answer was ironic. This form of verbal irony is *understatment* or *litotes.* By contrast, *overstatement* or *hyperbole* is exaggeration for effect, as in "I'll love you till the oceans go dry." Often verbal irony is ambiguous, having double meaning or *double entendre.* A foolish character named Witwoud in William Congreve's play *The Way of the World* enters to an intelligent group of people. He is disturbed, and says, "pity me." The character Mirabell responds, "I do from my soul." The response is socially acceptable, for it is the thing Witwoud asked for, but Mirabell is also saying that Witwoud is indeed a pathetic, pitiable character; this is not the sort of pity Witwoud wants. Mirabell makes one statement, in other words, but it has two meanings. Quite often *double entendre* is used in statements about sexuality and love.

The term *situational irony,* or *irony of situation,* refers to conditions that are measured against forces that transcend and overpower human capacities. These forces may be social, political, or environmental. Situational irony that is connected with a pessimistic or fatalistic view of life is sometimes called *irony of fate* or *cosmic irony.* Thomas Hardy was adept at this sort of irony, for he set up little accidents, chances, or misunderstandings that played a role, usually calamitous, far beyond their ordinary significance. Thus, in *The Return of the Native,* Eustacia appears at the window of her home briefly and glances at the visiting Mrs. Yeobright outside. Because a former suitor is visiting Eustacia, and also because she believes that her husband Clym will answer the door, she does not admit Mrs. Yeobright. Mrs. Yeobright has seen Eustacia at the window and misinterprets Eustacia's motives; she is disheartened and leaves for home, only to meet death on the heath. All subsequent disasters in the novel stem from this incident, and their effect on the tone of the novel is that the ill consequences are much more pathetic because they could have been easily avoided. The implication is that human beings are caught in a web of circumstances and that their lives are largely determined by these conditions, regardless of what they themselves do.

Situational irony could of course work in a more optimistic way. For example, a good person could go through a set of difficult circumstances and be on the verge of losing everything in life, but, through someone's perversity or through luck, might emerge successfully. Such a situation could reflect an author's conception of a benevolent universe. Most often, however, cosmic irony is more like that in Hardy.

*Dramatic irony* applies when a character perceives a situation in a limited way while the audience sees it in greater perspective. The audience sees double meaning whereas the character sees only one. The classic example of dramatic irony is found in *Oedipus Rex,* where Oedipus thinks he is about to discover that someone else murdered his father, while the audience knows, all along, that he himself is the murderer and that as he condemns the murderer he condemns himself.

## Irony, Laughter, and Tragedy

If you conclude that the incongruity of laughter and the ambiguity of irony are closely linked, you are right. Laughter is one product of irony, though more often of ironic expressions than ironic situations. In fact, however, many ironic situations verge on tragedy. In tragedy, all bright hopes for the future are blasted; the good person is brought to destruction by the forces unleashed around him. Tragic irony is thus based on a discrepancy between great potential and disastrous consequences. If there is laughter in tragedy, it is not the participants or the spectators who laugh, but some set of detached, remote, inhuman beings. Shakespeare's Gloucester in *King Lear* (IV.i, 42–43) describes this situation well:

> As flies to wanton boys are we to th' gods,
> They kill us for their sport.

## Studying Tone

The study of tone requires studying everything in a work that contributes to more than denotative statement. To perceive tone you should be constantly aware of the general impression that a passage leaves with you and be analytical enough to study the particular ways by which this effect is achieved. You must understand all the words and all the situations. Read the work carefully, and then study the passages you select for discussion to determine the connotations of the words and the rhythms of the cadence groups. Because many things in the work may affect tone, you should be alert to everything.

To see how everything can work at once, let us look at another passage from Swift's *Gulliver's Travels.* In the fourth voyage, Swift causes Gulliver to describe with pride the most recent weaponry, methods, and achievements in warfare:

> . . . being no stranger to the art of war, I gave . . . a description of cannons, culverins, muskets, carabines, pistols, bullets, powder, swords, bayonets, battles, sieges, retreats, attacks, undermines, countermines, bombardments, sea-fights; ships sunk with a thousand men, twenty thousand killed on each side; dying groans, limbs flying in the air, smoke, noise, confusion, trampling to death under horses' feet; flight, pursuit, victory; fields strewed with carcasses left for food to dogs, and wolves, and birds of prey; plundering, stripping, ravishing, burning and destroying. And to set forth the valour of my own dear countrymen, I assured him, that I had seen them blow up a hundred enemies at once in a siege, and as many in a ship, and beheld the dead bodies drop down in pieces from the clouds, to the great diversion of all the spectators.[2]

The tone is that of condemnation, angry but cold. Swift is in control. He achieves his tone in a number of ways. First, Gulliver thinks he is praising war while the sensitive reader receives entirely different signals. The reader and Swift provide a humane political and moral context against which Gulliver's words are to be measured. Thus we have an example of situational irony. Second, the texture of the passage is one of accumulation. Swift has Gulliver list all the death-dealing weapons and all the horrible consequences of warfare. The condemnation of war is achieved by the multiplication of examples alone, virtually overcoming all possible opposing views. Third, there is verbal irony in phrases like "the valour of my own dear countrymen" and "to the great diversion of all the spectators." This is hyperbole that cuttingly exposes the callousness to suffering that usually accompanies war. Fourth, the passage is capable of producing laughter—not happy laughter, but laughter of amazement and repulsion at the incongruity caused by the common moral pretensions of many people and their dereliction of these pretensions during warfare. When you read the passage, you respond to everything at once, yet analysis reveals a passage of high complexity. Swift's control of tone is the cause of your responses.

## Organizing Your Theme

### INTRODUCTION

State your central idea. You should not only define the tone briefly but also describe the force and conviction of the tone. Your thesis sentence should be a statement about the areas in which you plan to develop your

---

[2]*Gulliver's Travels and Other Writings*, ed. Landa, pp. 200–201.

discussion. If there are any particular obstacles to the proper determination of the tone, either in the work or in your personal attitudes, you should state these in your introduction also.

## BODY

In the body of your theme you should examine all aspects which in your judgment have a bearing on the tone of the work. Some of the things to cover are these:

1. *The audience, situation, and characters.* Is any person or group being directly addressed by the author? What attitude toward the audience seems to be expressed (love, respect, condescension, confidentiality, etc.)? What is the basic situation in the work? Is there any irony in it? If so, what type is it? What does the irony show about the author's attitudes (optimisim or pessimism, for example)? How does the author use the situation to shape your responses? That is, can any action, situation, or character be seen as an expression of attitude, or as a means of controlling attitude (as the Clown is Shakespeare's means of preserving sympathy for Cleopatra)? What is the nature of the author's voice or persona? Does the author seem to manipulate this voice to any degree to convey attitudes? How? Does the author seem to respect, admire, dislike, or otherwise evidence feeling about any characters or situations? Through what techniques are these feelings made clear?

2. *Descriptions, diction.* Analysis of these is stylistic, but your concern here is to relate stylistic technique to attitude. Are there any systematic references, such as to colors, sounds, noises, natural scenes, and so on, that collectively show or seem to reflect an attitude? Does the author manipulate connotation to control your responses? Is any special speech or dialect pattern used to indicate an attitude about speakers or their condition of life? Do the speech patterns conform to normal or standard usage? What can you make of this? Are there any unusual or noteworthy kinds of expression? What is their effect on the apparent attitude of the author? Does the author use verbal irony? To what effect?

3. *Humor.* Is there humor in the work? What is its intensity? Does the humor develop out of incongruous situations or out of language? Is there an underlying basis of attack in the humor, or are the objects of laughter still respected or even loved despite having humor directed against them?

4. *Ideas.* Ideas may be advocated, defended mildly, or attacked. Which do you seem to have in the work you have been studying? How does the author make his or her attitude clear—directly, by statement, or indirectly, through understatement, overstatement, or the language of a character?

5. *Unique characteristics of the work.* Each work has unique properties that may contribute to the tone. In Langston Hughes' "Theme for English B,"

for example, which is the work studied in the sample theme, the poetic form itself becomes a subject for study in the tone. In other works there might be some recurring word or theme that seems special. When you study your assigned work, be alert for anything unusual or individual that can be used in your discussion of tone.

## CONCLUSION

Here you might wish to go over again the main heads of your argument. You should also relate the tone to any evaluation you care to make about major ideas or situations in the work. You should try to emphasize the intensity with which the attitudes are brought out.

## Sample Theme

*The Confident Tone of Langston Hughes in the Poem "Theme for English B"*

[1] The entire poem "Theme for English B" is based on the situational irony of racial differences. The situation is the long-standing one of unequal opportunity, seen from the perspective of a college student whose race has been oppressed. This situation might easily produce bitterness, anger, outrage, or vengefulness. However, the poem is none of these. It is not angry or indignant; it is not an appeal for revenge or revolution. It is rather a declaration of personal independence and individuality. The tone is one of objectivity, daring, occasional playfulness, but above all, confidence.* These attitudes are made plain in Hughes' description of the speaker's situation, the ideas, the use of the poetic form itself, the diction, and the expressions.†

[2] Hughes' treatment of the situation is objective, factual, and personal, not emotional or political. The facts in the poem are these: The speaker is a black in an otherwise all-white English class. He has been displaced from his home in the South and now is living alone in a room at the Harlem YMCA, away from his family and roots. He is also, at 22, an older student. The class is a freshman class (English B), yet he is the age of many seniors. There is clear evidence

*Central idea
†Thesis sentence

here of disadvantage, yet Hughes does no more than present the facts objectively, without comment. He is in control, presenting the details straightforwardly, in a tone of total objectivity.

Hughes' thoughts about equality—the idea underlying the poem—are presented in the same objective, cool manner. He is speaking to his instructor, and he does so as an equal, not as an inferior. In describing his identity (for the assignment was to "let that page come out of" him) he does not deal in abstractions, but rather in reality. Thus he defines himself in terms of everyday abilities, needs, activities, and likes. He is cool and logical here, for his presentation has the form of a set of inclusive principles, which may be put thus:

[3]
> All the traits I have described about myself are normal. I have them; you have them; everyone has them. Therefore, I am like you, and you are like me. By extension, everyone is the same.

The clear idea is that people should follow their ideals and put away their prejudices. Yet Hughes, by avoiding emotionalism and controversy, makes counterarguments difficult if not impossible. He is so much in control that the facts themselves carry his argument.

[4]
The selection of the poetic form itself demonstrates bravery and confidence. One would normally expect a short prose essay in response to the instructor's assignment to write a page. But a poem is unexpected and therefore is daring and original. It is as though Hughes is showing his mettle and imagination, and thereby he is personally justifying his idea that he is on an equal footing with his instructor. The wit behind the use of the form itself justifies the granting of equality to the speaker.

Hughes' diction is in keeping with the tone of confidence and daring. The words are studiously simple, showing the confidence of the poet in the directness and truth of his ideas. A high number of words—85 percent—are of one syllable, while 12 percent are of two syllables. This high proportion reflects a conscious attempt to control the diction to achieve an effect of great simplicity. This is in keeping with Hughes' apparent wish to avoid ambiguity, as in the following, crucial part of the poem:

[5]
> Well, I like to eat, sleep, drink, and be in love.
> I like to work, read, learn, and understand life.
> I like a pipe for a Christmas present,
> or records—Bessie, bop, or Bach.                (21–24)

With the exception of what it means to "understand life," these words are direct, simple, descriptive, and relatively free of emotional overtones. They reflect the clear confidence that the time for reality has replaced the time for inequality and prejudice.

[6]
A number of Hughes' phrasings and expressions also show this same confidence. Although most of the material is expressed straightforwardly, one can perceive playfulness and irony, too. Thus, in lines 18–20 there seems to be a deliberate use of confusing language to bring about a verbal merging of the identities of the speaker, the instructor, Harlem, and the greater New York area:

> Harlem, I hear you:
> hear you, hear me—we two—you, me talk on this page.
> (I hear New York, too.) Me—who?

The confidence is strong enough to allow Hughes to write and keep in the poem an expression that seems almost childish. This is in line 26, the second line of the following quotation:

> I guess being colored doesn't make me not like
> the same things other folks like who are other races.

There is also a certain whimsicality in line 27, in which Hughes is treating the irony of the black–white situation:

> So will my page be colored that I write?

Underlying this last expression is an awareness that, despite the claim that people are equal and are tied to each other by the common bond of humanity, there are also strong differences. Hughes is confidently asserting grounds for individuality and independence as well as equality.

[7]     Thus, an examination of "Theme for English B" reveals vitality and confidence. In some respects the poem is a statement of trust, and an almost open challenge on the personal level to the American ideal of equality. Hughes is saying that since it is American to have such ideals, there is nothing to do but to live up to them. He makes this point through the almost conscious naiveté of his simple words and descriptions. Yet the poem is not without its ironies, particularly at the end, where the speaker mentions that the instructor is "somewhat more free" than he is. "Theme for English B" is complex and engaging. It shows the poet's confidence as it is evidenced in objectivity, daring, and playfulness. It is not incorrect to say that in the poem Hughes is, so to speak, feeling his poetic oats.

---

## Commentary on the Theme

The central idea in this theme is that the dominant attitude in "Theme for English B" is confidence and that this confidence is shown in the similar but separable attitudes of objectivity, daring, and playfulness. The purpose of the theme is to discuss how Hughes makes plain these and other related attitudes. The tone is studied as it is manifested in five separate aspects of the poem.

Paragraph two shows a consideration of situational irony. It is necessary to view the situation in relationship to some larger set of circumstances. In this case the circumstance is Hughes' response to the social fact of discrimination. The third paragraph considers the idea of equality as Hughes presents it. The aim of the paragraph, however, is not to consider equality as an idea, but to show how Hughes expresses his attitude toward it.

Paragraph four contains a discussion of how the selection of the poetic form is a mark of the poet's assurance. This quality is unique to the circumstances of this poem; hence, to consider the form as a mark of tone illustrates approach number 5 in the discussion of body (p. 148), that "unique characteristics" should be used. The fifth and sixth paragraphs consider the stylistic matters of word choice and expression. The attention given to monosyllabic words is justified by the high percentage of these words in the poem.

The concluding paragraph stresses again the tone of confidence in the poem and also notes additional attitudes of vigor, trust, challenge, ingenuousness, irony, objectivity, daring, playfulness, and enjoyment.

Because this theme deals with a number of approaches (situation, ideas, and style) by which tone may be studied in any work, it is typical of many themes on tone. The fourth paragraph is useful inasmuch as it shows how a topic that might ordinarily go unnoticed, such as the basic form of expression, can be seen as a feature of tone unique to the work being studied.

# chapter 13

# Three Themes
# Analyzing Prosody:
# (I) The theme on rhythm
# (II) The theme on segments
# (III) The theme on rhyme

*Prosody* is the word commonly used to describe the study of sound and rhythm in poetry. Other equally descriptive words are metrics, versification, mechanics of verse, and numbers. Some persons call sound and rhythm the *music* of poetry.

Sound and rhythm cannot be discussed in a vacuum. They are always integral in every good poem and are important only as they are related to the other parts. Words must be arranged for the maximum effects in the most important places. Poets utilize every linguistic skill to strike your mind and spirit, to fix the poem in your memory. Thus, prosodic study is an attempt to determine how the poet has arranged sound in the interests of sense.

You cannot undertake a study of prosody without a grasp of a few linguistic facts. Fortunately, you have the basic details readily at hand in your own speaking and reading knowledge. The pages that follow will therefore attempt to build on what you already know.

The three types of themes to be described here are on the topics of (1) rhythm, (2) segments, and (3) rhyme.

## I. The Theme on Rhythm

Rhythm refers to the relationship of words in groups. Large units are sentences and paragraphs; smaller units are *cadence groups* and *metrical feet*.

Principally we will be concerned here with cadence groups and feet, for these form the basic blocks of rhythmical analysis.

## CADENCE GROUPS

Words do not function alone but take on meaning only as they form a part of phrases or clauses. This is a fact of any language, and one should never ignore it in studying a poet's prosodic technique. The term used to describe a functioning group of words is *cadence group* (also discussed briefly on pp. 198–99). The word *in,* for example, is a preposition but is not very meaningful alone. In phrases like *in the dooryard* and *in the night,* however, it becomes part of a unit of meaning—prepositional phrases that are also cadence groups. The word *star* conveys a certain amount of meaning, but *the great star* forms a syntactic and rhythmical unit, a cadence group. When you speak, you do not utter words separately, but rather put them together into cadence groups which coincide syntactically and rhythmically. If we use separate lines and spaces to indicate the vocal pauses, noticeable and slight, that separate cadence groups, we can see approximately how individual sentences are made up of these units of both rhythm and meaning:

> Fourscore and seven years ago
> our fathers brought forth     on this continent
> a new nation
> conceived in liberty
> and dedicated to the proposition     that all men     are created equal.

This is, of course, famous prose, and you can see that it would be impossible to read it without bunching the words together approximately as it is laid out. The following lines by Walt Whitman are spaced according to such cadence groups:

> When lilacs last     in the dooryard bloom'd,
> And the great star     early droop'd     in the western sky
> in the night.

Such groups may or may not correspond to regular rhythmical demands in poetry. Here is an example of poetry in which the cadence groups are contained within a rhythmical norm:

> What passing-bells     for these who die as cattle?
> Only the monstrous anger     of the guns.
> Only the stuttering rifles     rapid rattle
> Can patter out     their hasty orisons.
>         Wilfred Owen, "Anthem for Doomed Youth"[1]

[1]Wilfred Owen, *Collected Poems.* Copyright Chatto & Windus, Ltd., 1946, © 1963. Reprinted by permission of New Directions Publishing Corporation, the Owen Estate, and Chatto & Windus, Ltd.

You may perceive a rhythmical similarity between the groups *What passing bells* and *can patter out;* the second and fourth syllables are more heavily pronounced (stressed) than the first and third. You may also perceive the rhythmical similarity (by verbal repetition) of *Only the monstrous anger* and *Only the stuttering rifles.* This kind of poetry, in which cadence groups form part of a recurring pattern, is loosely called *traditional.* Poetry like Whitman's, however, in which cadence groups behave more or less arbitrarily according to meaning and the poet's apparent wishes rather than to rhythmical regularity, is called *free verse.* Poets of both free and traditional verse share the desire to create effective, moving ideas through the manipulation of cadence groups. The difference between them is that the free-verse poet relies almost exclusively on the arrangement of cadence groups while the traditional poet merges cadence groups and rhythmical regularity. Thus, free verse takes no definite shape; lines may be long or short, as the poet wishes to expand or concentrate the ideas. Traditional verse takes on a more formal appearance, and its rhythms can be systematically measured.

## METRICAL FEET

When you speak, you naturally give more force or loudness to some syllables than to others. The syllables to which you give more force are *heavily stressed,* and those to which you give less are *lightly stressed.* In most English verse, poets have distributed the heavily and lightly stressed syllables into patterns called *feet.* They usually fill the lines with a specific number of the same feet, and that number determines the *meter* of the line. Thus five feet in a line make *pentameter,* four are *tetrameter,* three are *trimeter,* and two are *dimeter.* Frequently, rhetorical needs lead poets to substitute other feet for the regular feet. Whether there is *substitution* or not, the number and kind of feet in each line constitute the metrical description of that line. In order to discover the prevailing metrical system in any poem, you *scan* that poem. The act of scanning is called *scansion.*

## SCANNING A POEM

To scan a poem, read it aloud, several times if necessary, and mark the heavy and light stresses. Show heavily stressed syllables with a prime accent or acute accent mark ('). Show light syllables with a small circle or degree sign (°).

Once you have determined the relationship of light and heavy accents, you are ready to mark out your poem into the recurring metrical pattern. The names of the various metrical feet are derived from Greek poetry. In English, the most important are the two-syllable foot, the three-syllable foot, and the imperfect (or one-syllable) foot.

## The Two-Syllable Foot

1. **IAMB**.  A light stress followed by a heavy stress, as in

$$\overset{\circ}{\text{be}} \text{ - } \overset{\prime}{\text{have}}$$

The iamb is the most common foot in English poetry because it is capable of great variation. Within the same line of five iambic feet, each foot can be slightly different in intensity from the others. In this line from Words-worth, each foot is unique:

$$\overset{\circ}{\text{The}} \overset{\prime}{\text{winds}} \text{ / } \overset{\circ}{\text{that}} \overset{\prime}{\text{will}} \text{ / } \overset{\circ}{\text{be}} \overset{\prime}{\text{howl}} \text{ - / } \overset{\circ}{\text{ing}} \overset{\prime}{\text{at}} \text{ / } \overset{\circ}{\text{all}} \overset{\prime}{\text{hours}}.$$

Even though *will* and *at* are stressed syllables, they are not as heavily stressed as *winds, howl-,* and *hours*. Such variability, approximating the rhythms of actual speech, makes the iambic foot suitable for just about any purpose, serious or light.

2. **TROCHEE**.  A heavy accent followed by a light, as in

$$\overset{\prime}{\text{u}} \text{ - } \overset{\circ}{\text{nit}}$$

Because iambic meter is preferred in English (being called *rising, climactic, elevating,* or *masculine*) the trochee has created a problem for English poets. (Trochaic rhythm has been called *falling, dying, anti-climactic,* or *feminine*— a term in use before modern feminism.) The fact is that most English words of two syllables or more are trochaic. For example:

$$\overset{\prime}{\text{re}}\overset{\circ}{\text{gion}}, \overset{\prime}{\text{au}}\overset{\circ}{\text{thor}}, \overset{\prime}{\text{morn}}\overset{\circ}{\text{ing}}, \overset{\prime}{\text{ear}}\overset{\circ}{\text{ly}}$$

$$\overset{\circ}{\text{as}}\overset{\prime}{\text{sur}}\overset{\circ}{\text{ance}}, \overset{\circ}{\text{con}}\overset{\prime}{\text{si}}\overset{\circ}{\text{der}}, \overset{\circ}{\text{re}}\overset{\prime}{\text{turn}}\overset{\circ}{\text{ing}}, \overset{\circ}{\text{de}}\overset{\prime}{\text{pend}}\overset{\circ}{\text{ed}}$$

Exceptions, that is, polysyllabic words concluding with an accent and there-fore iambic, usually have prefixes, or else they are borrowed from a foreign language and their pronunciation is unchanged in English:

$$\overset{\circ}{\text{con}}\overset{\prime}{\text{trol}}, \overset{\circ}{\text{be}}\overset{\prime}{\text{cause}}, \overset{\circ}{\text{de}}\overset{\prime}{\text{spair}}, \overset{\circ}{\text{sub}}\overset{\prime}{\text{lime}}$$

$$\overset{\circ}{\text{ma}}\overset{\prime}{\text{chine}}, \overset{\circ}{\text{ga}}\overset{\prime}{\text{rage}}, \overset{\circ}{\text{tech}}\overset{\prime}{\text{nique}}$$

Because of this high frequency of "falling" rhythms, the problem has been to fit trochaic words into iambic patterns. A common way to solve the problem—and a way consistent with the natural word order of English—

is to place a definite or indefinite article or a possessive pronoun, or some other single-syllable word, before a trochaic word; for example:

$$\text{the building; a framework; their number}$$

Such additions produce an iamb followed by the light stress needed for the next iamb. See this line from Thomas Gray's "Elegy Written in a Country Churchyard" for the integration of three trochaic words in a regular iambic line:

$$\text{The plough - / man home - / ward plods / his wear - / y way.}$$

3. PYRRHIC.  Two unstressed syllables, as in *on their* in Pope's line:

$$\text{Now sleep - / ing flocks / on their / soft fleec - / es lie.}$$

The pyrrhic is usually substituted for an iamb or trochee and consists of weakly accented words like prepositions and articles. For this reason it is impossible in English for an entire poem to be in pyrrhics.

4. SPONDEE.  Two heavy accents, as in *rough winds* in Shakespeare's line

$$\text{Rough winds / do shake / the dar - / ling buds / of May.}$$

Like the pyrrhic, the spondee is primarily a substitute foot in English. An acceptable way to draw attention to a spondee is to link the two syllables with a chevronlike mark, as shown.

## The Three-Syllable Foot

1. ANAPAEST.  Two light stresses followed by a heavy:

$$\text{By the dawn's / ear - ly light}$$

2. DACTYL.  A heavy stress followed by two lights:

$$\text{might - i - est}$$

## The Imperfect Foot

The imperfect foot consists of a single syllable: (°) by itself, or (′) by itself. This foot is a variant or substitute occurring in a poem in which one of the major feet forms the metrical pattern. The second line of "The Star-Spangled

Banner," for example, is anapaestic, but it contains an imperfect foot at the end:

What so proud - / ly we hailed / at the twi - / light's last gleam - / ing.

Most scansion of English verse can be carried out with reference to the metrical feet described above. The following lines illustrate all the feet listed.

*trochee*  *iamb*  *iamb*  *anapaest*  *spondee*

How in / my thoughts / those hap - / pi - est days / shine forth—

*trochee*  *dactyl*  *iamb*  *pyrrhic*  *spondee*

Days of / mel - o - dy / and love / and a / great dream.

## Uncommon Meters

In many poems you might encounter variants other than those described above. Poets like Browning, Tennyson, Poe, and Swinburne experimented with uncommon meters. Other poets manipulated pauses or *caesurae* (discussed below) to create the effects of uncommon meters. For these reasons, you might need to refer to other metrical feet, such as the following:

1. **AMPHIBRACH.**  A light, heavy, and light, as in the following line from Swinburne's "Dolores":

Ah, feed me / and fill me / with plea - sure.

2. **AMPHIMACER OR CRETIC.**  A heavy, light, and heavy, as in Browning's lines:

Love is best

praise and pray

The amphimacer occurs mainly in short lines or refrains and also may be seen as a substitute foot.

3. **BACCHIUS OR BACCHIC.**  A light followed by two heavy stresses, as in *Some late lark* in W. E. Henley's line:

Some late lark / sing - ing.

Note: In scanning a poem to determine its formal meter, always try to explain the lines simply, by reference to the more common feet, before turning to the less common ones. If a line can be analyzed as iambic, for example, do not attempt to fit the bacchius or the amphibrach to it unless these feet are unmistakably indicated. The following line is iambic:

The file / of men / rode forth / a - mong / the hills./

It would be a mistake to scan it thus:

The / file of men / rode / forth a - mong / the hills. /

This incorrect analysis correctly accents *file of men* and *forth among*, but by describing these phrases as two amphimacers, it must resort to the explanation that *The* and *rode* are imperfect feet. Such an analysis creates unnecessary complications.

## THE CAESURA, OR PAUSE

In prosody the pause separating cadence groups, however brief, is called a *caesura* (the plural is *caesurae*). For noting scansion, the caesura is indicated by two diagonal lines or virgules (//) to distinguish it from the single virgule separating feet. The following line by Ben Jonson contains two caesurae:

Thou art / not, // Pens - / hurst, // built / to en - / vious show. //

If a caesura follows an accented syllable, it may be called a *masculine,* or *stressed* caesura; if it follows an unaccented syllable, *feminine* or *falling*. In the following line from William Blake, a stressed caesura follows the word *divine:*

With hands / divine // he mov'd / the gen - / tle Sod. //

The following line from the same poem ("To Mrs. Anna Flaxman") contains a falling caesura after the word *lovely:*

Its form / was love - / ly // but / its col - / ours pale. //

The word *caesura* is usually reserved for references to pauses within lines, but when a pause ends a line—usually marked by a comma, semicolon, or period—such a line is *end-stopped.* if you are writing about a poet's use of pauses, you should treat not only the caesurae but also the end-stopping; you might use the double virgules to show the concluding pause, as in the following line:

A thing / of beau - / ty // is / a joy / forever. //

If a line has no punctuation at the end and runs over to the next line, it is called *run-on*. A term also used to indicate run-on lines is *enjambement:*

> Its loveliness increases; // it will never
> Pass into nothingness; // but still will keep
> A bower quiet for us, // and a sleep
> Full of sweet dreams, // . . .
>
> —Keats, *Endymion,* lines 1–5

## EMPHASIS BY FORMAL
## SUBSTITUTION

Most poems are written in a pattern that can readily be perceived. Thus Shakespeare's plays usually follow the pattern of *blank verse* (unrhymed iambic pentameter) and Milton's *Paradise Lost* follows this same pattern. Such a pattern is no more than a rhythmical norm, however. For interest and emphasis (and perhaps because of the very nature of the English language) the norm is varied by *substituting* other feet for the normal feet.

The following line is from the "January" eclogue of Spenser's *Shepherd's Calendar.* Although the abstract pattern of the line is iambic pentameter, it is varied by the substitution of two other feet:

All in / a sun - / shine day, // as did / be - fall.

*All in* is a trochee, and *shine day* is a spondee. This line shows formal substitution; that is, a separate, formally structured foot is substituted for one of the original feet. The effect of these substitutions is to enable one's voice to emphasize *all* as a strong syllable, almost a separate imperfect foot. Then the phrase *in a sun* rolls off the tongue as an anapaest, and the spondee on *shine day* enables the voice to emphasize the words. In the context, Spenser has just been stressing the miseries of winter, and this line with its substitutions encourages the reader to think of spring as the voice lingers on the words:

> A shepherd's boy (no better do him call)
> When winter's wasteful spite was almost spent,
> All in a sunshine day, as did befall,
> Led forth his flock, that had been long ypent [enclosed].

When you study rhythm, try in this way to relate the substitutions to the ideas and attitudes of the poet.

EMPHASIS BY RHETORICAL
VARIATION

The effect of formal substitution is to create opposing or contrasting
internal rhythms. The same effect is also achieved by the manipulation of
the caesura. Placing the caesura in a perfectly regular line has the same
effect, in speaking the line, as if formal substitution had occurred. This
variation may be called *rhetorical substitution*. A noteworthy example in an
iambic pentameter line is this one by Pope:

$$\text{His ac - / tions', // pas - / sions', // be- / ing 's,// use / and end;}$$

Ordinarily there is one caesura in a line of this type, but in this one there
are three, each producing a strong pause. The line is regularly iambic and
should be scanned as regular. But in reading, the effect is different. Because
of the pauses in the middle of the second, third, and fourth feet, the line
is actually read as an amphibrach, a trochee, a trochee, and an amphimacer,
thus:

$$\text{His ac - tions', // pas- sions', // be - ing 's,// use and end;}$$

Although the line is regular, the practical effect—the rhetorical effect—is
of variation and tension.

## Choosing a Passage or Poem for Analysis

Because studying any aspect of prosody requires much detail, it is best to
pick a short passage. You might choose a sonnet, a stanza of a lyric poem,
or a fragment from a play or long poem. The fragment should be a self-
contained one, such as an entire speech or short episode.

The analysis of even a short fragment, however, can become very long
because of the need to describe the positions of words and stresses and
the need to discuss the various effects. For this reason you do not need to
aim at exhausting all aspects of your topic. Try instead to make your
discussion selective and representative—reasonably detailed, but brief.

## Preparing an Illustrative Worksheet

As a first page of your theme, provide a triple-spaced copy of the passage
being discussed.

Number each line of the passage, regardless of length, beginning
with 1.

Note the formal pattern, with the acute accent for heavily stressed syllables ('), and the degree sign for lightly stressed syllables (°). Use a corporal's chevron to show spondees (⌢).

Indicate the separate feet by a diagonal line or virgule (/). Indicate caesurae and the pauses at end-stopped lines by double virgules (//).

Underline any formal and rhetorical substitutions, and provide a numbered key, with the explanation of the numbering at the bottom of the page.

Throughout your theme, use your worksheet as a reference and guide for your reader. Even though you have the sheet as a reference, however, be sure to include words, phrases, or entire lines to illustrate points in your theme.

## Your Theme

### INTRODUCTION

As your central idea, relate the content of the poem or passage to the metrical form. Also, characterize the meter in terms of regularity, variation, or discontinuity. If your poem is in free verse, describe the control over cadence groups. Is your poem a lyric (song) in structure? Then you should relate line lengths to whatever rising and falling of emotion you find. Is the poem narrative or descriptive? Then you should look for varying metrical intensities as the subject matter reaches peaks or climaxes. Is your passage from a play? Then try to pinpoint the character and situation and the sort of emphases that might be expected. You should also establish the scope of your theme. That is, you might wish to discuss all aspects of rhythm, or perhaps just one, such as the poet's use of (1) regular meter, (2) a particular substitution, such as the anapaest or the spondee, and (3) the caesura and its effects. For comprehensiveness, the sample theme treats all these topics, but a separate theme might treat just one or two of them. Your thesis sentence should outline the aspects you plan to treat.

### BODY

In writing about meter you should first describe the formal metrical pattern. Is the poet successful in placing important words and syllables in stressed positions? What is the effect of any repeated rhythmical patterns? Generally, deal with the relationship between the formal pattern and the poet's ideas and attitudes.

In writing about substitutions, you should analyze the formal variations and the principal causes and effects of these. The aim is to relate substitutions to ideas and emotions emphasized by the poet. If you settle on a particular metrical substitution, like the spondee, try to find if there is any pattern in its use; that is, its locations, its recurrences, its effects on meaning and emphasis.

In the analysis of caesurae, treat the effectiveness of the poet's control. Can you see any pattern of use? Are the pauses regular, or do they seem randomly placed? Can you see any principle of variety in placement? Do the caesurae help the reader build up to important ideas and attitudes? How are the caesurae related to any rhetorical substitutions you find? What effects are achieved?

## CONCLUSION

Here you should attempt a short evaluation of the poet's metrical performance. Without going into detail, could you say any more than you have in the body? What has been the value of your study to your understanding and appreciation of this particular poem or passage? Do you believe that your study has helped you as you look at other poems?

---

## Sample Theme

*The Rhythms of Keats' Sonnet "Bright Star"*

---

Bright star! // would I / were stead- / fast // as / thou art/ — //          1

Not in / lone splen- / dor // hung / a- loft / the night, //          2

And watch- / ing, // with / e- ter- / nal lids / a- part, //          3

Like Na- / ture's pa- / tient // sleep-/ less E- / re- mite, //          4

The mov- / ing wa- / ters // at / their priest- / like task          5

Of pure / ab- lu- / tion // round / earth's hu- / man shores, //          6

Or gaz- / ing // on / the new / soft- fall- / en mask          7

Of snow / up- on / the moun- / tains // and / the moors-- //          8

No-- // yet / still stead- / fast, // still / un-change- / a- ble, //   9
—1—  —1—  – 3 –  —4—

Pill- owed / up- on / my fair / love's ripe- / ning breast, //   10
—1—  —1—

To feel / forev - / er // its / soft fall / and swell, //   11
—5—  —1—  — 2 —

A- wake / forev- / er // in / a sweet / un- rest, //   12
—5—  —6—

Still, // still // to hear / her ten- / der ta- / ken breath, //   13
—1—

And so / live ev- / er-- // or / else swoon / to death. //   14
—1—  — 2 —  —1—

1 = spondee
2 = effect of bacchius
3 = effect of imperfect foot
4 = effect of amphimacer

5 = effect of amphibrach
6 = effect of anapaest
7 = trochee
8 = effect of trochee

[1]    This personal poem, in which Keats describes the wish to be a "steadfast" lover like the "bright star" which is a witness to the earth's waters and snows, is a fourteen-line sonnet in form. Keats emphasizes steadiness and regularity, and his meter, too, is constant, even in its variations.* The regularity is apparent in the formal iambic pattern, the substitutions, and the caesurae.†

Because the sonnet, being made up of only one long sentence, is difficult to follow, Keats relies on metrical regularity to help the reader. Twelve of the fourteen lines are end-stopped, ending on stressed syllables in iambic feet, to climax particular ideas and descriptions. The two lines that are enjambed are 5 and 7. Even these create an identical pattern, however, because they are first and third in the second quatrain, and the carry-over words are alike

[2]    both grammatically and metrically (*task / Of pure,* and *mask / Of snow*). Keats uses parallel patterns in 3 and 7 (*And watch- / ing,* and *Or gaz- / ing*). The iambic-infinitives *to feel* and *to hear* appear in 11 and 13, and the accented single-syllable verbs *live* and *swoon* are balanced together in the last line. The iambic preposition *upon* is repeated in the second foot of 8 and 10, and the adverb *fore- / ver* recurs in 11 and 12.

*Central idea
†Thesis sentence

The same pattern of regularity can be seen in Keats' substitutions, mainly spondees. He frames his first line with opening and closing spondees (*Bright star* and *thou art*). For balance, he uses spondees again in the second and fourth feet of the concluding line, an effective inner frame. He uses a total of fourteen spondees. The spondee appears in the fourth foot of five separate lines (6, 7, 10, 11, and 14), enough to undergird his idea of stead-

fastness. Keats uses two successive spondees in the first line (*Bright star,* /

[3]     *would I* /) and uses this rhythm again at the start of line 9, as his thought shifts

from the star to himself (*No—yet* / *still stead-* /). He also uses a spondee at

the opening of the last couplet (*Still, still*), thus employing this substitution at

the beginning of each major grouping of the sonnet (lines 1–8 as group one;

9–12 as two; and 13 and 14 as three). He uses one spondee in 11 (*soft fall*)

to echo another one he uses in 7 (*soft fall-* / *en*). All these strategically placed spondees help to unify Keats' thought. The trochees in lines 1, 2, and 10 are not by themselves enough to be seen as part of any trochaic pattern of subtitution.

More to the effect of trochaic patterning is Keats' regularity in his use of caesurae. In eight lines, the caesura is in the middle, after the fifth syllable, thereby causing a trochaic or falling rhythm in the previous two syllables. This pattern is exemplified in line 4:

*falling rhythm*

Like Nat- / ure's (pa- / tient) // sleep- / less E- / re- mite,

[4]     The caesura in such a position creates not just apparent trochees, as in

*pa-tient* and *wa-ters* in 4 and 5, but also the effects of amphibrachs, as in

*ab-lu-tion* and *fore-ver* in 6 and 11. Keats also puts caesurae after uneven-numbered syllables in four of the other lines (1, 2, 5, and 13). Only two internal caesurae are rising ones after even-numbered syllables (1 and 13). Thus, the characteristic mode of caesurae for this poem is a falling one. In a real sense, the falling rhythm, balanced by the rising rhythm at the ends of the end-stopped lines, may be compared to the "fair love's" breathing described in lines 10 and 11.

It would be possible to add still more descriptions of other recurring rhythmical effects by which Keats unites the poem (for example, the effect of the bacchius  repeated  twice  in  the  opening  and  closing  lines:

[5]     *were stead-fast* and *as thou art,* and *and so live* and *or else swoon*). It is enough here, however, to restate that his metrics are used and varied with regularity. They reinforce his main theme—the wish to be as eternally steadfast as the bright star.

## Commentary on the Theme

Detailed as it is, this theme is a selective discussion of the rhythms of Keats' poem. It would be possible, for example, to extend the theme with a more searching study of the tension caused by the rhetorical variations which result from the placement of the caesurae.

The introductory paragraph relates the metrics to the constant, steadfast star. Paragraph two stresses the way in which the regularly placed accents help the reader to comprehend the poem, which consists of a single sentence. Note is made of the repeated words and grammatical forms which are also repeated rhythmical units.

The third paragraph treats the spondee as a regular substitution throughout the poem. Paragraph four deals with the caesurae, and relates these to the central idea by submitting that the falling rhythms before the caesurae, balanced by the rising rhythms of the end-stopped lines, can be likened to the regular breathing of the speaker's "fair love."

The final paragraph suggests, as has been already mentioned, that there might be other aspects of the rhythm that could be examined. The theme, however, concludes here, on the principle that the writer has demonstrated a satisfactory understanding of metrics.

# II. The Theme on Segments

Just as poetry stresses rhythm, it also emphasizes the sounds of individual words. These sounds have been classified by linguists as *segments*. Each segment is a sound essential to the meaningful understanding of words. Thus, in the word *top* there are three segments: *t, o,* and *p.* It takes three letters—*t, o,* and *p*—to spell *(graph)* the word, because each letter is identical with a segment. Sometimes it takes more than one letter to spell a segment. In *enough,* for example, there are four segments but six letters: *e, n, ou,* and *gh.* The last two segments (*ŭ* and *f*) require two letters each (two letters forming one segment are called a *digraph*). In the word *through* there are three segments but seven letters. To be correctly spelled in this word, the o͞o segment must have four letters, *ough.* Note, however, that in the word *flute* the o͞o segment requires only one letter, the *u.*

Segments may be treated as *vowel sounds* and *consonant sounds* (including *semivowels*). It is important to emphasize the word *sound* as distinguished from the letters of the alphabet, for, as you will see, the same letters often represent different sounds.

You should have an acceptable notational system for indicating sounds. The most readily available systems of pronunciation are those in the collegiate dictionaries; they take into account regional differences in pronunciation. If you have questions about syllabication and the position of stresses, you should use your dictionary as your authority.

## VOWEL SOUNDS

Vowel sounds are vibrations resonating in the space between the tongue and the top of the mouth. Some are relatively straight and "short," such as ĭ (whĭt), ŭ (fŭn), and ĕ (sĕt). Some are long, such as ō (snōw), ā (stāy), ē (flee), and ōō (food). There are three diphthongs—that is, sounds that begin with one vowel sound and move to another—namely ī (flȳ), ou (house), and oi (foĭl). A great number of vowel sounds in English are pronounced as a *schwa* (the e in "the boy"), despite their spellings. Thus "about," "stages," "rapid," "nation," and "circus" are spelled with the vowels a, e, i, o, and u, but all these different vowels make the same *schwa* sound.

## CONSONANT SOUNDS

There are various classifications of consonant sounds, but basically they are of three types: (1) *Stop* sounds are made by the momentary stoppage and release of breath either when the lips touch each other or when the tongue touches the teeth or palate. The stop sounds are p, b, t, d, k, and g. (2) *Spirant* or *continuant* sounds are produced by the breath in conjunction with certain positioning of the tongue in relation to the teeth and palate, as in n, l, th (thorn), th (the), s, z, ch (chew), j (jaw), sh (sharp), zh (pleasure), and ng; or with the touching of the lower lip and upper teeth for the sounds f and v; or with the touching of both lips for the sound m. (3) *Semivowel sounds* are midway between vowels and consonants. These are w (wagon), y (yes, union), and h (hope).

Another way of classifying consonant sounds is according to whether they are *voiced*, that is, produced with vibration of the vocal chords (b, d, v, z), or *voiceless*, produced by the breath alone (p, t, f, s).

## DISTINGUISHING SOUNDS FROM SPELLING

When discussing segments, it is important to distinguish between spelling, or *graphics*, and pronunciation, or *phonetics*. Thus the letter s has three very different sounds in the words *sweet, sugar,* and *flows:* s, sh, and z. On the other hand, the words *shape, ocean, nation, sure,* and *machine* use different letters or combinations of letters to spell the same *sh* sound.

Vowel sounds may also be spelled in different ways. The ē sound, for example, can be spelled with i in *machine,* ee in *speed,* ea in *eat,* e in *even,* and y in *funny,* yet the vowel sounds in *eat, break,* and *bear* are not the same even though they are spelled the same. Remember this: with both consonants and vowels, always be on the alert not to confuse spellings with actual sounds.

## SEGMENTAL POETIC DEVICES

You are now ready to apply your knowledge of segments to actual poems. A poet may use words containing the same segments and thereby impress your memory by merging sound and idea. In descriptive poetry, the segments may actually combine, with rhythm, to imitate some of the things being described. The segmental devices are *assonance, alliteration,* and *onomatopoeia.*

ASSONANCE. The repetition of identical *vowel* sounds in different words—for example, short *ĭ* in "swift Camĭlla skĭms," is called assonance. It is a strong means of emphasis, as in the following line, where the *ŭ* sound connects the two words *lull* and *slumber,* and the short *ĭ* connects *him, in,* and *his:*

> And more, to lull him in his slumber soft

In some cases you may discover that the poet has used assonance quite elaborately, as in this line from Pope:

> 'Tis hard to say, if greater want of skill

Here the line is framed and balanced with the short *ĭ* in *'Tis, if,* and *skill.* The *ä* in *hard* and *want* forms another, internal frame, and the *a* in *say* and *greater* creates still another. Such a balanced use of vowels is unusual, however, for in most lines the assonance will be a means by which the poet emphasizes certain words by making them stand out phonetically.

In looking for assonance, you should not select isolated instances of a sound. If, for example, you find three words in the same line that include a long *ā* sound, these form a pattern of assonance; but, if you find a word six lines later that includes a long *ā,* this word is too far away from the pattern to be significant.

ALLITERATION. Like assonance, alliteration is a means of highlighting ideas by the selection of words containing the same *consonant* sound—for example, the repeated *m* in "mixed with a murmuring wind," or the *s* sound in "your never-failing sword made war to cease," which emphasizes the connection between the words *sword* and *cease.*

There are two kinds of alliteration. (1) Most commonly, alliteration is regarded as the repetition of identical consonant sounds that begin syllables in relatively close patterns—for example, "Laborious, heavy, busy, bold, and blind," and "While pensive poets painful vigils keep." Used sparingly, alliteration gives strength to a poem by emphasizing key words, but too much can cause comic consequences. (2) Another form of alliteration occurs when a poet repeats identical or similar consonant sounds that do not begin syllables but nevertheless create a pattern and thus have prosodic importance—for example, the *z* segment in the line "In these places freezing breezes easily cause sneezes," or the *b, m,* and *p* segments (all of which are made *bilabially*, that is, with both lips) in "The *mum*bling and *mur*muring *b*eggar throws *p*egs and *pe*bbles in the *bu*bbling *p*ool." Such patterns, apparently deliberately organized, are hard to overlook.

ONOMATOPOEIA. Onomatopoeia is a blending of consonant and vowel sounds designed to imitate or suggest a sense or action. It is thus one of the most vivid and colorful aspects of poetry. Onomatopoeia depends on the fact that many words in English are *echoic*; that is, they are verbal echoes of the action they describe, such as *buzz, bump, slap,* and so on. In the following passage from John Donne's sonnet "Batter My Heart," we may see onomatopoeia in action:

> Batter my heart, three-personed God; for you
> As yet but knock, breathe, shine, and seek to mend,
> That I may rise, and stand, o'erthrow me, and bend
> Your force, to break, blow, burn, and make me new.

Notice here the words *batter, knock, seek, bend, break, blow,* and *burn.* These sounds, like the abrupt sounds of blows, provide a tactile illustration of the spiritual "violence" described in the lines.

Shakespeare created a memorable use of onomatopoeia in lines spoken by Cleopatra just before she commits suicide to avoid capture *(Antony and Cleopatra,* V.ii. 284–285):

> Now no more
> The juice of Egypt's grape shall moist this lip.

Here the bilabial *m* and *p* segments (like the sounds described in the previous section) in *more, Egypt's, grape, moist,* and *lip* all put spoken emphasis on the lips, to which people put glasses in the act of drinking. Shakespeare thus makes Cleopatra's reference to wine drinking a vivid verbal experience.

## Your Theme

Throughout, you should assume that all the words in a poem or passage are there because the poet chose them not only for meaning but also for sound. There is thus nothing accidental; all the effects were intended. Students sometimes have claimed that the relationship of sound to sense is subjective and murky. While there will always be an element of subjectivity, it is possible to show the objective basis for all conclusions. Thus, if a number of words with identical segments appear close together in a poem, this closeness justifies your study of them as a pattern.

Perhaps the greatest subjectivity occurs when you make observations about onomatopoeia. Should a poet be describing a strong wind, however, and if the description contains many words with *h, th, f,* and *s* segments (all of which, as spirants, require a constant, aspirated release of air), you would be justified in a claim that the sounds echo the description—an instance of onomatopoeia. If you are thus able to objectify your interpretation of sounds, your claims will stand most challenges.

Most of the time we read silently and are not fully aware of repeating sound patterns. *It is therefore important to read aloud for a full perception of segments in your poem.* You may use recurring letters in words to start your examination of a pattern, but you must check to make sure that you are really noting sounds. For example, a *c* will give a *k* in *calm*, a *ch* in *check*, a *sh* in *machine*, and an *s* in *cell*. Therefore, before you try to show a pattern of assonance or alliteration on the basis of *c* or any other letter, be sure that the sounds are truly spoken and not "paper" sounds.

## INTRODUCTION

In a sentence or two, make a brief overview of your poem or passage. Is it descriptive, reflective? Does it contain much action? Is it down to earth and "real," or is it romanticized or idealized? Is it about love, friendship, loyalty, selfishness, betrayal, or what? Try to fashion your central idea as a link between the subject matter and the sound. Is there a strong relationship, or does it seem that any segmental effects are unsystematic or unintended? Your thesis sentence should outline the topics you will discuss in the body.

## BODY

The body should be the report of your linkage of sound and sense. Be sure to establish that the instances you choose have really occurred systematically enough to be grouped as a pattern. You should illustrate sounds by including the relevant words within parentheses. You might wish to make separate paragraphs on alliteration, assonance, onomatopoeia, and any seemingly important pattern of segments. Also, because space in a theme is always at a premium, you might wish to concentrate on one noteworthy effect, like a certain pattern of assonance, rather than on everything in the poem. Throughout your discussion always keep foremost the relationship between the content and the sounds you are considering.

## CONCLUSION

Here you might make a brief evaluation of the poet's use of segments. A poem is designed not only to inform, but also to transfer attitudes and to stimulate the reader. To what degree did the use of sound contribute to these goals? Any personal reflections or discoveries that you have made as a result of your study would be appropriate here. If it seems too difficult to write an evaluation, it would be possible here, as in any theme, to conclude with a short summary.

## The Illustrative Worksheet

As for the theme on rhythm, provide a triple-spaced copy of the poem or passage and number each line of the passage beginning with 1. A well-prepared worksheet will simplify the preparation and writing of your theme.

To determine the various segmental patterns, use a set of different colored pencils or markers. Use one color for each separate segment, and draw lines to indicate connections. If you use only one pencil or marker, you might use a system of dotted, dashed, and unbroken lines (the method used, for this black and white text, in the sample theme). The colored pencil or marker method is best, but any easily recognized system convenient for you is acceptable.

Below your analysis, make an explanatory key to your circles and lines.

Use a standard pronunciation guide from one of the collegiate dictionaries to describe sounds. In a footnote, indicate which dictionary you are using.

Underline all sounds to which you are calling attention. If you use an entire word to illustrate a sound, underline only the sound and not the entire word, but put the word within quotation marks (e.g., The poet uses a *t* ["tip," "top," and "terrific"]). When you refer to entire words containing particular segments, however, underline these words (e.g., The poet uses a t in tip, top, and terrific.).

---

## Sample Theme

*A Study of Tennyson's Use of Segments in "The Passing of Arthur," 348–360*

---

NOTE: The other sample themes in this chapter analyze a sonnet and a lyric. For illustrative purposes, this theme analyzes a passage from a long poem: Tennyson's "The Passing of Arthur," which is part of Idylls of the King. Containing 469 lines, "The Passing of Arthur" describes the last battle and death of Arthur, legendary king of early Britain. After the fight, in which Arthur has been mortally wounded by the traitor Modred, only Arthur and his follower Sir Bedivere remain alive. Arthur commands Bedivere to throw the royal sword "Excalibur" into the lake from which it had been originally given to Arthur. After much hesitation, Bedivere does throw the sword into the lake, and a hand rises out of the water to catch it. Bedivere then carries Arthur to the shore of the lake, where the dying king is taken aboard a magical funeral barge by three queens, who are "black-hooded" and "black-stoled" and who wear "crowns of gold." The barge carries Arthur away to die, leaving Bedivere alone to tell the story.

The passage analyzed here is the description of Bedivere carrying Arthur from the chapel at the battlefield down the hills to the shore of the lake.

WORKSHEET NO. 1:   ALLITERATION

But the other (s) wiftly (s) trode from ridge to ridge,                1

Clothed with his breath, and looking, as (h) e walk'd,                 2

Larger than (h) uman on the frozen (h) ills.                           3

(H) e (h) eard the deep be (h) ind (h) im, and a cry                   4

Before. (H) is own thought drove him like a goad.                      5

Dry (c) lash'd (h) is (h) arness in the icy (c) aves                    6

And (b) arren (ch) asms, and all to left and right                     7

The (b) are (b) (l) ack (c) (l) iff (c) (l) ang'd round him, as he (b) ased    8

His feet on juts of s (l) ippery (c) rag that rang                     9

Sharp-smitten with the dint of armed heels—                            10

And on a sudden, (l) o! the (l) evel (l) ake,                          11

And the (l) ong g (l) ories of the winter moon.                        12


~~~~~~~~~  = s                          ——————  = b

– – – – –  = h aspirate                 ∿∿∿∿∿  = l as second consonant
                                                   sound in words

················  = k                   — · — · — ·  = l

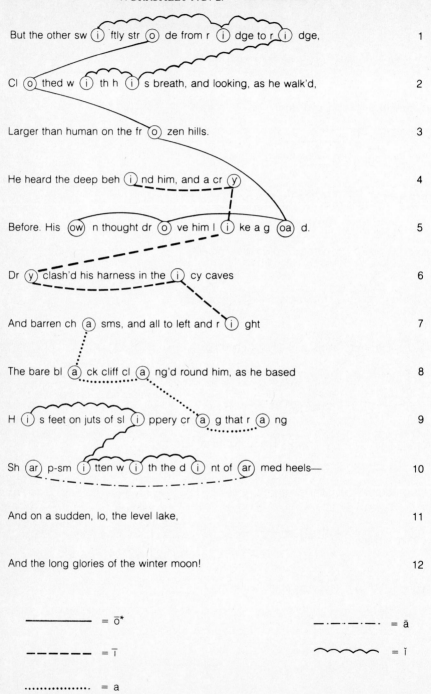

But the other sw (i) ftly str (o) de from r (i) dge to r (i) dge,    1

Cl (o) thed w (i) th h (i) s breath, and looking, as he walk'd,    2

Larger than human on the fr (o) zen hills.    3

He heard the deep beh (i) nd him, and a cr (y)    4

Before. His (ow) n thought dr (o) ve him l (i) ke a g (oa) d.    5

Dr (y) clash'd his harness in the (i) cy caves    6

And barren ch (a) sms, and all to left and r (i) ght    7

The bare bl (a) ck cliff cl (a) ng'd round him, as he based    8

H (i) s feet on juts of sl (i) ppery cr (a) g that r (a) ng    9

Sh (ar) p-sm (i) tten w (i) th the d (i) nt of (ar) med heels—    10

And on a sudden, lo, the level lake,    11

And the long glories of the winter moon!    12

──────── = ō*        ─·─·─·─· = ä

─ ─ ─ ─ ─ = ī        ∿∿∿∿ = ĭ

··············· = a

*Pronunciation symbols as in *Webster's New World Dictionary,* 2nd ed.

[1] In this passage from "The Passing of Arthur," Tennyson describes Sir Bedivere's effort in carrying the dying King Arthur from the chapel near the battlefield to the shores of the nearby lake. <u>Many of Tennyson's words contain sounds which support and echo his descriptions.*</u> <u>This blending of sound and meaning is shown in Tennyson's use of alliteration, assonance, general segmental texture, and onomatopoeia.†</u>

[2] <u>Tennyson's use of alliterative words ties together key ideas and assists in oral interpretation.</u> In line 1, <u>s</u>'s begin the words <u>swiftly</u> and <u>strode.</u> In 7 and 8, <u>b</u>'s connect <u>barren, bare, black,</u> and <u>based.</u> Aspirated <u>h</u>'s appear in 2–6 on <u>human, hills, heard, behind,</u> and <u>harness.</u> There are also <u>h</u>'s in <u>he, him,</u> and <u>his</u> in these lines, but these words do not require the same breathy <u>h</u> pronunciation. Hard <u>k</u> sounds are repeated in nouns and active verbs in 6–9 (<u>clash'd, caves, chasms, cliff, clang'd, crag</u>). Two sets of <u>l</u>'s appear. One is made up of the second segments in heavy, ringing words in 8 and 9 (<u>black, cliff, clang'd,</u> and <u>slippery</u>). The other is the first segment in words describing the lake in 11 and 12 (<u>lo, level, lake, long;</u> note also <u>glories</u>). In their contexts, these <u>l</u>'s assist in producing contrasting effects. They seem heavy and sharp in 8 and 9, but in 11 and 12 they help the voice to relax.

[3] <u>Through assonance, Tennyson achieves the same kind of emphasis.</u> To choose a notable example from many, the long <u>o̱</u> segment appears in six words in the first five lines. The first three words are descriptive and metaphoric (<u>strode, clothed,</u> and <u>frozen</u>), while the next three describe Bedivere's troubled spirit as he struggles on the barren crags (<u>own, drove,</u> and <u>goad</u>). By sound alone, therefore, the long <u>o̱</u> ties the physical to the psychological.

[4] Combining assonance with a skillful use of segmental texture, Tennyson creates a remarkable contrast at the end of the passage. In lines 8 through 10 he introduces a number of words containing vowels that are pronounced with the tongue forward and high in the mouth (<u>he, based, feet, heels;</u> and the short <u>ī</u> assonance in <u>cliff, him, his, slippery, smitten, with,</u> and <u>dint</u>). These segments are penetrating and sharp, in keeping with Bedivere's exertion as he climbs down the dreary hills. By contrast, in the last two lines Tennyson uses words that invite a lowering of vocal pitch and a relaxed and lingering pronunciation. These are <u>on, sudden, lo, long, glories, of,</u> and <u>moon</u> (particularly <u>long, glories,</u> and <u>moon</u>). In reading, the contrast is both sudden and effective, a memorable conclusion.

[5] Also in these last two lines, and elsewhere in the passage, onomatopoeia may be noted. The <u>l</u> sounds in <u>lo, level, lake, long,</u> and <u>glories</u> suggest the gentle lapping of waves on a shore. At the start of the passage, in line 2, Tennyson indicates that the mountainous ridges are so chilly that Bedivere's condensing breath resembles clothing. In the next five lines there are a number of words, already noted, that contain the breathy <u>h</u>. In the context, these sounds are literally identical with the sounds of Bedivere's labored breathing as he carries his royal burden. Similarly, the stop sounds in 6–10 (<u>b</u> and <u>k,</u> which

---

*Central idea
†Thesis sentence

have been noted, and also d̲ [in d̲ry̲, d̲int̲] and t̲ [clash'd̲, left̲, right̲, based̲, feet̲, jut̲s, smit̲t̲en, d̲int̲]) are like the sounds that Bedivere would have made in struggling to keep his feet on the "juts of slippery crag."

[6] Thus Tennyson's choice of words with identical or similar sounds is designed to undergird his descriptions of Bedivere's heroic efforts. It is right to claim that the sounds, in the context, have their own complementary meaning. They help Tennyson emphasize the grandeur of both Arthur and his faithful follower. As long as there are readers for the poem, this grandeur, if only for a moment, may be regained.

## Commentary on the Theme

The introductory paragraph briefly describes the topic material of the passage from Tennyson. The central idea connects many of the segments with his descriptions. The thesis sentence indicates that four topics will be developed in the theme.

Paragraph two examines all the instances of alliteration discovered in the analysis, with particular attention to the two groups of *l* sounds. Even within a comprehensive treatment, in other words, it is possible and desirable to go into detail on a single subtopic that is especially noteworthy.

The third paragraph considers assonance, not selecting all instances but instead providing detail about only a single pattern (the long *o*) and its effects. Such a treatment helps to keep the theme within a reasonably brief length. The worksheets, which pinpoint all the noted instances of assonance, protect the writer from a potential criticism that the discussion focuses on only one point because all the other points were not discovered.

Paragraph four deals with the specific effects of vowel quality in the last two lines. To make this treatment meaningful, the paragraph contrasts vowels in the preceding three lines with the vowels in the last two.

The fifth paragraph considers three separate instances of onomatopoeia, enough to justify the claim in the central idea that there is a close connection between sound and sense.

The concluding paragraph stresses the heroism and grandeur that Tennyson tried to evoke about his subject, and the paragraph also stresses the place of sound in this evocation.

Because confusion might result if both assonance and alliteration were marked together on only one worksheet, a single sheet is devoted to each aspect. The numbering, the circles, the connecting lines, and the key are all designed to assist readers in following the theme and in verifying the conclusions.

# III. *The Theme on Rhyme*

Rhyme, the most easily recognized physical characteristic of poetry, means the repetition of identical concluding syllables in different words, most often at the ends of lines. Words with the same concluding vowel sounds rhyme; such rhymes are a special kind of assonance. Thus *day* rhymes with *weigh, grey, bouquet,* and *matinee,* even though all these words are spelled differently. Rhyme may also combine assonance and identical consonant sounds, as in *ache, bake, break,* and *opaque,* or *turn, yearn, fern,* and *adjourn.*

Rhyme is a means of emphasis, a way of reinforcing and pointing up ideas. It is a powerful way of "clinching" a thought by the physical link of identical sounds. In its simplest form it jingles in the mind, with rhymes like *bells* and *tells.* Everyone has learned common jingles and sayings like "Five, six, / Pick up sticks," and "An apple a day / Keeps the doctor away." To hear such rhymes once is to know them forever, so strongly do they impress themselves in our memories.

## RHYME AND POETIC QUALITY

Wherever rhyme is used skillfully, it leads the mind into new, fresh, unusual, and even surprising turns of thought. Poets may thus be judged on their rhymes. Alexander Pope criticized "easy" rhymers who always paired obvious words like "trees" and "breeze." Such a rhymer was a follower of language, not a leader who saw rhyme in poetry as one means of reaching the goals of freshness and newness. The seventeenth-century poet John Dryden admitted that the need for rhymes led even him into turns of thought that he had not anticipated. In such a sense, rhyme had—and still has—a vital role in poetic creativity.

Rhyme not only has a serious role in poetry, but it may lead to witty, surprising, comic effects. The name *Julia* is rhymed with *peculiar* in a turn-of-the-century popular song. Samuel Butler rhymed *ecclesiastic* with *a stick* in his long poem *Hudibras.* Sometimes rhymes may involve puns, as *futile's* being used instead of *feudal* in a rhyme with *noodle.* A part of a word may be used as a rhyme, with the rest of the word carrying over to the next line, as in

> He would adorn
> Himself with orn-
> Aments.

Rhymes are often comic, as in this limerick:

> There once was a man from Tarentum
> Who gnashed his false teeth till he bent 'em.
>> When asked the cost
>> Of what he had lost,
> He said, "I can't say, for I rent 'em."

## RULES AND VARIANTS
## IN RHYME

Unlike languages such as Italian or French, English does not contain large numbers of rhyming words. Therefore there are not many "rules" for poets using rhymes. About the only restriction is that the same forms are not to be used, even if they appear in different words. *Turn* should not be matched with *taciturn, verse* with *universe,* or *stable* with *unstable.* Aside from this, the major guide is taste and propriety. A poet of serious verse would destroy a poem with rhymes like those in the limerick.

Also because of the difficulty of finding rhyming words in English, a wide latitude in rhyming forms has been accepted. There is *eye rhyme* or *sight rhyme,* the pairing of words that look alike but that do not sound alike. Thus according to sight rhyme "I *wind* [a clock]" may be joined to "the North *wind.*" In *slant rhyme* the rhyming vowel segments are different while the consonants are the same; for example *bleak* and *broke; could* and *solitude.*

## RHYME
## AND RHYTHM

The effects of rhyme are closely connected with those of rhythm. In general, rhymes falling on accented syllables lend themselves to serious effects. These rhymes have traditionally been called *masculine,* although terms like *heavy-stress rhyme* or *accented rhyme* are now more appropriate. The accenting of heavy-stress rhyme may be seen in the opening lines of Robert Frost's "Stopping by Woods on a Snowy Evening":

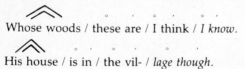

Whose woods / these are / I think / *I know.*

His house / is in / the vil- / *lage though.*

Rhymes concluding with either one or two light stresses have been called *feminine,* but this term may now be distasteful. Preferable terms are the accurate *trochaic* or *double rhyme* for rhymes of two syllables, and *dactylic* or *triple rhyme* for rhymes of three syllables. Abstractly, such rhymes are called *falling* or *dying.* Falling rhymes, like those in lines 1, 2, and 5 of the limerick above, are most appropriate in comic and light subject matter. It is difficult for any poet to use falling rhymes and maintain seriousness at the same time. The accents in falling rhyme, in this example trochaic or double rhyme, may be seen in the second and fourth lines of the first stanza of "Miniver Cheevy," by Edwin Arlington Robinson:

> Miniver Cheevy, child of scorn,
>
> Grew lean while he assailed the *seasons;*
>
> He wept that he was ever born
>
> And he had *reasons.*

Dactylic or triple rhyme is unusual. It may be seen in these lines from Browning's "The Pied Piper of Hamelin," which also illustrate *internal rhyme;* that is, a rhyming word within a line:

> Small feet were *pattering,* wooden shoes *clattering,*
>
> Little hands clapping and little tongues *chattering.*
>
> And, like fowls in a farm-yard when barley is *scattering,* . . .

## DESCRIBING RHYMES

In the description of rhymes, alphabetical letters are used. Each repeated letter indicates a rhyme (a, a). Each new letter indicates a new rhyme (b, b; c, c; d, d; etc.). An *x* indicates no rhyme. To formulate a rhyme pattern, you should include (1) the meter and number of feet of each line, and (2) the letters indicating rhymes. Here is such a formulation:

> Iambic pentameter: a, b, b, a, c, c, a.

This scheme shows that all the lines are iambic, with five feet in each line. The rhyming lines are 1, 4, and 7; 2 and 3; and 5 and 6.

Should the number of feet in lines vary, show this fact with a number in front of each letter:

> Iambic: 5a, 5b, 4a, 3a, 2b, 6a.

Always make a note of any deviations from the predominant pattern. If there is a variation in the meter of any of the rhymes, note that variation the first time you use the letter, as follows:

> Iambic: 5a, 4b (trochee), 5a, 4b, 5a, 5b.

Here the second, fourth, and sixth lines are rhyming trochees; there is no need to indicate this fact on any but the first use of the letter, because the following appearances of the letter automatically indicate the variation.

RHYME SCHEMES

Along with line length, rhyme is a determinant in the classification of poetic forms. Here are the major ones:

*1. The Couplet.*

> a, a; b, b; c, c; d, d; etc.

Couplets of iambic pentameter are called *heroic* or *neoclassic.* Also common, especially for light and satiric purposes, are couplets in iambic tetrameter (four iambic feet).

*2. The Italian or Petrarchan Sonnet.*

> Iambic pentameter: a, b, b, a, a, b, b, a, c, d, c, d, c, d.

The first eight lines form the *octave,* the last six the *sestet.* There is usually a shift in thought from the octave to the sestet.

*3. The Shakespearean Sonnet.*

> Iambic pentameter: a, b, a, b, c, d, c, d, e, f, e, f, g, g.

Note that the Shakespearean sonnet has seven rhyming sounds, contrasted with the four in the Italian sonnet. The rhyming groups of four lines, like any four-line group, are called *quatrains.* Each quatrain usually contains a separate development of the thought, with the couplet providing a conclusion or climax.

*4. Ballad Measure, or Common Measure.*

> Iambic: 4x, 3a, 4x, 3a; 4x, 3b, 4x, 3b; etc.

Each quatrain forms a separate unit, analogous to the paragraph, called a *stanza.* A typical ballad consists of many stanzas. Ballads are often narrative in development, like the anonymous "Sir Patrick Spens." Coleridge used ballad measure for "The Rime of the Ancient Mariner" and added variations with extra lines for some of his stanzas.

*5. The Song.*

The song is a free stanzaic form designed to be sung to a repeated melody. The scheme for one stanza therefore describes all the stanzas. There is no limit to the number of stanzas, although there are usually no more than five or six. Here are some rhyme schemes of song stanzas:

Donne's "The Canonization":

Iambic: 5a, 4b, 5b, 5a, 4c, 4c, 4a, 3a

Browning's "Two in the Campagna":

Iambic tetrameter: a, b, a, b, (3)x.

Note that line 5 is not paired in rhyme with any of the other lines and that this line has three rather than four feet.

Burns' "To a Mouse":

Iambic tetrameter: a, a, b, (2)c, b, (2)c.

In stanzas 1, 2, 4, and 6 the rhyming feet are in amphibrachs. In stanzas 3, 5, 7, and 8 the rhyming feet are iambic.

A regular variant of the song is the *hymn*, a song, often sung in unison, used in the service of religion. Hymns usually contain from three to six stanzas. Common measure is most frequently used, but there are many schemes. To enable hymns to be sung to a number of separate tunes, most hymnals contain an analytical table of the hymns based on the number of syllables in each line of the stanza.

### 6. The Ode.

The ode is a stanzaic form more complex than the song, with varying line lengths and sometimes intricate rhyme schemes. Some odes have repeating stanzaic patterns whereas others are totally free. Although some odes have been used as a setting for music, they usually do not fit repeating melodies. There is no set form for the ode; poets have developed their own types according to their needs. Keats' great odes were particularly congenial to his ideas, as in the "Ode to a Nightingale," which consists of ten stanzas in iambic pentameter, with the repeating form a, b, a, b, c, d, e, (3)c, d, e. By contrast, the pattern of none of Wordsworth's ten stanzas in the "Intimations of Immortality" ode is repeated.

### 7. Terza Rima.

Terza rima is a rhyming pattern of three lines in iambic pentameter: a, b, a; b, c, b; c, d, c; etc. Dante invented this form for *The Divine Comedy*. Shelley used it in the five stanzas of "Ode to the West Wind." Roethke used it in "The Waking."

## Your Theme

For your analysis, select either a short, representative passage from a long poem, or an entire shorter poem such as a sonnet or three-stanza song. At the beginning of the theme, as for the other themes on prosody, include a worksheet. This should contain a double-spaced copy of the poem or passage, with each line numbered beginning with 1. List the numbers of feet in each line (you do not need to provide a complete scansion), and mark any variations in the predominant meter of the rhymes. Letter each rhyme (a, b, b, a, etc.). Underline or otherwise draw attention to any particularly notable or outstanding aspect of the rhyme.

## INTRODUCTION

Here you should make any general remarks you wish about the poem, but concentrate on the relationship of the rhyme to the content. That is, does the rhyme seem to be no more than a decorative adjunct to the poem, or is it integrated in some way? Try to define and limit this relationship. Your thesis sentence should cover the topics in the body of the theme.

## BODY

While stressing your central idea, you should include the following aspects of rhyme:

1. The physical description, including the rhyme scheme and any variants, the lengths of the rhyming words, the rhythms of the rhymes, and any noteworthy segmental characteristics.

2. The grammatical features of the rhymes. As a general principle, the forms of rhyming words should not be the same but should vary. In your poem, what kinds of words are used for rhymes? Are they all the same? Does one form predominate? Is there variety? Can you determine the grammatical positions of the rhyming words? Is it possible to relate your discoveries to the idea or theme of the poem?

3. The qualities of the rhyming words. Are the words specific? Concrete? Abstract? Are there any particularly striking rhymes? Any surprises? Are there any rhymes that are clever or witty? Do any rhymes give unique comparisons or contrasts? How?

4. Any particularly striking or unique effects in the rhyme. Without becoming overly subtle or farfetched, you can make satisfying and sometimes even startling conclusions. Try to raise some of the following issues: Do any sounds in the rhymes appear (as assonance or alliteration) elsewhere in the poem to any appreciable degree? Do the rhymes assist in the achievement of any onomatopoeic effects? Generally, can you detect any aspects of the rhyme that are uniquely effective because they are at one with the thought and mood of your poem?

## CONCLUSION

Here you might include any additional observations about the rhyme as well as any comparisons between the rhyme in your poem and in other poems by the same poet or other poets. A short summary of your main headings is here, as always, appropriate.

---

## Sample Theme

### *The Rhymes in Christina Rossetti's Poem "Echo"*

---

| | | |
|---|---|---|
| 1 | Come to me in the silence of the *n* night; | 5a |
| 2 | Come in the speaking silence of a *n* dream; | 5b |
| 3 | Come with soft rounded cheeks and eyes as *adj* bright | 5a |
| 4 | As sunlight on a *n* stream; | 3b |
| 5 | Come back in *n* tears, | 2c |
| 6 | O memory, hope, love of finished *n* years. | 5c |
| 7 | O dream how sweet, too sweet, too bitter *adj* sweet, | 5d |
| 8 | Whose wakening should have been in *n* Paradise, | 5e |
| 9 | Where souls brimful of love abide and *v* meet; | 5d |
| 10 | Where thirsty longing *n* eyes | 3e |

Repeated words:

| | | |
|---|---|---|
| ~~~~~ | dream, dreams | n = noun |
| ——— | sweet | v = verb |
| –.–.–. | breath | adj = adjective |
| ...... | low | adv = adverb |
| – – – – | long ago | |
| ˘˘˘˘˘ | come | |

11      Watch the slow do$\overset{n}{\text{o}}$r                                    2f

12      That opening, letting in, lets out no m$\overset{adv}{\text{o}}$re.          5f


13      Yet come to me in dreams, that I may li$\overset{v}{\text{v}}$e             5g

14      My very life again though cold in d$\overset{n}{\text{e}}$ath:               5h

15      Come back to me in dreams, that I may gi$\overset{v}{\text{v}}$e            5g

16      Pulse for pulse, breath for br$\overset{n}{\text{e}}$ath:                    3h

17      Speak l$\overset{adj}{\text{o}}$w, lean low,                                 2i

18      As long ago, my love, how l$\overset{adj}{\text{o}}$ng ago!                  5i


[1]  In the three-stanza lyric poem "Echo," Christina Rossetti uses rhyme as a virtually coequal way of saying that one might regain in dreams a love that is lost in reality.* As the dream of love is to the real love, so is an echo to an original sound. From this comparison comes the title of the poem and also Rossetti's unique use of rhyme. Aspects of her rhyme are the lyric pattern, the forms and qualities of the rhyming words, and the special use of repetition.†

The rhyme pattern is simple, and, like rhyme generally, it may be thought of as a pattern of echoes. Each stanza contains four lines of alternating rhymes concluded by a couplet, as follows:

Iambic: 5a, 5b, 5a, 3b, 2c, 5c.

[2]  There are nine separate rhymes throughout the poem, three in each stanza. Only two words are used for each rhyme; no rhyme is used twice. Of the eighteen rhyming words, sixteen—almost all—are of one syllable. The remaining two words consist of two and three syllables. With such a great number of single-syllable words, the rhymes are all rising ones, on the accented halves of the iambic feet, and the end-of-line emphasis is on relatively simple words.

The grammatical forms and positions of the rhyming words lend support to the inward, introspective subject matter. Although there is variety, more than half of the rhyming words are nouns. There are ten in all, and eight are placed

[3]  within prepositional phrases as the objects of prepositions. Such enclosure is not unexpected in this lyric, personal poem, where the speaker states the yearning to relive her love within dreams. Also, the repeated verb "come" in stanzas one and three is in the form of commands to the absent lover. Thus,

*Central idea
†Thesis sentence

most of the verbal energy in the stanzas is in the first parts of the lines, leaving the rhymes to occur in elements modifying the verbs, as in these lines:

Come to me in the silence of the *night* (1)

Yet come to me in dreams, that I may live (13)
My very life again though cold in *death;* (14)

Most of the other rhymes are also in such internalized positions. The three rhyming verbs occur in subordinate and relative clauses, and the nouns that are not the objects of prepositions are the subject (10) and object (11) of the same relative clause.

[4] The qualities of the rhyming words are also consistent with the poem's emphasis on the speaker's internal life. Most of the words are impressionistic. Even the concrete words—*stream, tears, eyes, door,* and *breath*—reflect the speaker's mental condition rather than describe reality. In this regard, the rhyming words of 1 and 3 are starkly effective. These are *night* and *bright,* which contrast the bleakness of the speaker's condition, on the one hand, with the vitality of her inner life, on the other. Another effective contrast is in 14 and 16, where *death* and *breath* are rhymed. This rhyme may be taken to illustrate the sad fact that even though the speaker's love is past, it can yet live in present memory just as an echo continues to sound.

[5] It is in emphasizing how memory echoes experience that Rossetti creates the special use of rhyming words. There is an ingenious but not obtrusive repetition of a number of words—echoes. The major echoing word is of course the verb *come,* which appears six times at the beginnings of lines in stanzas one and three. But rhyming words, stressing as they do the ends of lines, are also repeated systematically. The most notable is *dream,* the rhyming word in 2. Rossetti repeats the word in 7 and uses the plural in 13 and 15. In 7 the rhyming word *sweet* is the third use of the word, a climax of "how *sweet,* too *sweet,* too bitter *sweet.*" Concluding the poem, Rossetti repeats *breath* (16), *low* (17), and the phrase *long ago* (18). This special use of repetition justifies the title "Echo," and it also stresses the major idea that it is only in one's memory that past experience has reality, even if dreams are no more than echoes of the past.

[6] Thus rhyme is not just ornamental in "Echo," but integral to it. The skill of Rossetti here is the same as in her half-serious, half-mocking poem "Eve," even though the two poems are totally different. In "Eve," she uses very plain rhyming words together with comically intended double rhymes. In "Echo," her subject might be called fanciful and maybe even morbid, but the easiness of the rhyming words, like the diction of the poem generally, keeps the focus on regret and yearning rather than self-indulgence. As in all rhyming poems, Rossetti's rhymes emphasize the conclusions of her lines. The rhymes go beyond this effect, however, because of the internal repetition—echoes—of the rhyming words. "Echo" is a poem in which rhyme is inseparable from meaning.

# Commentary on the Theme

Throughout the theme, illustrative words are italicized, and numbers are used to indicate the lines from which the illustrations are drawn.

The introductory paragraph asserts that rhyme is extremely important in Rossetti's poem. It also attempts to explain the title, "Echo." The thesis sentence indicates the four topics to be developed in the body.

Paragraph two deals with the mechanical, mathematical aspects of the poem's rhyme. The high number of monosyllabic rhyming words is used to explain the rising, heavy-stress rhyme.

The third paragraph treats the grammar of the rhymes. For example, a simple analysis and count reveals that there are ten rhyming nouns and three rhyming verbs. The verb of command "come" is mentioned in order to show that most of the rhyming words exist within groups modifying this word, and three lines from the poem illustrate this fact. The grammatical analysis is related to the internalized nature of the subject of the poem.

Paragraph four emphasizes the impressionistic nature of the rhyming words and also points out two instances in which rhymes stress the contrast between real life and the speaker's introspective life.

The fifth paragraph deals with repetitions within the poem of five rhyming words. This repetition is seen as a pattern of echoes, in keeping with the title of the poem.

In the concluding paragraph the rhymes in "Echo" are compared briefly with those in "Eve," another poem by Christina Rossetti. The conclusion is that Rossetti is a skilled rhymer because she uses rhyme appropriately in both poems. At the end of the theme, the central idea is reiterated.

# chapter 14

# Two Themes Based
# on a Close Reading:
# (I) The theme
# on general content
# (II) The theme on style

A theme on a close reading is a detailed study of a passage of prose or poetry. The passage may be a fragment of a longer work, such as an entire speech from a play, story, or novel, or it may be a paragraph of descriptive or analytic prose. It may also be an entire short poem, such as a sonnet or short lyric.

The close-reading theme is at once specific and general. It is specific because it requires you to concentrate on the selected passage. It is general because you do not need to study a single topic (such as character, setting, or point of view) but need to deal with any or all of those things that may be found in the passage. Should your passage describe a specific person, of course, you would need to discuss character, but your emphasis would be on what the passage itself brings out about the character. You would also stress action, setting, and ideas, or even make comparisons, if you find that these matters are important. In other words, the content of a close-reading theme is variable; your passage dictates your content.

## Studying Your Passage

Whenever you are to write a close-reading theme, you should first read the *entire* work, so that you can understand the relationship of all the parts. Read carefully. Then study the passage you are to write about. First, be sure to use a dictionary to help you understand all words that are even slightly obscure. Sometimes you may not get the sense of a passage on the first or second reading, perhaps because some of the words are not clear to you, even though they may appear so at first. Therefore, look up *all* the words, even the simple ones, in the obscure sentence or sentences. In Shakespeare's *Sonnet 73*, for example, this famous line occurs:

> Bare ruined choirs, where late the sweet birds sang.

If you think *choirs* means organized groups of singers (as you might at first), you will be puzzled by the line. The dictionary will tell you that *choirs* may also be an architectural term for that part of a church in which singers are often placed. Thus Shakespeare's word takes in the range of both empty branches and destroyed churches, and the phrase *sweet birds* refers to vanished human singers as well as birds that have flown away because of winter's cold. Let us take another line, this time from John Donne's first *Holy Sonnet:*

> And thou like Adamant draw mine iron heart.

Unless you look up *Adamant* and realize that Donne uses it to mean a magnet, you will not understand the sense of *draw*. You will thus miss Donne's image and his idea of God's immense power over human beings.

   Once you have mastered the words to the best of your ability, look at the sentence structures, particularly in poetry, where you will often find variations in the ordinary English subject-verb-object word order. If you read the line "Thy merit hath my duty strongly knit," be sure that you get the subject and object straight (i.e., "Thy merit hath strongly knit my duty"). Or, look at lines 15 and 16 from Pope's *Essay on Criticism:*

> Let such teach others who themselves excell,
> And censure freely who have written well.

On first reading these lines are difficult. A person might conclude that Pope is asking the critic to condemn those writers who have written well (but as an exercise, look up *censure* in the *Oxford English Dictionary*), until the lines are unraveled:

> Let such who themselves excell teach others,
> And [let such] who have written well censure freely.

There is a great difference here between the misreading and the correct reading. What you must keep in mind is that an initial failure to understand a sentence structure that is no longer common can prevent your full understanding of a passage. Therefore you must be sure, in your study, to untie all the syntactic knots.

## Types of Close-Reading Themes

There are two types of close-reading themes. The first deals with the general content of the passage and its relationship to the entire work. The second type is also concerned with the general content but goes on to deal with the style of the passage.

# I. The General Content of a Passage

This kind of close-reading theme emphasizes the content of the passage and the relationship of the passage to the rest of the work. The theme is designed as a first approach to close reading and does not require detailed knowledge about diction, grammar, and style. Thus, although you may wish to discuss a few special words and phrases, it should be your aim here to consider the content of your passage rather than its style.

Once you have clarified the passage to your satisfaction, you should develop materials for your theme. Try to make some general statements about your passage: Does the passage (1) describe a natural or artificial scene, (2) develop a character or characters, (3) describe an action, (4) describe or analyze a character's thoughts, or (5) develop an argument? Is the passage a speech by one character or a dialogue or discussion by two or more? What is the content of the passage? That is, are there themes and ideas that are brought up elsewhere in the work? In this respect, how does the passage connect to what has gone on before and to what comes after? (To deal with this question, you may assume that your reader is familiar in some detail with the entire work.) Some obvious points to think about are the following:

### For an Early Passage

Does the passage occur early in the work? If it does, you may reasonably expect that the author is using the passage to set things in motion. Thus you should try to determine how ideas, themes, characterizations, and arguments that you find in the passage are related to these matters as they appear later in the work. You may assume that everything in the passage is there for a purpose. Try to find that purpose.

### For a Later, Midpoint Passage

Does the passage come later in the work, at a time that you might characterize as a "pivot" or "turning point"? In such a passage a character's fortunes take either an expected or unexpected turn. If the change is expected, you should explain how the passage focuses the various themes or ideas and then propels them toward the climax. If the change is un-expected, however, it is necessary to show how the contrast is made in the passage. It may be that the work is one that features surprises, and the passage thus is read one way at first but on second reading may be seen to have a double meaning. Or it may be that the speaker has had one set of assumptions while the readers have had others, and that the passage marks a point of increasing self-awareness on the part of the speaker. Many parts of works are not what they seem at first reading, and it is your task here to determine how the passage is affected by events at or near the end of the work.

### For a Concluding Passage

If the passage occurs at or near the end of the work, you may assume that it is designed to solve problems or to be a focal point or climax for all the situations and ideas that have been building up in the work. You will need to show how the passage brings together all themes, ideas, and details. What is happening? Is any action described in the passage a major action, or a step leading to the major action? Has everything in the passage been prepared for earlier in the work?

## General Purposes of the Close-Reading Theme

In light of what we have seen, the general purposes of a close-reading theme should be clear. If you can read a paragraph, you can read the entire book; if you can read a speech, you can read the entire play or story; if you can read one poem by a poet, you can read other poems by the same poet. This is not to say that the writing of a close-reading theme auto-matically means that at first reading you will understand every work by the same author. Few people would insist that reading passages from Joyce's *Dubliners* makes it possible to understand *Finnegans Wake*. What a close-reading theme gives you is a skill upon which you can build, an approach to any other text you will encounter.

You will find use for the general technique of close reading in other courses also. In political science, for example, parts of political speeches can be, and should be, scrutinized carefully, not just for what is said but for what is half-said or left out entirely. A close study of a philosophical work or Biblical passage will yield much that might not be found in a casual first reading. No matter what course you are taking or what your personal interests may be, you can use close-reading techniques to improve your understanding.

## Organizing Your Theme

### INTRODUCTION

Because the close-reading theme is concerned with details in the passage, you may find a problem in creating a thematic structure. This difficulty is surmountable if you work either with a generalization about the passage itself or else with a central idea based on the relationship of the passage to the work. Suppose, for example, that the passage is factually descriptive, or intensely emotional, or that it introduces a major character or idea, or that it sets in motion forces that will create a climax later in the work. Any one of these observations may serve as your central idea.

### BODY

You may develop the body according to what you find in the passage. Suppose that you have a passage of character description; you might wish to analyze what is said about the character, together with a comparison of how these qualities are modified later. In addition, you might consider how these qualities are to affect other characters and/or later events in the work. Suppose your passage is particularly witty, and you decide to discuss the quality of the wit and then show how this wittiness bears upon earlier and later situations. The idea here is to focus on details in the passage and also on the relationship of these details to the entire work.

### CONCLUSION

As you make your major points for the body of the theme, you may also notice subpoints that are worth mentioning but do not merit full consideration. You might bring these points into your conclusion. For example, there may be a particular word or type of word, or there may be an underlying assumption that you found in the passage, or there may be some quality that you find hard to describe. The conclusion is the place for you to mention these things. If you haven't discussed anything about the way some of the things are said but want to say that the diction is plain and monosyllabic, or difficult and polysyllabic, and if you do not believe that you can go into great detail about these matters, then you can bring them up in your conclusion. You may also, of course, summarize your main points from the body of your theme.

## Numbers for Easy Reference

Include a copy of your passage at the beginning of your theme, as in the two samples. For the convenience of your reader, number lines in poetry and sentences in prose.

---

### Sample Theme (Study of a Prose Passage)

*An Analysis of a Paragraph from Frank O'Connor's "First Confession"*

---

Nora's turn came, and I heard the sound of something slamming, and then her voice as if butter wouldn't melt in her mouth, and then another slam, and out she came. [2] God, the hypocrisy of women. [3] Her eyes were lowered, her head was bowed, and her hands were joined very low down on her stomach, and she walked up the aisle to the side altar looking like a saint. [4] You never saw such an exhibition of devotion; and I remembered the devilish malice with which she had tormented me all the way from our door, and wondered were all religious people like that, really. [5] It was my turn now. [6] With the fear of damnation in my soul I went in, and the confessional door closed of itself behind me.

[1]

This paragraph from Frank O'Connor's "First Confession" appears midway in the story. It is transitional, coming between Jackie's recollections of his childhood troubles at home and his happier memory of his first confession. Although the short episode might have been painful for the child, the passage itself reflects geniality and good nature.* This mood is apparent in the comments of the narrator, the comic situation, and the narrator's apparent lack of self-awareness.†

[2]

More impressionistic than descriptive, the paragraph concentrates in a good-humored way on the direct but prejudiced responses of the narrator, Jackie. The two major events described are (1) that Nora enters the confessional, says her confession, and leaves, and (2) that Jackie then enters the confessional. But the narrator, now an adult, relates these details through his own disapproval and limited perceptions. Thus, he states that Nora, while confessing, sounds "as if butter wouldn't melt in her mouth." As he is about to describe her prayerful walk away from the confessional, he exclaims, "God, the hypocrisy of women" (2). When he himself enters the confessional, he does so with "the fear of damnation in . . . [his] soul" (6). These comments show

---

*Central idea
†Thesis sentence
For the text of this story, please see Appendix C, pp. 333–339.

prejudice and lack of understanding, but in the context of recollections of childhood they add to the charm and humor of the passage.

[3] It is from these remarks that the comedy of the passage develops. Much of the humor rests on the inconsistency between Nora's sisterly badgering of Jackie and her pietism at the confession. Since Jackie is careful here to stress Nora's "devilish malice" against him (4), readers might smile when thinking about her saintly pose. But readers surely know that Nora is not unusual; she has been behaving like any typical older brother or sister. So there is also a comic contrast between her normal actions and Jackie's opinion that she is "devilish." The humor is thus directed by the author toward the narrator.

[4] In fact, it may be that the narrator's lack of self-awareness is the major cause of humor in the passage. Jackie is an adult telling a story about his experience as a seven-year-old. Readers might expect him to be mature and therefore to be compassionate about his childhood anger against his sister. But his child's-eye view seems still to be controlling his responses. Comments about Nora such as "looking like a saint" (3) and "You never saw such an exhibition of devotion" (4) are not consistent with a person who has put childhood in perspective. Hence readers may smile not only at the obvious comedy of Nora's hypocrisy, but also at the narrator's lack of self-awareness. As he comments on his sister with his still jaundiced attitude, he shows his own limitation and in this way directs much amusement against himself.

[5] Readers are more likely to smile at Jackie's remarks, however, than to object to his adult character. The thrust of the paragraph is thus on the good-natured comedy of the situation. For this reason the paragraph is successful. In its context it is a turning point between Jackie's disturbing experiences with his sister, grandmother, and father, on the one hand, and the pleasant confession with the kind, thoughtful, and genial priest on the other. The child goes into confession with the fear of damnation in his thoughts, but after the farce that is to follow, he finds the assurances that his fears are not justified and that his anger is normal and can be forgiven. Surely, the good nature of the passage extends far beyond the simple, commmon episode described there.

---

## Commentary on the Theme

A number of central ideas might have been made about the passage chosen for analysis: that it is dramatic, that it centers on the religious hypocrisy of Jackie's sister, that it brings together the major themes of the story, or that it creates a problem in the character of the narrator. The central idea of the sample theme as brought out in the first paragraph, however, is that the passage reflects geniality and good nature. The theme does deal with Nora's hypocrisy and also with the problem in the narrator's character, but these points are brought out in connection with the central idea.

In the body of the theme, the second paragraph shows that the narrator's comments about his sister and his own spiritual condition add to the good nature of the passage. The third paragraph explains the relationship between Jackie's remarks and the comedy in the passage. In paragraph four the adult narrator's unwitting revelation of his own shortcomings is related to the good humor and comedy. The concluding paragraph connects the passage to the latter half of the story, suggesting that the good nature of the passage is like the divine forgiveness that is believed to follow the act of confession.

Because this theme is based on a close reading of the passage chosen for analysis, its major feature is the use of many specific details. Thus, the second paragraph stresses the action of the passage and some of the narrator's comments about it. The third paragraph stresses the details about Nora's posture and Jackie's comments about her. Paragraph four emphasizes more of the narrator's comments and the limitations of character that they show. Finally, the concluding paragraph includes the detail about Jackie's entering the confessional.

## II. *The Style of a Passage*

The second type of close-reading theme is like the first inasmuch as both deal with a passage in the context of the entire work. The second goes beyond the first, however, because it concentrates on the style of the passage rather than the content.

To carry out a discussion of style, you will need to apply many of the things that you have previously learned or are learning about the mechanics of language. You might feel hesitant at first, but you will unquestionably find that you know much more than you think you know. In addition, many of the approaches you might try are not especiallly difficult. As an instance, the sample theme shows what might be done with the application of no more than a moderate knowledge of language.

The word *style* is not easy to define to everyone's satisfaction, but for the present theme you may deal with it as an analysis of word choice and sentence development resulting from an author's judgment about the following matters:

1. The speaker, or narrator, of the work
2. The character being analyzed or described
3. The circumstances of the passage
4. The type or purpose of the work
5. The audience

Any close reading for style should take these and related elements into account as they become relevant to the details of the passage.

And they do become relevant. Authors do not always write in their own persons but take on the voice of a particular narrator, or they present the speech of a character just as they think that character would likely say it. (For further development of this fact, please see Chapter 5, on Point of View.) Also, the writer's perception of his or her audience governs the amount of detail and kinds of diction that you will find in your passage. It is not possible to write a close-reading theme for style without also considering the entire context of the passage.

## EXAMPLES OF STYLE AND ITS RELATION TO CHARACTER

To look at a specific example, let us consider the character of Portia from Shakespeare's *The Merchant of Venice*. Late in the play Portia masquerades brilliantly as a lawyer, and because of her ingenuity in argument she brings Antonio out of danger. It would seem natural that Shakespeare, in giving her speeches elsewhere in the play, would emphasize and demonstrate her intelligence. In I.ii, for example, Portia says the following:

> If to do were as easy as to know what were good to do, chapels had been churches and poor men's cottages princes' palaces. It is a good divine that follows his own instructions: I can easier teach twenty what were good to be done, than to be one of the twenty to follow mine own teaching.

From the style of this passage, one may conclude that Shakespeare is indeed showing that Portia has a rapid mind. Her first sentence uses simple diction but a complex structure. Of her first fourteen words, six are infinitives and two are verbs; that is, more than half of the words (about 57 percent) are verbs or verbals. One may conclude that such a proportion suggests great mental power. Also, the first fourteen words form an *if*-clause, dependent on the verb in the following main clause. The ability to control subordination in sentences is regarded as the mark of a good mind and a good style. Portia shows an ability to use rhetoric—in this sentence ellipsis in a parallel structure: the main clause of the first sentence equals two clauses, but the verb is used only once: "chapels had been churches and poor men's cottages [had been] princes' palaces." Portia's language is concrete and vivid, and she has control over her balanced sentence.

To be contrasted with Portia's speech is this one by Ophelia in *Hamlet*, IV. v:

> Well, God 'ild you. They say, the owl was a baker's daughter. Lord, we know what we are, but know not what we may be. God be at your table.

Ophelia makes this speech after she has gone mad. Her words are simple, and her sentences are disconnected. Just when she seems to become coherent (in sentence three) her thought is broken, and her last sentence seems as random as her first. Had Shakespeare introduced the mental toughness of Portia's speech here, he would not have shown a broken mind but an alert one in all its powers. Thus he gave Ophelia these disconnected sentences, so unlike her coherent speeches earlier in the play.

The point about both passages is that the differences in style are appropriate to the two characterizations and also to the differing dramatic situations. Please note that our analyses of style are related to the contexts of the plays. It would not be fruitful to discuss style independently of the context, particularly in a dramatic passage, for the language is likely to be indicative of the immediate situation and is also likely to involve comparisons with other sections of the work.

## TWO MAJOR APPROACHES TO STYLE

There are two major topics, or approaches, to close reading for style: (1) diction, and (2) rhetoric. Technically, rhetoric includes diction, but here they are separated for ease of analysis. Naturally, either approach can become complex and subtle, so much so that any aspect, such as connotation or parallelism, can furnish materials for an entire theme.

### Diction

The study of words is readily approached because you have the tools of understanding and verification available in your mind and in your dictionary. You should not rely simply on dictionary definitions, however, but should consider words in context and should try to characterize them. Look at the words carefully. Try to answer some of these questions: Who is speaking? Is it the author, some aspect of the author's personality, or a separately imagined speaker with individualized language traits? What is the speaker's background? How old is he or she? How does he or she function in the other parts of the work? What is the particular circumstance of the passage? How does it relate to earlier and later parts of the work? Does the speaker use standard English? Substandard? Dialect? Slang? Profanity? Does he or she seem to be articulate or inarticulate? Does the speech indicate any particular level of education? Any ethnic or social background?

**WORDS: SPECIFIC–CONCRETE AND GENERAL–ABSTRACT.** To the above questions you may add others: In describing events or situations, does the writer or speaker use words that are specific or general, concrete or abstract? Let us look at two examples of prose, the first from Hemingway's *A Farewell to Arms*, the second from Theodore Dreiser's *The Titan:*

> [1] In the late summer of that year we lived in a house in a village that looked across the river and the plain to the mountains. [2] In the bed of the river there were pebbles and boulders, dry and white in the sun, and the water was clear and swiftly moving and blue in the channels. [3]

Troops went by the house and down the road and the dust they raised powdered the leaves of the trees. [4] The trunks of the trees too were dusty and the leaves fell early that year and we saw the troops marching along the road and the dust rising and leaves, stirred by the breeze, falling and the soldiers marching and afterward the road bare and white except for the leaves.[1]

[1] From New York, Vermont, New Hampshire, Maine had come a strange company, earnest, patient, determined, unschooled in even the primer of refinement, hungry for something the significance of which, when they had it, they could not even guess, anxious to be called great, determined so to be without ever knowing how.[2]

Hemingway's diction is specific; that is, many of the words, such as *house, river, plain, mountains, dust, leaves,* and *trees,* describe something that can be seen or felt. In describing aspects of the scene, Hemingway uses concrete words, like *dry, clear, swiftly moving, dusty, stirred, falling, marching,* and *bare.* These words indicate clearly perceivable actions or states. Dreiser's words are in marked contrast. The names of states are specific, but *company* is a general word for a group of any sort, unlike Hemingway's troops. Dreiser's key descriptive words are *strange, earnest, patient, determined, hungry,* and *anxious.* Because none of these words describes anything that can be perceived, unlike *dry* and *dusty,* they are called *abstract.* Obviously the two passages are on different topics, and both are successful in their ways, but Hemingway's diction indicates an attempt to present a specific, concrete perception of things while Dreiser's indicates an attempt at psychological penetration.

**DENOTATION AND CONNOTATION.**   Denotation and connotation are a famous pair. Denotation refers to what a word means, and connotation to what the word suggests. Words with the same denotation usually have different connotations. Authors can manipulate these differences to create entirely different effects even though they might describe similar or even identical situations. Here is an example, the concluding paragraph of Joseph Conrad's novel *Nostromo* (1904):

In that true cry of love and grief that seemed to ring aloud from Punta Mala to Azuera and away to the bright line of the horizon, overhung by a big white cloud shining like a mass of solid silver, the genius of the magnificent *capataz de cargadores* dominated the dark gulf containing his conquests of treasure and love.[3]

[1]Reprinted with the permission of Charles Scribner's Sons and Jonathan Cape Ltd. from *A Farewell to Arms* by Ernest Hemingway, p. 3. Copyright 1929 Charles Scribner's Sons. Renewal copyright© 1957 Ernest Hemingway.
[2]New York: Dell Publishing Co., Inc. (Copyright World Publishing Co.), 1959, p. 25.
[3]New York: Modern Library, 1951, p. 631.

The situation is that Nostromo, the hero of the novel, has died, and the woman who loved him has cried out in grief. This circumstance is not uncommon, for people die every day, and their loved ones grieve for them. But through connotative words like *bright line, shining, solid silver, genius, magnificent,* and *dominated,* Conrad suggests that Nostromo was more than ordinary, a person of great worth and power, a virtual demi-god.

In contrast, here is the concluding paragraph of Hemingway's *A Farewell to Arms:*

> But after I had got them out and shut the door and turned off the light
> it wasn't any good. It was like saying good-by to a statue. After a while
> I went out and left the hospital and walked back to the hotel in the rain.

Hemingway's situation is similar to Conrad's. The heroine, Catherine Barclay, has died, and the hero, Frederick Henry, expresses his grief. He had loved her deeply, but their dreams for a happy future have been destroyed. Hemingway is interested in emphasizing the finality of the moment, and does so through phrases like *shut the door, turned out the light, went out,* and *walked back;* these are all everyday, common words, unlike some of the vocabulary of Conrad. Certainly Hemingway creates a touching, powerful, and memorable description, but he uses flat, bare words to express the idea that there is nothing glorious in death. The two passages show clearly the ways in which control over connotation may give different effects.

## Rhetoric

*Rhetoric* is a broad, inclusive word which means the art of persuasive writing. Thus, any aspect of a passage that seems to be worthy of mention falls into this category. The problem in discussing rhetoric is to develop both a method and a descriptive vocabulary with which to carry out your analysis. Here are some things you can do:

COUNTS. Simple counts can often lead to interesting observations about style, especially if you balance your counts with other analysis. These matters are always subjective, and conclusions usually reflect tendencies of authors rather than absolutes, but for illustration let us say that Author *A* uses an average of twelve words per sentence while Author *B* uses thirty. It is fair to conclude that Author *A* is brief while Author *B* is more expansive. Similarly, Author *C* might use words mainly of one or two syllables, while Author *D* includes many words of three, four, or five syllables. You can go even further, putting your counts into the contexts of the respective passages and then drawing conclusions about the qualities of writers. Let us say that a randomly chosen passage by Author *C* contains ten sentences of 100 words and 120 syllables. Because most of these words would be of one syllable, with an average of twelve words per sentence, it is fair to say that the passage would be simple, designed primarily for elementary reading levels. By contrast, a passage by Author *D* contains three sentences, 100 words, and 180 syllables. Such a passage, with a 33-word average sentence length and with many words of three or more syllables, would be completely different from Author *C*'s passage. It would likely be abstract and would be aimed at the highest levels of readers.

Once you complete counts like these, you can make more specific kinds of counts and observations. That is, how many nouns, adjectives, or adverbs are there? Are these words mainly monosyllabic, polysyllabic, or mixed. Are there many prepositions? Conjunctions? Articles? What sorts of conclusions can you draw as a result of your analysis?

**TYPES AND FIGURES.** There are four types of sentences (simple, compound, complex, and compound-complex). Many sentences correspond exactly to these types, but by no means all. Some are so detailed and involved that they can only be described as "more complex." You might, as you develop your skills, determine the mixtures of the types in your passage, and also determine the kinds of variations on the types.

A way to describe the structure of content in sentences is to use the terms *loose* and *periodic*. Loose sentences are those in which the principal thought comes first, with complements and modifiers coming afterward, as in this sentence:

> In America, the idea of equality was applied first only to white males.

Periodic sentences are those arranged so that the principal idea comes last, as a climax. Quite often the periodic sentence begins with a dependent clause, as in this sentence:

> Although in America the idea of equality was applied first only to white males, it has been extended, against great reluctance, to women and to persons of all races.

Within sentences there are shorter individual units, or *constituents*, that correspond to the various rhythmical structures. Thus, the relationship within a *prepositional phrase* is the subordination of a noun to a preposition (*in the boat*). This unit may be lengthened by additional words (in the *old, battered, and sunken* boat): thus the unit maintains its integrity, even though it has more words. A noun can be modified by a preceding adjective (the *sunken* boat), or by a following adjective phrase (the boat *at the bottom*) or clause (the boat *that I bought to replace the old one*). An *intransitive verb* may take adverbial modifiers (I ran *swiftly in the park*) but no object. A *transitive verb* takes direct objects and adverbial modifiers (I wrote *my theme in six hours*).

In combinations, such structures make up all sentences. They are the basis of internal sentence rhythms, and as such they are called *cadence groups*.[4] In analyzing prose style for rhythm, you should mark the cadence groups in order to observe whether they are short and rapid, long and leisurely, or something in between. Rely on your own vocal pauses as you read, being careful to mark the ends and beginnings of groups as suggested by punctuation marks, and the natural, if slight, pauses *(junctures)* between subjects and predicates, compound subjects, and so on. As you analyze the various groups, you might arrange them spatially to show how they are spoken. Thus one unit, say an opening phrase, might go on a separate line to indicate its uniqueness, and a clause might take an entire line but have extra long spaces between words to show where pauses occur. The following sentence is from the opening of Nathaniel Hawthorne's story "The Hollow of the Three Hills," and it is arranged to indicate possible vocal rhythms.

> In those strange old times
> when fantastic dreams          and madmen's reveries
>                         were realized
>         among the actual circumstances          of life,
>     two persons met together          at an appointed hour and place

With this layout may be compared a spatial arrangement of two sentences from Katherine Anne Porter's story "He":

> He did grow          and he never got hurt.
> A plank blew off the chicken house          and struck him on the head
>                and he never seemed to know it.[5]

While it is unwise to make extensive generalizations from only these two sentences, it is possible to observe in Hawthorne a tendency toward longer sentences, resulting in rhythmical units that are not self-contained clauses. Hawthorne's rhythmical units are embodied in phrases like the beginning prepositional-adverb phrase ("In those strange old times"), and the sentence is so extensive that it is made up of eight units. The rhythmical units in Katherine Anne Porter's sentences, by contrast, are coincidental with complete sentence structures. It is also possible to see in Hawthorne a tendency to arrange his diction and his stresses in patterns of two (*strange old; dreams . . . reveries; and hour and place*). Only an analysis of a greater number of sentences, however, would confirm whether these tentative conclusions have any validity. Your job in analyzing a prose passage is to

---

[4] See also above, pp. 153–54.

[5] In Sean O'Faolain, ed., *Short Stories: A Study in Pleasure* (Boston: Little, Brown and Co., 1961), p. 255.

make a similar attempt to discover and to characterize its rhythms. It is helpful to read the passage aloud and listen for its rises and falls, its lengths of utterance. It is also helpful to have another student read the passage aloud to you, so that you will be better able to observe its rhythms.

DEVICES. To create interest in their sentences, authors often rely on rhetorical figures, or "devices." There are many of these, but perhaps the commonest is *parallelism,* the repetition of the same grammatical forms (nouns, verbs, phrases, clauses and the like) with which to balance expressions. Here is a sentence by Samuel Johnson (*Rambler* No. 50) which uses four parallel infinitive phrases:

> I have always thought it the business of those who turn their speculations upon the living world, to commend the virtues, as well as to expose the faults of their contemporaries, and to confute a false as well as to support a just accusation.

Another favorite device of many authors is *chiasmus* or *antimetabole,* which takes the form AB BA, as follows:

*A*            *B*   *B*          *A*

When the *issue* deteriorates to *force, force* becomes the *issue.*

The goal in speaking about rhetoric is to determine the appropriateness and effectiveness of the writer's style as it pertains to the general content and aims of the work. When you make your study, you should watch to see what methods the writer uses to make his or her points. Let us look at a famous periodic sentence from a letter Samuel Johnson wrote to Lord Chesterfield. The Lord had offered Johnson financial help to write a dictionary after Johnson was almost done with it. Johnson was offended and wished to make this point as he rejected the belated offer of help. Here is the sentence:

> The notice which you have been pleased to take of my labours, had it been early, had been kind; but it has been delayed till I am indifferent, and cannot enjoy it; till I am solitary, and cannot impart it; till I am known, and do not want it.

Please observe that in this example, as in the first one, Johnson uses a number of parallel constructions, a characteristic of style for which he is famous. He writes *had it been . . . had been* and then the *till I am . . . and cannot* pattern three times. The last time, he varies the *cannot* with *do not* as a climax. It is as though he wished to stretch out and savor the indignation he felt, and because of the parallelism, variation, and climax, he achieved this goal memorably.

## PARAPHRASING FOR COMPARISON

In making your analysis, you might help yourself by making a paraphrase—usually of the bare, minimum content—and then by comparing your paraphrase with the original. Here is a famous sentence from President Franklin D. Roosevelt's first inaugural address (1933):

> So, first of all, let me assert my firm belief that the only thing we have to fear is fear itself—nameless, unreasoning, unjustified terror which paralyzes needed efforts to convert retreat into advance.

Let us try a paraphrase:

> I firmly believe that our only fear is to be afraid of terror which prevents us from advancing.

In comparison, Roosevelt's original assumes an even better light than at first reading. His sentence uses some effective repetitions: he changes the infinitive *to fear* to the noun *fear;* then he sets up the noun *terror* in apposition to *fear* and precedes it with three adjectives which point out his belief that the terror is irrational. The concluding clause builds up to the word *advance,* which aptly defines the goals he wanted the country to follow in 1933. You might wonder if Roosevelt would have persuaded people to accept his programs if he had written our paraphrase. What counts is the arrangement of his words and their power to interest and arouse his listeners.

### SEGMENTAL DEVICES

Another aspect of style that you might consider is the segments of the various words. These are explained in detail in the chapter on prosody (pp. 165–68). Often segments are not important in prose, but sometimes they are. You might note that the first passage from Hemingway, for example, uses assonance (*leaves, breeze, we, trees*). Johnson always relied on assonance and alliteration in his prose (*delayed, indifferent*).

## Organizing Your Theme

### INTRODUCTION

In your introduction you should try to establish the particular circumstances of the passage you are studying and should present a central idea that relates the manner of presentation to these circumstances. Things you should account for are the place of the passage in the work, the general subject matter of the passage, any special ideas, the speaker, the apparent audience (if any), and the basic method of presentation (that is, monologue, dialogue, argument, narration, description, comparison).

## BODY

In the body of your theme you should try to describe and evaluate the style. You should consider the style in relationship to the special circumstances of the work. For example, suppose the speaker is in a plane crashing to the ground, or in a racing car just approaching the winning line, or hurrying to meet a sweetheart; or suppose the speaker is recalling the past or considering the future. Such conditions must be kept foremost throughout your analysis of style. For example, the sample theme considers Hamlet's speech just after the Ghost of his father has left the stage. The Ghost is shown as the cause of Hamlet's shocked and contradictory state of mind.

To focus your theme, you might wish to single out one aspect of style, or to discuss everything, as you wish. In a discussion of diction, be sure to treat things like specific-general and concrete-abstract words, levels of simplicity or difficulty, length, and connotation-denotation. In discussing rhetorical features, go as far as you can with the nomenclature at your command. Consider things like length and subordination, and any specific rhetorical devices you notice and are able to describe. If you can discuss the elements in a parallel structure by using grammatical terms, do so. If you are able to detect the ways in which the sentences are kept simple or made complex, describe these ways. Be sure to use examples from the passage to illustrate your points.

The sort of theme envisaged here is one that is designed to sharpen your levels of awareness at your own particular stage of development as a reader. Later, when you gain sharper perception and a wider descriptive vocabulary, the sophistication of your analyses can increase.

## CONCLUSION

Whereas the body is the place for detailed descriptions of the author's style, the conclusion is the place for you to make your evaluations of the style. To what extent have your discoveries in your close reading increased or reinforced your appreciation of the work? Does the passage take on any added importance as a result of your study? Is anything elsewhere in the work comparable to the content, diction, or ideas that you have found in your passage?

# Sample Theme (Style in a Passage from a Play)

## Hamlet's Self Revelation: A Reading of Hamlet, I. v, 95–109[6]

| | |
|---|---|
| Remember thee? | 95 |
| Ay thou poor ghost, whiles memory holds a seat | 96 |
| In this distracted globe. Remember thee? | 97 |
| Yea, from the table of my memory | 98 |
| I'll wipe away all trivial fond records, | 99 |
| All saws of books, all forms, all pressures past, | 100 |
| That youth and observation copied there, | 101 |
| And thy commandment all alone shall live | 102 |
| Within the book and volume of my brain, | 103 |
| Unmixed with baser matter, yes, yes, by heaven: | 104 |
| O most pernicious woman! | 105 |
| O villain, villain, smiling, damned villain! | 106 |
| My tables, meet it is I set it down | 107 |
| That one may smile, and smile, and be a villain, | 108 |
| At least I am sure it may be so in Denmark. | 109 |

In this passage from Act I of *Hamlet,* Hamlet is alone after the Ghost of his father has left the stage. The speech builds upon the Ghost's command to be remembered, and Hamlet begins by addressing that departed figure. After the first ten lines, however, he moves into a soliloquy, really addressing himself.

[1] A close reading of the speech reveals Hamlet as an imaginative, reflective person undergoing great stress.* These qualities are apparent in the scholarly diction, the development of the "book and volume" comparison, the blending of grammatical structure and line, the poetic rhythms, and the contradiction within the speech.†

[2] The diction indicates Hamlet's background as a student, for many of his words might be expected from someone who has been immersed in arguments and ideas. *Table, records, saws* (sayings) *of books, copied, book and volume, set it down*—all these smack of the classroom. They show that Hamlet, who before the play's opening has returned from the university for his father's funeral (and his mother's marriage), turns naturally to the language of a student even under stress, or perhaps especially under stress.

[3] A turn of mind characteristic of a student is shown in the first ten lines of the speech. This is the knack of seizing a thought and developing it fully. Hamlet is promising to remember the Ghost, but he goes beyond that. He

[6]The edition of *Hamlet* used is from *Rebels and Lovers: Shakespeare's Young Heroes and Heroines,* ed. Alice Griffin (New York: New York University Press, 1976), p. 321.

*Central idea

†Thesis sentence

deals at great length with the thought that his memory is like a "book and volume" on which all his previous life's experiences have been written. He states that he will "wipe away" this entire record, which is "trivial" compared to the "commandment" for vengeance that the Ghost has just made. In short, Hamlet is the sort of person who pursues an idea to its logical extension, using the exactly right vocabulary.

<u>The grammatical control in the passage seems also designed to suggest Hamlet's mental strength.</u> Everything is correct. The adverbial clause *whiles . . . globe* modifies the opening verb *Remember* (95), which itself echoes the Ghost's departing words. The long sentence extending from 98 to 104 shows a perfect blending of grammar and poetic lines. Thus, 98 contains an adverb (prepositional) phrase modifying the main clause of 99. Line 100 contains three noun units which are in apposition to the noun complement in 99 *(records).* Lines 102 and 104 contain the second element in the compound

[4]  sentence, and the major parts of this, too, are coextensive with their respective lines. In 103 the phrase *Within . . . brain* modifies the verb *shall live* in 102, and the adjective phrase in 104 *(Unmixed . . . matter)* modifies the subject *(commandment)* in 102. The reader must here assume that Shakespeare in exerting this control over the lines to show that Hamlet's mind is powerful, and under the right circumstances capable of great control. Fortinbras says, after Hamlet's death, that the young Prince was potentially a great leader. Surely the control over language shown in this passage is evidence of the capacity for analysis and discernment that should characterize leadership.

Against this mental power, however, <u>there are many rhythmic indications that Hamlet is going through stress.</u> The large number of interjections throughout the speech create heavy interruptions in the thought, most likely to suggest a mind that is being upset and overwhelmed. These are: *Ay* (96) *Yea* (98); *Yes, yes, by heaven* (104); the exclamations against Gertrude and Claudius

[5]  which take up lines 105 and 106; and the repetition of *smile* (108). In addition, the major rhythm of the speech from 104 to the end is complementary to the morbidity that characterizes Hamlet in the rest of the play. This section contains many trochaic rhythms, which would have been described in Shakespeare's day as having a "dying fall." There are falling rhythms on

yes, by heaven

and

O villain, villain, smiling, damned villain.

The last two lines end with trochees *(villain Denmark).* These rhythms anticipate the interjections in the "To be or not to be" soliloquy, where Hamlet is so depressed that he thinks of suicide.

Along with these rhythmic indications, <u>a close reading of the content of the speech reveals great agitation.</u> Hamlet is obviously a person of normal sen-

[6]  sibility, and any normal person would be upset by much less than he has just been through. A natural result, however brief, would be a loss of composure, with wrong words, hesitations, or even contradictions in thought. While Shake-

speare sees to it that Hamlet's diction is perfect, he leads Hamlet into an apparent contradiction. Thus, after he exclaims that his mother is "pernicious" and his uncle is a "villain," he frantically writes in his "tables" that one "may smile, and smile, and be a villain." Here the contradiction between his promise to forget trivialities and his writing this platitude indicates his confused state after seeing the Ghost.

[7]

Because this passage reveals the disturbance in Hamlet's character so fully, it is important to the rest of the play. From this point on, Hamlet is goaded by his promise to the Ghost that he will think of nothing but revenge. He will feel guilty and will be overwhelmed with self-doubt and self-destructiveness, because he delays acting on this promise. His attitude toward Claudius, which previously was scorn, will now be hatred and the obsession for vengeance. His love for Ophelia will be wrecked by this obsession, and as a result Ophelia, a tender plant, will die. Truly, this passage may be regarded as the climax of the first act, and it points the way to the grim but inevitable outcome of the play.

## Commentary on the Theme

This theme is based on the details of style that may be discussed after a careful but not exhaustive close reading. Thus the discussion of diction in paragraph two deals only with those words that reflect Hamlet's concerns as a student. In paragraph three the "book and volume" analogy is related to this same studiousness. While the details of this analogy are mentioned, they are not examined extensively. The most detailed paragraph is the fourth, where the connection is made between grammar and Hamlet's mental power. An operative use of grammatical terms is illustrated here to describe constituent parts of sentences. Although the paragraph may seem detailed and hard to follow, the nomenclature is neither obscure nor difficult. To write a comparable paragraph, you would need to lay out the sentences of a passage grammatically, relying on whatever methods you have learned about parsing or structural analysis. The discussion of rhythm in paragraph five is focused on two prominent aspects of Hamlet's speech: the interjections to indicate mental turbulence, and the trochees to complement the growth of Hamlet's morbid frame of mind. The sixth paragraph is based on the interpretation (which the concentration in a close reading permits) that Hamlet's contradictory behavior is a normal response to his just having seen the Ghost. Throughout the theme there is an effort to fit the passage into the context of the play, and the concluding paragraph relates Hamlet's mental state, as revealed in the speech, to important aspects of the later acts.

*chapter 15*

# The Review

The review is a general essay on a literary work. It may also be thought of as a "critique," a "critical review," or simply an "essay." It is a free form, for in a review virtually everything is relevant—subject matter, technique, social and intellectual background, biographical facts, relationship to other works by the same author or by different authors, historical importance, and everything else. Because your aim in writing a review should be to judge generally the author's performance, the theme closest in purpose to the review is the theme of evaluation (Chapter 16). The review is different, however, because of its general nature. In the review, evaluation is only one of the aims, for there may be other elements of the work under surveillance that should be mentioned, special difficulties that you want to explain, and special features that you want to note.

Since the review is so free, it is also a challenge to the skills you have developed thus far as a disciplined reader. Much of your school experience to date has been assimilation—acquiring information and applying certain skills; your tasks have been mainly doing and deciding what to do. But with a review, you are left to your own devices; you must decide what to write about as well as what to say. Freedom of choice should be a constant goal, and it is important for you to realize that your experience is equipping you more and more to know what to do with this freedom. You should be able to synthesize the knowledge you are acquiring; you not only should know how to answer questions but should also decide on the questions to be asked.

Because the review is the most personal as well as general theme about literature, and also because of a close tie with the commercial side of literature and other forms of entertainment, it is one of the most common forms of critical writing. Most of the professional writing about literature in America today is reviewing. Performances of plays, musical compositions, art works, scholarly performances, scientific works, and of course works of imaginative literature are all subject to review. Of all the themes described in this book, the review is the one that you are most likely to be called on to write in your post-college careers, either by general publications or by publications of various organizations.

The review may be thought of as the "first wave" of criticism, with other, more deeply considered criticism to follow later. One immediate problem of the review is therefore to keep it from becoming too hasty, too superficial. Alexander Pope was probably considering this problem when he wrote the following couplet about the frequency of reviews and the stupidity of some of the reviewers (in the passage, substitute "works of art" for "verse," and "reviews" for "prose"):

> A *Fool* might once *himself* alone expose,
> Now *One* in *Verse* makes many more in *Prose*.
> *Essay on Criticism*, lines 7,8

## Types of Reviews

1. **GENERAL**   (First Sample Theme). Most reviews that you will be called on to write are general. For these you may assume that your readers are concerned not with specific occupational or professional matters, but with ideals, aspirations, daily living, success or failure, emotional well-being, and human relationships generally. If you touch on social, economic, or religious problems in your review, your focus should be broadly moral or ethical, not specifically political or sectarian. That is, you may be discussing a problem that has been treated by the political party you favor, but for your review you should keep in mind that many readers will have political views different from yours and may dismiss everything you write if you argue partially. Hence you should discuss the political problem in such a way that you appeal to a wide spectrum of political thought, not just to a narrow one.

2. **SPECIALIZED**  (Second Sample Theme). There is often a need for a specialized type of review. Suppose, for example, that you are planning to write reviews of the same nonfictional work for two magazines, one for psychologists and the other for a religious group. You will immediately see that your reviews would be different. The one for the psychologists would emphasize the psychological implications of the work, while the other would stress the religious ones. You might also be called on in another

course to write a review, say in sociology or history. Each discipline would require a different approach and selection of detail. Or it might be that you are writing a review of a recent novel—normally a subject for a general review—but your audience is to be a group of criminologists. While for the general reader you would focus on common human concerns, for the criminologists you would probably stress those conditions described in the novel that seemingly lead characters into delinquency and crime. You can see that the materials you select for discussion will necessarily be dictated by the group you are trying to reach.

3. PERSONAL (Third Sample Theme). In a personal review, reviewers are mainly interested in creating their own train of thought as prompted by the work. A review of this type may be properly considered as an artistic, moral, religious, science-related, or political essay, or a combination of these. Such an essay may take the following general forms:

  a. A consideration of the implications of the work. Here writers may either (1) begin with their own idea and then introduce references to the work when desirable or necessary, or else (2) begin with an idea in the work and let their discussion develop from that.
  b. A discussion stemming out of disagreement with something in the original work. Writers may take one major idea and contradict it, or they may wish to rebut a series of statements in the work.

## Your Readers and Your Selection of Material

No matter what type of review you write, you should perceive your role for the review as a guide and commentator. Do not try to make your review a substitute for the work itself. Thus it is necessary to refer to events or principal ideas in the work, but you should not make an exhaustive description. If the book you are reviewing has a surprise ending, it would be unforgivable to spoil the book for your readers by disclosing this ending, but you might justifiably intrigue your readers by indicating that they will be surprised when they come to the end of the work. If the author draws a number of important conclusions, do not describe every one. Concentrate only on one or two, leaving the rest for your readers themselves. If your subject is a book of poems, concentrate only on those poems that seem important or typical.

Perhaps the best frame of mind you can muster before you begin to write is this: imagine that you are preparing your readers to read the work themselves; imagine that you are providing them with parachute and rip cord, protective clothing, and the airplane ride, but that they must make the jump.

## Organizing Your Theme

Because reviews may become personal, you may wish to experiment with form and development. If you choose to develop only a single topic, be sure that you emphasize the various aspects with clear transitions. The third sample theme, for example, shows how the subject of faith or trust may be pursued throughout a theme. Should you be writing a general review, as in the first sample theme, and select a number of topics, be sure that your thesis sentence lists these topics.

### INTRODUCTION

In this section you should place the work in perspective. In what period was it written? What is the nationality of the author (if he or she is of another nationality)? What kind of background knowledge is needed for an understanding of the work, or what kind, and how much, is supplied by the author (for example, a knowledge of oil drilling, of conditions in the old West)? To what genre does the work belong? What general issues need explaining before you begin your discussion of the work? Although most frequently you will be asked to review a play or novel, it is good to bear in mind that you may also be reviewing techniques of acting and staging a play. If you are reviewing a new edition of an old work, you may be judging the relevance of the past to the present and also the apparatus supplied by the editor. Always try to show that your work has relevance to the present group of readers.

### BODY

In the body of your theme you should try to arouse interest in the work you are reviewing, or try to discourage readers from reading the work if the work itself dictates this conclusion. Beyond providing the introductory information, your principal objective is to describe the strengths and weaknesses of the work. To write such a description, you must call into play just about everything you have learned about analyzing literature for ideas, form, and style. In a sense, the review can be as specific as you wish to make it, for the greatest part of the body should be given to analysis. In this analysis you may bring out your own strengths and interests as a critical reader. It may be, for example, that you have become proficient in discussing structure. Suppose that you have observed a tightly knit structure in the work you are reviewing. You might choose to discuss that element in the body of your review, thereby appealing to your reader's response to artistic excellence. You should always recognize, however, that your discussion should be of limited extent. There is no need for a detailed, word-by-word analysis. It is not a theme on structure that you want, but a review emphasizing this element.

For specialized reviews you might call into play those disciplines that have interested you thus far in your college career. For example, you may feel competent in handling ideas connected with sociology. Hence, in your review of a novel you might bring your sociological awareness to bear on the work. Or you may have developed an interest in psychology and may wish to treat the characters in a work according to your understanding of psychological problems.

Whatever your personal interests and specialties may be, however, your best guide for subject matter is the work itself, which may very well channel your thinking along definite lines. For example, the second sample theme relates the obvious character flaw of the hero of "Young Goodman Brown" to concerns in the field of religion. The third sample theme adopts the position that the same story literally compels readers to consider the importance of security to life. In the work you are assigned, you may find similarly that certain features will point you in a specific direction (the humor, a connection with existential philosophy, reflections on economic or social conditions, the nature of life on the frontier, and so on).

CONCLUSION

Your conclusion should be an attempt to evaluate the work, certainly not as extensively as in a theme of evaluation, but at least you should give an outline of your responses and a suggestion to your readers of how they might respond, if you have shown that your interests coincide approximately with theirs. If the body of your review has emphasized evaluation, you should close your essay with a simple resume of your points. If you are ever asked to review a work in, say no more than 150 words, the greatest part of the review should be devoted to evaluation.

---

## First Sample Theme: A General Review

*Hawthorne's "Young Goodman Brown": A Timely Tale*

---

[1]    "Young Goodman Brown" is an allegorical story by Nathaniel Hawthorne (1804–1864), the New England writer who probed deeply into the relationships between religion and guilt. Hawthorne's setting is Puritan, colonial Salem. His major aim is to expose the weakness in the religious view that stresses the shortcomings and sins of human life. <u>Although this concern may seem narrow,</u>

the story itself is timely*, presenting a dreamlike narrative, a realistic analysis of the growth of intolerance, and a number of questions of permanent importance.†

On the surface, the apparent vagueness and dreamlike nature of Hawthorne's details may leave some readers a little baffled. The action is a nighttime trip by Young Goodman Brown to a mysterious Satanic gathering in a deep forest just outside the village of Salem. Brown begins his walk as a friendly youth, just three months married to a young woman named Faith. The cult-gathering disillusions and embitters him, however. He loses his faith, and he spends the rest of his life in pessimism and gloom. This much is clear, but the precise nature of Brown's experience is not. Does he really make a trip into [2] the woods? It would seem so, but by the story's end Hawthorne states that the whole episode may have been no more than a dream or nightmare, and he speaks about it as such. Yet when the morning comes, Brown walks back into town as though he is returning from an overnight trip, and he recoils in horror from a number of his fellow villagers, including his wife. Just as uncertain is the identity of the stranger whom Brown encounters on the path. The man resembles Brown's father, but his serpent-like walking stick suggests the devil, who later presides at the Satanic forest ritual.

The fact is, however, that Hawthorne was clearly not interested in producing a realistic imitation of life in detail, but rather wanted to get at the inward, psychological reality of persons who, like Goodman Brown, build a wall of anger and bitterness toward the people around them. From this perspective, Brown's walk into the forest is a symbol of one of the ways in which people [3] may turn sour. It is clear that Brown comes to be controlled by his will to condemn evil. So strong is his view that he rejects anyone not measuring up, even if he must live the rest of his life spiritually alone as a result. Although he is at the extreme edge, he is like many who cannot forgive and get along with anyone who is different.

While Brown is thus unacceptable, the story is nevertheless provocative and compelling, and it raises many timely questions. For example, how can something that is designed for human salvation, like the religious system that Brown inherited, become so ruinous? Is the failure that of the people who misunderstand the basic message of the system, or that of the system itself? To what degree can the religious structure of the story be related to political [4] and social institutions? Should any religious or political philosophy be given greater importance than the good will that is the cornerstone of society? Could any free society survive for long if it were composed of persons like Goodman Brown after his dream, or would it turn into some form of absolutism or despotism and soon be reduced to persecution on moral, religious, or political grounds? (This last question summarizes Hawthorne's judgment against colonial New England Puritanism.)

Although the story is laid in Puritan Salem—the location, one might remember, of the infamous witchcraft trials—it has many layers. It is a memorable study in spiritual deterioration and a vivid example of the need for trust and

*Central idea
†Thesis sentence
For the text of this story, please see Appendix C, pp. 292–301.

[5] goodwill in human relationships. Without such will, life itself would soon resemble the life lived by Goodman Brown, whose vision makes his world bleak and forbidding—a place controlled by negation and death rather than understanding and love.

---

## Commentary on the Theme

This general review follows a normal pattern of exposition. The introductory paragraph briefly presents essential background and states a central idea about the timeliness of Hawthorne's ideas. Paragraph two deals with the problem of the dreamlike vagueness of the narrative. Paragraph three contains an explanation of the vagueness inasmuch as Hawthorne's point is to dramatize the way in which people become intolerant. Paragraph four treats the timeliness of this analysis in terms of some of the important questions raised by the story. The last paragraph is a short tribute to the quality of Hawthorne's insights.

The aim throughout this sample review is not to examine any of the points in great depth, but rather to give readers topics to consider in detail whenever they might analyze the work themselves.

---

### Second Sample Theme: For a Specific Group (In This Example, a Religious Group)

*Hawthorne's "Young Goodman Brown" and Today's Christians*

---

[1] Even though Hawthorne's allegorical story "Young Goodman Brown" is set in early eighteenth-century colonial Massachusetts, it still has great significance for today's Christians.* The tale is about the shattering of Young Goodman Brown's illusions about human beings as a result of his witnessing a nightmarish witches' Sabbath in a forest. Brown becomes a despairing person, and deprives those around him of love and light. This material could easily be interpreted psychologically or politically, but the Christian context of the story invites discussion of Hawthorne's religious ideas. His significant message is both timely and Biblically sound.†

[2] The story is timely because it deals with—rather exposes—the development of religious intolerance. One would like to dismiss the topic as a dead issue in our modern, pluralistic society. The reality is otherwise. Intolerance has not

*Central idea
†Thesis sentence

vanished along with eighteenth-century Salem, but is still here, and will continue to be as long as misperception and distrust like Brown's can exist. He sets up his own religious standards, and no one else can measure up. Surely this formula spells intolerance, no matter what period of history in which it is applied.

[3]
A work that is at once both ancient and current, the Bible, is the basis for "Young Goodman Brown." It is true that the Bible can be used to justify intolerant views like those by which Goodman Brown judges his fellow Salem residents. We are told often to be perfect in our conduct (for example, Genesis 17:1; Matthew 5:48). Almost all the letters of Paul, together with the Pastoral and General epistles, give advice to Christians to purify life (see Romans 12; Ephesians 5:6; I Timothy 5:22; James 4:8). There is no shortage of such advice. Indeed, there is so much that one might believe, as Brown does, that persons seemingly ignoring it cannot continue to call themselves Christian.

More positively, however, the rigorous side of things seems to represent no more than a partial view of the Biblical message. Nowhere does the Bible say that those who do not measure up should be condemned by *people*. The task of judgment, and even of vengeance if necessary, belongs to God alone (see Psalms 94:1, and Romans 12:19, for example). For human beings, the Bible constantly stresses forgiveness, and this is what Brown lacks. Here are only two of the many passages emphasizing forgiveness:

[4]
> When ye stand praying, forgive, if ye have ought against any; that your Father also which is in heaven may forgive you your trespasses.
>
> Mark 11:25

> Forbearing one another, and forgiving one another, if any man have a quarrel against any: even as Christ forgave you, so also *do* ye.
>
> Colossians 3:13

One can go beyond advice like this to examples such as those of the Good Samaritan (Luke 10:29-31) and the Samaritan woman at the Well (John 4:7-42). These people were outsiders, not members of the same community, yet Jesus regarded them lovingly.

[5]
Charity, love, forgiveness, and toleration—these are virtues that Christians need today, and that Goodman Brown ignores. He suffers from the "holier-than-thou" symptom that does nothing so well as to alienate others. It is no wonder that his offspring following him to his grave "carved no hopeful verse upon his tombstone, for his dying hour was gloom." Certainly we should all keep trying to become perfect, but we should also leave judgment in greater Hands, and rather spend our time working toward understanding. In "Young Goodman Brown," Hawthorne has dramatized this point vividly and powerfully.

## Commentary on the Theme

This sample review is intended for an audience concerned about religious issues. As such it considers the story not as a general work of art, but as one with religious and moral implications. The theme works in two directions: first, as a presentation of arguments favoring religious tolerance, and, second, as an attempt to supply enough Biblical background to show that the views in Hawthorne's story are based in Scripture. The aim of the review is thus just as much persuasion as exposition and argument.

The first paragraph introduces the central idea about the story's religious significance, and it concludes with a thesis sentence. Paragraph two demonstrates that misperceptions such as Brown's can occur at any time; therefore the story is about a permanent human condition. Paragraphs three and four deal with possible Biblical passages that have a bearing, first, on explaining Brown's conduct (three) and, second, criticizing it (four). This material is not the sort that one might bring out in an analysis of, say, the ideas in the work, because it deals more with the Bible than with the story. Nevertheless it is appropriate here because a review is to be considered as a much freer form than an analysis. The last paragraph utilizes the negative example of Brown as an incentive for tolerance.

Although this sample review is specifically about a religious issue, it is so because of the intended audience. For an audience with other interests, a different treatment would be appropriate, even for the same work of literature.

---

## Third Sample Theme: A Personal Review

*Security and Hawthorne's "Young Goodman Brown"*

---

[1] The major prop of life is security, which depends on our hope, confidence, and trust in ourselves, the people around us, the economy, and the world generally. <u>The loss of any of our certainties destroys security and may produce panic.</u>* It is a kind of panic which Nathaniel Hawthorne portrays in his allegorical tale "Young Goodman Brown." The hero is Young Goodman Brown, who is a resident of colonial Salem. He witnesses a dreamlike Satanic cult meeting, and because he sees his wife there, and also sees the elders and dignitaries of the town, he loses the security which comes from confidence in the good will of others. <u>His story makes one think about the many things—personal, political, and natural—that affect our security.</u>†

[2] <u>Personal security can depend on almost as many situations as there are people.</u> Vital to Brown is his belief in the purity of his wife, Faith. Many people similarly base their lives on their confidence in those around them. But much can happen to disturb such security. Friends who are counted on might not be helpful when needed, because they were badly misjudged. A serious illness of someone close may have a devastating effect on faith in the continuity of

*Central idea
†Thesis sentence

life itself. And, like Brown, we might imprison ourselves in our own suspicions, and never be able to escape. Personal security is delicate, even though the example of Brown, who does not try to explore the truth of his shattered illusions, shows that efforts at understanding might help to restore personal security that is threatened.

[3]     If personal security is fragile, political security is even more so. At election times, there are always claims and counterclaims, so that we are never absolutely sure about the political wisdom we follow. Like many people, Brown loses faith in the local dignitaries, and he can never participate again with confidence in church and home. Today, on a world scale, we have even greater problems with our security, for our very lives may depend on the political stability of foreign governments who have the power to launch destructive missiles against us. Certainly, political security is worth the many hours and years spent by diplomats in trying to gain it.

[4]     In the natural world, too, we assume a great deal on which we depend absolutely. We cannot drive around a blind corner without the confidence that the road will continue, even though we cannot see it before we make our turns. We normally assume that the sun will rise and set, that rain will fall, that crops will grow (or at least appear in stores and cafés), that the air will be breatheable, and that the earth generally will be a good place. But often there are fires, tornadoes, earthquakes, floods, hurricanes, and even volcanic eruptions. It is the equivalent of these that occurs in the life of Young Goodman Brown. Such events can make people doubt the very ground they walk on.

[5]     The upshot of Hawthorne's story is that security—confidence about the world and people—is subject to accident and also design. It is true, nevertheless, that people can work to make themselves more secure. Perhaps Brown's greatest flaw is that he apparently does not try to get to the bottom of what he has seen. He accepts his vision without question and, with his security destroyed, he descends into a life of "gloom" and depression. It is the possibility that people can always try at least to make things better that provides a gauge by which to measure Brown and also ourselves. One should be grateful to Hawthorne for having pointed the way so memorably to these ideas.

---

## Commentary on the Theme

This sample review is a personal essay on a topic—security—suggested by Hawthorne's story. The material from "Young Goodman Brown" is thus introduced as a part, although a major part, of the train of thought. The method of development is primarily illustration.

Unlike the religiously based audience visualized for the second sample theme, the audience intended here is a general one concerned with many broad topics, such as the personal, political, and natural ones discussed. The goal is to cause readers to reconsider and redefine the topic of security. For this reason the review might be considered as an expanded definition theme.

Paragraph one introduces the topic of security, attempts a definition, relates the topic to Hawthorne's story, and concludes with a thesis sentence. Even though "Young Goodman Brown', is a religious story about how the hero's perceptions of life are destroyed by the Devil, the body of the sample theme does not deal with the religious issues, but instead goes into three separate though connected topics. The second paragraph deals with the first of these—personal situations which threaten personal security. Paragraph three considers political threats, and paragraph four brings in references to threats from the forces of nature. The concluding paragraph deals with more references to Goodman Brown, relating his passiveness to a need for a more aggressive pursuit of security.

# chapter 16

# The Theme of Evaluation

Evaluation is one of the major goals of literary study. It is closely allied with *judgment,* which is the faculty by which we can distinguish between good and bad, right and wrong, plausibility and implausibility, and so on. As used here, *evaluation* means the act of deciding what is good, bad, or mediocre. It requires a steady pursuit of the best—to be satisfied with less is to deny the best efforts of our greatest writers. Evaluation implies that there are ideal standards of excellence by which decisions about quality can be made, but it must be remembered that these standards are flexible, and may be applicable to works of literature written in all places and ages.

An evaluation is different from a theme on what you might like or dislike in a work (the subject of Chapter 3). While your preferences are important in your evaluation, they are not as important as your judgment, and your judgment may lead you into positions that seem contrary to your preferences. In other words, it is possible to grant the excellence of a work or writer that you personally do not like.

This claim is not as contradictory as it may at first seem, for perceptions about literary works constantly change. You may have found that works commonly adjudged as good do not seem good to you. If such has been the case, you should try to live with the work for a time. If you have ever played in a band or orchestra or sung in a chorus, you may have found a musical composition distasteful when you first read it through but discovered, as you worked on it and learned it, that you finally became fond of it. This process confirms the statement that you will learn to understand and like a good work of art when you have the opportunity to do so. If, however, you find that despite prolonged exposure to the work, you still do not concur in the general favorable judgment, be as certain as you can that your reaction is based on rational and logically defensible grounds.

Your ability to judge will be increased as you learn about more and more fine works. You must read and learn as much as you can, in order to establish the qualities of good literature firmly in your mind, and as these qualities become clearer to you, you will be able to evaluate with greater ease. In this chapter you have the task of evaluating a single work for your theme. This single assignment should have a definite bearing on your judgment in future years, because careful effort now will permanently improve your critical faculties.

## Rationale of Evaluation

There is no precise answer to the problem of how to justify an evaluation. Evaluation is the most abstract, philosophical, and difficult writing you will do about literature, just as it is the most necessary. Standards of taste, social mores, and even morals differ from society to society and age to age; nonetheless, some works of art have been adjudged good or even great by generation after generation whereas others have not. The student therefore asks, "By what standards may a work be judged a good or great work?" and, "How do I make this judgment by myself?"

## Standards for Evaluation

There are many standards to help you evaluate a literary work. Some of the major ones are described below, and many have been suggested in earlier chapters. The terms involved are used and defined here in the sense in which they are usually used in regard to literature.

### TRUTH

Although *truth* or *truthful* is used in speaking of literature to mean *realism* or *realistic* (e.g., does Flaubert give a truthful picture of Emma Bovary's society?), its meaning here is carefully restricted. To speak of the truth is to imply generality and universality. Let us take a concrete illustration.

Sophocles' *Antigone* is a play that has survived the passage of 2,400 years. It concerns a society (the Greek city-state with a ruling monarch) that no longer exists; it deals with a religious belief (that the souls of the unburied dead never find rest) that passed from currency centuries ago; it involves an idea (of a curse following an entire family) accepted now only by the least educated members of our society. Wherein, then, lies the appeal, the truth, of *Antigone,* which makes it as much alive for our age as it was for the Greeks of more than 2,000 years ago?

The answer is at least partly in the permanence of the human problem that Antigone faces: "How do I reconcile my duty to obey the state with my duty to obey my conscience? And if the two conflict, which do I follow?" This dilemma, and the suffering inevitable for any persons caught in it, regardless of which choice they make, is one that human beings have faced since the beginning of time; while humanity and states exist, this conflict between laws and conscience will endure. In short, the play embodies, lives in terms of, and comments on, one of the great *truths* of human life. It measures up to one standard we use in deciding whether a work of art is good or bad, great or mediocre.

## AFFIRMATIVENESS

*Affirmativeness* means here that human beings are worth caring about and writing about, no matter how debased the condition in which they live or how totally they abuse their state. All art should be affirmative. Although many works apparently say "no" to life, most say "yes," and a good argument can be made that the "no" works indirectly present a "yes." Thus, if a character like Macbeth falls to the depths of misfortune, despair, and death, the author must demonstrate that there is a loss of some sort worth lamenting. Human worth is here affirmed even as a major character loses it. If a character is happy at the end of the work, the author must show that this character's qualities have justified such good fortune. Life is again affirmed. If an unworthy character is fortunate at the end, the author still affirms human worth by suggesting a world in which such worth may become triumphant. In short, authors may portray the use and abuse of life, the love and the hate, the heights and the depths, but their vision is always that life is valuable and worthy of respect and dignity. The best works are those that make this affirmation forcefully, without being platitudinous or didactic.

## "THE JOINT FORCE AND FULL RESULT OF ALL"

This quotation is from Pope's *Essay on Criticism,* in which most of what can be said about evaluation is said. Pope insisted that a critic should not judge a work simply by its parts but should judge the *whole,* the entirety of the work. You can profit from Pope's wisdom. You should carefully consider the total effect of the work, both as an artistic form and as a cause of impressions and emotions in yourself. Bear in mind that a great work may be imperfect, but if the sum total of the work is impressive, the flaws assume minor importance. In other words, even if authors can be attacked on technical matters, the total effect of their works may overshadow adverse criticism.

Thus one cannot judge a work as good or bad by referring to only one element within it. An interesting plot, a carefully handled structure, a touching love story, a valid moral—none of these attributes alone can justify a total judgment of "good." One can say, for example, that Dickens' *Oliver Twist* has an extremely ingenious plot and that it arouses our emotions effectively, but to evaluate the novel fully one must take into consideration several questions. Foremost among them are these: How does the character of Oliver withstand modern knowledge of child development? Could a child subjected from birth to the brutal experiences that Oliver endures develop into the person that Dickens presents? You cannot make a final judgment on the work as a whole without taking all its important aspects into account.

Another important phase of the "joint force and full result of all" is the way in which you become involved as you read. Most of what you read, if it has merit, will cause you to become emotionally involved with the characters and actions. You have perhaps observed that characters in some works seem real to you or that incidents are described so vividly that you feel as though you had witnessed them. In these cases you were experiencing the pleasure of involvement. The problem here is whether your pleasure was fleeting and momentary or whether it has assumed more permanence (whether it resulted from a passage that is permanently, or spiritually, satisfying).

Closely integrated with the idea of involvement is the Aristotelian theory of *purgation* or *catharsis* in tragedy. How do you regard the character of Macbeth when he kills Duncan, or of Othello when he strangles Desdemona? Shakespeare causes you to become involved with both heroes, and when they perform evil deeds your own conscience cries out for them to stop. The result, when the play is over, is a "purgation" of your emotions; that is, if you experience these plays well, you will also have experienced an emotional "drain." You can see that the use to which a writer puts your involvement is important in your judgment of his or her works.

## VITALITY

A good work of literature has a life of its own and can be compared to a human being. You know that your friends are always changing and growing and that you learn more and more about them as your friendship progresses. A work of literature can grow in the sense that your repeated experience with it will produce insights that you did not have in your previous readings. A classic example of such a work is *Huckleberry Finn*, known to children as an exciting and funny story of adventure but known to adults as a profound story about the growth of a human soul. Another example is *Gulliver's Travels,* in which critics for two centuries have been finding new insights and beauties. It is naturally difficult for you to predict the future, but if you have based your present opinion on reasonable grounds and have determined that the work is good, you may conclude that within the work there will be what Wordsworth called "food for future years."

BEAUTY

Whole books have been devoted to an attempt to define *beauty.* Briefly, beauty is closely allied with unity, symmetry, harmony, and proportion. To discover the relationship of parts to whole—their logical and chronological and associational functions within the work—is to perceive beauty in a work.

In the eighteenth century there was an idea that "variety within order" constituted beauty; the extent to which Pope's couplets vary within the pattern of the neoclassic couplet is an illustration of the eighteenth-century ideal. The Romantic and post-Romantic periods held that beauty could be found only through greater freedom. This belief in freedom has produced such characteristics of modern literature as originality for its own sake, experimentation in verse and prose forms, freedom of syntax, stream-of-consciousness narration, and personal diction. Despite the apparent change of emphasis, however, the concepts of unity and proportion are still valid and applicable. Studies of style, structure, point of view, tone, and imagery are therefore all means to the goal of determining whether works are beautiful. Any one of these studies is an avenue toward evaluation. Remember, however, that an excellence in any one of them does not make a work excellent. Frequently critics use such terms as "facile" and "surface excellence" to describe what they judge to be technically correct but artistically imperfect works.

## Organizing Your Theme

In your theme you will attempt to answer the question of whether the work you have studied is good or not. If so, why? If not, why not? The grounds for your evaluation must be artistic. Although some works may be good pieces of political argument, or successfully controversial, your business is to judge them as works of art.

INTRODUCTION

In the introduction you briefly encapsulate your evaluation, which will be your central idea, and list the points by which you expect to demonstrate your central idea. To assist your reader's comprehension of your ideas, you should provide any unique facts or background about the work you are evaluating.

## BODY

In the body you attempt to demonstrate the grounds for your evaluation. Your principal points will be the excellences or deficiencies of the work you are evaluating. Such excellences might be qualities of style, idea, structure, character portrayal, logic, point of view, and so on. Your discussion will analyze the probability, truth, force, or power with which the work embodies these excellences.

Avoid analysis for its own sake, and do not merely retell stories. If you are showing the excellence or deficiency of a character portrayal, you must necessarily bring in a description of the character, but remember that your discussion of the character is to be pointed toward *evaluation*, not *description*, of the work as a whole. Therefore you must select details for discussion that will illustrate whether the work is good or bad. Similarly, suppose you are evaluating a sonnet of Shakespeare and mention that the imagery is superb. At this point you might introduce some of the imagery, but your purpose is not to analyze imagery as such; it should be used only for illustration. If you remember, as a cardinal rule, to keep your thematic purpose foremost, you should have little difficulty in making your discussion relate to your central idea.

## CONCLUSION

The conclusion should be a statement on the total result of the work you are evaluating. Your concern here is with total impressions. This part of evaluation should underline your central idea.

---

## Sample Theme

*A People's Dream: An Evaluation of* Black Elk Speaks

---

[1]   Those who read *Black Elk Speaks* might recall the excitement of discovery that Keats felt when he first read Chapman's translation of Homer. <u>The book is authenticity itself, a unique and powerful record of responses and recollec-</u>

All quotations and parenthetical page numbers refer to *Black Elk Speaks: Being the Life Story of a Holy Man of the Oglala Sioux, as told through John Neihardt (Flaming Rainbow), Illustrated by Standing Bear* (New York: Pocket Books, 1972).

tions of an Oglala Sioux warrior and visionary, Black Elk.* The period described is that between about 1867 and 1890, when the westward expansion produced the defeat and finally the humiliation of the Indian nations that had owned the western prairies before that time. In 1931, Black Elk, then a man of 68, related his story to his son, who translated it into English to be transcribed by John G. Neihardt. The account—is it autobiography, history, meditation, revelation, or all four?—is therefore both a translation and a transcription. Though the entire work is unique, Black Elk's reality and authenticity may be seen in his view of the Indian wars, his faith in his mystic powers, his value for life and the land, and his simple eloquence.†

[2]     As an historic account, *Black Elk Speaks* presents a view of history that is a truthful antidote to the view of the Indian wars that the western movie has promoted. As Black Elk saw it, the *Wasichu's* (white man's) thirst for gold and for land produced violence, conquest, and broken promises. The military defeats by the U.S. Army turned Indian against Indian and resulted in impoverishment, flight, and death by starvation or massacre. With their buffalo and their ponies gone, the Indians had little choice but to move onto reservations. Though the victor has always made "right," it has rarely been little more than half right, and the direct, personal account of Black Elk provides a truthful restorative.

[3]     The work is also an account of Black Elk's inner vision of truth. Feeling that he had a unique role to play in the betterment of his Sioux nation, he apparently thought that the descriptions of his visions—the most important being his great revelation at the age of nine—were of principal value. He was a man with mystic powers and apparently used them to effect cures and predict the future. Many sophisticated readers might dismiss this aspect of the work as superstition, but in an age of "Transcendental Meditation" and the "Relaxed Response," more and more people are coming to recognize the mysterious, hidden sources of human power. It would therefore be arbitrary to deny the authenticity of Black Elk's descriptions of his mysterious powers.

[4]     While Black Elk's visions may be admittedly controversial, there can be no controversy about the power and wisdom of his values. Principally, he expresses belief in valor and endurance and respect for life and for the land. Almost a thesis in his account is his claim that the Indians were living on their own land and desired only to be left alone, in a cooperative harmony between "two legs" (human beings) and "four legs" (the other animals). With such a value, it is natural that he would look with horror at the slaughter of the buffalo herds—a deliberate policy, incidentally, that the American government carried out in order to render the Indians helpless:

> . . . I can remember when the bison were so many that they could not be counted, but more and more Wasichus came to kill them until there were only heaps of bones scattered where they used to be. The Wasichus did not kill them to eat; they killed them for the metal that makes them crazy [gold], and they took only the hides to sell. Sometimes they did

*Central idea
†Thesis sentence

not even take the hides, only the tongues; and I have heard that fire-boats came down the Missouri River loaded with dried bison tongues. You can see that the men who did this were crazy. Sometimes they did not even take the tongues; they just killed and killed because they liked to do that. When we hunted bison, we killed only what we needed. And when there was nothing left but heaps of bones, the Wasichus came and gathered up even the bones and sold them (p. 181).

It is difficult to see how anyone with a grain of respect for life could see the slaughter in any other way, and yet, through such actions, the west was "won." But perhaps the gentler values of Black Elk, who provided shelter for a family of porcupines on a freezing night (p. 130) and who described his attitudes with such directness, may eventually become prominent.

It is, finally, Black Elk's straightforward, direct eloquence that is the best, most convincing aspect of the book. Everything that one might require from a great writer is here: conciseness, accuracy, strong feeling, irony, humor, pathos, use of images, vividness. Nothing is done to excess; Black Elk is a lover of detail, but just the right amount, and he did not engage in his emotions to the point of sentimentality. For example, his description of the dead after the senseless slaughter at Wounded Knee (December 29, 1890) displays controlled bitterness and pathos:

[5]    It was a good winter day when all this happened. The sun was shining. But after the soldiers marched away from their dirty work, a heavy snow began to fall. The wind came up in the night. There was a big blizzard, and it grew very cold. The snow drifted deep in the crooked gulch, and it was one long grave of butchered women and children and babies, who had never done any harm and were only trying to run away (p. 223).

One might quote many other examples from the book to show Black Elk's mastery. Expecially unforgettable are his description of the power of a circle (pp. 164 f.) and his lament over the loss of his people's dream (p. 230).

An evaluation of *Black Elk Speaks* would not be complete without an emphasis on its power to evoke an almost overwhelming sorrow and regret over the loss that it describes. Today people are finding much value in a pluralistic culture, and as a result the values represented by Black Elk seem more worthy than ever of being followed and cherished. It is painful to read in Black Elk's narrative just how the civilization that held these values was snuffed out. Truly, a book that so successfully provokes these thoughts is worthy of being enshrined in one's heart.

[6]

---

# Commentary on the Theme

The elements in any evaluation can be listed for convenience only. In an evaluation itself they are all brought together, as they are in this theme. The principal standard of evaluation here, however, is truth or authenticity.

Paragraph one includes the central idea and a brief description of what the book *Black Elk Speaks* is like. Paragraphs two and three emphasize Black Elk's adherence to historical and subjective truth. The fourth paragraph asserts the value of Black Elk's love of life and the land, and paragraph five discusses the directness of his style. The last paragraph praises the book for its power to stimulate sympathy and love of life.

*chapter 17*

# The Theme on Film

Film has today become the respected word for movies and motion pictures. It is a highly specialized kind of drama, utilizing, like drama, the techniques of dialogue, monologue, and action. Like drama also, it employs spectacle and pantomime. Unlike drama it embodies many additional techniques that are peculiarly a result of the technology of photography, editing, film development, and sound. If you are planning to write about film, many of your considerations may be purely literary, such as structure, tone, ideas, imagery, style. In addition, the techniques of film are so specialized—so much of an extension of what you normally see on a printed page—that a discussion of film requires more technical awareness than is normally needed by the disciplined reader.

## Film and Other Literary Forms

Film may be likened to a dramatic production. A typical production is a realization on stage of a dramatic text. The producer and director, together with actors, artists, scene designers, costume-makers, carpenters, choreographers, and lighting technicians, attempt to bring a dramatic text to life. Though occasionally a stage production may employ brief sections of film, slides, and tape recordings for special effects (such as the witches in *Macbeth,* the ghost in *Hamlet*), the stage itself limits the freedom of the

production. Aside from budget, the makers of film have few such limitations. In this respect film is like the novel or the story, in which the absence
of any restrictions other than the writer's imagination permits the inclusion
of any detail whatever, from the description of a chase to the reenactment
of a scene in the Napoleonic wars. In reading, when you attempt to visualize a scene, you are using your imagination. When you look at a film,
the film-maker has in effect provided you with a ready-made imagination.
Is there to be a scene on a desert island? The film-maker has gone on
location to such an island, and in the film the island itself is presented,
complete with beach, sand dunes, palm trees, native huts, and authentic
natives-turned-actors. Little is left to your imagination. Is there to be a
scene on a distant planet? Obviously the film-maker cannot go on location
there but will create a working location in the studio, with lighting, props,
and costumes. Film, in short, enables a dramatic production to achieve
something approaching the complete freedom that one finds in novels and
stories.

## Film and Art

To the degree that film is confined to a screen, it may visually be compared
to the art of the painter or the still photographer. There is a whole language
of visual art. Paintings and photographs have compositional balance. One
object may appear in relationship to another as a background forces the
eye upon a visual center of attention. A color used in one part of a painting
may be balanced with the same color, or its complement, in another part
of the painting. The use of certain details may have particularly symbolic
significance. Paintings may become allegorical by including certain mythical
figures or other objects in the background. Particular effects may be achieved
with the use of the textures of the paint. The techniques and effects are
virtually endless.

Still photographers have many of the same resources as the painter,
except that they cannot create quite the same textures with their cameras
and developers that the painter can with paint. Basically photographers
transfer an image of reality to a finished print or slide. However, they do
have freedom of focus with lenses and can throw one object into focus
while putting others out. They also have the freedom to select camera
speeds and can either stop an action at 1/1,000 of a second or let it remain
blurred at 1/25 of a second. With the exacting control of developers, they
can create many monochromatic, polychromatic, blurred, or textured sur-
faces, and with techniques such as these they truly have a great deal of
interpretive freedom in handling the initial photographic reality that is the
basis of their art.

The film-maker is able to utilize almost all the resources of the still photographer, and most of those of the painter. Artistically, the most confining aspect of film is the rectangular screen, but aside from that, film is quite free. With a basis in a dramatic text called a "script" or "film-script," it employs words and their effects, but it also employs the language of art and especially the particular verisimilitude and effectiveness of moving pictures. In discussing a film, then, you should see that film communicates not just by words, but also by use of its unique and various techniques. You can treat the ideas, the problems, and the symbolism in a film, but while treating them you should recognize that the visual presentation is inseparable from the medium of film itself.

## Techniques

There are many techniques of film, and a full description and documentation of them could, and have, become extensive.[1] In preparing to write a theme about film, however, you should try to familiarize yourself only with those aspects of technique that have an immediate bearing on your responses to the film and your interpretations of it. Film is both visual and audial.

### VISUAL

Camera technique permits great freedom in presenting scenes. If you are seeing a stage production of a play, your distance from the actors is fixed by your seat in the theater. In a film, on the other hand, the visual viewpoint is constantly shifting. The film may begin with a distant shot of the actors—a "longshot"—much like the sight you might have on a stage. But then the camera may zoom in or out to present you with a sudden closeup or panorama. Usually an actor speaking will be the subject of a closeup, but the camera may also show closeups of other actors who are reacting to the first actor's statements. You must decide on the effects of closeups and longshots yourself, but it should be plain that the frequent use of either—or of middle-distance photographs—is a means by which film directors specifically convey meaning.

The camera may also be moved rapidly, or slowly, from character to character, or from character to some natural or manufactured object. In this way a film may show a series of reactions to an event. It may also show visually the attitude of a particular character or it may represent a visual commentary on his or her actions. If a young couple is in love, as

---

[1]See, for example, Rudolph Arnheim, *Film as Art* (Berkeley: University of California Press, 1969); Daniel Talbot, ed., *Film: An Anthology* (Berkeley: University of California Press, 1969); and Louis D. Giannetti, *Understanding Movies* (Englewood Cliffs, N.J.: Prentice-Hall, Inc., 1982).

an example, the camera may shift from the couple to flowers, trees, and water, thus associating their love visually with objects of beauty and growth. Should the flowers be wilted and the trees be without leaves and the water brackish, the visual commentary might well be that the love is doomed and hopeless. Because characters are constantly seen in settings, real or symbolic, you should always be aware that the cinematic manipulation of setting is even more a part of the statement of the film than it might be in a story, in which even an alert reader may often lose awareness of such relationships.

The camera may also be used to create effects that no other medium can convey. Slow motion, for example, can focus on a certain aspect of a person's character. A girl running in slow motion happily through a meadow enables the viewer to concentrate on the possible joy conveyed by the slow rhythms of her body and the patterns of her dress and her hair.

There are many other techniques of camera use and of editing that have a bearing on action and character. The focus may be made sharp at one point, fuzzy at another. Moving a speaking character out of focus may suggest that listeners are beginning to get bored. The use of sharp or fuzzy focus may also show that a character has seen things exactly or inexactly. In an action sequence, the camera may follow the moving character, a technique that is called "tracking." It is possible to track from a car or truck, which may follow the movement of running human beings or horses or the movement of cars. A camera operator on foot may be the tracker, or the camera may shoot movement from a helicopter or an airplane. Movement may also be captured by a fixed camera that follows a character from one point to another in a panoramic view. Then, too, the camera may be held fixed and the moving character may simply walk, run, or ride across the screen. If the character is moving in a car, the car may become blurred. For special comic effects, the film may be reversed in order to emphasize the illogicality of the actions being filmed. Reversing, of course, is a result of the developing, editing, and cutting processes. Through these same processes film-makers can create many other visual effects, such as *fading* or *dissolving* from one scene to another, or superimposing one scene upon another.

The process of editing deserves special consideration, for it is the soul of the film-maker's art. A typical film is made up of many separate sequences, all put together during editing sessions. In one scene a character may be seen boarding a plane. Then there may be a scene showing the plane taking off, then flying. Then may follow a scene of the landing, followed by the character's getting off the plane. The entire action may conclude with several different views of the character riding in a taxi to a specific destination. In the film, the whole sequence may take no more than half a minute, yet the episode may consist of perhaps a dozen separate views from the camera. It is editing that puts everything together. The camera records many views; the director selects from among these in creating a film.

## LIGHT, SHADOW, COLOR

As in the theater, the film-maker utilizes light, shadow, and color as a means of communication. Characters filmed in a bright light are presumably being examined fully, whereas characters in shadow or darkness may be hiding some of their motives. The use of flashing light might show a changeable, mercurial, and perhaps sinister character or situation. In color, the use of greenish-tinted light may suggest ghoulish motivations. Colors, of course, have much the same meaning that they have in any other artistic medium. Always, colors are carefully arranged. Like the stage director, the film-maker will arrange the blocking of characters and scenery to create a pleasing arrangement and complementing of colors. However, clashing colors may suggest a disharmony in the mind of one or several characters. The director may also employ light for similar effects. A scene in sunshine, which brings out all the colors, and the same scene in rain and clouds or in twilight, all of which mute the colors, create different moods.

## PANTOMIME AND ACTION

In film there are often many periods in which action takes place with no dialogue. The camera may show a man reacting to a situation, or a boy running through a woods, or a couple walking in a park. The scene may run on for several minutes, with all the footage being devoted to movement. Such wordless action is essentially *pantomime* rather than drama. To some degree, all actors employ pantomime by gesture and facial expression. In a dramatic production, pantomime is featured mainly as "business," and many dramas call for pageantry and swordplay. The unspoken devices of the stage are soon exhausted (unless the production happens to be ballet or actual pantomime), and any production must soon return to spoken dialogue. In film, however, there is great potentiality for rhapsodical focus on movement. In addition, musical accompaniments can be so interwoven with the action that dramatic statement can be rendered effectively without the use of the spoken word.

The strength of film has always been the portrayal of direct action. Love affairs, chases, trick effects, fights, ambushes, movement of all sorts—all these make an immediate appeal to the viewer's sense of reality. Actions of love and violence are immediately stimulating. Obviously one of the things you should look for in film is the effectiveness of the portrayal of the action: What is the relationship of the action to the theme of the film?

Does the action have any bearing on the characters, or does it seem to have departed from character into an indulgence in action for its own sake? Is the action particularly realistic? Does the camera stay at a distance, showing the persons as relatively small in a vast natural or artificial world? Do closeups show smiles, frowns, eagerness, or anxiety? Is any attempt made to render temperature by action, say cold by a character's stamping of feet, or warmth by the character's removing a coat or shirt? Does the action show any changing of mood, from sadness to happiness, or from indecision to decision? What particular aspects of the action point toward these changes?

Closely related to the portrayal of action is the way in which the film shows the human body. The closeup is a technique for rendering certain aspects of the drama. Other methods, too, can be employed. A photograph showing an actor in complete proportion may be emphasizing the normality of that person, or it may show the views toward humanity of the film-maker. The film may also create certain distortions. The "fisheye" lens creates such a distortion, usually of the center of a face, which often shows a character's view of another character, or shows the film-maker's thoughts about a character. Sometimes the view creates bodily distortions, emphasizing certain limbs or other parts of the body, or focusing on a scolding mouth or a suspicious eye. If distortion is used, it invites interpretation: perhaps the film-maker is attempting to show that certain human beings, even when supposedly normal, bear weaknesses and even psychological disturbances.

## MONTAGE

Montage is to film as imagery is to literature; it may demonstrate a character's thoughts or dreams, or it may embody the director's commentary on situation or character. Physically, montage refers to an abrupt changing of scene, but it should be distinguished from a narrative change of scene and also from camera movement for narrative purposes. Exclusively a result of editing and therefore a unique property of film, montage provides commentary or illustration by association. For example, an early sequence in Sir Charles Chaplin's *Modern Times* shows a large group of workingmen rushing to their factory jobs. Immediately following this scene is a view of a large, milling herd of sheep. By this montage, Chaplin is suggesting that the men are being herded and dehumanized by modern industry.

While montage is different from a narrative change of scene, it may be used as a "flashback" to explain present, ongoing actions or characteristics. In this respect it retains its nature as a mode of commentary or explanation. Thus, a character suffering from amnesia may suddenly undergo brief recollections from an unremembered past, and these may be shown in brief, almost subliminal montages. A famous montage occurs in *Citizen Kane*, by Orson Welles. One of the final scenes shows the protagonist Kane's boyhood sled, which bore the brand name "Rosebud." This montage clarifies Kane's dying word by indicating that he still maintained a fond connection with the long-departed innocence of his boyhood.

SOUND

The first business of the sound track in a film is naturally to include the spoken dialogue, but there are many other effects that become a part of the sound track. Music is selected to suit the mood of the film. Special sound effects are used to augment the action; the sound of a blow, for example, will be enhanced electronically in order to cause an impact on the viewer's ears that is similar to the force of the blow itself. If a character is engaged in introspection, muted strings may create a mellow sound to complement the mood. But if the character is going insane, the sound may become percussive and cacophonous. At times the sound may be played through a mechanical apparatus of some sort in order to create weird or ghostly effects. Often a character's words will be echoed rapidly and sickeningly in order to show dismay or anguish. In a word, sound is a vital part of film. Once you leave the theater, or the television set if you have been watching the film on TV, it is difficult to remember all aspects of sound, say a certain melody that serves as mood or background to the action, but you should make the effort to observe some of the various uses to which the sound is put.

## Preparing Your Theme

Obviously the first requirement is to see a film. It is wise to see it twice or more if you can, because your discussion will take on value the more thoroughly you know the material. It is difficult to take notes in a darkened theater, but you should make an immediate effort, after leaving, to take notes on the various aspects of the film that impressed you. Take the program or write down the names of the director and the principal actresses and actors. Try to make your notes as complete as you can, for when you write your theme you will not be able to verify details and make illustrative quotations as you can with a written work that you can recheck. If any particular speeches were worth quoting from the movie, you should try to remember the general circumstances of the quotation, and also, if possible, any key words. Try to recall uses of costume and color, or (if the film was in black and white) particularly impressive uses of light and shade. An effort of memory will be required in writing a theme on film.

# Organizing Your Theme

## INTRODUCTION

Here state your central idea and thesis sentence as usual. You should also include background information necessary for understanding what you will bring out in the body of your theme. It is appropriate to include here the names of the director, or director-producer, and the actresses and actors worthy in your judgment of particular mention.

## BODY

The most difficult choice that you will face in writing about film is deciding on a topic. If you have no other instructions, you might conveniently decide on subjects like those described in other chapters of this book, such as characterization, ideas, structure, or problems. Remember, however, to widen your discussion of such topics to a consideration of the techniques of film as well as to the dialogue.

Then, too, you may choose to confine your attention to special cinematographic techniques, stressing their relationship to the theme of the film, their appropriateness, and their quality. If you have never paid particular attention to techniques of film or to photography, you might find some difficulties here. But if you concentrate on certain scenes, you may be able to recall enough to describe some of the techniques, particularly if you have helped yourself with good notes.

In judging a film you might also choose to emphasize the quality of the acting. How well did the actors adapt to the medium of film? How convincing were their performances? Did they possess good control over their facial expressions? Did their appearance lend anything to your understanding of the characters they portrayed? How well did they control bodily motion? Were they graceful? Awkward? Did it seem that the actors were genuinely creating their roles, or just reading through the parts?

Or you may wish to write a general review, bringing in all these various aspects that go into the total package that is the film. If you write a review, consult Chapter 15 for ideas on how to proceed.

## CONCLUSION

You might best conclude by evaluating the effectiveness of the cinematographic form to the story and to the idea. Were all the devices of film used in the best possible way? Was anything particularly overdone? Was anything underplayed? Was the film good, bad, or indifferent up to a point, and then did it change? Why? How? The development of answers to questions like these will be appropriate in the conclusion of your theme.

## Sample Theme

*Ingmar Bergman's* Virgin Spring: *An Affirmation of Complexity*

[1]
*Virgin Spring* (1959), a black-and-white film in Swedish with English subtitles, is directed by Ingmar Bergman, filmed by Sven Nykvist, and written by Ulla Isaksson. It is a complex but affirmative rendering of an old Scandinavian folk tale.* The fabric of the film is woven out of violence, horror, revenge, and mystery. Against this background, however, there is a pattern of purpose and affirmation. On the surface the story of the film is simple enough: In medieval times a young virgin girl is permitted to ride alone to church to deliver candles, but on her way she is murdered by three herdsmen. The three take her clothes and ask shelter for the night at her home, where they try to sell the clothes to her parents. The father concludes that the three men have murdered his daughter, and he kills them in revenge. Going to recover his daughter's body, the father vows to build a church on the spot where she fell. When the body is removed, a spring of water gushes forth from the point where her head lay. While the film could thus be regarded as a religious play, the impact of the characterizations and cinematic techniques is that any faith, or any commitment whatsoever, is difficult and sometimes self-contradictory.†

[2]
The characterizations bring out the complexity. For example, the girl Ingeri, (acted by Gunnel Lindblom) is ostensibly a malcontent, a dark-haired figure of evil committed to Odin, the god of battles and death. She is to be contrasted with the fair-haired Karin, the favorite daughter, and her half-sister (Birgitta Petersson). But Ingeri is not seen so simplistically, for she is a menial whose freedom is restricted and whose potential beauty is useless. Desiring fine clothes and servants herself, she has nothing. Her approaching motherhood will not be accompanied by marriage. Her resentment and her worship of the mysterious Odin bring death to Karin, but are nevertheless understandable responses to her condition. Her placing the frog in the bread loaf is not an act of evil, despite its consequences, but rather an act of extreme frustration and disgust. Such complexity marks Bergman's uniquely modern handling of the old story.

[3]
The same complexity may be found in Karin, the daughter who gives the film its name. She is the sacrificial victim, and her rape and death arouse the horror and indignation that one feels at seeing purposeless violence. But before she leaves for church, Karin is shown as having some of the haughtiness and spitefulness of a spoiled person. She is vain, and wheedles herself into favorable positions with her parents. She is fussy, and will not go to church until

---

*Central idea
†Thesis sentence
*Virgin Spring* is available for rental in 16mm from Janus Films, 745 Fifth Avenue, New York, N.Y. 10022.

her clothes are just right. She is not bad, however, but human, and the fullness of this characterization lends even more pity to her death than if she had been no more than a simple figure on a tapestry.

The most complex characterization is that of the father, Herr Töre (Max von Sydow). It is Töre's lot to kill the three crazed herdsmen and to make vows to build a church where his daughter was killed. Töre does not go easily to either task, however, for he performs a ritual cleansing before attacking the three men, and his regret and horror after his deed are made apparent. Similarly, his prayers alongside his daughter's corpse indicate his bewilderment and frustration. His previous quiet manner is thus shown as covering greater, almost philosophic capabilities. He is a man forced into a situation he cannot under-stand or control, and he tries to do his best. Of particular interest is his dec-laration of inability to comprehend God's ways. In view this admission, his promise to build a church may be seen as a human commitment, a compromise solution, rather than a simple memorial act.

[4]

While these characterizations strongly undergird the complexity of Berg-man's treatment of the tale, the film's major strength is in Bergman's direction and in the filming, done by Sven Nykvist. It was clearly Bergman's intention to use photography to dramatize the complex, mysterious forces that swirl around the centers of human motivation. In what is in effect the epigraph of the film, for example, Nykvist photographs Ingeri from above as she calls on Odin. This downward view conditions our attitudes toward her. When she meets the gnomic man in the woods, however, even she demonstrates fear of the grotesque, distorted forces shown by the man. The same kind of mad force is suggested in the actions of the three herdsmen when they first see Karin. Their attitudes are conveyed through an irrational and depraved set of actions, augmented by the closeups of the bizarre mute herdsman when he tries to speak. Even so, their violence is restrained until they see the frog in the bread. Here the forces that were controlling Ingeri are unleashed on the herdsmen, for the sight of the frog triggers the rape and murder of Karin.

[5]

Such forces can be beaten only by much greater, if equally vague forces, and it is here that Bergman and Nykvist gain the utmost from camera and light. The views of Karin riding along the shore of the lake show beauty and innocence; she is clothed in light, and her horse is white. The lake is clear, and the scene is beautiful. By contrast, when Nykvist focuses the camera on Töre before the vengeance scene, he portrays a more complex and powerful set of forces. First, Töre is at the gate when the three murderers approach; he is in darkness but appears to be a stolid, guardian-like figure. Later, Töre is shown tearing up a young tree in preparation for his ritualistic bath and switching. Bergman and Nykvist in this scene suggest that Töre gets his strength directly from the earth. The scene is portrayed as a union of man, earth, and sky, in a vague, ghostly light, as though the forces of right are equally as vast, vague, and ambiguous as those of evil.

[6]

In the face of this ambiguity, the virgin spring itself is to be seen as an affirmation of the difficulty and mystery of life. Bergman stresses the beauty of the gushing spring in both sight and sound. It would be easy to accept this water as a new birth, a new baptism, a sign that horror and sacrifice are over.

But it seems more reasonable, because of the main actions of the film, to see the spring as a sign that there is value in trying to overcome hostile forces. The spring, like the tree, gives strength, and both come from the earth, which is shown throughout by Bergman and Nykvist as hill, vale, mud, and shore.

[7] As a symbol, the spring cannot guarantee that evil can ever be eliminated or that violence can be stopped. The future will hold many reenactments of just such situations as Karin encounters on her innocent journey, but if persons like Herr Töre make the commitment and the effort, evil at least will not overcome.

Bergman has done well with a good script. At first one might wonder at the extent of Karin's preparations before she leaves home, but as the tale unfolds it may be seen that this preparation serves (a) to establish involvement with her character, and (b) to show her clothing, which later becomes proof that

[8] the three herdsmen have murdered her. Similarly, the extensive movement of the three shepherds when they first see Karin, which may seem unnecessary, creates an impression of their sinister irrationality. Logically, there is nothing done to excess, nor is there anything wanting in the film. In just about every technical matter from acting, to photography, to editing, *Virgin Spring* is a major film.

## Commentary on the Theme

Paragraph one gives essential background material about the film. It also includes a brief summary of the story.

In keeping with the first point of the thesis sentence, paragraphs two, three, and four discuss the characters. There is not much difference between these discussions and those that could be carried out for a story, novel, or play. The main difference is that the actions and decisions of the characters are all drawn from observation of the film, not from descriptions in a printed text. Paragraphs five, six, and seven discuss the second aspect of the thesis sentence, namely the film's cinematic techniques. Paragraph five emphasizes camera angle and closeups. Paragraph six draws attention to the uses of light. Paragraph seven treats the visual symbols of water and earth. The concluding paragraph evaluates the film in the light of Bergman's integration of scene and action.

# chapter 18

# Research Themes

Research, as distinguished from pure criticism, refers to using primary and secondary sources for assistance in solving a literary problem. That is, in criticizing a work, pure and simple, you consult only the work in front of you, whereas in doing research on the work, you consult not only the work but many other works that were written about it or that may shed light on it. Typical research tasks are to find out more about the historical period in which a work was written, or about prevailing opinions of the times, or about what modern (or earlier) critics have said about the work. It is obvious that a certain amount of research is always necessary in any critical job, or in any theme about a literary work. Looking up words in a dictionary, for example, is only a minimal job of research, which may be supplemented by reading introductions, critical articles, encyclopedias, biographies, critical studies, histories, and the like. There is, in fact, a point at which criticism and research merge.

It is necessary that you put the job of doing research in perspective. In general, students and scholars do research in order to uncover some of the accumulated "lore" of our civilization. This lore—the knowledge that presently exists—may be compared to a large cone that is constantly being filled. At the beginnings of human existence there was little knowledge of anything, and the cone was at its narrowest point. As civilization progressed, more and more knowledge appeared, and the cone thus began to fill. Each time a new piece of information or a new conclusion was recorded, a little more knowledge or lore was in effect poured into the cone, which accordingly became slightly fuller and wider. Though at present our cone of knowledge is quite full, it appears to be capable of infinite growth. Knowledge keeps piling up and new disciplines keep developing. It becomes more and more difficult for one person to accumulate more than a small portion of the entirety. Indeed, historians generally agree that the last person to know virtually everything about every existing discipline was Aristotle—2,400 years ago.

If you grant that you cannot learn everything, you can make a positive start by recognizing that research can provide two things: (1) a systematic understanding of a portion of the knowledge filling the cone, and (2) an understanding of, and ability to handle, the methods by which you might someday be able to make your own contributions to the filling of the cone. The principal goal of education is to help you reach a state where you are prepared to make your own contributions. Research is a key method of reaching this goal.

Thus far we have been speaking broadly about the relevance of research to any discipline. The chemist, the anthropologist, the ecologist, the marine biologist—all employ research. Our problem here, however, is literary research. A critical paper on a primary source without any external aids is one kind of research. In the sense usually applied in literature courses, however, research is the systematic study of library sources in order to illuminate a literary topic.

## Selecting a Topic

Frequently your instructor will ask for a research paper on a specific topic. However, if you have only a general research assignment, your first problem is to select a topic. It may be helpful to have a general notion of the kind of research paper you would find most congenial. There are five types:

1. *A paper on a particular work.* You might treat character (for example, "The Character of Strether in James' *The Ambassadors*," or "Kurtz as a type of antihero in Conrad's *Heart of Darkness*"), or tone, ideas, form, problems, and the like. A research paper on a single work is similar to a theme on the same work, except that the research paper takes into account more views and facts than those you are likely to have without the research. This type of paper is particularly attractive if you are studying a novelist or a playwright, whose works are usually quite long.

2. *A paper on a particular author.* The paper could be about an idea, or some facet of style, imagery, tone, or humor of the author, tracing the origins and development of the topic through a number of different works by the author. An example might be "The idea of the true self as developed

by Frost in his poetry before 1920." This type of paper is particularly suitable if you are writing on a poet whose works are short, though a topic like "Shakespeare's idea of the relationships between men and women as dramatized in *The Winter's Tale, All's Well That Ends Well, A Midsummer Night's Dream,* and *As You Like It*" would also be workable.

3. *A paper based on comparison and contrast.* There are two types:

a. *A paper on an idea of some artistic quality common to two or more authors.* Your intention might be to show points of similarity or contrast, or to show that one author's work may be read as a criticism of another's. A typical subject of such a paper might be "The 'hollow-man' theme in Eliot, Auden, and Dreiser," or "Goldsmith's *She Stoops to Conquer* as a response to selected sentimental dramas of the eighteenth century." Consult the second sample theme in Chapter 10 for an example of this type.

b. *A paper concentrating on opposing critical views of a particular work or body of works.* Sometimes much is to be gained from an examination of differing critical opinions, say "The conflict over *Lolita,*" "The controversy over Book IV of *Gulliver's Travels,*" or "Pro and con over Lina Wertmüller's film *Swept Away.*" Such a study would attempt to determine the critical climate of opinion and taste to which a work did or did not appeal, and it might also aim at conclusions about whether the work was in the advance or rear guard of its time.

4. *A paper showing the influence of an idea, an author, a philosophy, a political situation, or an artistic movement on specific works of an author or authors.* A paper on influences can be fairly cut-and-dried, as in "The influence of Italian army customs and operations on the details in Hemingway's *A Farewell to Arms,*" or else it can be more abstract and psychological, as "The influence of the World War I psyche on the narrator in *A Farewell to Arms.*"

5. *A paper on the origins of a particular work or type of work.* One avenue of research for such a paper might be to examine an author's biography to discover the germination and development of a work—for example, "*Heart of Darkness* as an outgrowth of Conrad's experience in the Belgian Congo." Another way of discovering origins might be to relate a work to a particular type or tradition: "*Hamlet* as revenge tragedy," or "*Mourning Becomes Electra* and its origins in the story of Agamemnon."

If you consider these types, an idea of what to write may come to you. Perhaps you have particularly liked one author, or several authors. If so, you might start to think along the lines of types 1, 2, and 3. If you are interested in influences or in origins, then types 4 or 5 may suit you better. If you still have not decided on a topic after rereading the works you have liked, then you should carry your search for a topic into your school library. Look up your author or authors in the card catalogue. Usually the works written by the authors are included first, followed by works written about the authors. Your first goal should be to find a relatively recent book-length critical study published by a university press. Use your judgment here: look for a title indicating that the book is a general one dealing with the author's major works rather than just one work. Study those chapters relevant to your base work. Most writers of critical studies describe their purpose and plan in their introductions or first chapters, so read the first part of the book. If there is no separate chapter on the base work, use the index and go to the relevant pages. Reading in this way should soon supply you with sufficient knowledge about the issues and ideas raised by the base work to enable you to select a topic you will wish to study further. Once you have made your decision, you are ready to go ahead and gather a working bibliography.

## Setting Up a Bibliography

The best way to gather a working bibliography of books and articles is to begin with major critical studies of the writer or writers. Again, go to the card catalogue and pick out books that have been published by university presses. These books will usually contain selective bibliographies. Be particularly careful to read the chapters on your base work or works and to look for the footnotes. Quite often you can save time if you record the names of books and articles listed in these footnotes. Then refer to the bibliographies included at the ends of the books, and select any likely looking titles. Now, look at the dates of publication of the critical books you have been using. Let us suppose that you have been looking at three, published in 1951, 1963, and 1980. The chances are that the bibliography in a book published in 1980 will be fairly complete up through about 1978, for the writer will usually have completed the manuscript about two years before the book actually was published. What you should do then is aim at gathering a bibliography of works published since 1978; you may assume that writers of critical works will have done the selecting for you of the most relevant works published before that time.

### BIBLIOGRAPHICAL GUIDES

Fortunately for students doing literary research, the Modern Language Association of America has been providing a virtually complete bibliography of literary studies for years, not just in English and American literatures, but in the literatures of most modern foreign languages. The

Association started achieving completeness in the late 1950's and by 1969 had reached such an advanced state that it divided the bibliography into four parts. The first volume of the *1980 MLA International Bibliography* is devoted to "General, English, American, Medieval and Neo-Latin, Celtic Literatures, and Folklore," and it contains 18,574 entries. All four volumes are bound together in library editions, just as the earlier bibliographies were bound separately for reference-room use. Most university and college libraries have a set of these bibliographies readily available on open shelves or tables. There are, of course, many other bibliographies that are useful for students doing research, many more than can be mentioned here meaningfully. As an entry into the vast field of bibliography on English studies, you might consult Donald F. Bond, compiler, *A Reference Guide to English Studies* [A Revision of the *Bibliographical Guide to English Studies* by Tom Peete Cross] (Chicago: University of Chicago Press [Phoenix Books], 1962). This work lists a total of 1,230 separate studies and bibliographies on which further research may be based. Section VII lists 100 "Periodical Publications Containing Reviews and Bibliographies." There is more here than can be readily imagined. For most purposes, however, the *MLA International Bibliography* is more than adequate. Remember that as you progress in your reading, the footnotes and bibliographies in the works you consult also will constitute an unfolding bibliography.

The *MLA International Bibliography* is conveniently organized. If your author is Richard Wright, for example, look him up under "American Literature V. Twentieth Century," the relevant listing for all twentieth-century American writers. If your author is Shakespeare, refer to "English Literature VI. Renaissance and Elizabethan." So many books and articles appear each year on Shakespeare that the bibliography lists the separate plays alphabetically under the Shakespeare entry. Depending on your topic, of course, you will find most of the bibliography you need under the author's last name. Journal references are abbreviated, but a lengthy list explaining abbreviations appears at the beginning of the volume. Using the MLA bibliographies, you should begin with the most recent one and then go backward to your stopping point. Be sure to get the complete information, especially volume numbers and years of publication, for each article and book you wish to consult.

If your research carries you into a great number of primary sources, then you should rely on *The Cambridge Bibliography of English Literature*, in five volumes. The *CBEL* is selective for secondary sources but is invaluable as a general guide to the canon and the various editions of individual authors' works. If you want to see a first edition of poems by the eighteenth-century poet Christopher Smart, for example, the *CBEL* will describe the edition, and it also will describe an acceptable or standard modern edition of the poems if you want the best reading edition.

You are now ready to consult your sources and to take notes.

## Taking Notes and Paraphrasing Material

There are many ways of taking notes, but the consensus is that the best method is to use note cards. If you have never used cards before, you might profit from consulting any one of a number of handbooks and special workbooks on research. Robert M. Gorrell and Charlton Laird present a lucid and methodical explanation of taking notes on cards in their *Modern English Handbook,* 6th ed. (Englewood Cliffs, N.J.: Prentice-Hall, Inc., 1976), pp. 369–373. The principal virtue of using cards is that they may be classified, numbered, renumbered, shuffled, tried out in one place, rejected, and then used in another ( or thrown away), and arranged in order when you start to write. If you can do without the flexibility and freedom of cards, however, and would like to use some other way, do so.

### *Write the Source on Each Card*

As you take notes, do not forget to write down the source of your information on each card. This may sound like a lot of bother, but it is easier than finding out as you write that you will need to go back to the library to get the correct source. And if you have not recorded the source, how will you know where to start?

You can save time if you take the complete data on one card—a "master card" for that source—and then make up an abbreviation to be used in your notes. Here is an example:

---

Donovan, Josephine, ed. <u>Feminist Literary</u>

<u>Criticism: Explorations in Theory.</u>

Lexington, Ky.: The University Press of

Kentucky, 1975. 81 pp.


DONOVAN

---

If you plan to use many notes from this book, then the name "Donovan" will work as the right identification. Be sure not to lose your complete master card, because you will need it for bibliographical information on your theme.

*Record the Page Number*
*for Each Note*

It would be hard to guess how much exasperation has been caused by the failure to record page numbers of notes. Be sure to get the page number down first, *before* you begin to take your note. If the detail you are noting goes from one page to the next in your source, record the exact spot where the page changes, as in this example:

---

Heilbrun & Stimson, in DONOVAN, pp. 63–64

[63]After the raising of the feminist consciousness

it is necessary to develop / [64]"the growth of

moral perception" through anger and the

correction of social inequality.

---

The reason for being so careful is that you may, in your theme, wish to use only a part of a note, and when there are two pages you will need to be accurate in your location of what goes where.

*Record Only One Fact or*
*Opinion Per Card*

Record only one thing on each card—one quotation, one paraphrase, one observation—never two or more. You might be tempted to fill up the entire card, but such a try at economy often causes trouble because you might want to use the same card in different places in your theme. One element per card keeps flexibility and convenience. Two per card causes strain and inconvenience.

### Use Quotation Marks for All
### Quoted Material

A major problem in taking notes, one that can cause grief later on in writing, is to distinguish copied material from your own words. Here you must be super-cautious. Always—*always*—put quotation marks around *every direct quotation you copy verbatim from a source.* Make the quotation marks immediately, before you forget, so that you will always know that the words of your notes within quotation marks are the words of another writer.

Often, as you take a note, you may use some of your own words and some of the words from your source. In cases like this it is even more important to be cautious. Put quotation marks around *every word* that you take directly from the source, even if you find yourself literally with a note that resembles a picket fence. Later when you begin writing your paper, your memory of what is yours and not yours will become dim, and if you use another's words in your own paper but do not grant recognition, you lay yourself open to the charge of plagiarism.

## PARAPHRASING

When you take notes, it is best to rephrase or paraphrase the sources. A paraphrase is a restatement in your own words, and because of this it is actually a first step in the writing of the theme. Chapter 1 in this book has a full treatment on making a précis or abstract. If you work on this technique, you will be well prepared to paraphrase for your research theme.

A big problem in paraphrasing is to capture the idea in the source without duplicating the words. (This problem is also considered in Chapter 1, p. 36.) It is not easy to find better words than those in the original. If you have already found out this difficulty, do not be surprised: The writer of your source made a great effort to put things in the best way he or she could. It is therefore hard to escape the original wording, but even so, you must try.

The best way to handle the problem is this: Read and reread the passage you are noting. Turn over the book or journal and write out the idea, in *your own words*, as accurately as you can, with the original out of sight. Once you have this note, compare it with the original and make corrections to improve your thought and emphasis. Add a short quotation if you believe it is needed, but be sure to use quotation marks. If your paraphrase uses too many words from the source, or if your own words are in the exact same order as in the original, throw out the note and try again in your own words. It is worth making this effort, because often you can transform much of your note directly to the appropriate place in your theme. The time spent with the notes, in short, is almost the same as time spent in writing your theme.

To see the problems of paraphrase, let us look at a paragraph of original criticism and then see how a student doing research might take notes on it. The paragraph is by Professor Maynard Mack, from an essay entitled "The World of Hamlet," originally published in *The Yale Review*, 41 (1952) and reprinted in *Twentieth Century Interpretations of Hamlet.* David Bevington, ed. (Englewood Cliffs, N.J.: Prentice-Hall, Inc., 1968), p. 57:

> The powerful sense of mortality in *Hamlet* is conveyed to us, I think, in three ways. First, there is the play's emphasis on human weakness, the instability of human purpose, the subjection of humanity to fortune— all that we might call the aspect of failure in man. Hamlet opens this theme in Act I, when he describes how from that single blemish, perhaps not even the victim's fault, a man's whole character may take corruption. Claudius dwells on it again, to an extent that goes far beyond the needs of the occasion, while engaged in seducing Laertes to step behind the arras of a seemer's world and dispose of Hamlet by a trick. Time qualifies everything, Claudius says, including love, including purpose. As for love— it has a "plurisy" in it and dies of its own too much. As for purpose— "That we would do, We should do when we would, for this 'would' changes, And hath abatements and delays as many As there are tongues, are hands, are accidents; And then this 'should' is like a spendthrift's sigh, That hurts by easing." The player-king, in his long speeches to his queen in the play within the play, sets the matter in a still darker light. She means these protestations of undying love, he knows, but our purposes depend on our memory, and our memory fades fast. Or else, he suggests, we propose something to ourselves in a condition of strong feeling, but then the feeling goes, and with it the resolve. Or else our fortunes change, he adds, and with these our loves: "The great man down, you mark his favorite flies." The subjection of human aims to fortune is a reiterated theme in *Hamlet,* as subsequently in *Lear.* Fortune is the harlot goddess in whose secret parts men like Rosencrantz and Guildenstern live and thrive; the strumpet who threw down Troy and Hecuba and Priam; the outrageous foe whose slings and arrows a man of principle must suffer or seek release in suicide. Horatio suffers them with composure: he is one of the blessed few "Whose blood and judgment are so well co-mingled That they are not a pipe for fortune's finger To sound what stop she please." For Hamlet the task is of a greater difficulty.

It is obvious that no note can do full justice to such a well-substantiated paragraph of criticism. There are subtleties and shades, and a mingling of discourse with interpretive and appreciative reminiscences and quotations from the play, that cannot be duplicated briefly and that will be lost when put into other words. However, the task of taking notes forces you to shorten and interpret, and there are some things that can guide you in the face of the large amount of reading in your sources.

### Think of the Purpose of Your Theme

It is true that you may not know exactly what you are "fishing for" when you start to take notes, for you cannot prejudge what your theme will contain. Research is a form of discovery. But soon you will develop a topic, and you should use that as your guide in all your note-taking.

For example, let us suppose that you have started to take notes on *Hamlet* criticism, and after a certain amount of reading you have decided on "Shakespeare's tragic views in *Hamlet*." This decision would prompt you to take a note when you come to Mack's thought about morality and death in the quoted passage. If you wanted mainly this topic, without recording the detail in the development of Mack's idea, the following note would be enough:

---

Mack, in Bevington, p. 57            Death and
                                                              Mortality

Mack cites three ways in which <u>Hamlet</u> stresses

death and mortality. The first (p. 57) is an

emphasis on human shortcomings and "weakness."

Corruption, loss of memory and enthusiasm, bad

luck, misery—all suit the sense of the closeness of

death to life.

---

This note focuses on the early part of Mack's paragraph rather than the middle or end. For short notes like this one, it is best to rephrase the first part of a paragraph in your source, for it is there that you will most often find the author's topic idea.

Let us now suppose that you wanted a fuller note in the expectation that you would need not just the topic but also some of Mack's detail. Such a note might look like this:

Mack, in Bevington, p. 57                                    Death and
                                                            Mortality

The first of Mack's "three ways" in which a
"powerful sense of mortality" is shown in <u>Hamlet</u>
is the illustration of human "weakness," "instability,"
and helplessness before fate. In support, Mack
refers to Hamlet's early speech on a single fault
leading to corruption, also to Claudius' speech
(in the scene persuading Laertes to trick Hamlet).
The player-king also talks about his queen's
forgetfulness and therefore inconstancy by default.
As slaves to fortune, Rosencrantz and Guildenstern
are examples. Horatio is not a slave, however. Hamlet's
case is by far the worst of all.       Mack, p. 57

When the actual theme-writing is done, any part of this note would be useful. The words are almost all the note-taker's own, and the few quotations are within quotation marks. Note that Mack, the critic, is properly recognized as the source of the criticism, so that the note could be adapted readily to a research theme.

The key here is that your taking of notes should be guided by your developing plan for your theme. For another example, let us assume different plans. If you decided to write about the character of Claudius, for example, you would take a note from Mack's essay relating the theme of mortality to Claudius' overemphasis on the idea of the limitations of life. Or suppose that you were studying the Player scene. Then you would take a note on the "darker light" this scene casts over the theme of morbidity. The things you take notes on would all change according to your plan for a theme subject.

It should be clear that your taking of notes is part of your thinking and composing process. You may not always know whether you will be able to use each note that you take, and you will throw away many notes when you write your theme. You will always find, however, that taking notes is easier once you have determined your purpose. For example, you might not need an entire article because, despite its merits, it may have nothing to offer for your theme. You might also discover that you need to go back over books or articles because you remember something that you have later decided to use, even though you had not thought at first that you would need it.

## *Title Your Notes*

To help you in developing the various parts of your theme, write a title for each of your notes. This practice is a form of outlining. Let us assume that you have chosen to write about Jonathan Swift's *A Modest Proposal* (the subject of the sample theme in this chapter) and that your topic is Swift's speaker, the "economic projector."[1] As you have been reading, you discover that there are good points and bad points about this projector. Here is a note about one of the bad qualities:

---

Hunting, p. 91                                                    character—BAD

91. Hunting claims that the projector is a

"monster" because he speaks about women and

men as "breeders" [Swift's word] and thinks of

babies as nothing more than meat.                                           91

---

Notice that this title classifies the topic of the note. Once all the note-taking is done, a number of such cards would form the substance of a section in the theme about the bad qualities of Swift's speaker. (If you look at the sample theme, p. 255–259, you will see that this note has been fitted into the section there.) In addition, once you have decided that "character—BAD" is one of the topics you would like to explore, you would be helped in further note-taking. The use of titles for notes, in short, is both a constructive and creative part of writing a research theme.

---

[1]A modern equivalent of the word *projector* would be a theorist, a person who runs a think tank. Swift clearly believed that such people valued statistics and ideas before human beings and thus they were potentially harmful despite the avowed good intentions of some of their plans.

## Write Your Own Comments
## as They Occur to You

As you take your notes, you will find many thoughts of your own. Do not let these go, to be remembered later (maybe), but write them down at the time you get them. Often you may notice a detail that your source does not mention, or you may get a hint for an idea that the critic does not develop. Often, too, you may get thoughts which can serve as "bridges" between details in your notes or as introductions or concluding observations for the details. Be sure to title your comment and also to mark it as your own thought. Here is such a note, on the bad quality again of Swift's projector in *A Modest Proposal*. (This note appears, as modified, in the sample theme, p. 257):

---

MY OWN                                                    character—BAD


If the projector's way of considering human beings

as statistics were only private, there could be no

harm done. But he is a public speaker, and therefore

he is dangerous.

---

## Make Groups, or Piles,
## of Your Cards

If you have taken your notes well, your theme will have been taking shape in your mind already. The titles of your cards will suggest areas to be developed in your theme. Once you have assembled a stack of note cards derived from a reasonable number of sources (your instructor may have assigned the minimum number), you can distribute your cards in groups, or piles, according to your titles. For the sample theme, after some shuffling and retitling, the following groups of cards were distributed:

1. Character—GOOD          2. Character—BAD

3. Irony                             4. Satire

5. Inconsistent Voice          6. Consistent Voice

If you look at the major sections of the sample theme, you will see that the topics there were taken right from these groups of cards.

### Arrange the Cards in Each Group

There is still much to be done with your individual groups. You cannot use the details as they happened to fall randomly in your "deal." You need to decide which cards you can use and which ones you must throw out. You might also need to retitle some cards and put them into another pile. Of those that remain in the group, you will need to lay them out in an order, or progression, in which you can put them into your theme.

Once you have your cards in order, you can write whatever comments or transitions you think you will need to get you from detail to detail. Write this material directly on your cards, and be sure to use a different color ink so that you will be able to know what was on the original card and what you added at this stage of your composing process. Here is an example of such a "developed" note card, with the original note together with a comment:

---

Kernan, p. 89                                                    character—BAD


89. "a smug, emotionless, completely self-centered

and dangerous dunce"                                                             89


*Kernan is wrong about "emotionless" (see the opening of the Proposal, where the projector expresses melancholy). But K. is right about the projector being a "self-centered and dangerous dunce."*

---

Observe how the ideas on this card have been expressed as they appear in the sample theme (p. 257):

> It is not right to claim that he is "emotionless," as Kernan states, for the projector does express emotions in his opening paragraphs. But it is right to agree with Kernan that the projector is a "completely self-centered and dangerous dunce."

From this movement from note card to finished sentence, you can see how working with these cards is a necessary part of the writing of your theme. Once you have a complete and organized set of cards, the writing of the theme is really a revision of the material on your cards.

### Be Creative and Original in Research Themes

This is not to say that you can settle for the direct movement of the cards to your theme. You should do your writing with the following ideas in mind, realizing as you go that you will need to make changes, reorder details, revise language, and perhaps go back to the library to get new notes or recheck sources.

The major concern in a research paper is that your use of sources can become an end in itself and therefore a shortcut for your own thinking and writing. Quite often students introduce details in a research theme the way a master of ceremonies introduces performers in a variety show. This is unfortunate because it is the writer whose paper will be judged, even though the sources, like the performers, do all the work.

It is important, then, to try to recognize how you can be creative and original in a research theme even though you are relying heavily on your sources. Here are four major ways:

1. SELECTION. In each major section of your theme you will include a number of details from your sources. To be creative you should select different but related details and should not repeat anything. Your theme will be judged on the basis of the thoroughness with which you make your point with different details (which in turn will represent the completeness of your research "spade work"). Even though you are relying on published materials and cannot be original on that score, your selection is original because you are bringing the materials together, as far as you are concerned, for the first time. In paragraph thirteen of the sample theme (p. 259), you can see how four separate details have been brought

together to illustrate the point that *A Modest Proposal* has been praised as literature.

2. DEVELOPMENT. A closely related way of being original is the development of your various points. Your arrangement is an obvious area of originality: One detail seems naturally to precede another, and certain conclusions stem out of certain details. As you present the details, conclusions, and arguments from your sources, you may also add your own original stamp by using supporting details that are different from those in your sources. You may also wish to add your own emphasis to particular points—an emphasis that you do not find in your sources.

Naturally, the words that you use will be original with you. Your topic sentences, for example, will all be your own. As you introduce details and conclusions, you will need to write "bridges" to get yourself from point to point. These may be introductory remarks or transitions. In other words, as you write, you are not just stringing things out but are actively tying thoughts together in a variety of creative ways. Your efforts to do this will constitute the area of your greatest originality.

As you develop your points, you will be grateful for all the attention you gave to your note cards. A thorough job on these will supply you with many introductions, comments, and transitions that are already written. You can develop your topic sentences, of course, from the titles of your piles of cards.

3. EXPLANATION OF CONTROVERSIAL VIEWS. Also closely related to selection is the fact that in your research you may have found conflicting or differing views on a topic. It is original for you, as you describe and distinguish these views, to explain the reasons for the differences. In other words, as you explain a conflict or difference, you are writing an original analysis. To see how differing views may be handled, see paragraphs nine to twelve of the sample theme (pp. 258–259).

4. CREATION OF YOUR OWN INSIGHTS AND POSITIONS. There are three possibilities here, all related to how well you have learned the primary texts on which your research in secondary sources is based.

a. *Your Own Interpretations and Ideas.* Remember that an important part of taking notes is to make your own points precisely when they occur to you. Often you can expand these as truly original parts of your theme. Your originality does not need to be extensive; it may consist of no more than an insight expressed in a word or in a sentence. Here is such a card, which was written during the research on *A Modest Proposal:*

MY OWN                                                      introductory?

A Modest Proposal is above all unforgettable.
Social schemes are easy to forget, like political
platform planks, but the suggestion to eat babies
is so outrageous and shocking that it can't be
forgotten. The shocking nature of the Proposal
has unquestionably caused great interest in Swift
himself, the author of the work in which the suggestion
is made.

The originality here boils down to the word "unforgettable." This is perhaps not a startling discovery, but it does represent the result of some original thought about *A Modest Proposal*. When expanded, the ideas in the card supply the substance of the opening three paragraphs of the sample research theme (pp. 255–256).

b. *Gaps in the Sources.* As you read your secondary sources it may dawn on you that a certain, obvious conclusion is not being made, or that a certain detail is not being stressed. Here is an area which you can develop on your own. Your conclusions may involve a particular interpretation or major point of comparison, or it may rest on a particularly important but somehow overlooked or understressed word or fact. In the sample theme, for example, it is claimed that the concluding words of *A Modest Proposal* are more significant as a means of understanding the speaker's character than the "modest proposal" itself (pp. 258–259). Critics have acknowledged these words as a "twist" but have not made the strong connection with the speaker's character. In the light of such a critical "vacuum," it is right to move in with whatever is necessary to fill it. A great deal of scholarship is created in this way.

c. *Disputes with the Sources.* You may also find that your sources present certain arguments with which you wish to dispute. As you develop your disagreement, you will be arguing originally, for you will be using details in a different way from that of the critic or critics whom you are disputing, and your conclusions will be your own. This area of originality is of course similar to the laying out of controversial critical views, except that you furnish one of the opposing views yourself. The approach is limited, because it is difficult to find many substantive points of interpretation on which there are not already clearly delineated opposing views. Paragraph six of the sample theme shows a small point of disagreement, but one that is nevertheless original (p. 257).

## Organizing Your Theme

INTRODUCTION

The introduction of a research theme may be expanded beyond the length of that for an ordinary theme because of the need to relate the problem of research to your topic. You may wish to bring in historical or biographical information as long as you can show its relevance. You might also wish to summarize critical opinion or to describe any particular critical problems as they pertain to your topic. The idea is to lead your reader into your topic by providing interesting and significant materials that you have uncovered during your research. Obviously, you should include your usual guides—your central idea and your thesis sentence.

Because of the greater length of most research themes, some instructors require a topic outline, which is in effect a table of contents. This pattern is followed in the sample theme, including subheadings at the various sections. Inasmuch as this method is a matter of choice with various instructors, be sure that you understand whether your instructor requires it.

BODY, CONCLUSION

Your development both for the body and the conclusion will be governed by your choice of topic. Please consult the relevant chapters in this book about what to include for whatever topic you select (setting, idea, comparison-contrast, or any other).

The research theme is usually assigned as a longer paper of from five to fifteen or more pages, although it may be shorter, depending on your topic. It seems reasonable to assume that a theme based on only one work would be shorter than one based on several. If you narrow the scope of your topic, as suggested in the five approaches described above, you can readily keep your theme within the assigned length. The sample theme, for example, is on the point of view in Swift's *A Modest Proposal* (first approach). Were you to write on the points of view in a number of other works by Swift (second approach), you could limit your total number of pages by stressing comparative treatments and by avoiding excessive detail about problems pertaining to only one work. In short, you will decide to include or exclude materials by compromising between the importance of the materials and the limits of your assignment.

Although you limit your topic yourself in consultation with your instructor, your sources may get out of your control when you plan and organize your theme. It is important therefore to keep your central idea foremost. By making this emphasis you can keep in control of your sources and prevent their controlling you.

The sources also add to the usual complications of writing, for you will be dealing not with one text alone but with many. The sources will of course be the basis of your details and of many of your ideas. The problem will be to handle the many strands and still preserve thematic unity. Once again, a constant stressing of your central idea will help you. Your introductory remarks, observations and assessments, bridges from one detail to another, comparisons, and conclusions should all proceed logically and naturally as long as you keep concentrating on the development of your central idea.

Because of the sources, there is something of a problem about your authority, and that problem is plagiarism. Your reader will automatically assume that everything you write is your own material unless you indicate otherwise. You leave yourself open to a charge of plagiarism, however, if you give no recognition to a detail or interpretation that seems clearly to have been derived from a source.

To handle this problem, you need to be especially careful in your documentation. (Consult Appendix B for a full treatment of this topic.) Most commonly, if you are simply presenting facts and details, you can write straightforwardly and let footnotes or parenthetical references suffice as your authority, as follows:

> *A Modest Proposal* stemmed from Jonathan Swift's outrage against the political and economic system which kept the Irish masses in a constant condition of poverty, starvation, and despair.[1]

Here the footnote to a reliable secondary text is sufficient recognition of an authority beyond your own.

If you are using an interpretation that is unique to a particular writer, however, or if you are relying on a significant quotation from your source, you should grant recognition as a necessary part of your own development, as in this sentence:

> [The projector] therefore justifies Ricardo Quintana's observation that he is a "public-spirited" author who even as he makes his outrageous proposal seems to be "well intentioned" and "motivated solely by a concern for the public good."[2]

Here the idea of the critic is clearly located, and key phrases are included within quotation marks. If you grant recognition in this way, no confusion can possibly arise about the authority underlying your theme.

If you plan to introduce a section detailing any controversy among your sources, be sure to connect it to your central idea. The sample theme includes such a section, on the topic of conflicting views about the character of the narrator (paragraphs nine to twelve). This section reviews the two positions on the topic and accepts the one holding that the projector is a separate and integrated character. In this way the controversy is explored but the thematic wholeness of the theme is retained.

---

## Sample Theme (Research on a Single Work)

*Jonathan Swift's Projector in* A Modest Proposal: *A Study in Point of View*

---

### Contents

### I. INTRODUCTION

[1]  No one who has read *A Modest Proposal* (1729),[1] Jonathan Swift's pamphlet response to the Irish poverty and misery that were worsened by crop failures in 1727 and later,[2] can ever forget it. It is "that work" in which the eating of year-old infants is recommended as a solution to a number of social and

In this sample theme, *for illustrative purposes only*, three different reference systems are used. These are all described in Appendix B, pp. 279–285. The first is the footnote system, used in paragraphs one through eight. The second is that of the American Psychological Association (APA), used in paragraphs nine through eleven. The third is the abbreviation system, used in paragraphs twelve through fourteen. It is not expected that you would combine systems in your own theme, unless your instructor specifically requires such a combination.

For the text of Swift's work, please see Appendix C, pp. 287–292.

economic problems. The sale and consumption of babies is offered as the means to eliminate starvation, solidify families, aid the Irish economy, and improve the fare at the tables of the ruling landlords. The proposal, anything but modest, is unforgettable.

[2]
It is also curious, for great interest is generated in the author of a work in which such a suggestion is made. Obviously a sympathetic reader cannot accept the *Proposal* as anything other than an outrageous way of drawing attention to the miserable plight of the Irish poor. But this reading of the work has not always been accepted. The "history of the criticism of *A Modest Proposal* is proof," as Jack S. Gilbert says, that Swift himself has been attacked as a "savage misanthrope" because of the cannibalistic suggestion.[3]

[3]
It seems clear that Swift knew that the "unique horror" of the proposal[4] might cause misinterpretations. He therefore sought to separate himself from possible attack by the creation of a distinct and consistent point of view, even though he himself was deeply involved in the situation of the people of Ireland. He wrote from the standpoint of a mouthpiece, speaker, writer, or *persona* who had a separate background and also was pursuing his own interests. Critical doubts have been raised whether Swift applied the point of view consistently. There seems little doubt, however, that his speaker has traits that mark him as a unique, clearly realized individual.* This theme will examine both the positive and negative sides of this speaker, Swift's use of these sides in the creation of irony and satire, and the critical dispute over the consistency of the voice.†

## II. THE PROJECTOR'S POSITIVE SIDE

[4]
On the positive side, Swift's unnamed speaker is a character with keen analytic ability who honestly thinks that he is a person of good will. William Ewald, who has written on Swift's literary masks, notes that the speaker is an "economic projector."[5] This is not to say that he is a professional arithmetician or economist—an impression that some critics give.[6] Rather he is an amateur, a "learned gentleman interested in the welfare of his nation."[7] He sincerely believes that one can use science to solve human problems. His opening description of the miseries of the Irish poor, in fact, shows that he has much sympathy and compassion.[8]

[5]
Thus this character at first encourages the trust of the reader.[9] He seems never to exaggerate, even when he is making his "modest" proposal, and he uses facts and figures so that his argument is grounded in reality. Because of his claim that he has nothing to gain personally from the proposal,[10] his motives seem above suspicion.[11] He therefore justifies Ricardo Quintana's observation that he is a "public-spirited" author who even as he makes his outrageous proposal seems to be "well intentioned" and "motivated solely by a concern for the public good."[12]

*Central idea
†Thesis sentence

### III. THE PROJECTOR'S NEGATIVE SIDE

[6] On the negative side, and this is the side that Swift brings out strongly, the projector is unable to understand the horror of his own proposal. It is not right to claim that he is "emotionless," as Kernan states,[13] for the projector does express emotions in his opening paragraphs. But it is right to agree with Kernan that the projector is a "completely self-centered and dangerous dunce."[14] If his way of thinking about human beings as statistics were only private, there could be no harm done. But the projector is a public speaker, and therefore he is dangerous. It is threatening that he treats human beings in the same way as cattle; that is, in "exclusively quantitative" terms.[15] He genuinely does not know that his serious suggestion is really "inhuman."[16] Robert Hunting goes so far as to say that the projector is a "monster" because he speaks about women and men as "breeders" and thinks of babies as nothing more than meat.[17] This totally blind side is the projector's destructive flaw. The way in which Swift brings out the flaw is the mark of his genius in *A Modest Proposal.*

### IV. SWIFT'S IRONY AND THE PROJECTOR

[7] As A. L. Rowse observes, *A Modest Proposal* is "the most savage" of Swift's "essays in irony,"[18] and it is the projector's flaw on which the irony of the work is based. Swift's realistic goal, historically speaking, was to wake people up to the misery of the Irish poor as a political way to begin help. His mood is anger, and he uses the projector to plant in the reader a "feeling of horror" that is equal to his anger.[19] The factual, unexaggerated opening by the projector, who seems at first above suspicion, elevates the horror that the unsuspecting reader feels.[20] The irony, as William Ewald notes, is that "the reader sees, as the *persona* does not, the incongruity between . . . [the projector's] sympathy and his proposal."[21] The projector speaks on and on, all the while making an "unconscious and involuntary revelation of brutality which creates the terrifying ironic contradiction."[22]

### V. THE PROJECTOR AND SWIFT'S SATIRE

[8] This irony, so important a quality of *A Modest Proposal,* carries the thrust of Swift's satire. Swift is striking out not only at the conditions of the Irish poor, but also at the people in power who allowed the conditions to exist. The projector is one of these. Ironically, he combines the characteristics of good intentions with total inability to think in terms of real solutions. Out of such limited perspective there were many pamphlet analyses at the time, and these, as might be expected, were distant from reality. The projector's essay is a parody of these works.[23] The projector does not offer any proposal for breaking the cycle of poverty. In fact, he specifically denies some very practical ideas that Swift himself had been urging for years. The projector rather accepts the policies which produced poverty, and he "carries them to extremes."[24] This gap between the speaker's intentions and his understanding makes him a symbol of the insensitivity of the ruling classes. Swift, by using his projector in this way, satirically attempts to cause his readers to admit fault for the poverty and inequality under which the Irish poor suffered.[25]

## VI. POSSIBLE INCONSISTENCY IN SWIFT'S PROJECTOR

Although the effectiveness of Swift's satire depends on the consistency of his speaker, some critics have observed inconsistency, indicating that the projector is no more than an occasional voice. Ernest Tuveson grants the projector a certain independence (1972, p. 69) but also claims that he may "be thought of as Swift himself, purposely adopting the ironic mode" (p. 66). Tuveson also states that the projector is "vaguely outlined" and is "little more than a voice" (p. 65). William Ewald indicates that Swift "exploits his mask . . . extensively" (1954, p. 168), but Ewald also notes some limitations in [9] the voice. He describes a merging of the projector and Swift inasmuch as the projector "speaks for Swift" when detailing the misery of the Irish (p. 165). Moreover, Ewald believes that Swift steps "somewhat out of his pose" to describe the practical solutions in the "I can think of no one objection" section (p. 171; MP, pp. 445–446). Kathleen Williams draws attention to the limited life of Swift's narrators, noting that their "purpose is purely satiric" and that they "may from time to time disappear altogether" (1968, p. 131). The implication here is that the projector of *A Modest Proposal* is one of these, and that he has nothing more than an occasional life.

## VII. THE CONSISTENCY OF SWIFT'S VIEWPOINT

The view that the speaker is not a consistent voice is not persuasive. It is the same as the admission that Swift failed in the work. The view would have [10] it that Swift had been trying to create a consistent voice in the projector but was not able to do so. Thus, the "I can think of no one objection" section would be an artistic breakdown from which Swift recovers at the end.

The more convincing argument, and one that upholds the artistic integrity of *A Modest Proposal,* is that the projector is consistently and fully realized. Thus, one may grant that the opening details are those that Swift might himself have used. In the biographical light of Swift's "terrible anger" against the politicians who allowed poverty and injustice, however (Ferguson, 1962, p. 171), and also against the indifference of the Irish to improve their own condition, it is not possible to admit that the opening would contain no anger if [11] Swift had written in his own voice rather than the projector's. Also, it is true that the "I can think of no one objection" passage describes those remedies which Swift himself had long urged for relief of the poor (Murry, 1955, p. 428; Ewald, 1954, p. 171; Hunting, 1967, p. 89; Landa, 1960, p. 548). But it is also true that the remedies are presented as being unworkable (MP, p. 445). Thus, as Ferguson notes, the voice of the projector is "the same" throughout all parts of the *Proposal* (1962, p. 175). Swift does not interrupt "the projector's voice with his own," but preserves the character of his demented persona without any inconsistencies.

Although the case may be made, then, that Swift uses his projector inconsistently, the better case is that the projector is consistent and complete. One can go even further to claim that the main strength of the work is the consistency of the projector's voice. He is always true to himself. Thus his closing words (that he cannot profit from his scheme because his wife is too old to have children, and his youngest child is beyond the edible year) are even more incredible than his proposal itself. This "crowning revelation" (B, 62) confirms Robert Hunting's previously noted statement that the projector is a "monster" (Hu, 91). It also poses the tragic dilemma that the persons who were proposing [12] solutions—"the aristocracy, merchants, clergy, lawyers, all the responsible classes" (T, 67)—are also part of the problem. Hunting accounts for the power of *A Modest Proposal* in the expression of this dilemma, claiming that Swift uses his point of view as part of a grim warning:

> . . . the easy way to solve the problem of human misery is to give it to some modest-seeming, prudent-talking, thing-oriented political arithmetician and plug the ears when the screams begin.
>
> Hu, 91

## VIII. CONCLUSION: THE EXCELLENCE OF *A MODEST PROPOSAL* AND THE PROJECTOR

Thus the work's great force, the creation of which stems largely from the central mind of the quietly insane projector, has occasioned great critical acclaim, even though the admiration is mixed with a degree of distress. John Middleton Murry compliments Swift's skill in taking his readers into "a realm of lucid nightmare" (M, 427). William Ewald notes that Swift merges a "mad world" with the "real world of Irish misery" (E, 169). It is F. R. Leavis who states [13] that "a remarkably disturbing energy is generated" in the satire that Swift creates with the projector's bizarre scheme (LI, 125). To this mixed praise, however, may be added Herbert Davis's tribute that the work is "the most perfect piece of writing that ever came from . . . [Swift's] pen" (D, 167), and also Edward Rosenheim's conclusion that *A Modest Proposal* is "certainly the most widely read of . . . [Swift's] works" (R, 47).

It would be hard to account for such general recognition of merit and power if the critics were talking about a flawed work. The praise would then have to depend on the content alone and not on the work's artistic integrity. The actual proposal itself can be called shocking, startling, horrible, depraved, memorable, and other similar words, but it could hardly justify praise as great lit- [14] erature. Instead, it would seem that the context of the work, the suggestion of the scheme, the ironic development of the idea as a concrete proposal, and, most important, the totally consistent point of view, all together have earned the work the high esteem it now holds. It is Swift's projector who makes the work coherent and who justifies William Ewald's recognition that *A Modest Proposal* is a "landmark among all the ironical works of literature" (E, 168).

## FOOTNOTES

[1]In Louis A. Landa, ed., *Gulliver's Travels and Other Writings* (Boston: Houghton Mifflin, 1960), pp. 439–446. Cited throughout this theme as *MP*.

[2]Louis A. Landa, *Swift and the Church of Ireland* (Oxford: Clarendon Press, 1954), p. 143.

[3]*Jonathan Swift, Romantic and Cynic Moralist* (Austin: University of Texas Press, 1966), p. 21.

[4]John M. Bullitt, *Jonathan Swift and the Anatomy of Satire* (Cambridge: Harvard University Press, 1953), p. 61.

[5]*The Masks of Jonathan Swift* (Oxford: Basil Blackwell, 1954), p. 164.

[6]Matthew Hodgart, *Satire* (New York: McGraw-Hill, 1969), p. 130.

[7]Alvin Kernan, *The Plot of Satire* (New Haven: Yale University Press, 1965), p. 89.

[8]MP, pp. 439–440.

[9]Ernest Tuveson, "Swift: The View from Within the Satire," in H. James Jenson and Malvin R. Zirker, Jr., eds., *The Satirist's Art* (Bloomington: Indiana University Press, 1972), p. 69.

[10]MP, p. 446.

[11]Tuveson, p. 60.

[12]*Two Augustans: John Locke, Jonathan Swift* (Madison: University of Wisconsin Press, 1978), p. 115.

[13]Kernan, p. 89.

[14]Kernan, p. 89.

[15]Quintana, *Two Augustans*, p. 115.

[16]Hodgart, p. 130.

[17]*Jonathan Swift* (New York: Twayne, 1967), p. 91.

[18]*Jonathan Swift* (New York: Charles Scribner's Sons, 1975), p. 210.

[19]Oliver W. Ferguson, *Jonathan Swift and Ireland* (Urbana: University of Illinois Press, 1962), p. 175.

[20]Tuveson, pp. 60, 69.

[21]Ewald, p. 170.

[22]Bullitt, p. 61.

[23]Hodgart, p. 130; Ronald Paulson, *The Fictions of Satire* (Baltimore: Johns Hopkins University Press, 1967), p. 138; and Ricardo Quintana, *Swift, An Introduction* (London: Oxford University Press, 1962), p. 177.

[24]Ewald, p. 167.

[25]Tuveson, p. 67.

## REFERENCES

B        Bullitt, John M. *Jonathan Swift and the Anatomy of Satire: A Study of Satiric Technique.* Cambridge: Harvard University Press, 1953.

D        Davis, Herbert. "Swift's Use of Irony." In Brian Vickers, ed., *The World of Jonathan Swift.* Cambridge: Harvard University Press, 1968, pp. 154–170.

E        Ewald, William. *The Masks of Jonathan Swift.* Oxford: Basil Blackwell, 1954.

F        Ferguson, Oliver. *Jonathan Swift and Ireland.* Urbana: University of Illinois Press, 1962.

G        Gilbert, Jack. *Jonathan Swift, Romantic and Cynic Moralist.* Austin: University of Texas Press, 1966.

Ho       Hodgart, Matthew. *Satire.* New York: McGraw-Hill, 1969.

Hu       Hunting, Robert. *Jonathan Swift.* New York: Twayne, 1967.

K        Kernan, Alvin. *The Plot of Satire.* New Haven: Yale University Press, 1965.

LC      Landa, Louis. *Swift and the Church of Ireland.* Oxford: Clarendon Press, 1954.

LG      Landa, Louis, ed. *Gulliver's Travels and Other Writings.* Boston: Houghton Mifflin, 1960. *LG* refers to Landa's critical apparatus, as distinguished from the text of *A Modest Proposal,* which is abbreviated as *MP.*

LI      Leavis, F. R. "The Irony of Swift." In A. Norman Jeffares, ed., *Swift: Modern Judgements.* Nashville: Aurora, 1970, pp. 121–134.

M      Murry, John Middleton. *Jonathan Swift, A Critical Biography.* New York: Noonday Press, 1955.

MP      Please see *LG.*

P      Paulson, Ronald. *The Fictions of Satire.* Baltimore: Johns Hopkins University Press, 1967.

QS      Quintana, Ricardo. *Swift, An Introduction.* London: Oxford University Press, 1962.

QT      ———. *Two Augustans: John Locke, Jonathan Swift.* Madison: University of Wisconsin Press, 1978.

R      Rosenheim, Edward W., Jr. *Swift and the Satirist's Art.* Chicago: University of Chicago Press, 1963.

Rw      Rowse, Alfred Leslie. *Jonathan Swift.* New York: Charles Scribner's Sons, 1975.

T      Tuveson, Ernest. "Swift: The View from Within the Satire." In H. James Jensen, and Malvin R. Zirker, Jr., eds. *The Satirist's Art.* Bloomington: Indiana University Press, 1972, pp. 55–85.

W      Williams, Kathleen. *Jonathan Swift and the Age of Compromise.* Lawrence: University Press of Kansas, 1968.

---

## Commentary on the Theme

This theme is a response to an assignment visualized as requiring 1,500 to 2,000 words with a minimum of fifteen sources. Because of this length, the first two paragraphs raise important historical and critical perspectives which are relevant to the topic of point of view in *A Modest Proposal.* Particular attention is given to some of the adverse criticism against Swift because of the apparent harshness of the work. The third paragraph of the theme specifically introduces the topic of point of view and raises the issues to be explored in the theme.

Paragraphs four and five deal with the positive aspects of Swift's speaker. Five critical references are cited in addition to the references to *A Modest Proposal* itself.

Paragraph six describes the negative aspects of the speaker. Here, four authorities are cited. Please note that the second sentence contains a point of disagreement (and the third, a point of agreement) with one of the sources.

Paragraphs seven and eight contain, respectively, a discussion of the irony and the satire of Swift as they are brought about through the point of view. Paragraph seven explains the irony with the help of five critical sources. Paragraph eight is less dependent on sources in its first half and thus is more a result of the writer's original thoughts. The latter half of the paragraph introduces three authorities for the conclusions reached there.

Paragraphs nine through twelve constitute the *con* and *pro* of a critical controversy, derived from the sources, about whether Swift made his speaker consistent. The ninth paragraph utilizes the ideas of three critics who have noted an inconsistency in Swift's voice. The tenth paragraph is a transition to the argument in paragraphs eleven and twelve. Paragraph ten is entirely original, using no sources at all but attempting to show the basis for an argument in favor of consistency. Paragraph eleven points toward the conclusion announced in its concluding two sentences. For one of the factual references, four sources are cited. The twelfth paragraph goes beyond the eleventh by relating the quality of the work to the consistency of the speaker's voice.

The concluding two paragraphs cite references in support of the conclusion in paragraph twelve that "the main strength of the work is the consistency of the projector's voice." In defining the quality of *A Modest Proposal,* paragraph thirteen cites three critics who note the work's disturbing effect, but paragraph thirteen offsets these critics by citing two other critics who praise the work. The last paragraph is largely original, concluding with praise from one of the sources.

# Taking Examinations on Literature

Taking an examination on literature is not difficult if you prepare in the right way. Preparing means (1) studying the material assigned, studying the comments made in class by your instructor and by fellow students in discussion, and studying your own thoughts; (2) anticipating the questions by writing some of your own on the material to be tested and by writing practice answers to these questions; and (3) understanding the precise function of the test in your education.

You should realize that the test is not designed to plague you or to hold down your grade. The grade you receive is in fact a reflection of your achievement at a given point in the course. If your grades are low, you can probably improve them by studying in a coherent and systematic way. Those students who can easily do satisfactory work might do superior work if they improve their method of preparation. From whatever level you begin, you can increase your achievement by improving your method of study.

Your instructor has three major concerns in evaluating your tests (assuming literate English): (1) to see the extent of your command over the subject material of the course ("How good is your retention?"), (2) to see how well you are able to think about the material ("How well are you educating yourself?"), and (3) to see how well you can actually respond to a question or address yourself to an issue.

There are many elements that go into writing good answers on tests, but this last point, about responsiveness, is perhaps the most important.

A major cause of low exam grades is that students really do not *answer* the questions asked. Does that seem surprising? The problem is that some students do no more than retell the story, never confronting the issues in the question. This is the common problem that has been treated throughout this book. Therefore, if you are asked, "Why does . . . ," be sure to emphasize the *why*, and use the *does* only to exemplify the *why*. If the question is about organization, focus on that. If a problem has been raised, deal with the problem. In short, always *respond* directly to the question or instruction. Let us compare two answers to the same question:

> Q. How does the setting of Stephen Crane's "Horses—One Dash" contribute to the action of the story?

### A

The setting is essential to the action of "Horses—One Dash." The scene opens on the Mexican desert. It is lovely, with mesquite and distant hills that are beautiful in the setting sun. Richardson and Jose, his servant and guide, are riding through this desert. As night comes on, so do the shadows and the cold, so Richardson and Jose go to a nearby village for shelter. The village looks ghostly in the twilight gloom. The men find a house, an inn, in which to spend the night. There, Richardson's expensive looking gun and saddle excite the local gang of men, who apparently decide to rob him and likely kill him. There is a good deal of tension in the house as Richardson believes that the men are closing in, but the main action is that Jose is beaten. Soon the gang is distracted by guitar music and laughing women, and so Richardson gets some disturbed sleep. In the early morning it is back to the horses for Richardson and Jose, who flee into the surrounding desert and hills. They push their horses to topmost speed and they are pursued closely by the bandits from the village. It is in the hills that the two men are about to be caught and killed, but a patrol of *Rurales* (soldiers) stops the chase and makes the rescue. "Horses—One Dash" is an action story, and the setting is indispensable in this action.

### B

The setting is both a cause and location for the action of "Horses—One Dash." The coldness and darkness of the Mexican desert at night force Richardson and Jose into the nearby village to find a house or inn (cause). This inn, with its force of young men, hoodlums really, is the location for the first part of the action. The men aim to rob and likely kill Richardson and Jose for Richardson's expensive equipment (cause). Because the inn also supplies music and women, however (cause), the locals settle at first for beating poor Jose (location). But the inn is not a refuge for long, and the threat makes Richardson wake Jose and ride away before sunup (cause). The desert and nearby hills are the natural place of their flight, and thus the scene of action (location). Fortunately, the isolation and lawlessness of this natural setting justify the patrolling *Rurales* (cause). Therefore, just as the chase is about to end in death for Richardson and Jose, the *Rurales* stop the pursuers (location). "Horses—One Dash" is an action story, and the setting is indispensable to the action both as a cause and location.

While column *A* relates the action to the various scenes of the story, it does not focus on the relationship. It is also cluttered by details that have no bearing on the question. Column *B,* on the other hand, focuses directly on the connection and uses parenthetical words for emphasis. Because of this emphasis, *B* is shorter than *A.* That is, with the focus directly on the issue, there is no need for irrelevant narrative details. Thus, *A* is unresponsive and unnecessarily long, while *B* is responsive and includes only enough detail to exemplify the major points.

## Preparation

Your problem is how best to prepare yourself to have a knowledgeable and ready mind at examination time. If you simply cram facts into your head for the examination in hopes that you will be able to adjust to whatever questions are asked, you will likely flounder.

### READ AND REREAD

Above all, keep in mind that your preparation should begin not on the night before the exam but as soon as the course begins. When each assignment is given, you should complete it by the date due, for you will understand your instructor's lecture and the classroom discussion only if you know the material being discussed. Then, about a week before the exam, you should review each assignment, preferably rereading everything completely. With this preparation, your study on the night before the exam will be fruitful, for it might be viewed as a climax of preparation, not the entire preparation itself.

### MAKE YOUR OWN QUESTIONS: GO ON THE ATTACK

Just to read or reread is too passive to give you the masterly preparation you want for an exam. You should instead go on the attack by trying to anticipate the specific conditions of the test. The best way to reach this goal is to compose and answer your own practice questions. Do not waste your time trying to guess the questions you think your instructor might ask. That might happen—and wouldn't you be happy if it did?—but do not turn your study into a game of chance. What is of greatest importance is to arrange the subject matter by asking yourself questions that help you get things straight.

How can you make your own questions? It is not as hard as you might think. Your instructor may have announced certain topics or ideas to be tested on the exam. You might develop questions from these. Or you might apply general questions to the specifics of your assignments, as in the following examples:

1. About a character: What sort of character is *A*? How does *A* grow, or change in the work? What does *A* learn, or not learn, that brings about the conclusion? To what degree is *A* the representative of any particular type?
2. About the interactions of characters: How does *B* influence *A*? Does a change in *C* bring about any corresponding change in *A*?
3. About events or situations: What relationship does episode *A* have to situation *B*? Does *C*'s thinking about situation *D* have any influence on the outcome of event *E*?
4. About a problem: Why is character *A* or situation *X* this way and not that way? Is the conclusion justified by the ideas and events leading up to it?

## ADAPT YOUR NOTES
## TO MAKE QUESTIONS

Perhaps the best way to construct questions is to use your classroom notes, for notes are the fullest record you have about your instructor's views of the subject material. As you work with your notes, you should refer to passages from the text that were studied by the class or mentioned by your instructor. If there is time, try to memorize as many important phrases or lines as you can; plan to incorporate these into your answers as evidence to support the points you make. Remember that it is good to work not only with main ideas from your notes, but also with matters such as style, imagery, and organization.

Obviously you cannot make questions from all your notes, and you will therefore need to select from those that seem most important. As an example, here is a short but significant note from a class about John Dryden's poem *Absalom and Achitophel* (1681): "A political poem—unintelligible unless one knows the politics of the time." It is not difficult to use this note to make two practice questions:

1. Why is *Absalom and Achitophel* unintelligible unless one knows the politics of the time?
2. What knowledge of the politics of the time is needed to make *Absalom and Achitophel* intelligible?

The first question consists of the simple adaptation of the word *why* to the phrasing of the note. For the second, the word *what* has been adapted. Either question would force pointed study. The first would require an explanation of how various parts of Dryden's poem become clear only when they are related to aspects of the politics of 1681. The second would emphasize the politics, with less reference to the poem. If you spent fifteen or twenty minutes writing practice answers to these questions, you could be confident in taking an examination on the material. It is likely that you could adapt your preparation to any question related to the politics of the poem.

## WORK WITH QUESTIONS EVEN
## WHEN TIME IS SHORT

Whatever your subject, it is important that you spend as much study time as possible making and answering your own questions. Of course, you will have limited time and will not be able to write extensive answers indefinitely. Even so, do not give up on the question method. If time is too short for full answers, write out the main heads, or topics, of an answer. When the press of time (or the need for sleep) no longer permits you to make even such a brief outline answer, keep thinking of questions, and think about the answers on the way to the exam. Try never to read passively or unresponsively, but always with a creative, question-and-answer goal. Think of studying as a potential writing experience.

Whatever time you spend in this way will be of great value, for as you practice, you will develop control and therefore confidence. If you have ever known anyone who has had difficulty with tests, or who has claimed a phobia about them, you may find that a major cause has been passive rather than active preparation. The process is about like this: A passively prepared student finds that test questions compel thought, arrangement, and responsiveness; but the student is not ready for this challenge and therefore writes answers that are both unresponsive and filled with summary. The grade, needless to say, is low, and the student's general fear of tests is reinforced. It seems clear that active, creative study is the best way to break any such long-standing patterns of fear or uncertainty, because it is the best form of preparation. There is no moral case to make against practice question-and-answer study, either, for everyone has the right and obligation to prepare—and all of this is preparation—in the best way possible.

## STUDY WITH A FELLOW STUDENT

Often the thoughts of another person can help you understand the material to be tested. Try to find a fellow student with whom you can work, for both of you can help each other. In view of the need for steady preparation throughout a course, keep in mind that regular conversations (over coffee or some other beverage to your liking) are a good idea. Also, you might wish to make your joint study genuinely systematic and thus might set aside a specific evening or afternoon for detailed work sessions. Make the effort; working with someone else can be stimulating and rewarding.

# Two Basic Types of Questions About Literature

There are two types of questions that you will find on any examination about literature. Keep them in mind as you prepare. The first type is *factual,* or *mainly objective,* and the second is *general, comprehensive, broad,* or *mainly subjective.* In a literature course very few questions are purely objective, except multiple-choice questions.

## FACTUAL QUESTIONS

**MULTIPLE-CHOICE QUESTIONS.** These are the most purely factual questions. In a literature course your instructor will most likely reserve them for short quizzes, usually on days when an assignment is due, to make sure that you are keeping up with the reading. Multiple choice can test your knowledge of facts, and it also can test your ingenuity in perceiving subtleties of phrasing in certain choices, but on a literature exam this type of question is rare.

**IDENTIFICATION QUESTIONS.** These questions are decidedly of more interest. They test not only your factual knowledge but also your ability to relate this knowledge to your understanding of the work assigned. This type of question will frequently be used as a check on the depth and scope of your reading. In fact, an entire exam could be composed of only identification questions, each demanding perhaps five minutes to write. Typical examples of what you might be asked to identify are:

1. *A character,* for example, Nora in O'Connor's "First Confession." It is necessary to describe briefly the character's position and main activity (i.e., she is Jackie's older sister who gets him in trouble at home and who takes him to his confession). You should then go on to emphasize the character's importance (i.e., her values help keep Jackie confused throughout most of the story, but by the end it is clear that O'Connor shows that it is really her values that are confused).
2. *Incidents or situations,* which may be illustrated as follows: "A woman mourns the death of her husband." After giving the location of the situation or incident (Mrs. Popov in Chekhov's play *The Bear*), try to demonstrate its significance in the work. (That is, Mrs. Popov is mourning the death of her husband when the play opens, and in the course of the play Chekhov uses her feelings to show amusingly that life with real emotion is stronger than devotion or duty to the dead.)
3. *Things, places, and dates.* Your instructor may ask you to identify an "overcoat" (Gogol's "Overcoat"), or a train station (Cheever's "The Five Forty-Five"), or the date of *Paradise Lost* (1672). For dates, you might often be given a leeway of five or ten years if you must guess.

4. *Quotations.* Theoretically, you should remember enough of the text to identify a passage taken from it, or at least to make an informed guess. Generally, you should try to locate the quotation, if you remember it, or else to describe the probable location, and to show the ways in which the quotation is typical of the work you have read, with regard to both content and style. You can often salvage much from a momentary lapse of memory by writing a reasoned and careful explanation of your guess, even if the guess is incorrect.

TECHNICAL AND ANALYTICAL QUESTIONS AND PROBLEMS. In a scale of ascending importance, the third and most difficult type of factual question is on those matters with which this book has been concerned: technique, analysis, and problems. You might be asked to discuss the *setting, images, point of view,* or *principal idea* of a work; you might be asked about a *specific problem;* you might be asked to analyze a poem that may or may not be duplicated for your benefit (if it is not duplicated, woe to students who have not studied their assignments). Questions like these are difficult, because they usually assume that you have a fairly technical knowledge of some important terms, while they also ask you to examine the text quite rigidly within the limitations imposed by the terms.

Obviously, technical questions will occur more frequently in advanced courses than in elementary ones, and the questions will become more subtle as the courses become more advanced, Instructors of elementary courses may frequently use main-idea or special-problem questions but will probably not use many of the others unless they specifically state their intentions to do so in advance, or unless technical terms have been studied in class.

Questions of this type are fairly long, perhaps with from fifteen to twenty-five minutes allowed for each. If you have two or more of these questions, try to space your time sensibly; do not devote 80 percent of your time to one question and leave only 20 percent for the rest.

## BASIS OF JUDGING
## FACTUAL QUESTIONS

IDENTIFICATION QUESTIONS. In all factual questions, literate English being assumed, your instructor is testing (1) your factual command, and (2) your quickness in relating a part to the whole. Thus, suppose that you are identifying the incident "A woman refuses to go on tour with a traveling show" (assuming that you are being quizzed on Dreiser's novel *Sister Carrie*). You would identify Sister Carrie as the woman and say that she is advised by her friend Lola to stay in New York (where the big opportunity is) and not to go on tour, where nobody important will see her. You would also try to show that the incident occurs when Carrie is just a minor dancer, during her early years in show business. But more important, you should show that her decision leaves her in New York, where a new opportunity develops, quickly enabling Carrie to become a star. You should conclude by saying that the incident prepares the way for all Carrie's later successes and show how far she has advanced above Hurstwood's deteriorating state, monetarily speaking. The incident can therefore be seen as one of the most significant in the entire novel.

Your answers should all take this general pattern, Always try to show the *significance* of the things you are identifying. Significance, of course, works in many directions, but for a short identification question you should try to refer to (1) major events in the book, (2) major ideas, (3) the structure of the work, and (4) for a quotation, the style. Time is short; therefore you must be selective, but if you can set your mind toward producing answers along these lines, you will probably approach what your instructor expects.

Here are three answers that were written to an identification question. The students were asked to identify "The thing which was not," from the fourth voyage of Swift's *Gulliver's Travels*.

*Answer 1.* This quotation serves as an example of a typical saying in the language of the Houyhnhnms. It means that the thing was false. It shows their roundabout method of saying things.

*Answer 2.* This quotation is found in Chapter IV of "A Voyage to the Country of the Houyhnhnms." Gulliver is told this by his Master, one of the Houyhnhnms (a horse). It is brought out when the two of them are discussing their own customs and culture, and Gulliver is telling his Master how he sailed over to this country. The Master finds it hard to believe. He tells Gulliver that lying is altogether foreign to the culture of the Houyhnhnms. He says speech is for the purpose of being understood and he cannot comprehend lying and is unfamiliar with doubt. He goes on to say that if someone says "the thing which was not," the whole end of speech is defeated. I think what the Master has said to Gulliver clearly illustrates Swift's thought that people should use language as a means to communicate truth or otherwise its purpose is defeated. We can also see Swift's thought that this very beautiful concept of language and its use is not taken up by people. This degrades humankind.

*Answer 3. The thing which was not,* a variation on *"is* not," is used throughout the fourth voyage of Gulliver by the Houyhnhnm Master as a term for lying—telling a thing contrary to fact. The term is interesting because it shows a completely reasonable reaction (represented by that of the Houyhnhnm Master) toward a lie, with all the subtle variations on the word we have in English. By whatever term we use, a lie is <u>a thing which is not</u> (except in the mind of the person who tells it) and destroys the chief end of speech—truthful communication. The term is therefore an integral part of Swift's attack in *Gulliver* on the misuse of reason. A lie misleads the reason and thereby destroys all the processes of reason (e.g., logic, science, law) by supplying it with nonexistent things. Because our civilization depends on the reasonable pursuit of truth, a lie about anything is thus actually an attack on civilization itself. Swift's Houyhnhnms have this value, then, that they provide us with a reasonable basis for judging elements in our own life, and for improving them where reason can improve them.

The first answer is not satisfactory, since it is inaccurate in sentences one and three and does not indicate much thought about the meaning of the quotation. The second answer is satisfactory; despite faults of style, it shows knowledge of the conditions under which the quotation is delivered, and it also indicates some understanding of the general meaning of the quotation. The third answer is superior, for it relates the quotation to Swift's satiric purposes in *Gulliver's Travels* and also shows how lying becomes a perversion of language and reason. The distinguishing mark of the third answer is that it shows *thorough* understanding.

One thing is clear from these sample answers: *really superior answers cannot be written if your thinking originates entirely at the time you are faced with the question;* the more thinking and practicing you do before the exam, the better your answers will be. Obviously the writer of the third answer was not caught unprepared. You should reduce surprise on an exam to an absolute minimum.

LONGER FACTUAL QUESTIONS. The more extended factual questions also require more thoroughly developed organization. Remember that here your knowledge of essay writing is important, for the quality of your composition will determine a major share of your instructor's evaluation of your answers. It is therefore best to take several minutes to gather your thoughts together before you begin to write, because a 10-minute planned answer is preferable to a 25-minute unplanned answer. You do not need to write down every possible fact on each particular question. Of greater significance is the use to which you put the facts you know and the organization of your answer. When the questions are before you, use a sheet of scratch paper to jot down the facts you remember and your ideas about them in relation to the question. Then put them together, phrase a thesis sentence, and use your facts to illustrate or prove your thesis.

It is always necessary to begin your answer pointedly, using key words or phrases from the question or direction if possible, so that your answer will have thematic shape. You should never begin an answer with "Because" and then go on from there without referring again to the question. To be most responsive during the short time available for writing an exam, you should use the question as your guide for your answer. Let us suppose that you have the following question on your test: "What are some reasons for which Dick Diver loses his professional abilities and therefore his strength and security?" (Fitzgerald's novel *Tender Is the Night*). You should use some of the phrases here to launch yourself. Here are some possible opening sentences, with phrases from the question underlined:

Dick Diver <u>loses his professional abilities</u> for at least two <u>reasons.</u> Fitzgerald indicates that Nicole absorbs Dick's <u>strength</u> as he loses it by helping her back to mental health. A more plausible <u>reason</u> is the sapping of his <u>strength and security</u> by his living so superficially among the international set.

From this opening you could go on to develop Fitzgerald's reason (Dick's relationship with his wife) and then your own (Dick's lifestyle among the wealthy). What is important here is that these first three sentences have set the aims and limits of the answer, so that the entire response will be self-contained. The problem with many answers is that they are not self-contained; they seem to exist in a vacuum, totally apart from the question. Your reader or readers must always know what you are about, and there is no way they can know unless *you* tell them. Your best approach is to think of every one of your answers as an essay, no matter how short, demanding good thinking, clear organizing, and pointed writing.

For comparison, here are two paragraphs from a 25-minute question on Fitzgerald's story "The Rich Boy." The question was: "What do Anson's two love affairs contribute to your understanding of his character?" Both paragraphs are about Anson's first love affair, with Paula Legendre:

1

2

The Paula affair helps understand Anson. Paula best understood him through their relationship. Anson was searching for stability and security in life; he felt he could achieve these with Paula. This was shown through the following idea: if only he could be with Paula he would be happy. Paula saw him as a mixture of solidity and self-indulgence and cynicism. She deeply loved him, but it was impossible for him to form a lasting relationship with her. The reason for this was his drinking and his code of superiority. This was shown in the fact that he felt hopeless despair before his pride and his self-knowledge. His superiority can be further observed through his physical and emotional relationship with Paula. His entire relationship with Paula was based on his feelings that emotion was sufficient, and why should he commit himself? Her marriage greatly affected Anson; it made a cynic out of him.

Fitzgerald brings out Anson's strength and weakness through the Paula affair. In one way, Anson sees in Paula everything he needs for a full, satisfying life: love, equal social and economic position, a purpose in life, and conservatism. His earnest, low talks with her show how positive his life could be if he were to marry her. But Paula also brings out Anson's weakness. Because his life as a rich boy has been without motivation or responsibility, he is a man of shallow and superficial emotions. Thus, he cannot face the responsibility of marriage with Paula. He gets drunk and embarrasses her. He delays proposing to her at the right moment, and therefore the right moment is lost forever. When Paula marries another man, Anson is deeply disturbed, but secretly he is happy. He is really no better than a child, for his emotions are undeveloped. Paula is his opportunity, and he knows it, but he cannot summon the necessary strength to come to grips with maturity, and thus he becomes an emotional failure.

Column 2 is superior to column 1. If column 1 were judged as part of an outside-class theme, it would be a failure, but as part of a test it would probably receive a passing grade. Column 2 is clearer; it develops its point well and uses evidence more accurately as illustration.

## GENERAL OR COMPREHENSIVE QUESTIONS

General or comprehensive questions are particularly important on final examinations, when your instructor is interested in testing your total comprehension of the course material. You have much freedom of choice in deciding what to write, but you must constantly bear in mind that your instructor is looking for intelligence and knowledge in what you choose to say.

Considerable time is usually allowed for answering a comprehensive question, perhaps 45 minutes or more, depending on the scope and depth that your instructor expects. Questions may be phrased in a number of ways:

1. A direct question asking about philosophy, underlying attitudes, "schools" of literature or literary movements, main ideas, characteristics of style, backgrounds, and so on. Here are some typical questions in this category: "Define and characterize Metaphysical poetry," or "Discuss the influences of science on literature in the Restoration," or "Describe the dramatic prose of the Jacobean dramatists."
2. A "comment" question, usually based on an extensive quotation, borrowed from a critic or written by your instructor for the occasion, about a broad class of writers, or about a literary movement, or the like. Your instructor may ask you to treat this question broadly (taking in many writers) or else to apply the quotation to a specific writer.
3. A "suppose" question, such as "Suppose Rosalind were in Desdemona's place; what would she do when Othello accused her of infidelity?" or "What would Pope say about Joyce's *Ulysses?*"

## BASIS OF JUDGING GENERAL QUESTIONS

In dealing with a broad, general question you are in fact dealing with an unstructured situation, and you must not only supply an *answer* but—almost more important—must also create a *structure* within which your answer can have meaning. You might say that you make up your own question, which will be derived from the original, broadly expressed question. If you were asked to "Consider Shakespeare's thoughts about the ideal monarch," for example, you would do well to structure the question by narrowing its limits. A possible narrowing might be put as follows: "Shakespeare dramatizes thoughts about the ideal monarch by setting up a contrast between, on one side, monarchs who fail either by alienating their close supporters or by becoming tyrannical, and, on the other side, monarchs who succeed by securing faithful supporters and by creating confidence in themselves." With this sort of focus, you would be able to proceed point by point, introducing supporting data as you went. Without such a structure, you would experience difficulty.

As a general rule, the best method to adopt in answering a comprehensive question is that of comparison-contrast. The reason is that in dealing with, say, a general question on Yeats, Eliot, and Auden, it is too easy to write *three* separate essays rather than one. Thus, you should force yourself to consider a topic like "The Treatment of Alienation," or "The Attempt to Find Truth," and then to treat such a topic point by point rather than author by author. If you were answering the question posed on Shakespeare's thoughts about the ideal monarch, you might try to show the failures of Richard II and Richard III against the successes of Henry IV and Henry V. It would also be relevant to introduce, by way of comparison and contrast, references to Antony, and even to King Lear or to Prospero (from *The Tempest*). By moving from point to point, you would bring in these references as they are germane to your topic. But if you treated each figure separately, your comprehensive answer would become diffuse and ineffective. Fur further ideas on this method, see Chapter 10.

In judging your response to a general question, your instructor is interested in seeing: (1) how intelligently you select material, (2) how well you organize your material, (3) how adequate and intelligent are the generalizations you make about the material, and (4) how relevant are the facts you select for illustration.

Bear in mind that in comprehensive questions, though you are ostensibly free, the freedom you have been extended has been that of creating your own structure. The underlying idea of the comprehensive, general question is that you personally possess special knowledge and insights that cannot be discovered by more factual questions. You must therefore try to formulate your own responses to the material and try to introduce evidence that reflects your own particular insights and command of information.

# *appendix b*

# *A Note on Documentation*

This section will not present a complete discussion of documentation but only as much as is necessary for typical themes about literature. You will find complete discussions in most writing handbooks and guidebooks to research, and in the latest edition of the *MLA Style Sheet*. Whenever you are in doubt about documentation, always ask your instructor.

In any writing not derived purely from your own mind, you must document your facts. In writing about literature, you must base your conclusions on material in particular literary works and must document this material. If you refer to secondary sources, you must be especially careful to document your facts. To document properly, you must use illustrative material in your discussion and mention your sources either in your discussion or in footnotes to it.

## Integration and Mechanics of Quotations

DISTINGUISH YOUR THOUGHTS FROM THOSE OF YOUR AUTHOR. Ideally your themes should reflect your own thought as it is prompted and illustrated by an author's work. Sometimes a problem arises, however, because it is hard for your reader to know when *your* ideas have stopped and your *author's* have begun. You must therefore arrange things to make the distinction clear, but you must also create a constant blending of materials that will make your themes easy to follow. You will be moving from paraphrase, to general interpretation, to observation, to independent application of everything you choose to discuss. It is not always easy to keep these various elements integrated. Let us see an example in which the writer moves from reference to an author's ideas—really paraphrase—to an independent application of the idea:

> [1] In the "Preface to the Lyrical Ballads," Wordsworth stated that the language of poetry should be the same as that of prose. [2] That is, poetic diction should not be artificial or contrived in any sense, but should consist of the words normally used by people in their everyday lives (pp. 791–793). [3] If one follows this principle in poetry, then it would be improper to refer to the sun as anything but *the sun*. [4] To call it a *heavenly orb* or the *source of golden gleams* would be inadmissible because these phrases are not used in common speech.

Here the first two sentences present a paraphrase of Wordsworth's ideas about poetic diction, the second going so far as to locate a particular spot where the idea is developed. The third and fourth sentences apply Wordsworth's idea to examples chosen by the writer. Here the blending is provided by the transitional clause, "If one follows this principle," and the reader is thus not confused about who is saying what.

INTEGRATE MATERIAL BY USING QUOTATION MARKS.   Sometimes you will use short quotations from your author to illustrate your ideas and interpretations. Here the problem of distinguishing your thoughts from the author's is solved by quotation marks. In this sort of internal quotation you may treat prose and poetry in the same way. If a poetic quotation extends from the end of one line to the beginning of another, however, indicate the line break with a virgule (/) and use a capital letter to begin the next line, as in the following:

> Wordsworth states that in his boyhood all of nature seemed like his own personal property. Rocks, mountains, and woods were almost like food to him, and he claimed that "the sounding cataract/Haunted . . . [him] like a passion" (76–80).

BLEND QUOTATIONS INTO YOUR OWN SENTENCES.   Making internal quotations still creates the problem of blending materials, however, for quotations should never be brought in unless you prepare your reader for them in some way. Do not, for example, bring in quotations in the following manner:

> The sky is darkened by thick clouds, bringing a feeling of gloom that is associated with the same feeling that can be sensed at a funeral. "See gloomy clouds obscure the cheerful day."

This abrupt quotation throws the reader off balance. It is better to prepare the reader to move from the discourse to the quotation, as in the following revision:

> The scene is marked by sorrow and depression, as though the spectator, who is asked to "See gloomy clouds obscure the cheerful day," is present at a funeral.

Here the quotation is made an actual part of the sentence. This sort of blending is satisfactory, provided the quotation is brief.

**SET OFF AND INDENT LONG QUOTATIONS.** The standard for how to place quotations should be not to quote within your own sentence any passage longer than 20 or 25 words. Quotations of greater length demand so much separate attention that they interfere with your own sentence. When your quotation is long, you should set it off separately, remembering to introduce it in some way. It is possible but not desirable to have one of your sentences conclude with an extensive quotation, but you should never make an extensive quotation in the middle of your sentence. By the time you finish such an unwieldy sentence, your reader will have lost sight of how it began.

The physical layout of extensive quotations should be as follows: Leave three blank lines between your own discourse and the quotation. Single-space the quotation and make a special indention for it to set off from the rest of your theme. After the quotation leave a three-line space again and resume your own discourse. Here is a specimen, from a theme about John Gay's *Trivia*, an early eighteenth-century poem:

> In keeping with this general examination of the anti-heroic side of life, Gay takes his description into the street, where constant disturbance and even terror were normal conditions after dark. A person trying to sleep was awakened by midnight drunkards, and the person walking late at night could be attacked by gangs of thieves and cutthroats who waited in dark corners. The reality must have been worse than Gay implies in his description of these sinister inhabitants of the darkened streets:
>
>> Now is the time that rakes their revels keep;
>> Kindlers of riot, enemies of sleep.
>> His scattered pence the flying Nicker flings,
>> And with the copper shower the casement rings.
>> Who has not heard the Scourer's midnight fame?
>> Who has not trembled at the Mohock's name?
>>                     —lines 321–326
>
> Gay mentions only those who have "trembled" at the Mohocks, not those who have experienced their brutality.

This same layout applies also when you are quoting prose passages. When quoting lines of poetry, always remember to quote them *as lines*. Do not run them together. When you set off the quotation by itself, as in the example above, you do *not* need quotation marks.

USE THREE SPACED PERIODS (AN ELLIPSIS) TO SHOW OMISSIONS.  Whether your quotation is long or short, you will often need to change some of the material in it to conform to your own thematic requirements. You might wish to omit something from the quotation that is not essential to your point. Indicate such omissions with three spaced periods ( . . . ). If your quotation is very brief, however, do not use spaced periods, as they might be more of a hindrance than a help. See, for example, the absurdity of using an ellipsis in a sentence like this one:

> Keats asserts that "a thing of beauty . . ." always gives joy.

USE SQUARE BRACKETS FOR YOUR OWN WORDS WITHIN QUOTATIONS.  If you add words of your own to integrate your quotation into your own train of discourse or to explain words that may seem obscure, put square brackets around these words, as in the following passage:

> In the "Tintern Abbey Lines," Wordsworth refers to a trance-like state of illumination, in which the "affections gently lead . . . [him] on." He is unquestionably describing a state of extreme relaxation, for he mentions that the "motion of . . . human blood [was]/Almost suspended [his pulse slowed]" and that in these states he became virtually "a living soul" (lines 42–49).

DO NOT CHANGE YOUR SOURCE.  Always reproduce your source exactly. Because most freshman anthologies and texts modernize the spelling in works that are old, you may never see any old-spelling editions. But if you use an unmodernized text, as in many advanced courses, duplicate everything exactly as you find it, even if this means spelling words like *achieve* as *atchieve* or *joke* as *joak*. A student once spelled out fully the word *an* in the construction "an I were" in an Elizabethan text. The result was unnecessary, because *an* really meant *if* (or *and if*) and not *and*. Difficulties like this one are rare, but you will avoid them if you reproduce the text as you find it. Should you think that something is either misspelled or confusing as it stands, you may do one of two things:

1. Within brackets, clarify or correct the confusing word or phrase, as in the following:

   In 1714, fencing was considered a "Gentlemany [i.e., gentlemanly] subject."

2. Use the word *sic* [Latin for *thus*, meaning "It is this way in the text"] immediately after the problematic word or obvious mistake:

   He was just finning [sic] his way back to health when the next disaster struck.

DO NOT OVERQUOTE.  A word of caution: Do not use too many quotations. You will be judged on your own thought and on the continuity and development of your own theme. It is tempting to use many quotations on the theory that you need to use examples from the text to illustrate your ideas. Naturally, it is important to illustrate your ideas, but please remember that too many quotations can disturb the flow of your own thought.

## Formal Documentation

It is essential to acknowledge any source from which you have derived factual or interpretive information. If you fail to grant recognition, you run the risk of being challenged for representing as your own the results of other people's work. To indicate the source of all derived material, you must, formally, use footnotes at the bottom of the page or at the end of your theme, or informally, embody some form of recognition in the body of your paper. Although the care necessary for noting book titles and page numbers can be annoying, you should realize that footnotes and informal references exist to help your readers. First, your readers may want to consult your source in order to assure themselves that you have not misstated any facts. Second, they may dispute your conclusions and wish to see your source in order to arrive at their own conclusions. Third, they may become so interested in one of your points that they might wish to read more about it for their own pleasure or edification. For these reasons, you must show the sources of all material that you use.

If you are using many sources in a research report, the standard method is to document your paper formally. The procedures discussed here will be sufficient for most papers requiring formal documentation. For especially difficult problems, consult the latest edition of the *MLA Style Sheet* or the section on documentation in your writing handbook.

The first time you quote from a source or refer to the source, you should provide a footnote giving the following information in the order listed below.

### FOR A BOOK

1. The author's name, first name or initials first.
2. The title: in quotation marks for a story or poem; underlined for a book.
3. The edition (if indicated) abbreviated thus: *2nd ed.*, *3rd ed.*, etc.
4. The name of the editor or translator. Abbreviate "editor" or "edited by" as *ed.;* "editors" as *eds.* Use *trans.* for "translator" or "translated by."

5. The publication facts should be given in parentheses in the following order:
   a. City (not the state) of publication, followed by a colon (the state need not be included unless the city might be confused with another).
   b. Publisher. This information is frequently not given, but it is wise to include it.[1]
   c. Year of publication.
6. The page number(s), for example, *p. 65, pp. 65f., pp. 6–10*. For books commonly reprinted (like *Gulliver's Travels*) and for well-known long poems (like *Paradise Lost*) you should include the chapter or part number and the line numbers, so that readers using a different edition may be able to locate your quotation.

## FOR A MAGAZINE ARTICLE

1. The author, first name or initials first.
2. The title of the article, in quotation marks.
3. The name of the magazine, underlined.
4. The volume number, in Arabic numerals (no longer Roman).
5. The year of publication, within parentheses.
6. The page number(s), for example, *65, 65f., 6–10*. (It is not necessary to include *p.* or *pp.* when you have included the volume number of the periodical.)

To prepare for subsequent footnotes, mention at the end of the first footnote that you will hereafter use a shortened reference to the source, such as the author's last name, or the title of the work, or some abbreviation, according to your preference. This practice is illustrated in the sample footnotes that follow.

Footnotes may be positioned either at the bottom of each page (separated from the text by a line) or else at the end of the theme in a list. Some instructors request that each footnote go right into the text at the appropriate position, with lines setting the footnote apart from the text. Ask your instructor about the practice you should adopt.

The first line of a footnote should be paragraph indented, and continuing lines should be flush with the left margin of your theme. Footnote numbers are positioned slightly above the line. Generally, you may single-space footnotes, but be sure to ask your instructor about how to proceed.

---

[1]If faced with a choice, some editors prefer citing the publisher rather than the city of publication, on the assumption that several publishers in cities like London or New York will often have published editions of the same work. For identification purposes, citing the publisher is therefore more helpful than citing the city, but as yet this practice has not been widely adopted. In this as in all matters connected with your course, be guided by the advice of your instructor.

SAMPLE FOOTNOTES

In the examples below, book titles and periodicals, which are usually italicized in print, are shown underlined, as they would be in your type-written paper.

[1]Joseph Conrad, The Rescue: A Romance of the Shallows (New York: Doubleday & Co., Inc., 1960), p. 103. Hereafter cited as The Rescue.

[2]George Milburn, "The Apostate," An Approach to Literature, 3rd ed., Cleanth Brooks, John Thibaut Purser, and Robert Penn Warren, eds. (New York: Appleton-Century-Crofts, Inc., 1952), p. 74. Hereafter cited as "The Apostate."

[3]Carlisle Moore, "Conrad and the Novel as Ordeal," Philological Quarterly, 42 (1963), 59. Hereafter cited as Moore.

[4]Moore, p. 61.

[5]The Rescue, p. 171.

[6]"The Apostate," p. 76.

As a general principle, you do not need to repeat in a footnote any material that you have already incorporated into your theme. For example, if in your theme you mention the author and title of your source, then your footnote should merely give the data about publication. Here is an example:

In *Charles Macklin: An Actor's Life*, William W. Appleton points out that Macklin had been "reinstated at Drury Lane" by December 19, 1744, and that he was playing his stellar role of Shylock.[7]

---

[7](Cambridge, Mass.: Harvard University Press, 1961), p. 72.

# Informal Documentation

To make for a smoother flowing text and to eliminate the sometimes cumbersome apparatus of footnotes, many editors today recommend the incorporation of as many references as possible directly within the paper itself. If you are using many sources, of course, formal footnotes can eliminate possible confusion and misreadings. Even so, you should include the names of authors, articles, and books in the body of your theme whenever possible, as in the example just given.

When you are writing about only one work of literature—as you will be in most of your themes—it is desirable to include virtually all documentation within the text of the theme. The principle is to give complete documentation but to avoid footnotes which distract your reader for no other reason than to list page numbers. This principle has been applied in most of the sample themes in this book.

The method is easy: In a single footnote (the only one you will need), state that all later page numbers, parenthetical and otherwise, will refer to the work you are citing in the footnote:

> ¹Lucian, *True History and Lucius or the Ass*, trans. Paul Turner (Bloomington: Indiana University Press, 1958), p. 49. All page numbers in this theme refer to this edition.

The next time you refer to the source, do the following:

1. For an indented (set off) quotation, indicate the page number, line number, or chapter number, preceded by a dash, immediately below the quotation, as follows:
   > Nobody grows old there, for they all stay the age they were when they first arrived, and it never gets dark. On the other hand, it never gets really light either, and they live in a sort of perpetual twilight such as we have just before sunrise.
   >
   > —p. 39

2. For a quotation blended into your own discussion:
   a. If your sentence ends with the quotation, put the reference in parentheses immediately following the quotation marks and immediately before the period concluding your sentence:
      > Sidney uses the example that "the Romaine lawes allowed no person to be carried to the warres but hee that was in the Souldiers role" (p. 189).
   b. If the quotation ends near the conclusion of your sentence, put the reference in parentheses at the end of your sentence before the period:
      > William Webbe states that poetry originated in the needs for "eyther exhortations to vertue, dehortations from vices, or the prayses of some laudable thing"; that is, in public needs (p. 248).
   c. If the quotation ends far from the end of your sentence, put the reference in parentheses immediately following the quotation mark but before your own punctuation mark:
      > If we accept as a truth Thomas Lodge's statement, "Chaucer in pleasant vein can rebuke sin vncontrold" (p. 69), then satire and comedy are the most effective modes of moral persuasion in literature.

## Shorter Reference Systems

Some instructors recommend shorter reference systems like the above even when many works are being used, as in an extended research theme. The mechanics are simple. First, a first-page list of references should contain all the works—and *only* those works—used in the theme, arranged alphabetically according to abbreviations that stand for the works. All necessary bibliographical information should be included in this list, in the following order:

> For a book:
>> Author, last name first, period.
>>
>> Title, underlined, period.
>>
>> City of publication, colon; publisher, comma; and date, period.
>
> For an article:
>> Author, last name first, period.
>>
>> Title of article, in quotation marks, period.
>>
>> Name of journal, underlined, comma; volume number, together with series number if there is one, in Arabic numerals, no punctuation; year of publication, including month and day of weekly or daily publications, all within parentheses, comma; and inclusive page numbers, period.

Here is a model entry:

Sp      Spacks, Patricia Meyer. An Argument of Images: The Poetry of Alexander Pope. Cambridge: Harvard University Press, 1971.

Whenever a reference to this book is necessary, the abbreviation *Sp* followed by the page number should appear within parentheses, for example: (Sp, 24). The following is a short list of references arranged in this manner:

D      Dixon, Peter. The World of Pope's Satires. London: Methuen, 1968.

G      Gneiting, Teona Tone. "Pictorial Imagery and Satiric Inversion in Pope's Dunciad." Eighteenth-Century Studies, 8 (1975), 420–430.

K      Kallich, Martin I. Heav'ns First Law. DeKalb: Northern Illinois University Press, 1967.

R      Russo, John. Alexander Pope: Tradition and Identity. Cambridge: Harvard University Press, 1972.

Sit      Sitter, John E. The Poetry of Pope's *Dunciad*. Minneapolis: University of Minnesota Press, 1971.

Sp      Spacks, Patricia Meyer. An Argument of Images: The Poetry of Alexander Pope. Cambridge: Harvard University Press, 1971.

W      Wellington, James E. "Pope and Charity." Philological Quarterly, 46 (1967), 225–235.

**NOTE:** When references are made to page numbers in these works, the abbreviations and the page numbers are given in parentheses; e.g., "(D, 24)" refers to page 24 in Peter Dixon's book.

Some instructors prefer that the reference list be numbered and that the numbers be used with the appropriate pages. Let us assume that we number our list, with *D* as *1* and *W* as *7*. Then the parenthetical references "(3, 45)" and "(6, 64)" would refer to page 45 of the Kallich book, and to page 64 of the Spacks book.

Here is a sample paragraph showing the use of the abbreviation system, based on our list of references:

> In the midst of fragmentation and disunity, Alexander Pope held to the ideal that the universe was a whole, an entirety, which provided a "viable benevolent system for the salvation of everyone who does good," as Martin Kallich has stated (K, 24). Pope's view was therefore positive, but it was not passive. It required that people in power use their Christian charity to help the poor, who did not have power (W, 235). In this way, the system worked through an intricate network of human dependency. Pope saw a "common humanity" in life (Sp, 149), and therefore he was tolerant of persons incapable of reason, like Sir Plume, but he was also filled with "a sense of outrage" against those who attempted to destroy art and beauty (G, 421).

## The Reference Method of the American Psychological Association (APA)

A system of references is detailed in the *Publication Manual of the American Psychological Association,* 2nd ed. (Washington: American Psychological Association, 1974, with "Change Sheets" dated 1975 and 1977). The method, used in all the APA journals and in many other publications in the social and natural sciences, is the "author-date method of citation." By this method, all footnotes are eliminated, and the last name of the author or authors, date of publication, and page numbers are included within the article itself. This information may all be included within parentheses, or some of it may appear as part of the discourse, as in the example to follow. The full bibliographical data for each reference are to be found in the bibliography at the end of the article (arranged by the last names of the authors). Nothing is to be included in this list that is not used in the article. Here is a sample paragraph employing the APA method, based on the previous list of seven references:

> Underlying Pope's satires was a complex set of intellectual, psychological, and moral ideals. In the intellectual sphere, Pope measured contemporary wits against the "Augustan conception of cultural progress" (Sitter, 1971, p. 100) and satirized them when they did not measure up. On the personal level, there was a need, in Russo's words, for the "active harmonization of conflicting emotions and ideas" (1972, p. 204). To go too far either toward emotion or reason was to cause psychological disharmony, and therefore to become the butt of Pope's satiric attack. Dixon, in 1968, drew attention to the standards of "genuine hospitality"

and "human dignity" (p. 58) that determined whether Pope's subjects were failing in their moral obligations to love and respect one another, not only personally but socially.

## Final Words

As long as all that you want from a reference is the page number of a quotation or of a paraphrase, any of the shorter methods is suitable and easy, but always remember to use them consistently. They save your reader the trouble of glancing at the bottom of the page or of thumbing through pages to find a long list of footnotes. Obviously, these systems are not adequate if you wish to add more details or if you wish to refer your reader to additional materials that you are not using directly in your theme. In such cases you must use full footnotes.

Whatever method you use, there is un unchanging need to grant recognition to sources. Remember that whenever you begin to write and to make references, you might forget a number of specific details about documentation, and you will certainly discover that you have many questions. Be sure then to ask your instructor, who is your final authority.

*appendix c:*

# Works Used
# *for the*
# *Sample Themes*

## William Shakespeare (1564–1616)

### Sonnet 116

| | |
|---|---|
| Let me not to the marriage of true minds | 1 |
| Admit impediments. Love is not love | 2 |
| Which alters when it alteration finds, | 3 |
| Or bends with the remover to remove: | 4 |
| O, no! it is an ever-fixed mark, | 5 |
| That looks on tempests and is never shaken; | 6 |
| It is the star to every wand'ring bark, | 7 |
| Whose worth's unknown, although his height be taken. | 8 |
| Love's not Time's fool, though rosy lips and cheeks | 9 |
| Within his bending sickle's compass come; | 10 |
| Love alters not with his brief hours and weeks, | 11 |
| But bears it out even to the edge of doom:— | 12 |
|   If this be error and upon me proved, | 13 |
|   I never writ, nor no man ever loved. | 14 |

Not included here are *Black Elk Speaks* (Ch. 16) and the filmscript of *Virgin Spring* (Ch. 17). For illustrative purposes, some works are included with their respective sample themes. These are: Shakespeare's Sonnet 30 (Ch. 9, pp. 107f.), Keats' sonnet "Bright Star" (Ch. 13, pp. 162f.), Rossetti's poem "Echo" (Ch. 13, pp. 181f.), and a passage of Tennyson's "The Passing of Arthur" from *Idylls of the King* (Ch. 13, pp. 171f.).

## Jonathan Swift (1667–1744)

# *A Modest Proposal*

FOR *Preventing the Children of poor People in* Ireland, *from being a Burden to their Parents or Country; and for making them beneficial to the Publick*

WRITTEN IN THE YEAR 1729

IT is a melancholly Object to those, who walk through this great Town, or travel in the Country; when they see the *Streets,* the *Roads,* and *Cabbin-doors* crowded with *Beggars* of the Female Sex, followed by three, four, or six Children, *all in Rags,* and importuning every Passenger for an Alms. These *Mothers,* instead of being able to work for their honest Livelyhood, are forced to employ all their Time in stroling to beg Sustenance for their *helpless Infants;* who, as they grow up, either turn *Thieves* for want of Work; or leave their *dear Native Country, to fight for the Pretender in* Spain, or sell themselves to the *Barbadoes.*

I THINK it is agreed by all Parties, that this prodigious Number of Children in the Arms, or on the Backs, or at the *Heels* of their *Mothers,* and frequently of their *Fathers,* is *in the present deplorable State of the Kingdom,* a very great additional Grievance; and therefore, whoever could find out a fair, cheap, and easy Method of making these Children sound and useful Members of the Commonwealth, would deserve so well of the Publick, as to have his Statue set up for a Preserver of the Nation.

BUT my Intention is very far from being confined to provide only for the Children of *professed Beggars:* It is of a much greater Extent, and shall take in the whole Number of Infants at a certain Age, who are born of Parents, in effect as little able to support them, as those who demand our Charity in the Streets.

AS to my own Part, having turned my Thoughts for many Years, upon this important Subject, and maturely weighed the several *Schemes of other Projectors,* I have always found them grosly mistaken in their Computation. It is true a Child, *just dropt from its* Dam, may be supported by her Milk, for a Solar Year with little other Nourishment; at most not above the Value of two Shillings; which the Mother may certainly get, or the Value in *Scraps,* by her lawful Occupation of *Begging:* And, it is exactly at one Year old, that I propose to provide for them in such a Manner, as, instead of being a Charge upon their *Parents,* or the *Parish,* or *wanting Food and Raiment* for the rest of their Lives; they shall, on the contrary, contribute to the Feeding, and partly to the Cloathing, of many Thousands.

THERE is likewise another great Advantage in my *Scheme,* that it will prevent those *voluntary Abortions,* and that horrid Practice of *Women murdering their Bastard Children;* alas! too frequent among us; sacrificing the *poor innocent Babes,* I doubt, more to avoid the Expence than the Shame; which would move Tears and Pity in the most Savage and inhuman Breast.

THE Number of Souls in *Ireland* being usually reckoned one Million and a half; of these I calculate there may be about Two hundred Thousand Couples whose Wives are Breeders; from which Number I subtract thirty thousand Couples, who are able to maintain their own Children; although I apprehend there cannot be so many, under *the present Distresses of the Kingdom;* but this being granted, there will remain an Hundred and Seventy Thousand Breeders. I again subtract Fifty Thousand, for those Women who miscarry, or whose Children die by Accident, or Disease, within the Year. There only remain an Hundred and Twenty Thousand Children of poor Parents, annually born: The Question therefore is, How this Number shall be reared, and provided for? Which, as I have already said, under the present Situation of Affairs, is utterly impossible, by all the Methods hitherto proposed: For we can *neither employ them in Handicraft* or *Agriculture;* we neither build Houses, (I mean in the Country) nor cultivate Land: They can very seldom pick up a Livelyhood by *Stealing* until they arrive at six Years old; except where they are of towardly Parts; although, I confess, they learn the Rudiments much earlier; during which Time, they can, however, be properly looked upon only as *Probationers;* as I have been informed by a principal Gentleman in the County of *Cavan,* who protested to me, that he never knew above one or two Instances under the Age of six, even in a Part of the Kingdom *so renowned for the quickest Proficiency in that Art.*

I AM assured by our Merchants, that a Boy or a Girl before twelve Years old, is no saleable Commodity; and even when they come to this Age, they will not yield above Three Pounds, or Three Pounds and half a Crown at most, on the Exchange; which cannot turn to Account either to the Parents or the Kingdom; the Charge of Nutriment and Rags, having been at least four Times that Value.

I SHALL now therefore humbly propose my own Thoughts; which I hope will not be liable to the least Objection.

I HAVE been assured by a very knowing *American* of my Acquaintance in *London;* that a young healthy Child, well nursed, is, at a Year old, a most delicious, nourishing, and wholesome Food; whether *Stewed, Roasted, Baked,* or *Boiled;* and, I make no doubt, that it will equally serve in a *Fricasie,* or *Ragoust.*

I DO therefore humbly offer it to *publick Consideration,* that of the Hundred and Twenty Thousand Children, already computed, Twenty thousand may be reserved for Breed; whereof only one Fourth Part to be Males; which is more than we allow to *Sheep, black Cattle,* or *Swine;* and my Reason is, that these Children are seldom the Fruits of Marriage, *a Circumstance not much regarded by our Savages;* therefore, *one Male* will be sufficient to serve *four Females.* That the remaining Hundred thousand, may, at a Year old, be offered in Sale to the *Persons of Quality* and *Fortune,* through the Kingdom; always advising the Mother to let them suck plentifully in the last Month, so as to render them plump, and fat for a good Table. A Child will make two Dishes at an Entertainment for Friends; and when the Family dines alone, the fore or hind Quarter will make a reasonable Dish; and seasoned with a little Pepper or Salt, will be very good Boiled on the fourth Day, especially in *Winter.*

I HAVE reckoned upon a Medium, that a Child just born will weigh Twelve Pounds; and in a solar Year, if tolerably nursed, encreaseth to twenty eight Pounds.

I GRANT this Food will be somewhat dear, and therefore very *proper for Landlords;* who, as they have already devoured most of the Parents, seem to have the best Title to the Children.

INFANTS Flesh will be in Season throughout the Year; but more plentiful in *March,* and a little before and after: For we are told by a grave Author, an eminent *French* Physician, that *Fish being a prolifick Dyet,* there are more Children born in

*Roman Catholick Countries* about Nine Months after *Lent,* than at any other Season: Therefore reckoning a Year after *Lent,* the Markets will be more glutted than usual; because the Number of *Popish Infants,* is, at least, three to one in this Kingdom; and therefore it will have one other Collateral Advantage, by lessening the Number of *Papists* among us.

I HAVE already computed the Charge of nursing a Beggar's Child (in which List I reckon all *Cottagers, Labourers,* and Four fifths of the *Farmers*) to be about two Shillings *per Annum,* Rags included; and I believe, no Gentleman would repine to give Ten Shillings for the *Carcase of a good fat Child;* which, as I have said, will make four Dishes of excellent nutritive Meat, when he hath only some particular Friend, or his own Family, to dine with him. Thus the Squire will learn to be a good Landlord, and grow popular among his Tenants; the Mother will have Eight Shillings net Profit, and be fit for Work until she produceth another Child.

THOSE who are more thrifty *(as I must confess the Times require)* may flay the Carcase; the Skin of which, artifically dressed, will make admirable *Gloves for Ladies,* and *Summer Boots for fine Gentlemen.*

AS to our City of *Dublin;* Shambles may be appointed for this Purpose, in the most convenient Parts of it; and Butchers we may be assured will not be wanting; although I rather recommend buying the Children alive, and dressing them hot from the Knife, as we do *roasting Pigs.*

A VERY worthy Person, *a true Lover of his Country,* and whose Virtues I highly esteem, was lately pleased, in discoursing on this Matter, to offer a Refinement upon my Scheme. He said, that many Gentlemen of this Kingdom, having of late destroyed their Deer; he conceived, that the Want of Venison might be well supplied by the Bodies of young Lads and Maidens, not exceeding fourteen Years of Age, nor under twelve; so great a Number of both Sexes in every County being now ready to starve, for Want of Work and Service: And these to be disposed of by their Parents, if alive, or otherwise by their nearest Relations. But with due Deference to so excellent a Friend, and so deserving a Patriot, I cannot be altogether in his Sentiments. For as to the Males, my *American* Acquaintance assured me from frequent Experience, that their Flesh was generally tough and lean, like that of our School-boys, by continual Exercise, and their Taste disagreeable; and to fatten them would not answer the Charge. Then, as to the Females, it would, I think, with humble Submission, *be a Loss to the Publick,* because they soon would become Breeders themselves: And besides it is not improbable, that some scrupulous People might be apt to censure such a Practice (although indeed very unjustly) as a little bordering upon Cruelty; which, I confess, hath always been with me the strongest Objection against any Project, how well soever intended.

BUT in order to justify my Friend; he confessed, that this Expedient was put into his Head by the famous *Salmanazor,* a Native of the Island *Formosa,* who came from thence to *London,* above twenty Years ago, and in Conversation told my Friend, that in his Country, when any young Person happened to be put to Death, the Executioner sold the Carcase to *Persons of Quality,* as a prime Dainty; and that, in his Time, the Body of a plump Girl of fifteen, who was crucified for an Attempt to poison the Emperor, was sold to his Imperial *Majesty's prime Minister of State,* and other great *Mandarins* of the Court, *in Joints from the Gibbet,* at Four hundred Crowns. Neither indeed can I deny, that if the same Use were made of several plump young girls in this Town, who, without one single Groat to their Fortunes, cannot stir Abroad without a Chair, and appear at the *Play-house*, and *Assemblies* in foreign Fineries, which they never will pay for; the Kingdom would not be the worse.

SOME Persons of a desponding Spirit are in great Concern about that vast Number of poor People, who are Aged, Diseased, or Maimed; and I have been desired to employ my Thoughts what Course may be taken, to ease the Nation of so grievous an Incumbrance. But I am not in the least Pain upon that Matter; because it is very well known, that they are every Day *dying*, and *rotting*, by *Cold* and *Famine*, and *Filth*, and *Vermin*, as fast as can be reasonably expected. And as to the younger Labourers, they are now in almost as hopeful a Condition: They cannot get Work, and consequently pine away for Want of Nourishment, to a Degree, that if at any Time they are accidentally hired to common Labour, they have not Strength to perform it; and thus the Country, and themselves, are in a fair Way of being soon delivered from the Evils to come.

I HAVE too long digressed; and therefore shall return to my Subject. I think the Advantages of the Proposal which I have made, are obvious, and many, as well as of the highest Importance.

FOR, *First*, as I have already observed, it would greatly lessen the *Number of Papists*, with whom we are yearly overrun; being the principal Breeders of the Nation, as well as our most dangerous Enemies; and who stay at home on Purpose, with a Design to *deliver the Kingdom to the Pretender;* hoping to take their Advantage by the Absence *of so many good Protestants*, who have chosen rather to leave their Country, than stay at home, and pay Tithes against their Conscience, to an idolatrous *Episcopal Curate*.

SECONDLY, The poorer Tenants will have something valuable of their own, which, by Law, may be made liable to Distress, and help to pay their Landlord's Rent; their Corn and Cattle being already seized, and *Money a Thing unknown*.

THIRDLY, Whereas the Maintenance of an Hundred Thousand Children, from two Years old, and upwards, cannot be computed at less than ten Shillings a Piece *per Annum*, the Nation's Stock will be thereby encreased Fifty Thousand Pounds *per Annum*; besides the Profit of a new Dish, introduced to the Tables of all *Gentlemen of Fortune* in the Kingdom, who have any Refinement in Taste; and the Money will circulate among ourselves, the Goods being entirely of our own Growth and Manufacture.

FOURTHLY, The constant Breeders, besides the Gain of Eight Shillings *Sterling per Annum*, by the Sale of their Children, will be rid of the Charge of maintaining them after the first Year.

FIFTHLY, This Food would likewise bring great *Custom to Taverns*, where the Vintners will certainly be so prudent, as to procure the best Receipts for dressing it to Perfection; and consequently, have their Houses frequented by all the *fine Gentlemen*, who justly value themselves upon their Knowledge in good Eating; and a skilful Cook, who understands how to oblige his Guests, will contrive to make it as expensive as they please.

SIXTHLY, This would be a great Inducement to Marriage, which all wise Nations have either encouraged by Rewards, or enforced by Laws and Penalties. It would encrease the Care and Tenderness of Mothers towards their Children, when they were sure of a Settlement for Life, to the poor Babes, provided in some Sort by the Publick, to their annual Profit instead of Expence. We should soon see an honest Emulation among the married Women, *which of them could bring the fattest Child to the Market.* Men would become as *fond* of their Wives, during the Time of their Pregnancy, as they are now of their *Mares* in Foal, their *Cows* in Calf, or *Sows* when they are ready to farrow; nor offer to beat or kick them, (as it is too *frequent* a Practice) for fear of a Miscarriage.

MANY other Advantages might be enumerated. For instance, the Addition of some Thousand Carcasses in our Exportation of barrelled Beef: The Propagation of *Swines Flesh,* and Improvement in the Art of making good *Bacon;* so much wanted among us by the great Destruction of *Pigs,* too frequent at our Tables, which are no way comparable in Taste, or Magnificence, to a well-grown fat yearling Child; which, roasted whole, will make a considerable Figure at a *Lord Mayor's Feast,* or any other publick Entertainment. But this, and many others, I omit; being studious of Brevity.

SUPPOSING that one Thousand Families in this City, would be constant Customers for Infants Flesh; besides others who might have it at *merry Meetings,* particularly *Weddings* and *Christenings;* I compute that *Dublin* would take off, annually, about Twenty Thousand Carcasses; and the rest of the Kingdom (where probably they will be sold somewhat cheaper) the remaining Eighty Thousand.

I CAN think of no one Objection, that will possibly be raised against this Proposal; unless it should be urged, that the Number of People will be thereby much lessened in the Kingdom. This I freely own; and it was indeed one principal Design in offering it to the World. I desire the Reader will observe, that I calculate my Remedy *for this one individual Kingdom of* IRELAND, *and for no other that ever was, is, or I think ever can be upon Earth.* Therefore, let no man talk to me of other Expedients: *Of taxing our Absentees at five Shillings a Pound: Of using neither Cloaths, nor Houshold Furniture except what is of our own Growth and Manufacture: Of utterly rejecting the Materials and Instruments that promote foreign Luxury: Of curing the Expensiveness of Pride, Vanity, Idleness, and Gaming in our Women: Of Introducing a Vein of Parsimony, Prudence and Temperance: Of learning to love our Country, wherein we differ even from* LAPLANDERS, *and the Inhabitants of* TOPINAMBOO: *Of quitting our Animosities, and Factions; nor act any longer like the Jews, who were murdering one another at the very Moment their City was taken: Of being a little cautious not to sell our Country and Consciences for nothing: Of teaching Landlords to have, at least, one Degree of Mercy towards their Tenants. Lastly, Of putting a Spirit of Honesty, Industry, and Skill into our Shop-keepers; who, if a Resolution could now be taken to buy only our native Goods, would immediately unite to cheat and exact upon us in the Price, the Measure, and the Goodness; nor could ever yet be brought to make one fair Proposal of just Dealing, though often and earnestly invited to it.*

THEREFORE I repeat, let no Man talk to me of these and the like Expedients; till he hath, at least, a Glimpse of Hope, that there will ever be some hearty and sincere Attempt to put *them in Practice.*

BUT, as to my self; having been wearied out for many Years with offering vain, idle, visionary Thoughts; and at length utterly despairing of Success, I fortunately fell upon this Proposal; which, as it is wholly new, so it hath something *solid* and *real,* of no Expence, and little Trouble, full in our own Power; and whereby we can incur no Danger in *disobliging* ENGLAND: For, this Kind of Commodity will not bear Exportation; the Flesh being of too tender a Consistence, to admit a long Continuance in Salt; *although, perhaps, I could name a Country, which would be glad to eat up our whole Nation without it.*

AFTER all, I am not so violently bent upon my own Opinion, as to reject any Offer proposed by wise Men, which shall be found equally innocent, cheap, easy, and effectual. But before something of that Kind shall be advanced, in Contradiction to my Scheme, and offering a better; I desire the Author, or Authors, will be pleased maturely to consider two Points. *First,* As Things now stand, how they will be able to find Food and Raiment, for a Hundred Thousand useless Mouths and Backs? And *secondly,* There being a round Million of Creatures in human Figure, throughout this Kingdom; whose whole Subsistence, put into a common Stock, would leave them in Debt two Millions of Pounds *Sterling;* adding those, who are Beggars by Profession, to the Bulk of Farmers, Cottagers, and Labourers, with their Wives and Children, who are Beggars in Effect; I desire those Politicians, who dislike my Overture, and may perhaps be so bold to attempt an Answer, that they will first ask the Parents of these Mortals, Whether they would not, at this Day, think it a great Happiness to have been sold for Food at a Year old, in the Manner I prescribe; and thereby have avoided such a perpetual Scene of Misfortunes, as they have since gone through; by the *Oppression of Landlords;* the Impossibility of paying Rent, without Money or Trade; the Want of common Sustenance, with neither House nor Cloaths, to cover them from the Inclemencies of Weather, and the most inevitable Prospect of intailing the like, or greater Miseries upon their Breed for ever.

I PROFESS, in the Sincerity of my Heart, that I have not the least personal Interest, in endeavouring to promote this necessary Work; having no other Motive than the *publick Good of my Country, by advancing our Trade, providing for Infants, relieving the Poor, and giving some Pleasure to the Rich.* I have no Children, by which I can propose to get a single penny; the youngest being nine Years old, and my Wife past Childbearing.

# Nathaniel Hawthorne (1804–1864)

---

# *Young Goodman Brown*

Young Goodman Brown came forth at sunset, into the street of Salem village, but put his head back, after crossing the threshold, to exchange a parting kiss with his young wife. And Faith, as the wife was aptly named, thrust her own pretty head into the street, letting the wind play with the pink ribbons of her cap, while she called to Goodman Brown.

"Dearest heart," whispered she, softly and rather sadly, when her lips were close to his ear, "prithee, put off your journey until sunrise, and sleep in your own bed to-night. A lone woman is troubled with such dreams and such thoughts, that she's afeard of herself, sometimes. Pray, tarry with me this night, dear husband, of all nights in the year!"

"My love and my Faith," replied young Goodman Brown, "of all nights in the year, this one night must I tarry away from thee. My journey, as thou callest it, forth and back again, must needs be done 'twixt now and sunrise. What, my sweet, pretty wife, dost thou doubt me already, and we but three months married!"

"Then God bless you!" said Faith with the pink ribbons, "and may you find all well, when you come back."

"Amen!" cried Goodman Brown. "Say thy prayers, dear Faith, and go to bed at dusk, and no harm will come to thee."

So they parted; and the young man pursued his way, until, being about to turn the corner by the meeting-house, he looked back and saw the head of Faith still peeping after him, with a melancholy air, in spite of her pink ribbons.

"Poor little Faith!" thought he, for his heart smote him. "What a wretch am I, to leave her on such an errand! She talks of dreams, too. Methought, as she spoke, there was trouble in her face, as if a dream had warned her what work is to be done to-night. But no, no! 't would kill her to think it. Well; she's a blessed angel on earth; and after this one night, I'll cling to her skirts and follow her to Heaven."

With this excellent resolve for the future, Goodman Brown felt himself justified in making more haste on his present evil purpose. He had taken a dreary road, darkened by all the gloomiest trees of the forest, which barely stood aside to let the narrow path creep through, and closed immediately behind. It was all as lonely as could be; and there is this peculiarity in such a solitude, that the traveller knows not who may be concealed by the innumerable trunks and the thick boughs overhead; so that, with lonely footsteps, he may yet be passing through an unseen multitude.

"There may be a devilish Indian behind every tree," said Goodman Brown to himself; and he glanced fearfully behind him, as he added, "What if the devil himself should be at my very elbow!"

His head being turned back, he passed a crook of the road, and looking forward again, beheld the figure of a man, in grave and decent attire, seated at the foot of an old tree. He arose at Goodman Brown's approach, and walked onward, side by side with him.

"You are late, Goodman Brown," said he. "The clock of the Old South was striking, as I came through Boston; and that is full fifteen minutes agone."

"Faith kept me back awhile," replied the young man, with a tremor in his voice, caused by the sudden appearance of his companion, though not wholly unexpected.

It was now deep dusk in the forest, and deepest in that part of it where these two were journeying. As nearly as could be discerned, the second traveller was about fifty years old, apparently in the same rank of life as Goodman Brown, and bearing a considerable resemblance to him, though perhaps more in expression than features. Still, they might have been taken for father and son. And yet, though the elder person was as simply clad as the younger, and as simple in manner too, he had an indescribable air of one who knew the world, and would not have felt abashed at the governor's dinner-table, or in King William's court, were it possible that his affairs should call him thither. But the only thing about him that could be fixed upon as remarkable, was his staff, which bore the likeness of a great black snake, so curiously wrought, that it might almost be seen to twist and wriggle itself like a living serpent. This, of course, must have been an ocular deception, assisted by the uncertain light.

"Come, Goodman Brown!" cried his fellow-traveller, "this is a dull pace for the beginning of a journey. Take my staff, if you are so soon weary."

"Friend," said the other, exchanging his slow pace for a full stop, "having kept covenant by meeting thee here, it is my purpose now to return whence I came. I have scruples, touching the matter thou wot'st of."

"Sayest thou so?" replied he of the serpent, smiling apart. "Let us walk on, nevertheless, reasoning as we go, and if I convince thee not, thou shalt turn back. We are but a little way in the forest, yet."

"Too far, too far!" exclaimed the goodman, unconsciously resuming his walk. "My father never went into the woods on such an errand, nor his father before him. We have been a race of honest men and good Christians, since the days of the martyrs. And shall I be the first of the name of Brown that ever took this path and kept—"

"Such company, thou wouldst say," observed the elder person, interrupting his pause. "Well said, Goodman Brown! I have been as well acquainted with your family as with ever a one among the Puritans; and that's no trifle to say. I helped your grandfather, the constable, when he lashed the Quaker woman so smartly through the streets of Salem. And it was I that brought your father a pitch-pine knot, kindled at my own hearth, to set fire to an Indian village, in King Philip's war. They were my good friends, both; and many a pleasant walk have we had along this path, and returned merrily after midnight. I would fain be friends with you, for their sake."

"If it be as thou sayest," replied Goodman Brown, "I marvel they never spoke of these matters. Or, verily, I marvel not, seeing that the least rumor of the sort would have driven them from New England. We are a people of prayer, and good works to boot, and abide no such wickedness."

"Wickedness or not," said the traveller with twisted staff, "I have a very general acquaintance here in New England. The deacons of many a church have drunk the communion wine with me; the selectmen, of divers towns, make me their chairman; and a majority of the Great and General Court are firm supporters of my interest. The governor and I, too—but these are state secrets."

"Can this be so!" cried Goodman Brown, with a stare of amazement at his undisturbed companion. "Howbeit, I have nothing to do with the governor and council; they have their own ways, and are no rule for a simple husbandman like me. But, were I to go on with thee, how should I meet the eye of that good old man, our minister, at Salem village? Oh, his voice would make me tremble, both Sabbath-day and lecture-day!"

Thus far, the elder traveller had listened with due gravity, but now burst into a fit of irrepressible mirth, shaking himself so violently, that his snakelike staff actually seemed to wriggle in sympathy.

"Ha! ha! ha!" shouted he, again and again; then composing himself, "Well, go on, Goodman Brown, go on; but, prithee, don't kill me with laughing!"

"Well, then, to end the matter at once," said Goodman Brown, considerably nettled, "there is my wife, Faith. It would break her dear little heart; and I'd rather break my own!"

"Nay, if that be the case," answered the other, "e'en go thy ways, Goodman Brown. I would not, for twenty old women like the one hobbling before us, that Faith should come to any harm."

As he spoke, he pointed his staff at a female figure on the path, in whom

Goodman Brown recognized a very pious and exemplary dame, who had taught him his catechism in youth, and was still his moral and spiritual adviser, jointly with the minister and Deacon Gookin.

"A marvel, truly, that Goody Cloyse should be so far in the wilderness, at nightfall!" said he. "But, with your leave, friend, I shall take a cut through the woods, until we have left this Christian woman behind. Being a stranger to you, she might ask whom I was consorting with, and whither I was going."

"Be it so," said his fellow-traveller. "Betake you to the woods, and let me keep the path."

Accordingly, the young man turned aside, but took care to watch his companion, who advanced softly along the road, until he had come within a staff's length of the old dame. She, meanwhile, was making the best of her way, with singular speed for so aged a woman, and mumbling some indistinct words, a prayer, doubtless, as she went. The traveller put forth his staff, and touched her withered neck with what seemed the serpent's tail.

"The devil!" screamed the pious old lady.

"Then Goody Cloyse knows her old friend?" observed the traveller, confronting her, and leaning on his writhing stick.

"Ah, forsooth, and is it your worship, indeed?" cried the good dame. "Yea, truly is it, and in the very image of my old gossip, Goodman Brown, the grandfather of the silly fellow that now is. But, would your worship believe it? My broomstick hath strangely disappeared, stolen, as I suspect, by that unhanged witch, Goody Cory, and that, too, when I was all anointed with the juice of smallage and cinquefoil and wolf's-bane—"

"Mingled with fine wheat and the fat of a new-born babe," said the shape of old Goodman Brown.

"Ah, your worship knows the recipe," cried the old lady, cackling aloud. "So, as I was saying, being all ready for the meeting, and no horse to ride on, I made up my mind to foot it; for they tell me there is a nice young man to be taken into communion to-night. But now your good worship will lend me your arm, and we shall be there in a twinkling."

"That can hardly be," answered her friend. "I will not spare you my arm, Goody Cloyse, but here is my staff, if you will."

So saying, he threw it down at her feet, where, perhaps, it assumed life, being one of the rods which its owner had formerly lent to the Egyptian Magi. Of this fact, however, Goodman Brown could not take cognizance. He had cast up his eyes in astonishment, and looking down again, beheld neither Goody Cloyse nor the serpentine staff, but his fellow-traveller alone, who waited for him as calmly as if nothing had happened.

"That old woman taught me my catechism!" said the young man; and there was a world of meaning in this simple comment.

They continued to walk onward, while the elder traveller exhorted his companion to make good speed and persevere in the path, discoursing so aptly, that his arguments seemed rather to spring up in the bosom of his auditor, than to be suggested by himself. As they went he plucked a branch of maple, to serve for a walking-stick, and began to strip it of the twigs and little boughs, which were wet with evening dew. The moment his fingers touched them, they became strangely withered and dried up, as with a week's sunshine. Thus the pair proceeded, at a good free pace, until suddenly, in a gloomy hollow of the road, Goodman Brown sat himself down on the stump of a tree, and refused to go any farther.

"Friend," said he, stubbornly, "my mind is made up. Not another step will I budge on this errand. What if a wretched old woman do choose to go to the devil, when I thought she was going to Heaven! Is that any reason why I should quit my dear Faith, and go after her?"

"You will think better of this by and by," said his acquaintance, composedly. "Sit here and rest yourself a while; and when you feel like moving again, there is my staff to help you along."

Without more words, he threw his companion the maple stick, and was as speedily out of sight as if he had vanished into the deepening gloom. The young man sat a few moments by the roadside, applauding himself greatly, and thinking with how clear a conscience he should meet the minister, in his morning walk, nor shrink from the eye of good old Deacon Gookin. And what calm sleep would be his, that very night, which was to have been spent so wickedly, but purely and sweetly now, in the arms of Faith! Amidst these pleasant and praiseworthy meditations, Goodman Brown heard the tramp of horses along the road, and deemed it advisable to conceal himself within the verge of the forest, conscious of the guilty purpose that had brought him thither, though now so happily turned from it.

On came the hoof-tramps and the voices of the riders, two grave old voices, conversing soberly as they drew near. These mingled sounds appeared to pass along the road, within a few yards of the young man's hiding-place; but owing, doubtless, to the depth of the gloom, at that particular spot, neither the travellers nor their steeds were visible. Though their figures brushed the small boughs by the wayside, it could not be seen that they intercepted, even for a moment, the faint gleam from the strip of bright sky, athwart which they must have passed. Goodman Brown alternately crouched and stood on tiptoe, pulling aside the branches, and thrusting forth his head as far as he durst, without discerning so much as a shadow. It vexed him the more, because he could have sworn, were such a thing possible, that he recognized the voices of the minister and Deacon Gookin, jogging along quietly, as they were wont to do, when bound to some ordination or ecclesiastical council. While yet within hearing, one of the riders stopped to pluck a switch.

"Of the two, reverend Sir," said the voice like the deacon's, "I had rather miss an ordination dinner than to-night's meeting. They tell me that some of our community are to be here from Falmouth and beyond, and others from Connecticut and Rhode Island; besides several of the Indian powwows, who, after their fashion, know almost as much deviltry as the best of us. Moreover, there is a goodly young woman to be taken into communion."

"Mighty well, Deacon Gookin!" replied the solemn old tones of the minister. "Spur up, or we shall be late. Nothing can be done, you know, until I get on the ground."

The hoofs clattered again, and the voices, talking so strangely in the empty air, passed on through the forest, where no church had ever been gathered, nor solitary Christian prayed. Wither, then, could these holy men be journeying, so deep into the heathen wilderness? Young Goodman Brown caught hold of a tree, for support, being ready to sink down on the ground, faint and over-burthened with the heavy sickness of his heart. He looked up to the sky, doubting whether there really was a Heaven above him. Yet, there was the blue arch, and the stars brightening in it.

"With Heaven above, and Faith below, I will yet stand firm against the devil!" cried Goodman Brown.

While he still gazed upward, into the deep arch of the firmament, and had lifted his hands to pray, a cloud, though no wind was stirring, hurried across the zenith, and hid the brightening stars. The blue sky was still visible, except directly overhead, where this black mass of cloud was sweeping swiftly northward. Aloft in the air, as if from the depths of the cloud, came a confused and doubtful sound of voices. Once, the listener fancied that he could distinguish the accents of town's-people of his own, men and women, both pious and ungodly, many of whom he had met at the communion-table, and had seen others rioting at the tavern. The next moment, so indistinct were the sounds, he doubted whether he had heard aught but the murmur of the old forest, whispering without a wind. Then came a stronger swell of those familiar tones, heard daily in the sunshine, at Salem village, but never, until now, from a cloud at night. There was one voice, of a young woman, uttering lamentations, yet with an uncertain sorrow, and entreating for some favor, which, perhaps, it would grieve her to obtain. And all the unseen multitude, both saints and sinners, seemed to encourage her onward.

"Faith!" shouted Goodman Brown, in a voice of agony and desperation; and the echoes of the forest mocked him, crying—"Faith! Faith!" as if bewildered wretches were seeking her, all through the wilderness.

The cry of grief, rage, and terror was yet piercing the night, when the unhappy husband held his breath for a response. There was a scream, drowned immediately in a louder murmur of voices fading into far-off laughter, as the dark cloud swept away, leaving the clear and silent sky above Goodman Brown. But something fluttered lightly down through the air, and caught on the branch of a tree. The young man seized it and beheld a pink ribbon.

"My Faith is gone!" cried he, after one stupefied moment. "There is no good on earth, and sin is but a name. Come, devil! for to thee is this world given."

And maddened with despair, so that he laughed loud and long, did Goodman Brown grasp his staff and set forth again, at such a rate, that he seemed to fly along the forest path, rather than to walk or run. The road grew wilder and drearier, and more faintly traced, and vanished at length, leaving him in the heart of the dark wilderness, still rushing onward, with the instinct that guides mortal man to evil. The whole forest was peopled with frightful sounds; the creaking of the trees, the howling of wild beasts, and the yell of Indians; while, sometimes, the wind tolled like a distant church bell, and sometimes gave a broad roar around the traveller, as if all Nature were laughing him to scorn. But he was himself the chief horror of the scene, and shrank not from its other horrors.

"Ha! ha! ha!" roared Goodman Brown, when the wind laughed at him. "Let us hear which will laugh loudest! Think not to frighten me with your deviltry! Come witch, come wizard, come Indian powwow, come devil himself! and here comes Goodman Brown. You may as well fear him as he fear you!"

In truth, all through the haunted forest, there could be nothing more frightful than the figure of Goodman Brown. On he flew, among the black pines, brandishing his staff with frenzied gestures, now giving vent to an inspiration of horrid blasphemy, and now shouting forth such laughter, as set all the echoes of the forest laughing like demons around him. The fiend in his own shape is less hideous, than when he rages in the breast of man. Thus sped the demoniac on his course, until, quivering among the trees, he saw a red light before him, as when the felled trunks and branches of a clearing have been set on fire, and throw up their lurid blaze against the sky, at the hour of midnight. He paused, in a lull of the tempest that had driven him onward, and heard the swell of what seemed a hymn, rolling solemnly from a distance, with the weight of many voices. He knew the tune. It was a familiar one in the choir of the village meeting-house. The verse died heavily away, and was lengthened by a chorus, not of human voices, but of all the sounds of the benighted wilderness, pealing in awful harmony together. Goodman Brown cried out; and his cry was lost to his own ear, by its unison with the cry of the desert.

In the interval of silence, he stole forward, until the light glared full upon his eyes. At one extremity of an open space, hemmed in by the dark wall of the forest, arose a rock, bearing some rude, natural resemblance either to an altar or a pulpit, and surrounded by four blazing pines, their tops aflame, their stems untouched, like candles at an evening meeting. The mass of foliage, that had overgrown the summit of the rock, was all on fire, blazing high into the night, and fitfully illuminating the whole field. Each pendent twig and leafy festoon was in a blaze. As the red light arose and fell, a numerous congregation alternately shone forth, then disappeared in shadow, and again grew, as it were, out of the darkness, peopling the heart of the solitary woods at once.

"A grave and dark-clad company!" quoth Goodman Brown.

In truth, they were such. Among them, quivering to-and-fro, between gloom and splendor, appeared faces that would be seen, next day, at the council-board of the province, and others which, Sabbath after Sabbath, looked devoutly heavenward, and benignantly over the crowded pews, from the holiest pulpits in the land. Some affirm that the lady of the governor was there. At least, there were high dames well known to her, and wives of honored husbands, and widows a great multitude, and ancient maidens, all of excellent repute, and fair young girls, who trembled lest their mothers should espy them. Either the sudden gleams of light, flashing over the obscure field, bedazzled Goodman Brown, or he recognized a score of the church members of Salem village, famous for their especial sanctity. Good old Deacon Gookin had arrived, and waited at the skirts of that venerable saint, his reverend pastor. But, irreverently consorting with these grave, reputable, and pious people, these elders of the church, these chaste dames and dewy virgins, there were men of dissolute lives and women of spotted fame, wretches given over to all mean and filthy vice, and suspected even of horrid crimes. It was strange to see, that the good shrank not from the wicked, nor were the sinners abashed by the saints. Scattered, also, among their pale-faced enemies, were the Indian priests, or powwows, who had often scared their native forest with more hideous incantations than any known to English witchcraft.

"But, where is Faith?" thought Goodman Brown; and, as hope came into his heart, he trembled.

Another verse of the hymn arose, a slow and mournful strain, such as the pious love, but joined to words which expressed all that our nature can conceive of sin, and darkly hinted at far more. Unfathomable to mere mortals is the lore of fiends. Verse after verse was sung, and still the chorus of the desert swelled between, like the deepest tone of a mighty organ. And, with the final peal of that dreadful anthem, there came a sound, as if the roaring wi.d, the rushing streams, the howling beasts, and every other voice of the unconverted wilderness were mingling and according with the voice of guilty man, in homage to the prince of all. The four blazing pines threw up a loftier flame, and obscurely discovered shapes and visages of horror on the smoke-wreaths, above the impious assembly. At the same moment, the fire on the rock shot redly forth, and formed a glowing arch above its base, where now appeared a figure. With reverence be it spoken, the apparition bore no slight similitude, both in garb and manner, to some grave divine of the New England churches.

"Bring forth the converts!" cried a voice, that echoed through the field and rolled into the forest.

At the word, Goodman Brown stepped forth from the shadow of the trees, and approached the congregation, with whom he felt a loathful brotherhood, by the sympathy of all that was wicked in his heart. He could have well-nigh sworn, that the shape of his own dead father beckoned him to advance, looking downward from a smoke-wreath, while a woman, with dim features of despair, threw out her hand to warn him back. Was it his mother? But he had no power to retreat one step, nor to resist, even in thought, when the minister and good old Deacon Gookin seized his arms, and led him to the blazing rock. Thither came also the slender form of a veiled female, led between Goody Cloyse, that pious teacher of the catechism, and Martha Carrier, who had received the devil's promise to be queen of hell. A rampant hag was she! And there stood the proselytes, beneath the canopy of fire.

"Welcome, my children," said the dark figure, "to the communion of your race! Ye have found, thus young, your nature and your destiny. My children, look behind you!"

They turned; and flashing forth, as it were, in a sheet of flame, the fiend-worshippers were seen; the smile of welcome gleamed darkly on every visage.

"There," resumed the sable form, "are all whom ye have reverenced from youth. Ye deemed them holier than yourselves, and shrank from your own sin, contrasting it with their lives of righteousness and prayerful aspirations heavenward. Yet, here are they all, in my worshipping assembly! This night it shall be granted you to know their secret deeds; how hoary-bearded elders of the church have whispered wanton words to the young maids of their households; how many a woman, eager for widow's weeds, has given her husband a drink at bedtime, and let him sleep his last sleep in her bosom; how beardless youths have made haste to inherit their father's wealth; and how fair damsels—blush not, sweet ones!—have dug little graves in the garden, and bidden me, the sole guest, to an infant's funeral. By the sympathy of your human hearts for sin, ye shall scent out all the places—whether in church, bed-chamber, street, field, or forest—where crime has been committed, and shall exult to behold the whole earth one stain of guilt, one mighty blood-spot. Far more than this! It shall be yours to penetrate, in every bosom, the deep mystery of sin, the fountain of all wicked arts, and which inexhaustibly supplies more evil impulses than human power—than my power, at its utmost!—can make manifest in deeds. And now, my children, look upon each other."

They did so; and, by the blaze of the hell-kindled torches, the wretched man beheld his Faith, and the wife her husband, trembling before that unhallowed altar.

"Lo! there ye stand, my children," said the figure, in a deep and solemn tone, almost sad, with its despairing awfulness, as if his once angelic nature could yet mourn for our miserable race. "Depending upon one another's hearts, ye had still hoped that virtue were not all a dream! Now are ye undeceived!—Evil is the nature of mankind. Evil must be your only happiness. Welcome, again, my children, to the communion of your race!"

"Welcome!" repeated the fiend-worshippers, in one cry of despair and triumph.

And there they stood, the only pair, as it seemed, who were yet hesitating on the verge of wickedness, in this dark world. A basin was hollowed, naturally, in the rock. Did it contain water, reddened by the lurid light? or was it blood? or, perchance, a liquid flame? Herein did the Shape of Evil dip his hand, and prepare to lay the mark of baptism upon their foreheads, that they might be partakers of the mystery of sin, more conscious of the secret guilt of others, both in deed and thought, than they could now be of their own. The husband cast one look at his pale wife, and Faith at him. What polluted wretches would the next glance show them to each other, shuddering alike at what they disclosed and what they saw!

"Faith! Faith!" cried the husband. "Look up to Heaven, and resist the Wicked One!"

Whether Faith obeyed, he knew not. Hardly had he spoken, when he found himself amid calm night and solitude, listening to a roar of the wind, which died heavily away through the forest. He staggered against the rock, and felt it chill and damp, while a hanging twig, that had been all on fire, besprinkled his cheek with the coldest dew.

The next morning, young Goodman Brown came slowly into the street of Salem village staring around him like a bewildered man. The good old minister was taking a walk along the grave-yard, to get an appetite for breakfast and meditate his sermon, and bestowed a blessing, as he passed, on Goodman Brown. He shrank from the venerable saint, as if to avoid an anathema. Old Deacon Gookin was at domestic worship, and the holy words of his prayer were heard through the open window. "What God doth the wizard pray to?" quoth Goodman Brown. Goody Cloyse, that excellent old Christian, stood in the early sunshine, at her own lattice, catechising a little girl, who had brought her a pint of morning's milk. Goodman Brown snatched away the child, as from the grasp of the fiend himself. Turning the corner by the meetinghouse, he spied the head of Faith, with the pink ribbons, gazing anxiously forth, and bursting into such joy at sight of him that she skipt along the street, and almost kissed her husband before the whole village. But Goodman Brown looked sternly and sadly into her face, and passed on without a greeting.

Had Goodman Brown fallen asleep in the forest, and only dreamed a wild dream of a witch-meeting?

Be it so, if you will. But, alas! it was a dream of evil omen for young Goodman Brown. A stern, a sad, a darkly meditative, a distrustful, if not a desperate man did he become, from the night of that fearful dream. On the Sabbath day, when the congregation were singing a holy psalm, he could not listen, because an anthem of sin rushed loudly upon his ear, and drowned all the blessed strain. When the minister spoke from the pulpit, with power and fervid eloquence, and with his hand on the open Bible, of the sacred truths of our religion, and of saint-like lives and triumphant deaths, and of future bliss or misery unutterable, then did Goodman Brown turn pale, dreading lest the roof should thunder down upon the gray blasphemer and his hearers. Often, awaking suddenly at midnight, he shrank from the bosom of Faith, and at morning or eventide, when the family knelt down at prayer, he scowled, and muttered to himself, and gazed sternly at his wife, and turned away. And when he had lived long, and was borne to his grave, a hoary corpse, followed by Faith, an aged woman, and children and grandchildren, a goodly procession, besides neighbors not a few, they carved no hopeful verse upon his tombstone; for his dying hour was gloom.

# Matthew Arnold (1822–1888)

## *Dover Beach*

| | |
|---|---|
| The sea is calm to-night. | 1 |
| The tide is full, the moon lies fair | 2 |
| Upon the straits:—on the French coast the light | 3 |
| Gleams and is gone; the cliffs of England stand, | 4 |
| Glimmering and vast, out in the tranquil bay. | 5 |
| Come to the window, sweet is the night air! | 6 |
| Only, from the long line of spray | 7 |
| Where the sea meets the moon-blanched land, | 8 |
| Listen! you hear the grating roar | 9 |
| Of pebbles which the waves draw back, and fling, | 10 |
| At their return, up the high strand, | 11 |
| Begin, and cease, and then again begin, | 12 |
| With tremulous cadence slow, and bring | 13 |
| The eternal note of sadness in. | 14 |
| | |
| Sophocles long ago | 15 |
| Heard it on the Ægean, and it brought | 16 |
| Into his mind the turbid ebb and flow | 17 |
| Of human misery; we | 18 |
| Find also in the sound a thought, | 19 |
| Hearing it by this distant northern sea. | 20 |
| The Sea of Faith | 21 |
| Was once, too, at the full, and round earth's shore | 22 |
| Lay like the folds of a bright girdle furled. | 23 |
| But now I only hear | 24 |
| Its melancholy, long, withdrawing roar, | 25 |
| Retreating, to the breath | 26 |
| Of the night wind, down the vast edges drear | 27 |
| And naked shingles of the world. | 28 |

| | |
|---|---:|
| Ah, love, let us be true | 29 |
| To one another! for the world, which seems | 30 |
| To lie before us like a land of dreams, | 31 |
| So various, so beautiful, so new, | 32 |
| Hath really neither joy, nor love, nor light, | 33 |
| Nor certitude, nor peace, nor help for pain; | 34 |
| And we are here as on a darkling plain | 35 |
| Swept with confused alarms of struggle and flight | 36 |
| Where ignorant armies clash by night. | 37 |

## Thomas Hardy (1840–1928)

# *The Three Strangers*

Among the few features of agricultural England which retain an appearance but little modified by the lapse of centuries may be reckoned the high, grassy and furzy downs, coombs, or ewe-leases, as they are indifferently called, that fill a large area of certain counties in the south and southwest. If any mark of human occupation is met with hereon, it usually takes the form of the solitary cottage of some shepherd.

Fifty years ago such a lonely cottage stood on such a down, and may possibly be standing there now. In spite of its loneliness, however, the spot, by actual measurement, was not more than five miles from a county-town. Yet that affected it little. Five miles of irregular upland, during the long inimical seasons, with their sleets, snows, rains, and mists, afford withdrawing space enough to isolate a Timon or a Nebuchadnezzar; much less, in fair weather, to please that less repellent tribe, the poets, philosophers, artists, and others who "conceive and meditate of pleasant things."

Some old earthen camp or barrow, some clump of trees, at least some starved fragment of ancient hedge is usually taken advantage of in the erection of these forlorn dwellings. But, in the present case, such a kind of shelter had been disregarded. Higher Crowstairs, as the house was called, stood quite detached and undefended. The only reason for its precise situation seemed to be the crossing of two footpaths at right angles hard by, which may have crossed there and thus for a good five hundred years. Hence the house was exposed to the elements on all sides. But, though the wind up here blew unmistakably when it did blow, and the rain hit hard whenever it fell, the various weathers of the winter season were not quite so formidable on the coomb as they were imagined to be by dwellers on low ground. The raw rimes were not so pernicious as in the hollows, and the frosts

From *Wessex Tales* (1888), reprinted with the permission of the Trustees of the Hardy Estate, Macmillan & Co. Ltd. of London and The Macmillan Company of Canada Limited, Toronto.

were scarcely so severe. When the shepherd and his family who tenanted the house were pitied for their sufferings from the exposure, they said that upon the whole they were less inconvenienced by "wuzzes and flames" (hoarses and phlegms) than when they had lived by the stream of a snug neighboring valley.

The night of March 28, 182–, was precisely one of the nights that were wont to call forth these expressions of commiseration. The level rainstorm smote walls, slopes, and hedges like the clothyard shafts of Senlac and Crécy. Such sheep and outdoor animals as had no shelter stood with their buttocks to the winds; while the tails of little birds trying to roost on some scraggy thorn were blown inside-out like umbrellas. The gable-end of the cottage was stained with wet, and the eavesdroppings flapped against the wall. Yet never was commiseration for the shepherd more misplaced. For that cheerful rustic was entertaining a large party in glorification of the christening of his second girl.

The guests had arrived before the rain began to fall, and they were all now assembled in the chief or living room of the dwelling. A glance into the apartment at eight o'clock on this eventful evening would have resulted in the opinion that it was as cozy and comfortable a nook as could be wished for in boisterous weather. The calling of its inhabitant was proclaimed by a number of highly polished sheep crooks without stems that were hung ornamentally over the fireplace, the curl of each shining crook varying from the antiquated type engraved in the patriarchal pictures of old family Bibles to the most approved fashion of the last local sheep-fair. The room was lighted by half a dozen candles having wicks only a trifle smaller than the grease which enveloped them, in candlesticks that were never used but at high-days, holy-days, and family feasts. The lights were scattered about the room, two of them standing on the chimney piece. This position of candles was in itself significant. Candles on the chimney piece always meant a party.

On the hearth, in front of a back-brand to give substance, blazed a fire of thorns, that crackled "like the laughter of the fool."

Nineteen persons were gathered here. Of these, five women, wearing gowns of various bright hues, sat in chairs along the wall; girls shy and not shy filled the window-bench; four men, including Charley Jake the hedge-carpenter, Elijah New the parish-clerk, and John Pitcher, a neighboring dairyman, the shepherd's father-in-law, lolled in the settle; a young man and maid, who were blushing over tentative *pourparlers* on a life-companionship, sat beneath the corner-cupboard; and an elderly engaged man of fifty or upward moved restlessly about from spots where his betrothed was not to the spot where she was. Enjoyment was pretty general, and so much the more prevailed in being unhampered by conventional restrictions. Absolute confidence in each other's good opinion begat perfect ease, while the finishing stroke of manner, amounting to a truly princely serenity, was lent to the majority by the absence of any expression or trait denoting that they wished to get on in the world, enlarge their minds, or do any eclipsing thing whatever—which nowadays so generally nips the bloom and *bonhomie* of all except the two extremes of the social scale.

Shepherd Fennel had married well, his wife being a dairyman's daughter from a vale at a distance, who brought fifty guineas in her pocket—and kept them there, till they should be required for ministering to the needs of a coming family. This frugal woman had been somewhat exercised as to the character that should be given to the gathering. A sit-still party had its advantages; but an undisturbed position of ease in chairs and settles was apt to lead on the men to such an unconscionable deal of toping that they would sometimes fairly drink the house dry. A dancing-party was the alternative; but this, while avoiding the foregoing objection on the score of good drink, had a counterbalancing disadvantage in the matter of good victuals, the ravenous appetites engendered by the exercise causing immense havoc in the buttery. Shepherdess Fennel fell back upon the intermediate plan of mingling short dances with short periods of talk and singing, so as to hinder any ungovernable rage in either. But this scheme was entirely confined to her own gentle mind: the shepherd himself was in the mood to exhibit the most reckless phases of hospitality.

The fiddler was a boy of those parts, about twelve years of age, who had a wonderful dexterity in jigs and reels, though his fingers were so small and short as to necessitate a constant shifting for the high notes, from which he scrambled back to the first position with sounds not of unmixed purity of tone. At seven the shrill tweedle-dee of this youngster had begun, accompanied by a booming ground-bass from Elijah New, the parish-clerk, who had thoughtfully brought with him his favorite musical instrument, the serpent. Dancing was instantaneous, Mrs. Fennel privately enjoining the players on no account to let the dance exceed the length of a quarter of an hour.

But Elijah and the boy, in the excitement of their position, quite forgot the injunction. Moreover, Oliver Giles, a man of seventeen, one of the dancers, who was enamored of his partner, a fair girl of thirty-three rolling years, had recklessly handed a new crown-piece to the musicians, as a bribe to keep going as long as they had muscle and wind. Mrs. Fennel, seeing the steam begin to generate on the countenances of her guests, crossed over and touched the fiddler's elbow and put her hand on the serpent's mouth. But they took no notice, and fearing she might lose her character of genial hostess if she were to interfere too markedly, she retired and sat down helpless. And so the dance whizzed on with cumulative fury, the performers moving in their planet-like courses, direct and retrograde, from apogee to perigee, till the hand of the well-kicked clock at the bottom of the room had traveled over the circumference of an hour.

While these cheerful events were in course of enactment within Fennel's pastoral dwelling, an incident having considerable bearing on the party had occurred in the gloomy night without. Mrs. Fennel's concern about the growing fierceness of the dance corresponded in point of time with the ascent of a human figure to the solitary hill of Higher Crowstairs from the direction of the distant town. This personage strode on through the rain without a pause, following the little-worn path which, further on in its course, skirted the shepherd's cottage.

It was nearly the time of full moon, and on this account, though the sky was lined with a uniform sheet of dripping cloud, ordinary objects out of doors were readily visible. The sad, wan light revealed the lonely pedestrian to be a man of supple frame; his gait suggested that he had somewhat passed the period of perfect and instinctive agility, though not so far as to be otherwise than rapid of motion when occasion required. At a rough guess, he might have been about forty years of age. He appeared tall, but a recruiting sergeant, or other person accustomed to the judging of men's heights by the eye, would have discerned that this was chiefly owing to his gauntness, and that he was not more than five-feet-eight or nine.

Notwithstanding the regularity of his tread, there was caution in it, as in that of one who mentally feels his way; and despite the fact that it was not a black coat nor a dark garment of any sort that he wore, there was something about him which suggested that he naturally belonged to the black-coated tribes of men. His clothes were of fustian, and his boots hobnailed, yet in his progress he showed not the mud-accustomed bearing of hobnailed and fustianed peasantry.

By the time that he had arrived abreast of the shepherd's premises the rain came down, or rather came along, with yet more determined violence. The outskirts of the little settlement partially broke the force of wind and rain, and this induced him to stand still. The most salient of the shepherd's domestic erections was an empty sty at the forward corner of his hedgeless garden, for in these latitudes the principle of masking the homelier features of your establishment by a conventional frontage was unknown. The traveler's eye was attracted to this small building by the pallid shine of the wet slates that covered it. He turned aside, and, finding it empty, stood under the pent-roof for shelter.

While he stood, the boom of the serpent within the adjacent house, and the lesser strains of the fiddler, reached the spot as an accompaniment to the surging hiss of the flying rain on the sod, its louder beating on the cabbage-leaves of the garden, on the eight or ten beehives just discernible by the path, and its dripping from the eaves into a row of buckets and pans that had been placed under the walls of the cottage. For at Higher Crowstairs, as at all such elevated domiciles, the grand difficulty of housekeeping was an insufficiency of water; and a casual rainfall was utilized by turning out, as catchers, every utensil that the house contained. Some queer stories might be told of the contrivances for economy in suds and dishwaters that are absolutely necessitated in upland habitations during the droughts of summer. But at this season there were no such exigencies; a mere acceptance of what the skies bestowed was sufficient for an abundant store.

At last the notes of the serpent ceased and the house was silent. This cessation of activity aroused the solitary pedestrian from the reverie into which he had elapsed, and, emerging from the shed, with an apparently new intention, he walked up the path to the house-door. Arrived here, his first act was to kneel down on a large stone beside the row of vessels, and to drink a copious draught from one of them. Having quenched his thirst, he rose and lifted his hand to knock, but paused with his eye upon the panel. Since the dark surface of the wood revealed absolutely nothing, it was evident that he must be mentally looking through the door, as if he wished to measure thereby all the possibilities that a house of this sort might include, and how they might bear upon the question of his entry.

In his indecision he turned and surveyed the scene around. Not a soul was anywhere visible. The garden path stretched downward from his feet, gleaming like the track of a snail; the roof of the little well (mostly dry), the well-cover, the top rail of the garden-gate, were varnished with the same dull liquid glaze; while, far away in the vale, a faint whiteness of more than usual extent showed that the rivers were high in the meads. Beyond all this winked a few bleared lamplights through the beating drops—lights that denoted the situation of the county-town from which he had appeared to come. The absence of all notes of life in that direction seemed to clinch his intentions, and he knocked at the door.

Within, a desultory chat had taken the place of movement and musical sound.

The hedge-carpenter was suggesting a song to the company, which nobody just then was inclined to undertake, so that the knock afforded a not unwelcome diversion.

"Walk in!" said the shepherd, promptly.

The latch clicked upward, and out of the night our pedestrian appeared upon the door-mat. The shepherd arose, snuffed two of the nearest candles, and turned to look at him.

Their light disclosed that the stranger was dark in complexion and not unprepossessing as to feature. His hat, which for a moment he did not remove, hung low over his eyes, without concealing that they were large, open, and determined, moving with a flash rather than a glance round the room. He seemed pleased with his survey, and, baring his shaggy head, said, in a rich, deep voice: "The rain is so heavy, friends, that I ask leave to come in and rest awhile."

"To be sure, Stranger," said the shepherd. "And faith, you've been lucky in choosing your time, for we are having a bit of a fling for a glad cause—though, to be sure, a man could hardly wish that glad cause to happen more than once a year."

"Nor less," spoke up a woman. "For 'tis best to get your family over and done with, as soon as you can, so as to be all the earlier out of the fag o't."

"And what may be this glad cause?" asked the stranger.

"A birth and christening," said the shepherd.

The stranger hoped his host might not be made unhappy either by too many or too few of such episodes and, being invited by a gesture to a pull at the mug, he readily acquiesced. His manner, which, before entering, had been so dubious, was now altogether that of a careless and candid man.

"Late to be traipsing athwart this coomb—hey?" said the engaged man of fifty.

"Late it is, Master, as you say.—I'll take a seat in the chimney corner, if you have nothing to urge against it, Ma'am; for I am a little moist on the side that was next the rain."

Mrs. Shepherd Fennel assented, and made room for the self-invited comer, who, having got completely inside the chimney corner, stretched out his legs and arms with the expansiveness of a person quite a home.

"Yes, I am rather cracked in the vamp," he said freely, seeing that the eyes of the shepherd's wife fell upon his boots, "and I am not well fitted either. I have had some rough times lately, and have been forced to pick up what I can get in the way of wearing, but I must find a suit better fit for working-days when I reach home."

"One of hereabouts?" she inquired.

"Not quite that—further up the country."

"I thought so. And so be I; and by your tongue you come from my neighborhood."

"But you would hardly have heard of me," he said quickly. "My time would be long before yours, Ma'am, you see."

This testimony to the youthfulness of his hostess had the effect of stopping her cross-examination.

"There is only one thing more wanted to make me happy," continued the newcomer, "and that is a little baccy, which I am sorry to say I am out of."

"I'll fill your pipe," said the shepherd.

"I must ask you to lend me a pipe likewise."

"A smoker, and no pipe about 'ee?"

"I have dropped it somewhere on the road."

The shepherd filled and handed him a new clay pipe, saying, as he did so, "Hand me your baccy-box—I'll fill that too, now I am about it."

The man went through the movement of searching his pockets.

"Lost that too?" said his entertainer, with some surprise.

"I am afraid so," said the man with some confusion. "Give it to me in a screw of paper." Lighting his pipe at the candle with a suction that drew the whole flame into the bowl, he resettled himself in the corner and bent his looks upon the faint steam from his damp legs, as if he wished to say no more.

Meanwhile the general body of guests had been taking little notice of this visitor by reason of an absorbing discussion in which they were engaged with the band about a tune for the next dance. The matter being settled, they were about to stand up when an interruption came in the shape of another knock at the door.

At sound of the same the man in the chimney corner took up the poker and began stirring the brands as if doing it thoroughly were the one aim of his existence; and a second time the shepherd said, "Walk in!" In a moment another man stood upon the straw-woven door-mat. He too was a stranger.

This individual was one of a type radically different from the first. There was more of the commonplace in his manner, and a certain jovial cosmopolitanism sat upon his features. He was several years older than the first arrival, his hair being slightly frosted, his eyebrows bristly, and his whiskers cut back from his cheeks. His face was rather full and flabby, and yet it was not altogether a face without power. A few grog-blossoms marked the neighborhood of his nose. He flung back his long drab greatcoat, revealing that beneath it he wore a suit of cinder-gray shade throughout, large heavy seals, of some metal or other that would take a polish, dangling from his fob as his only personal ornament. Shaking the water drops from his low-crowned glazed hat, he said, "I must ask for a few minutes' shelter, comrades, or I shall be wetted to my skin before I get to Casterbridge."

"Make yourself at home, Master," said the shepherd, perhaps a trifle less heartily than on the first occasion. Not that Fennel had the least tinge of niggardliness in his composition; but the room was far from large, spare chairs were not numerous, and damp companions were not altogether desirable at close quarters for the women and girls in their bright-colored gowns.

However, the second comer, after taking off his greatcoat, and hanging his hat on a nail in one of the ceiling-beams as if he had been specially invited to put it there, advanced and sat down at the table. This had been pushed so closely into the chimney corner, to give all available room to the dancers, that its inner edge grazed the elbow of the man who had ensconced himself by the fire; and thus the two strangers were brought into close companionship. They nodded to each other by way of breaking the ice of unacquaintance, and the first stranger handed his neighbor the family mug—a huge vessel of brown ware, having its upper edge worn away like a threshold by the rub of whole generations of thirsty lips that had gone the way of all flesh, and bearing the following inscription burnt upon its rotund side in yellow letters:

THERE IS NO FUN
UNTIL i CUM.

The other man, nothing loth, raised the mug to his lips, and drank on, and on, and on—till a curious blueness overspread the countenance of the shepherd's wife, who had regarded with no little surprise the first stranger's free offer to the second of what did not belong to him to dispense.

"I knew it!" said the toper to the shepherd with much satisfaction. "When I walked up your garden before coming in, and saw the hives all of a row, I said to myself, 'Where there's bees there's honey, and where there's honey there's mead.' But mead of such a truly comfortable sort as this I really didn't expect to meet in my older days." He took yet another pull at the mug, till it assumed an ominous elevation.

"Glad you enjoy it!" said the shepherd, warmly.

"It is goodish mead," assented Mrs. Fennel, with an absence of enthusiasm which seemed to say that it was possible to buy praise for one's cellar at too heavy a price. "It is trouble enough to make—and really I hardly think we shall make any more. For honey sells well, and we ourselves can make shift with a drop o' small mead and metheglin for common use from the comb-washings."

"Oh, but you'll never have the heart!" reproachfully cried the stranger in cinder-gray, after taking up the mug a third time and setting it down empty. "I love mead, when 'tis old like this, as I love to go to church o' Sundays, or to relieve the needy any day of the week."

"Ha, ha, ha!" said the man in the chimney corner, who, in spite of the taciturnity induced by the pipe of tobacco, could not or would not refrain from this slight testimony to his comrade's humor.

Now the old mead of those days, brewed of the purest first-year or maiden honey, four pounds to the gallon—with its due complement of white of eggs, cinnamon, ginger, cloves, mace, rosemary, yeast, and processes of working, bottling, and cellaring—tasted remarkably strong; but it did not taste so strong as it actually was. Hence, presently, the stranger in cinder-gray at the table, moved by its creeping influence, unbuttoned his waistcoat, threw himself back in his chair, spread his legs, and made his presence felt in various ways.

"Well, well, as I say," he resumed, "I am going to Casterbridge, and to Casterbridge I must go. I should have been almost there by this time; but the rain drove me into your dwelling, and I'm not sorry for it."

"You don't live in Casterbridge?" said the shepherd.

"Not as yet; though I shortly mean to move there."

"Going to set up in trade, perhaps?"

"No, no," said the shepherd's wife. "It is easy to see that the gentleman is rich, and don't want to work at anything."

The cinder-gray stranger paused, as if to consider whether he would accept that definition of himself. He presently rejected it by answering, "Rich is not quite the word for me, Dame. I do work, and I must work. And even if I only get to Casterbridge by midnight I must begin work there at eight tomorrow morning. Yes, het or wet, blow or snow, famine or sword, my day's work tomorrow must be done."

"Poor man! Then, in spite o' seeming, you be worse off than we," replied the shepherd's wife.

" 'Tis the nature of my trade, men and maidens. 'Tis the nature of my trade more than my poverty. . . . But really and truly I must up and off, or I shan't get a lodging in the town." However, the speaker did not move, and directly added, "There's time for one more draught of friendship before I go; and I'd perform it at once if the mug were not dry."

"Here's a mug o' small," said Mrs. Fennel. "Small, we call it, though to be sure 'tis only the first wash o' the combs."

"No," said the stranger, disdainfully. "I won't spoil your first kindness by partaking o' your second."

"Certainly not," broke in Fennel. "We don't increase and multiply every day, and I'll fill the mug again." He went away to the dark place under the stairs where the barrel stood. The shepherdess followed him.

"Why should you do this?" she said, reproachfully, as soon as they were alone. "He's emptied it once, though it held enough for ten people; and now he's not contented wi' the small, but must needs call for more o' the strong! And a stranger unbeknown to any of us. For my part, I don't like the look o' the man at all."

"But he's in the house, my honey; and 'tis a wet night, and a christening. Daze it, what's a cup of mead more or less? There'll be plenty more next bee-burning."

"Very well—this time, then," she answered, looking wistfully at the barrel. "But what is the man's calling, and where is he one of, that he should come in and join us like this?"

"I don't know. I'll ask him again."

The catastrophe of having the mug drained dry at one pull by the stranger in cinder-gray was effectually guarded against this time by Mrs. Fennel. She poured out his allowance in a small cup, keeping the large one at a discreet distance from him. When he had tossed off his portion the shepherd renewed his inquiry about the stranger's occupation.

The latter did not immediately reply, and the man in the chimney corner, with sudden demonstrativeness, said, "Anybody may know my trade—I'm a wheelwright."

"A very good trade for these parts," said the shepherd.

"And anybody may know mine—if they've the sense to find it out," said the stranger in cinder-gray.

"You may generally tell what a man is by his claws," observed the hedge-carpenter, looking at his own hands. "My fingers be as full of thorns as an old pincushion is of pins."

The hands of the man in the chimney corner instinctively sought the shade, and he gazed into the fire as he resumed his pipe. The man at the table took up the hedge-carpenter's remark, and added smartly, "True; but the oddity of my trade is that, instead of setting a mark upon me, it sets a mark upon my customers."

No observation being offered by anybody in elucidation of this enigma, the shepherd's wife once more called for a song. The same obstacles presented themselves as at the former time—one had no voice, another had forgotten the first verse. The stranger at the table, whose soul had now risen to a good working temperature, relieved the difficulty by exclaiming that, to start the company, he would sing himself. Thrusting one thumb into the armhold of his waistcoat, he waved the other hand in the air, and, with an extemporizing gaze at the shining sheepcrooks above the mantelpiece, began:

> *O my trade it is the rarest one,*
>> *Simple shepherds all—*
> *My trade is a sight to see;*
> *For my customers I tie, and take them up on high,*
> *And waft 'em to a far countree!*

The room was silent when he had finished the verse—with one exception, that of the man in the chimney corner, who at the singer's word, "Chorus!" joined him in a deep bass voice of musical relish:

> *And waft 'em to a far countree!*

Oliver Giles, John Pitcher the dairyman, the parish-clerk, the engaged man of fifty, the row of young women against the wall, seemed lost in thought not of the gayest kind. The shepherd looked meditatively on the ground, the shepherdess gazed keenly at the singer, and with some suspicion; she was doubting whether this stranger were merely singing an old song from recollection, or was composing one there and then for the occasion. All were as perplexed at the obscure revelation as the guests at Belshazzar's Feast, except the man in the chimney corner, who quietly said, "Second verse, stranger," and smoked on.

The singer thoroughly moistened himself from his lips inward, and went on with the next stanza as requested:

> *My tools are but common ones,*
>> *Simple shepherds all—*
> *My tools are no sight to see:*
> *A little hempen string, and a post whereon to swing,*
> *Are implements enough for me!*

Shepherd Fennel glanced round. There was no longer any doubt that the stranger was answering his question rhythmically. The guests one and all started back with suppressed exclamations. The young woman engaged to the man of fifty fainted halfway, and would have proceeded, but finding him wanting in alacrity for catching her she sat down trembling.

"Oh, he's the———!" whispered the people in the background, mentioning the name of an ominous public officer. "He's come to do it! 'Tis to be at Casterbridge jail tomorrow—the man for sheep-stealing—the poor clockmaker we heard of, who used to live at Shottsford and had no work to do—Timothy Summers, whose family were astarving, and so he went out of Shottsford by the highroad, and took a sheep in open daylight, defying the farmer and the farmer's wife and the farmer's lad, and every man jack among 'em. He" (and they nodded toward the stranger of the deadly trade) "is come from up the country to do it because there's not enough to do in his own county-town, and he's got the place here now our own county-man's dead; he's going to live in the same cottage under the prison wall."

The stranger in cinder-gray took no notice of this whispered string of observations, but again wetted his lips. Seeing that his friend in the chimney corner was the only one who reciprocated his joviality in any way, he held out his cup toward that appreciative comrade, who also held out his own. They clinked together, the eyes of the rest of the room hanging upon the singer's actions. He parted his lips for the third verse; but at that moment another knock was audible upon the door. This time the knock was faint and hesitating.

The company seemed scared; the shepherd looked with consternation toward the entrance, and it was with some effort that he resisted his alarmed wife's deprecatory glance, and uttered for the third time the welcoming words, "Walk in!"

The door was gently opened, and another man stood upon the mat. He, like those who had preceded him, was a stranger. This time it was a short, small personage, of fair complexion, and dressed in a decent suit of dark clothes.

"Can you tell me the way to———?" he began: when, gazing round the room to observe the nature of the company among whom he had fallen, his eyes lighted on the stranger in cinder-gray. It was just at the instant when the latter, who had thrown his mind into his song with such a will that he scarcely heeded the interruption, silenced all whispers and inquiries by bursting into his third verse:

> *Tomorrow is my working day,*
> > *Simple shepherds all—*
> *Tomorrow is a working day for me:*
> *For the farmer's sheep is slain, and the lad who did it ta'en,*
> *And on his soul may God ha' merc-y!*

The stranger in the chimney corner, waving cups with the singer so heartily that his mead splashed over on the hearth, repeated in his bass voice as before:

> *And on his soul may God ha' merc-y!*

All this time the third stranger had been standing in the doorway. Finding now that he did not come forward or go on speaking, the guests particularly regarded him. They noticed to their surprise that he stood before them the picture of abject terror—his knees trembling, his hand shaking so violently that the door-latch by which he supported himself rattled audibly: his white lips were parted, and his eyes fixed on the merry officer of justice in the middle of the room. A moment more and he had turned, closed the door, and fled.

"What a man can it be?" said the shepherd.

The rest, between the awfulness of their late discovery and the odd conduct of this third visitor, looked as if they knew not what to think, and said nothing. Instinctively they withdrew further and further from the grim gentleman in their midst, whom some of them seemed to take for the Prince of Darkness himself, till they formed a remote circle, an empty space of floor being left between them and him—

> . . . *circulas, cujus centrum diabolus.*[1]

The room was so silent—though there were more than twenty people in it—that nothing could be heard but the patter of the rain against the window-shutters, accompanied by the occasional hiss of a stray drop that fell down the chimney into the fire, and the steady puffing of the man in the corner, who had now resumed his pipe of long clay.

---

[1] . . . circles, whose center [is] the devil.

The stillness was unexpectedly broken. The distant sound of a gun reverberated through the air—apparently from the direction of the county-town.

"Be jiggered!" cried the stranger who had sung the song, jumping up.

"What does that mean?" asked several.

"A prisoner escaped from the jail—that's what it means."

All listened. The sound was repeated, and none of them spoke but the man in the chimney corner, who said quietly, "I've often been told that in this county they fire a gun at such times; but I never heard it till now."

"I wonder if it is *my* man?" murmured the personage in cinder-gray.

"Surely it is!" said the shepherd involuntarily. "And surely we've zeed him! That little man who looked in at the door by now, and quivered like a leaf when he zeed ye and heard your song!"

"His teeth chattered, and the breath went out of his body," said the dairyman.

"And his heart seemed to sink within him like a stone," said Oliver Giles.

"And he bolted as if he'd been shot at," said the hedge-carpenter.

"True—his teeth chattered, and his heart seemed to sink; and he bolted as if he'd been shot at," slowly summed up the man in the chimney corner.

"I didn't notice it," remarked the hangman.

"We were all awondering what made him run off in such a fright," faltered one of the women against the wall, "and now 'tis explained!"

The firing of the alarm-gun went on at intervals, low and sullenly, and their suspicions became a certainty. The sinister gentleman in cinder-gray roused himself. "Is there a constable here?" he asked, in thick tones. "If so, let him step forward."

The engaged man of fifty stepped quavering out from the wall, his betrothed beginning to sob on the back of the chair.

"You are a sworn constable?"

"I be, Sir."

"Then pursue the criminal at once, with assistance, and bring him back here. He can't have gone far."

"I will, Sir, I will—when I've got my staff. I'll go home and get it, and come sharp here, and start in a body."

"Staff!—never mind your staff; the man'll be gone!"

"But I can't do nothing without my staff—can I, William, and John, and Charles Jake? No; for there's the king's royal crown apainted on en in yaller and gold, and the lion and the unicorn, so as when I raise en up and hit my prisoner, 'tis made a lawful blow thereby. I wouldn't 'tempt to take up a man without my staff—no, not I. If I hadn't the law to gie me courage, why, instead o' my taking up him he might take up me!"

"Now, I'm a king's man myself, and can give you authority enough for this," said the formidable officer in gray. "Now then, all of ye, be ready. Have ye any lanterns?"

"Yes—have ye any lanterns?—I demand it!" said the constable.

"And the rest of you able-bodied—"

"Able-bodied men—yes—the rest of ye!" said the constable.

"Have you some good stout staves and pitchforks—"

"Staves and pitchforks—in the name o' the law! And take 'em in yer hands and go in quest, and do as we in authority tell ye!"

Thus aroused, the men prepared to give chase. The evidence was, indeed, though circumstantial, so convincing, that but little argument was needed to show the shepherd's guests that after what they had seen it would look very much like connivance if they did not instantly pursue the unhappy third stranger, who could not as yet have gone more than a few hundred yards over such uneven country.

A shepherd is always well provided with lanterns; and, lighting these hastily, and with hurdle-staves in their hands, they poured out of the door, taking a direction along the crest of the hill, away from the town, the rain having fortunately a little abated.

Disturbed by the noise, or possibly by unpleasant dreams of her baptism, the child who had been christened began to cry heart-brokenly in the room overhead. These notes of grief came down through the chinks of the floor to the ears of the women below, who jumped up one by one, and seemed glad of the excuse to ascend and comfort the baby, for the incidents of the last half-hour greatly oppressed them. Thus in the space of two or three minutes the room on the ground-floor was deserted quite.

But it was not for long. Hardly had the sound of footsteps died away when a man returned round the corner of the house from the direction the pursuers had taken. Peeping in at the door, and seeing nobody there, he entered leisurely. It was the stranger of the chimney corner, who had gone out with the rest. The motive of his return was shown by his helping himself to a cut piece of skimmer-cake that lay on a ledge beside where he had sat, and which he had apparently forgotten to take with him. He also poured out half a cup more mead from the quantity that remained, ravenously eating and drinking these as he stood. He had not finished when another figure came in just as quietly—his friend in cinder-gray.

"Oh—you here?" said the latter, smiling. "I thought you had gone to help in the capture." And this speaker also revealed the object of his return by looking solicitously round for the fascinating mug of old mead.

"And I thought you had gone," said the other, continuing his skimmer-cake with some effort.

"Well, on second thoughts, I felt there were enough without me," said the first confidentially, "and such a night as it is, too. Besides, 'tis the business o' the Government to take care of its criminals—not mine."

"True; so it is. And I felt as you did, that there were enough without me."

"I don't want to break my limbs running over the humps and hollows of this wild country."

"Nor I neither, between you and me."

"These shepherd-people are used to it—simple-minded souls, you know, stirred up to anything in a moment. They'll have him ready for me before the morning, and no trouble to me at all."

"They'll have him, and we shall have saved ourselves all labor in the matter."

"True, true. Well, my way is to Casterbridge; and 'tis as much as my legs will do to take me that far. Going the same way?"

"No, I am sorry to say! I have to get home over there" (he nodded indefinitely to the right), "and I feel as you do, that it is quite enough for my legs to do before bedtime."

The other had by this time finished the mead in the mug, after which, shaking hands heartily at the door, and wishing each other well, they went their several ways.

In the meantime the company of pursuers had reached the end of the hog's-back elevation which dominated this part of the down. They had decided on no particular plan of action; and, finding that the man of the baleful trade was no longer in their company, they seemed quite unable to form any such plan now. They descended in all directions down the hill, and straightway several of the party fell into the snare set by Nature for all misguided midnight ramblers over this part of the cretaceous formation. The "lanchets," or flint slopes, which belted the escarpment at intervals of a dozen yards, took the less cautious ones unawares, and losing their footing on the rubbly steep they slid sharply downward, the lanterns rolling from their hands to the bottom, and there lying on their sides till the horn was scorched through.

When they had again gathered themselves together, the shepherd, as the man who knew the country best, took the lead, and guided them round these treacherous inclines. The lanterns, which seemed rather to dazzle their eyes and warn the fugitive than to assist them in the exploration, were extinguished, due silence was observed; and in this more rational order they plunged into the vale. It was a grassy, briery, moist defile, affording some shelter to any person who had sought it; but the party perambulated it in vain, and ascended on the other side. Here they wandered apart, and after an interval closed together again to report progress. At the second time of closing in they found themselves near a lonely ash, the single tree on this part of the coomb, probably sown there by a passing bird some fifty years before. And here, standing a little to one side of the trunk, as motionless as the trunk itself appeared the man they were in quest of, his outline being well defined against the sky beyond. The band noiselessly drew up and faced him.

"Your money or your life!" said the constable sternly to the still figure.

"No, no," whispered John Pitcher. " 'Tisn't our side ought to say that. That's the doctrine of vagabonds like him, and we be on the side of the law."

"Well, well," replied the constable, impatiently; "I must say something, mustn't I? and if you had all the weight o' this undertaking upon your mind, perhaps you'd say the wrong thing, too!—Prisoner at the bar, surrender in the name of the Father—the Crown, I mane!"

The man under the tree seemed now to notice them for the first time, and, giving them no opportunity whatever for exhibiting their courage, he strolled slowly toward them. He was, indeed, the little man, the third stranger; but his trepidation had in a great measure gone.

"Well, travelers," he said, "did I hear you speak to me?"

"You did; you've got to come and be our prisoner at once!" said the constable. "We arrest 'ee on the charge of not biding in Casterbridge jail in a decent proper manner to be hung tomorrow morning. Neighbors, do your duty, and seize the culprit!"

On hearing the charge, the man seemed enlightened, and, saying not another word, resigned himself with preternatural civility to the search-party, who, with their staves in their hands, surrounded him on all sides, and marched him back toward the shepherd's cottage.

It was eleven o'clock by the time they arrived. The light shining from the open door, a sound of men's voices within, proclaimed to them as they approached the house that some new events had arisen in their absence. On entering they discovered the shepherd's living-room to be invaded by two officers from Casterbridge jail, and a well-known magistrate who lived at the nearest county-seat, intelligence of the escape having become generally circulated.

"Gentlemen," said the constable, "I have brought back your man—not without risk and danger; but everyone must do his duty! He is inside this circle of able-bodied persons, who have lent me useful aid, considering their ignorance of Crown work.—Men, bring forward your prisoner!" And the third stranger was led to the light.

"Who is this?" said one of the officials.

"The man," said the constable.

"Certainly not," said the turnkey; and the first corroborated his statement.

"But how can it be otherwise?" asked the constable. "Or why was he so terrified at sight o' the singing instrument of the law who sat there?" Here he related the strange behavior of the third stranger on entering the house during the hangman's song.

"Can't understand it," said the officer coolly. "All I know is that it is not the condemned man. He's quite a different character from this one; a gauntish fellow, with dark hair and eyes, rather good-looking, and with a musical bass voice that if you heard it once you'd never mistake as long as you lived."

"Why, souls—'twas the man in the chimney corner!"

"Hey—what?" said the magistrate, coming forward after inquiring particulars from the shepherd in the background. "Haven't you got the man after all?"

"Well, Sir," said the constable, "he's the man we were in search of, that's true; and yet he's not the man we were in search of. For the man we were in search of was not the man we wanted, Sir, if you understand my everyday way; for 'twas the man in the chimney corner!"

"A pretty kettle of fish altogether!" said the magistrate. "You had better start for the other man at once."

The prisoner now spoke for the first time. The mention of the man in the chimney corner seemed to have moved him as nothing else could do. "Sir," he said, stepping forward to the magistrate, "take no more trouble about me. The time is come when I may as well speak. I have done nothing; my crime is that the condemned man is my brother. Early this afternoon I left home at Shottsford to tramp it all the way to Casterbridge jail to bid him farewell. I was benighted, and called here to rest and ask the way. When I opened the door I saw before me the very man, my brother, that I thought to see in the condemned cell at Casterbridge. He was in this chimney corner; and jammed close to him, so that he could not have got out if he had tried, was the executioner who'd come to take his life, singing a song about it and not knowing that it was his victim who was close by, joining in to save appearances. My brother looked a glance of agony at me, and I know he meant, 'Don't reveal what you see; my life depends on it.' I was so terror-struck that I could hardly stand, and, not knowing what I did, I turned and hurried away."

The narrator's manner and tone had the stamp of truth, and his story made a great impression on all around. "And do you know where your brother is at the present time?" asked the magistrate.

"I do not. I have never seen him since I closed this door."

"I can testify to that, for we've been between ye ever since," said the constable.

"Where does he think to fly to?—what is his occupation?"

"He's a watch-and-clock-maker, Sir."

" 'A said 'a was a wheelwright—a wicked rogue," said the constable.

"The wheels of clocks and watches he meant, no doubt," said Shepherd Fennel. "I thought his hands were palish for's trade."

"Well, it appears to me that nothing can be gained by retaining this poor man in custody," said the magistrate; "your business lies with the other, unquestionably."

And so the little man was released off-hand; but he looked nothing the less sad on that account, it being beyond the power of magistrate or constable to raze out the written troubles in his brain, for they concerned another whom he regarded with more solicitude than himself. When this was done, and the man had gone his way, the night was found to be so far advanced that it was deemed useless to renew the search before the next morning.

Next day, accordingly, the quest for the clever sheep-stealer became general and keen, to all appearance at least. But the intended punishment was cruelly disproportioned to the transgression, and the sympathy of a great many country-folk in that district was strongly on the side of the fugitive. Moreover, his marvelous coolness and daring in hob-and-nobbing with the hangman, under the unprecedented circumstances of the shepherd's party, won their admiration. So that it may be questioned if all those who ostensibly made themselves so busy in exploring woods and fields and lanes were quite so thorough when it came to the private examination of their own lofts and outhouses. Stories were afloat of a mysterious figure being occasionally seen in some old overgrown trackway or other, remote from turnpike roads, but when a search was instituted in any of these suspected quarters nobody was found. Thus the days and weeks passed without tidings.

In brief, the bass-voiced man of the chimney corner was never recaptured. Some said that he went across the sea, others that he did not, but buried himself in the depths of a populous city. At any rate, the gentleman in cinder-gray never did his morning's work at Casterbridge, nor met anywhere at all, for business purposes, the genial comrade with whom he had passed an hour of relaxation in the lonely house on the coomb.

The grass has long been green on the graves of Shepherd Fennel and his frugal wife; the guests who made up the christening party have mainly followed their entertainers to the tomb; the baby in whose honor they all had met is a matron in the sere and yellow leaf. But the arrival of the three strangers at the shepherd's that night, and the details connected therewith, is a story as well-known as ever in the country about Higher Crowstairs.

# Thomas Hardy (1840–1928)

## *Channel Firing*

| | |
|---|---|
| That night your great guns unawares, | 1 |
| Shook all our coffins as we lay, | 2 |
| And broke the chancel window squares. | 3 |
| We thought it was the Judgment-day | 4 |
| | |
| And sat upright. While drearisome | 5 |
| Arose the howl of wakened hounds: | 6 |
| The mouse let fall the altar-crumb, | 7 |
| The worms drew back into the mounds, | 8 |
| | |
| The glebe cow drooled. Till God called, "No; | 9 |
| It's gunnery practice out at sea | 10 |
| Just as before you went below; | 11 |
| The world is as it used to be: | 12 |
| | |
| "All nations striving strong to make | 13 |
| Red war yet redder. Mad as hatters | 14 |
| They do no more for Christés sake | 15 |
| Than you who are helpless in such matters. | 16 |
| | |
| "That this is not the judgment-hour | 17 |
| For some of them's a blessed thing, | 18 |
| For if it were they'd have to scour | 19 |
| Hell's floor for so much threatening . . . | 20 |
| | |
| "Ha, ha. It will be warmer when | 21 |
| I blow the trumpet (if indeed | 22 |
| I ever do; for you are men, | 23 |
| And rest eternal sorely need)." | 24 |
| | |
| So down we lay again. "I wonder, | 25 |
| Will the world ever saner be," | 26 |
| Said one, "than when He sent us under | 27 |
| In our indifferent century!" | 28 |
| | |
| And many a skeleton shook his head. | 29 |
| "Instead of preaching forty year," | 30 |
| My neighbor Parson Thirdly said, | 31 |
| "I wish I had stuck to pipes and beer." | 32 |
| | |
| Again the guns disturbed the hour, | 33 |
| Roaring their readiness to avenge, | 34 |
| As far inland as Stourton Tower, | 35 |
| And Camelot, and starlit Stonehenge. | 36 |

April 1914

# Guy De Maupassant (1850–1893)

# *The Necklace*

She was one of those pretty and charming women, born, as if by an error of destiny, into a family of clerks and copyists. She had no dowry, no prospects, no way of getting known, courted, loved, married by a rich and distinguished man. She finally settled for a marriage with a minor clerk in the Ministry of Education.

She was a simple person, without the money to dress well, but she was as unhappy as if she had gone through bankruptcy, for women have neither rank nor race. In place of high birth or important family connections, they can rely only on their beauty, their grace, and their charm. Their inborn finesse, their elegant taste, their engaging personalities, which are their only power, make working-class women the equals of the grandest duchesses.

She suffered constantly, feeling herself destined for all delicacies and luxuries. She suffered because of her grim apartment with its drab walls, threadbare furniture, ugly curtains. All such things, which most other women in her situation would not even have noticed, tortured her and filled her with despair. The sight of the young country girl who did her simple housework awakened in her only a sense of desolation and lost hopes. She daydreamed of large, silent anterooms, decorated with oriental tapestries and lighted by high bronze floor lamps, with two elegant valets in short culottes dozing in large armchairs under the effects of forced-air heaters. She visualized large drawing rooms draped in the most expensive silks, with fine end tables on which were placed knickknacks of inestimable value. She dreamed of the perfume of dainty private rooms, which were designed only for intimate tête-à-têtes with the closest friends, who because of their achievements and fame would make her the envy of all other women.

When she sat down to dinner at her round little table covered with a cloth that had not been washed for three days, in front of her husband who opened the kettle while declaring ecstatically, "Oh boy, beef stew, my favorite," she dreamed of expensive banquets with shining placesettings, and wall hangings depicting ancient heroes and exotic birds in an enchanted forest. She imagined a gourmet-prepared main course carried on the most exquisite trays and served on the most beautiful dishes, with whispered gallantries which she would hear with a sphinxlike smile as she dined on the pink meat of a trout or the delicate wing of a quail.

She had no decent dresses, no jewels, nothing. And she loved nothing but these; she believed herself born only for these. She burned with the desire to please, to be envied, to be attractive and sought after.

She had a rich friend, a comrade from convent days, whom she did not want to see anymore because she suffered so much when she returned home. She would weep for the entire day afterward with sorrow, regret, despair, and misery.

Well, one evening, her husband came home glowing and carrying a large envelope.

Translated by Edgar V. Roberts.

"Here," he said, "this is something for you."

She quickly tore open the envelope and took out a card engraved with these words:

> The Chancellor of Education and Mrs. George Ramponneau request that Mr. and Mrs. Loisel do them the honor of coming to dinner at the Ministry of Education on the evening of January 8.

Instead of being delighted, as her husband had hoped, she threw the invitation spitefully on the table while muttering:

"What do you expect me to do with this?"

"But Honey, I thought you'd be glad. You never get to go out, and this is a special occasion! I had a lot of trouble getting the invitation. Everyone wants one; the demand is high and not many clerks get invited. Everyone important will be there."

She looked at him angrily and stated impatiently:

"What do you want me to wear to go there?"

He had not thought of that. He stammered:

"But your theatre dress. That seems nice to me . . ."

He stopped, amazed and bewildered, as his wife began to cry. Large tears fell slowly from the corners of her eyes to her mouth. He said falteringly:

"What's wrong? What's wrong?"

But with a strong effort she had recovered, and she answered calmly as she wiped her damp cheeks:

"Nothing, except that I have nothing to wear and therefore can't go to the party. Give your invitation to someone else at the office whose wife will have nicer clothes than mine."

Distressed, he responded:

"Well, okay, Mathilde. How much would a new dress cost, something you could use at other times, but not anything fancy?"

She thought for a few moments, adding things up and thinking also of an amount that she could ask without getting an immediate refusal and a frightened outcry from the frugal clerk.

Finally she responded tentatively:

"I don't know exactly, but it seems to me that I could get by on four hundred francs."

He blanched slightly at this, because he had set aside just that amount to buy a shotgun and go with a few friends to Nanterre on Sundays the next summer to shoot larks.

However, he said:

"Okay, you've got four hundred francs, but make it a pretty dress."

As the day of the party drew near, Mrs. Loisel seemed sad, uneasy, anxious, even though her dress was all ready. One evening her husband said to her:

"What's up? You've been acting strangely for several days."

She answered:

"It's awful, but I don't have any jewels, not a single stone, nothing for matching jewelry. I'm going to look impoverished. I'd almost rather not go to the party."

He responded:

"You can wear a corsage of cut flowers. This year that's really the in thing. For no more than ten francs you can get two or three gorgeous roses."

She was not convinced.

"No . . . there's nothing more humiliating than to look ragged in the middle of rich women."

But her husband exclaimed:

"God, but you're silly! Go to your friend Mrs. Forrestier, and ask her to lend you some jewelry. You know her well enough to do that."

She uttered a cry of joy:

"That's right. I hadn't thought of that."

The next day she went to her friend's house and described her problem.

Mrs. Forrestier went to her glass-plated wardrobe, took out a large jewel box, opened it, and said to Mrs. Loisel:

"Choose, my dear."

She saw bracelets, then a pearl necklace, then a Venetian cross of finely worked gold and gems. She tried on the jewelry in front of a mirror, and hesitated, unable to make up her mind about which ones to give back. She kept asking:

"Do you have anything else?"

"Certainly. Look to your heart's content. I don't know what will please you most."

Suddenly she found, in a black satin box, a superb diamond necklace, and her heart throbbed with desire for it. Her hands shook as she took it up. She fastened it around her neck, watched it gleam at her throat, and looked at herself ecstatically.

Then she asked, haltingly and anxiously:

"Could you lend me this, nothing but this?"

"Why yes, certainly."

She jumped up, hugged her friend joyfully, then hurried away with her treasure.

The day of the party came. Mrs. Loisel was a success. She was prettier than anyone else, stylish, graceful, smiling, and wild with joy. All the men saw her, asked her name, and sought to be introduced. All the important administrators stood in line to waltz with her. The Chancellor watched her.

She danced joyfully, passionately, intoxicated with pleasure, thinking of nothing but the moment, in the triumph of her beauty, in the glory of her success, in a cloud-nine of happiness made up of all the admiration, of all the aroused desire, of this victory so complete and so sweet to the heart of any woman.

She did not leave until four o'clock in the morning. Her husband, since midnight, had been sleeping in a little empty room with three other men whose wives had also been enjoying themselves.

He threw over her shoulders the shawl that he had brought for the trip home, modest clothing from everyday life, the poverty of which contrasted sharply with the elegance of the party dress. She felt it and hurried away to avoid being noticed by the other women who luxuriated in rich furs.

Loisel tried to hold her back:

"Wait a while. You'll catch cold outdoors. I'll call a cab."

But she paid no attention and hurried down the stairs. When they reached the street they found no carriages. They began to look for one, shouting at cabmen passing by at a distance.

They walked toward the Seine, desperate, shivering. Finally, on a quay, they found one of those old night-going buggies that are seen in Paris only after dark, as if they were ashamed of their wretched appearance in daylight.

It took them to their door, on the Street of Martyrs, and they sadly climbed the stairs to their flat. For her, it was finished. As for him, he could think only that he had to begin work at the Ministry of Education at ten o'clock.

She took the shawl off her shoulders, in front of the mirror, to see herself once more in her glory. But suddenly she cried out. The necklace was no longer around her neck!

Her husband, already half undressed, asked:

"What's wrong with you?"

She turned toward him frantically:

"I . . . I . . . I no longer have Mrs. Forrestier's necklace."

He stood up, bewildered:

"What! . . . How! . . . It's not possible!"

And they looked in the folds of the dress, in the creases of the shawl, in the pockets, everywhere. They found nothing.

He asked:

"You're sure you still had it when you left the party?"

"Yes. I checked it in the vestibule of the Ministry."

"But if you had lost it in the street, we would have heard it fall. It must be in the cab."

"Yes, probably. Did you notice the number?"

"No. Did you see it?"

"No."

Overwhelmed, they looked at each other. Finally, Loisel got dressed again:

"I'm going out to retrace all our steps," he said, "to see if I can find the necklace that way."

And he went out. She stayed in her evening dress, without the energy to get ready for bed, prostrated in a chair, drained of strength and thought.

Her husband came back at about seven o'clock. He had found nothing.

He went to Police Headquarters and to the newspapers to announce a reward. He went to the small cab companies, and finally he followed up even the slightest hopeful lead.

She waited the entire day, in the same enervated state, in the face of this frightful disaster.

Loisel came back in the evening, his face pale and haggard. He had found nothing.

"You'll have to write to your friend," he said, "that you broke a fastening on her necklace and that you will have it fixed. That will give us time to look around."

She wrote as he dictated.

At the end of a week they had lost all hope.

And Loisel, seemingly five years older, declared:

"We'll have to see about replacing the jewels."

The next day, they took the case which had contained the necklace, and went to the jeweler whose name was inside. He looked at his books:

"I wasn't the one, Madam, who sold the necklace. I only made the case."

Then they went from jeweler to jeweler, searching for a necklace like the other one, racking their memories, both of them sick with worry and anguish.

In a shop in the Palais-Royal, they found a string of diamonds that seemed to them exactly like the one they were seeking. It was priced at forty thousand francs. They could buy it for thirty-six thousand.

They got the jeweler to promise not to sell it for three days. And they made an agreement that he would buy it back for thirty-four thousand francs if the original was recovered before the end of February.

Loisel had saved eighteen thousand francs that his father had left him. He would have to borrow the rest.

He borrowed, asking a thousand francs from one, five hundred from another, five louis[1] here, three louis here. He made promissory notes, undertook ruinous obligations, did business with loan sharks and the whole tribe of finance companies. He compromised himself for the remainder of his days, risked his signature without knowing whether he would be able to honor it, and, terrified by anguish over the future, by the black misery that was about to descend on him, by the prospect of all kinds of physical deprivations and moral tortures, he went to get the new necklace, and put down thirty-six thousand francs on the jeweler's counter.

Mrs. Loisel took the necklace back to Mrs. Forrestier, who said with an offended tone:

"You should have brought it back sooner, because I might have needed it."

She did not open the case, as her friend feared she might. If she had noticed the substitution, what would she have thought? What would she have said? Would she not have taken her for a thief?

Mrs. Loisel soon discovered the horrible life of the needy. She did her share, however, completely, heroically. That horrifying debt had to be paid. She would pay. They dismissed the maid; they changed their address; they rented an attic flat.

She learned to do heavy housework, dirty kitchen jobs. She washed the dishes, wearing away her manicured fingernails on greasy pots and encrusted baking dishes. She handwashed dirty linen, shirts, and dish towels that she hung out on the line to dry. Each morning, she took the garbage down to the street, and she carried up water, stopping at each floor to catch her breath. And, dressed in cheap house dresses, she went to the fruit dealer, the grocer, the butcher, with her basket under her arms, haggling, insulting, defending her measly cash penny by penny.

They had to make installment payments every month, and, to buy more time, to refinance loans.

The husband worked evenings to make fair copies of tradesmen's accounts, and late into the night he made copies at five cents a page.

And this life lasted ten years.

At the end of ten years, they had paid back everything—everything—including the extra charges imposed by loan sharks and the accumulation of compound interest.

Mrs. Loisel seemed old now. She had become the strong, hard, and rude woman of poor households. Her hair unkempt, with uneven skirts and rough, red hands, she spoke loudly, washed floors with large buckets of water. But sometimes, when

---

[1]A louis was a twenty-franc coin.

her husband was at work, she sat down near the window, and she dreamed of that evening so long ago, of that party, where she had been so beautiful and so admired.

What would life have been like if she had not lost that necklace? Who knows? Who knows? Life is so peculiar, so uncertain. How little a thing it takes to destroy you or to save you!

Well, one Sunday, as she had gone on a stroll along the Champs-Elysées to relax from the cares of the week, she suddenly noticed a woman walking with a child. It was Mrs. Forrestier, always youthful, always beautiful, always attractive.

Mrs. Loisel felt moved. Would she speak to her? Yes, certainly. And now that she had paid, she could tell all. Why not?

She walked closer.

"Hello, Jeanne."

The other did not recognize her at all, being astonished to be addressed so intimately by this working woman. She stammered:

"But . . . Madam! . . . I don't know. . . . You must have made a mistake."

"No. I'm Mathilde Loisel."

Her friend cried out:

"Oh! . . . My poor Mathilde, you've changed so much."

"Yes. I've had some hard times since I saw you last; in fact, miseries . . . and all this because of you! . . ."

"Of me . . . how so?"

"You remember the diamond necklace that you lent me to go to the party at the Ministry of Education?"

"Yes. What then?"

"Well, I lost it."

"How, since you gave it back to me?"

"I brought back another exactly like it. And for ten years we've been paying for it. You understand that this wasn't easy for us, who have nothing. . . . Finally it's over, and I'm mighty damned glad."

Mrs. Forrestier stopped her.

"You say that you bought a diamond necklace to replace mine?"

"Yes. You didn't notice it, eh? They were exactly like yours."

And she smiled with proud and childish joy.

Mrs. Forrestier, deeply moved, took both her hands.

"Oh, my poor Mathilde! But mine was false. At the most, it was worth five hundred francs! . . . "

# Anton Chekhov (1860–1904)

## *The Bear:*
## *A Joke in One Act*

### Cast of Characters

Mrs. Popov. *A widow of seven months*, Mrs. Popov *is small and pretty, with dimples. She is a landowner. At the start of the play, she is pining away in memory of her dead husband.*

Grigory Stepanovich Smirnov. *Easily angered and loud*, Smirnov *is older. He is a landowner, too, and a gentleman farmer of some substance.*

Luka. Luka *is* Mrs. Popov's *footman (a servant whose main tasks were to wait table and attend the carriages, in addition to general duties). He is old enough to feel secure in telling* Mrs. Popov *what he thinks.*

Gardener, Coachman, Workmen, *who enter at the end.*

*The drawing room of* MRS. POPOV'S *country home.*

(MRS. POPOV, *in deep mourning, does not remove her eyes from a photograph.*)

LUKA. It isn't right, madam . . . you're only destroying yourself. . . . The chambermaid and the cook have gone off berry picking; every living being is rejoicing; even the cat knows how to be content, walking around the yard catching birds, and you sit in your room all day as if it were a convent, and you don't take pleasure in anything. Yes, really! Almost a year has passed since you've gone out of the house!

MRS. POPOV. And I shall never go out. . . . What for? My life is already ended. *He* lies in his grave; I have buried myself in these four walls . . . we are both dead.

LUKA. There you go again! Your husband is dead, that's as it was meant to be, it's the will of God, may he rest in peace. . . . You've done your mourning and that will do. You can't go on weeping and mourning forever. My wife died when her time came, too. . . . Well? I grieved, I wept for a month, and that was enough for her; the old lady wasn't worth a second more. (*Sighs.*) You've forgotten all your neighbors. You don't go anywhere or accept any calls. We live, so to speak, like spiders. We never see the light. The mice have eaten my uniform. It isn't as if there weren't any nice neighbors—the district is full of them . . . there's a regiment stationed at Riblov, such officers—they're like candy—you'll never get your fill of them! And in the barracks, never a Friday goes by without a dance; and, if you please, the military band plays music every day. . . . Yes, madam, my dear lady: you're young, beautiful, in the full bloom of youth—if only you took a little pleasure in life . . . beauty doesn't last forever, you know! In ten years' time, you'll be wanting to wave your fanny in front of the officers—and it will be too late.

Slightly altered from the Bantam Press edition of *Ten Great One-Act Plays*, Morris Sweetkind, ed. (1968).

MRS. POPOV (*determined*). I must ask you never to talk to me like that! You know that when Mr. Popov died, life lost all its salt for me. It may seem to you that I am alive, but that's only conjecture! I vowed to wear mourning to my grave and not to see the light of day. . . . Do you hear me? May his departed spirit see how much I love him. . . . Yes, I know, it's no mystery to you that he was often mean to me, cruel . . . and even unfaithful, but I shall remain true to the grave and show him I know how to love. There, beyond the grave, he will see me as I was before his death. . . .

LUKA. Instead of talking like that, you should be taking a walk in the garden or have Toby or Giant harnessed and go visit some of the neighbors . . .

MRS. POPOV. Ai! (*She weeps.*)

LUKA. Madam! Dear lady! What's the matter with you! Christ be with you!

MRS. POPOV. Oh, how he loved Toby! He always used to ride on him to visit the Korchagins or the Vlasovs. How wonderfully he rode! How graceful he was when he pulled at the reins with all his strength! Do you remember? Toby, Toby! Tell them to give him an extra bag of oats today.

LUKA. Yes, madam.

(*Sound of loud ringing.*)

MRS. POPOV (*shudders*). Who's that? Tell them I'm not at home!

LUKA. Of course, madam. (*He exits.*)

MRS. POPOV (*alone. Looks at the photograph*). You will see, Nicholas, how much I can love and forgive . . . my love will die only when I do, when my poor heart stops beating. (*Laughing through her tears.*) Have you no shame? I'm a good girl, a virtuous little wife. I've locked myself in and I'll be true to you to the grave, and you . . . aren't you ashamed, you chubby cheeks? You deceived me, you made scenes, for weeks on end you left me alone . . .

LUKA (*enters, alarmed*). Madam, somebody is asking for you. He wants to see you. . . .

MRS. POPOV. But didn't you tell them that since the death of my husband, I don't see anybody?

LUKA. I did, but he didn't want to listen; he spoke about some very important business.

MRS. POPOV. I am *not at home!*

LUKA. That's what I told him . . . but . . . the devil . . . he cursed and pushed past me right into the room . . . he's in the dining room right now.

MRS. POPOV (*losing her temper*). Very well, let him come in . . . such manners! (LUKA *goes out.*) How difficult these people are! What does he want from me? Why should he disturb my peace? (*Sighs.*) But it's obvious I'll have to go live in a convent. . . . (*Thoughtfully.*) Yes, a convent. . . .

SMIRNOV (*to* LUKA). You idiot, you talk too much. . . . Ass! (*Sees* MRS. POPOV *and changes to dignified speech.*) Madam, may I introduce myself: retired lieutenant of the artillery and landowner, Grigory Stepanovich Smirnov! I feel the necessity of troubling you about a highly important matter. . . .

MRS. POPOV (*refusing her hand*). What do you want?

SMIRNOV. Your late husband, whom I had the pleasure of knowing, has remained in my debt for two twelve-hundred-ruble notes. Since I must pay the interest at the agricultural bank tomorrow, I have come to ask you, madam, to pay me the money today.

MRS. POPOV. One thousand two hundred. . . . And why was my husband in debt to you?

SMIRNOV. He used to buy oats from me.

MRS. POPOV (*sighing, to* LUKA). So, Luka, don't you forget to tell them to give Toby an extra bag of oats.

(LUKA *goes out.*)

(*To* SMIRNOV.) If Nikolai, my husband, was in debt to you, then it goes without saying that I'll pay; but please excuse me today. I haven't any spare cash. The day after tomorrow, my steward will be back from town and I will give him instructions to pay you what is owed; until then I cannot comply with your wishes. . . . Besides, today is the anniversary—exactly seven months ago my husband died, and I'm in such a mood that I'm not quite disposed to occupy myself with money matters.

SMIRNOV. And I'm in such a mood that if I don't pay the interest tomorrow, I'll be owing so much that my troubles will drown me. They'll take away my estate!

MRS. POPOV. You'll receive your money the day after tomorrow.

SMIRNOV. I don't want the money the day after tomorrow. I want it today.

MRS. POPOV. You must excuse me. I can't pay you today.

SMIRNOV. And I can't wait until after tomorrow.

MRS. POPOV. What can I do, if I don't have it now?

SMIRNOV. You mean to say you can't pay?

MRS. POPOV. I can't pay. . . .

SMIRNOV. Hm! Is that your last word?

MRS. POPOV. That is my last word.

SMIRNOV. Positively the last?

MRS. POPOV. Positively.

SMIRNOV. Thank you very much. We'll make a note of that. (*Shrugs his shoulders.*) And people want me to be calm and collected! Just now, on the way here, I met a tax officer and he asked me: why are you always so angry, Grigory Stepanovich? Goodness' sake, how can I be anything but angry? I need money desperately . . . I rode out yesterday early in the morning, at daybreak, and went to see all my debtors; and if only one of them had paid his debt . . . I was dog-tired, spent the night God knows where—a Jewish tavern beside a barrel of vodka. . . . Finally I got here, fifty miles from home, hoping to be paid, and you treat me to a "mood." How can I help being angry?

MRS. POPOV. It seems to me that I clearly said: My steward will return from the country and then you will be paid.

SMIRNOV. I didn't come to your steward, but to you! What the hell, if you'll pardon the expression, would I do with your steward?

MRS. POPOV. Excuse mé, my dear sir, I am not accustomed to such unusual expressions nor to such a tone. I'm not listening to you any more. (*Goes out quickly.*)

SMIRNOV (*alone*). Well, how do you like that? "A mood." . . ."Husband died seven months ago"! Must I pay the interest or mustn't I? I ask you: Must I pay, or must I not? So, your husband's dead, and you're in a mood and all that finicky stuff . . . and your steward's away somewhere; may he drop dead. What do you want me to do? Do you think I can fly away from my creditors in a balloon or something? Or should I run and bash my head against the wall? I go to Gruzdev—and he's not at home; Yaroshevich is hiding, with Kuritsin it's a quarrel to the death and I almost throw him out the window; Mazutov has diarrhea, and this one is in a "mood." Not one of these swine wants to pay me! And all because I'm too nice to them. I'm a sniveling idiot, I'm spineless, I'm an old lady! I'm too delicate with them! So, just you wait! You'll find out what I'm like! I won't let you play around with me, you devils! I'll stay and stick it out until she pays. Rrr! . . . How furious I am today, how furious! I'm shaking inside from rage and I can hardly catch my breath. . . . Damn it! My God, I even feel sick! *(He shouts.)* Hey, you!

LUKA *(enters).* What do you want?

SMIRNOV. Give me some beer or some water! (LUKA *exits.*) What logic is there in this! A man needs money desperately, it's like a noose around his neck—and she won't pay because, you see, she's not disposed to occupy herself with money matters! . . . That's the logic of a woman! That's why I never did like and do not like to talk to women. I'd rather sit on a keg of gunpowder than talk to a woman. Brr! . . . I even have goose pimples, this broad has put me in such a rage! All I have to do is see one of those spoiled bitches from a distance, and I get so angry it gives me a cramp in the leg. I just want to shout for help.

LUKA *(entering with water).* Madam is sick and won't see anyone.

SMIRNOV. Get out! (LUKA *goes.*) Sick and won't see anyone! No need to see me . . . I'll stay and sit here until you give me the money. You can stay sick for a week, and I'll stay for a week . . . if you're sick for a year, I'll stay a year. . . . I'll get my own back, dear lady! You can't impress me with your widow's weeds and your dimpled cheeks . . . we know all about those dimples! *(Shouts through the window.)* Semyon, unharness the horses! We're not going away quite yet! I'm staying here! Tell them in the stable to give the horses some oats! You brute, you let the horse on the left side get all tangled up in the reins again! *(Teasing.)* "Never mind" . . . I'll give you a never mind! *(Goes away from the window.)* Shit! The heat is unbearable and nobody pays up. I slept badly last night and on top of everything else this broad in mourning is "in a mood" . . . my head aches . . . *(Drinks, and grimaces.)* Shit! This is water! What I need is a drink! *(Shouts.)* Hey, you!

LUKA *(enters).* What is it?

SMIRNOV. Give me a glass of vodka. (LUKA *goes out.*) Oof! *(Sits down and examines himself.)* Nobody would say I was looking well! Dusty all over, boots dirty, unwashed, unkempt, straw on my waistcoat. . . . The dear lady probably took me for a robber. *(Yawns.)* It's not very polite to present myself in a drawing room looking like this; oh well, who cares? . . . I'm not here as a visitor but as a creditor, and there's no official costume for creditors. . . .

LUKA *(enters with vodka).* You're taking liberties, my good man. . . .

SMIRNOV *(angrily).* What?

LUKA. I . . . nothing . . . I only . . .

SMIRNOV. Who are you talking to? Shut up!

LUKA *(aside).* The devil sent this leech. An ill wind brought him. . . . (LUKA *goes out.*)

SMIRNOV. Oh how furious I am! I'm so mad I could crush the whole world into a powder! I even feel faint! *(Shouts.)* Hey, you!

MRS. POPOV *(enters, eyes downcast).* My dear sir, in my solitude, I have long ago grown unaccustomed to the masculine voice and I cannot bear shouting. I must request you not to disturb my peace and quiet!

SMIRNOV. Pay me my money and I'll go.

MRS. POPOV. I told you in plain language: I haven't any spare cash now; wait until the day after tomorrow.

SMIRNOV. And I also told you respectfully, in plain language: I don't need the money the day after tomorrow, but today. If you don't pay me today, then tomorrow I'll have to hang myself.

MRS. POPOV. But what can I do if I don't have the money? You're so strange!

SMIRNOV. Then you won't pay me now? No?

MRS. POPOV. I can't. . . .

SMIRNOV. In that case, I can stay here and wait until you pay. . . . *(Sits down.)* You'll pay the day after tomorrow? Excellent! In that case I'll stay here until the day after tomorrow. I'll sit here all that time . . . *(Jumps up.)* I ask you: Have I got to pay the interest tomorrow, or not? Or do you think I'm joking?

MRS. POPOV. My dear sir, I ask you not to shout! This isn't a stable!

SMIRNOV. I wasn't asking you about a stable but about this: Do I have to pay the interest tomorrow or not?

MRS. POPOV. You don't know how to behave in the company of a lady!

SMIRNOV. No, I don't know how to behave in the company of a lady!

MRS. POPOV. No, you don't! You are an ill-bred, rude man! Respectable people don't talk to a woman like that!

SMIRNOV. Ach, it's astonishing! How would you like me to talk to you? In French, perhaps? *(Lisps in anger.)* Madam, je vous prie[1] . . . how happy I am that you're not paying me the money. . . . Ah, pardon, I've made you uneasy! Such lovely weather we're having today! And you look so becoming in your mourning dress. *(Bows and scrapes.)*

MRS. POPOV. That's rude and not very clever!

SMIRNOV *(teasing).* Rude and not very clever! I don't know how to behave in the company of ladies. Madam, in my time I've seen far more women than you've seen sparrows. Three times I've fought duels over women; I've jilted twelve women, nine have jilted me! Yes! There was a time when I played the fool; I became sentimental over women, used honeyed words, fawned on them, bowed and scraped. . . . I loved, suffered, sighed at the moon; I became limp, melted, shivered . . . I loved passionately, madly, every which way, devil take me, I chattered away like a magpie about the emancipation of women, ran through half my fortune as a result of my tender feelings; but now, if you will excuse me, I'm on to your ways! I've had enough! Dark eyes, passionate eyes, ruby lips, dimpled cheeks; the moon, whispers, bated breath—for all that I wouldn't give a good goddamn. Present company excepted, of course, but all women, young and old alike, are affected clowns, gossips, hateful, consummate liars to the marrow of their bones, vain, trivial, ruthless, outrageously illogical, and as far as this is concerned *(taps on his forehead)*, well, excuse my frankness, any sparrow could give pointers to a philosopher in petticoats! Look at one of those romantic creatures: muslin, ethereal demigoddess, a thousand raptures, and you look into her soul—a common crocodile! *(Grips the back of a chair; the chair cracks and breaks.)* But the most revolting part of it all is that this crocodile imagines that she has, above everything, her own privilege, a monopoly on tender feelings. The hell with it—you can hang me upside down by that nail if a woman is capable of loving anything besides a lapdog. All she can do when she's in love is slobber! While the man suffers and sacrifices, all her love is expressed in playing with her skirt and trying to lead him around firmly by the nose. You have the misfortune of being a woman, you know yourself what the

[1]Madam, I beg you.

nature of a woman is like. Tell me honestly; Have you ever in your life seen a woman who is sincere, faithful, and constant? You never have! Only old and ugly ladies are faithful and constant! You're more liable to meet a horned cat or a white woodcock than a faithful woman!

MRS. POPOV. Pardon me, but in your opinion, who is faithful and constant in love? The man?

SMIRNOV. Yes, the man!

MRS. POPOV. The man! *(Malicious laugh.)* Men are faithful and constant in love! That's news! *(Heatedly)* What right have you to say that? Men are faithful and constant! For that matter, as far as I know, of all the men I have known and now know, my late husband was the best. . . . I loved him passionately, with all my being, as only a young intellectual woman can love; I gave him my youth, my happiness, my life, my fortune; he was my life's breath; I worshipped him as if I were a heathen, and . . . and, what good did it do—this best of men himself deceived me shamelessly at every step of the way. After his death, I found his desk full of love letters; and when he was alive—it's terrible to remember—he used to leave me alone for weeks at a time, and before my very eyes he paid court to other women and deceived me. He squandered my money, made a mockery of my feelings . . . and, in spite of all that, I loved him and was true to him . . . and besides, now that he is dead, I am still faithful and constant. I have shut myself up in these four walls forever and I won't remove these widow's weeds until my dying day. . . .

SMIRNOV *(laughs contemptuously)*. Widow's weeds! . . . I don't know what you take me for! As if I didn't know why you wear that black outfit and bury yourself in these four walls! Well, well! It's no secret, so romantic! When some fool of a poet passes by this country house, he'll look up at your window and think: "Here lives the mysterious Tamara, who, for the love of her husband, buried herself in these four walls." We know these tricks!

MRS. POPOV *(flaring)*. What? How dare you say that to me?

SMIRNOV. You may have buried yourself alive, but you haven't forgotten to powder yourself!

MRS. POPOV. How dare you use such expressions with me?

SMIRNOV. Please don't shout. I'm not your steward! You must allow me to call a spade a spade. I'm not a woman and I'm used to saying what's on my mind! Don't you shout at me!

MRS. POPOV. I'm not shouting, you are! Please leave me in peace!

SMIRNOV. Pay me my money and I'll go.

MRS. POPOV. I won't give you any money!

SMIRNOV. Yes, you will.

MRS. POPOV. To spite you, I won't pay you anything. You can leave me in peace!

SMIRNOV. I don't have the pleasure of being either your husband or your fiancé, so please don't make scenes! *(Sits down.)* I don't like it.

MRS. POPOV *(choking with rage)*. You're sitting down?

SMIRNOV. Yes, I am.

MRS. POPOV. I ask you to get out!

SMIRNOV. Give me my money . . . *(Aside.)* Oh, I'm so furious! Furious!

MRS. POPOV. I don't want to talk to impudent people! Get out of here! *(Pause.)* You're not going? No?

SMIRNOV. No.

MRS. POPOV. No?

SMIRNOV. No!

MRS. POPOV. We'll see about that. *(Rings.)*

(LUKA *enters.*)

Luka, show the gentleman out!

LUKA *(goes up to* SMIRNOV*).* Sir, will you please leave, as you have been asked. You mustn't . . .

SMIRNOV *(jumping up).* Shut up! Who do you think you're talking to? I'll make mincemeat out of you!

LUKA *(his hand to his heart).* Oh my God! Saints above! *(Falls into chair.)* Oh, I feel ill! I feel ill! I can't catch my breath!

MRS. POPOV. Where's Dasha? Dasha! *(She shouts.)* Dasha! Pelagea! Dasha! *(She rings.)*

LUKA. Oh! They've all gone berry picking . . . there's nobody at home . . . I'm ill! Water!

MRS. POPOV. Will you please get out!

SMIRNOV. Will you please be more polite?

MRS. POPOV *(clenches her fist and stamps her feet).* You're nothing but a crude bear! A brute! A monster!

SMIRNOV. What? What did you say?

MRS. POPOV. I said that you were a bear, a monster!

SMIRNOV *(advancing toward her).* Excuse me, but what right do you have to insult me?

MRS. POPOV. Yes, I am insulting you . . . so what? Do you think I'm afraid of you?

SMIRNOV. And do you think just because you're one of those romantic creations, that you have the right to insult me with impunity? Yes? I challenge you!

LUKA. Lord in Heaven! Saints above! . . . Water!

SMIRNOV. Pistols!

MRS. POPOV. Do you think just because you have big fists and you can bellow like a bull, that I'm afraid of you? You're such a bully!

SMIRNOV. I challenge you! I'm not going to let anybody insult me, and I don't care if you are a woman, a delicate creature!

MRS. POPOV *(trying to get a word in edgewise).* Bear! Bear! Bear!

SMIRNOV. It's about time we got rid of the prejudice that only men must pay for their insults! Devil take it, if women want to be equal, they should behave as equals! Let's fight!

MRS. POPOV. You want to fight! By all means!

SMIRNOV. This minute!

MRS. POPOV. This minute! My husband had some pistols . . . I'll go and get them right away. *(Goes out hurriedly and then returns.)* What pleasure I'll have putting a bullet through that thick head of yours! The hell with you! *(She goes out.)*

SMIRNOV. I'll shoot her down like a chicken! I'm not a little boy or a sentimental puppy. I don't care if she is delicate and fragile.

LUKA. Kind sir! Holy father! *(Kneels.)* Have pity on a poor old man and go away from here! You've frightened her to death and now you're going to shoot her?

SMIRNOV *(not listening to him).* If she fights, then it means she believes in equality of rights and emancipation of women. Here the sexes are equal! I'll shoot her like a chicken! But what a woman! *(Imitates her.)* "The hell with you! . . . I'll put a bullet through that thick head of yours! . . ." What a woman! How she blushed, her eyes shone . . . she accepted my challenge! To tell the truth, it was the first time in my life I've seen a woman like that. . . .

LUKA. Dear sir, please go away! I'll pray to God on your behalf as long as I live!

SMIRNOV. That's a woman for you! A woman like that I can understand! A real woman! Not a sour-faced nincompoop but fiery, gunpowder! Fireworks! I'm even sorry to have to kill her!

LUKA *(weeps)*. Dear sir . . . go away!

SMIRNOV. I positively like her! Positively! Even though she has dimpled cheeks, I like her! I'm almost ready to forget about the debt. . . . My fury has diminished. Wonderful woman!

MRS. POPOV *(enters with pistols)*. Here they are, the pistols. Before we fight, you must show me how to fire. . . . I've never had a pistol in my hands before . . .

LUKA. Oh dear Lord, for pity's sake. . . . I'll go and find the gardener and the coachman. . . . What did we do to deserve such trouble? *(Exit.)*

SMIRNOV *(examining the pistols)*. You see, there are several sorts of pistols . . . there are special dueling pistols, the Mortimer with primers. Then there are Smith and Wesson revolvers, triple action with extractors . . . excellent pistols! . . . they cost a minimum of ninety rubles a pair. . . . You must hold the revolver like this . . . *(Aside.)* What eyes, what eyes! A woman to set you on fire!

MRS. POPOV. Like this?

SMIRNOV. Yes, like this . . . then you cock the pistol . . . take aim . . . put your head back a little . . . stretch your arm out all the way . . . that's right . . . then with this finger press on this little piece of goods . . . and that's all there is to do . . . but the most important thing is not to get excited and aim without hurrying . . . try to keep your arm from shaking.

MRS. POPOV. Good . . . it's not comfortable to shoot indoors. Let's go into the garden.

SMIRNOV. Let's go. But I'm giving you advance notice that I'm going to fire into the air.

MRS. POPOV. That's the last straw! Why?

SMIRNOV. Why? . . . Why . . . because it's my business, that's why.

MRS. POPOV. Are you afraid? Yes? Aahhh! No, sir. You're not going to get out of it that easily! Be so good as to follow me! I will not rest until I've put a hole through your forehead . . . that forehead I hate so much! Are you afraid?

SMIRNOV. Yes, I'm afraid.

MRS. POPOV. You're lying! Why don't you want to fight?

SMIRNOV. Because . . . because you . . . because I like you.

MRS. POPOV *(laughs angrily)*. He likes me! He dares say that he likes me! *(Points to the door.)* Out!

SMIRNOV *(loads the revolver in silence, takes cap and goes; at the door, stops for half a minute while they look at each other in silence; then he approaches MRS. POPOV hesitantly)*. Listen. . . . Are you still angry? I'm extremely irritated, but, do you understand me, how can I express it . . . the fact is, that, you see, strictly speaking . . . *(He shouts.)* Is it my fault, really, for liking you? *(Grabs the back of a chair, which cracks and breaks.)* Why the hell do you have such fragile furniture! I like you! Do you understand? I . . . I'm almost in love with you!

MRS. POPOV. Get away from me—I hate you!

SMIRNOV. God, what a woman! I've never in my life seen anything like her! I'm lost! I'm done for! I'm caught like a mouse in a trap!

MRS. POPOV. Stand back or I'll shoot!

SMIRNOV. Shoot! You could never understand what happiness it would be to die under the gaze of those wonderful eyes, to be shot by a revolver which was held by those little velvet hands. . . . I've gone out of my mind! Think about it and decide right away, because if I leave here, then we'll never see each other again! Decide . . . I'm a nobleman, a respectable gentleman, of good family. I have an income of ten thousand a year. . . . I can put a bullet through a coin tossed in the air . . . I have some fine horses. . . . Will you be my wife?

MRS. POPOV *(indignantly brandishes her revolver).* Let's fight! I challenge you!

SMIRNOV. I'm out of my mind . . . I don't understand anything . . . *(Shouts.)* Hey, you, water!

MRS. POPOV *(shouts).* Let's fight!

SMIRNOV. I've gone out of my mind. I'm in love like a boy, like an idiot! *(He grabs her hand, she screams with pain.)* I love you! *(Kneels.)* I love you as I've never loved before! I've jilted twelve women, nine women have jilted me, but I've never loved one of them as I love you. . . . I'm weak, I'm a limp rag. . . . I'm on my knees like a fool, offering you my hand. . . . Shame, shame! I haven't been in love for five years, I vowed I wouldn't; and suddenly I'm in love, like a fish out of water. I'm offering my hand in marriage. Yes or no? You don't want to? You don't need to! *(Gets up and quickly goes to the door.)*

MRS. POPOV. Wait!

SMIRNOV *(stops).* Well?

MRS. POPOV. Nothing . . . you can go . . . go away . . . wait. . . . No, get out, get out! I hate you! But—don't go! Oh, if you only knew how furious I am, how angry! *(Throws revolver on table.)* My fingers are swollen from that nasty thing. . . . *(Tears her handkerchief furiously.)* What are you waiting for? Get out!

SMIRNOV. Farewell!

MRS. POPOV. Yes, yes, go away! *(Shouts.)* Where are you going? Stop. . . . Oh, go away! Oh, how furious I am! Don't come near me! Don't come near me!

SMIRNOV *(approaching her).* How angry I am with myself! I'm in love like a student. I've been on my knees. . . . It gives me the shivers. *(Rudely.)* I love you! A lot of good it will do me to fall in love with you! Tomorrow I've got to pay the interest, begin the mowing of the hay. *(Puts his arm around her waist.)* I'll never forgive myself for this. . . .

MRS. POPOV. Get away from me! Get your hands away! I . . . hate you! I . . . challenge you!

(*Prolonged kiss.* LUCA *enters with an ax, the* GARDENER *with a rake, the* COACHMAN *with a pitchfork, and* WORKMEN *with cudgels.)*

LUCA *(catches sight of the pair kissing).* Lord in heaven! *(Pause.)*

MRS. POPOV *(lowering her eyes).* Luka, tell them in the stable not to give Toby any oats today.

CURTAIN

## Robert Frost (1875–1963)

# *Desert Places*

| | |
|---|---|
| Snow falling and night falling fast, oh, fast | 1 |
| In a field I looked into going past, | 2 |
| And the ground almost covered smooth in snow, | 3 |
| But a few weeds and stubble showing last. | 4 |
| | |
| The woods around it have it—it is theirs. | 5 |
| All animals are smothered in their lairs. | 6 |
| I am too absent-spirited to count; | 7 |
| The loneliness includes me unawares. | 8 |
| | |
| And lonely as it is that loneliness | 9 |
| Will be more lonely ere it will be less— | 10 |
| A blanker whiteness of benighted snow | 11 |
| With no expression, nothing to express. | 12 |
| | |
| They cannot scare me with their empty spaces | 13 |
| Between stars—on stars where no human race is. | 14 |
| I have it in me so much nearer home | 15 |
| To scare myself with my own desert places. | 16 |

## Frank O'Connor (1903–1966)

# *First Confession*

All the trouble began when my grandfather died and my grandmother—my father's mother—came to live with us. Relations in the one house are a strain at the best of times, but, to make matters worse, my grandmother was a real old country-woman and quite unsuited to the life in town. She had a fat, wrinkled old face, and, to Mother's great indignation, went round the house in bare feet—the boots had her crippled, she said. For dinner she had a jog of porter and a pot of potatoes with—sometimes—a bit of salt fish, and she poured out the potatoes on the table and ate them slowly, with great relish, using her fingers by way of a fork.

Now, girls are supposed to be fastidious, but I was the one who suffered most from this. Nora, my sister, just sucked up to the old woman for the penny she got every Friday out of the old-age pension, a thing I could not do. I was too honest, that was my trouble; and when I was playing with Bill Connell, the sergeant-major's son, and saw my grandmother steering up the path with the jug of porter sticking out from beneath her shawl I was mortified. I made excuses not to let him come into the house, because I could never be sure what she would be up to when we went in.

When Mother was at work and my grandmother made the dinner I wouldn't touch it. Nora once tried to make me, but I hid under the table from her and took the bread-knife with me for protection. Nora let on to be very indignant (she wasn't, of course, but she knew Mother saw through her, so she sided with Gran) and came after me. I lashed out at her with the bread-knife, and after that she left me alone. I stayed there till Mother came in from work and made my dinner, but when Father came in later Nora said in a shocked voice: "Oh, Dadda, do you know what Jackie did at dinnertime?" Then, of course, it all came out; Father gave me a flaking; Mother interfered, and for days after that he didn't speak to me and Mother barely spoke to Nora. And all because of that old woman! God knows, I was heart-scalded.

Then, to crown my misfortune, I had to make my first confession and communion. It was an old woman called Ryan who prepared us for these. She was about the one age with Gran; she was well-to-do, lived in a big house on Montenotte, wore a black cloak and bonnet, and came every day to school at three o'clock when we should have been going home, and talked to us of hell. She may have mentioned the other place as well, but that could only have been by accident, for hell had the first place in her heart.

She lit a candle, took out a new half-crown, and offered it to the first boy who would hold one finger—only one finger!—in the flame for five minutes by the school clock. Being always very ambitious I was tempted to volunteer, but I thought it might look greedy. Then she asked were we afraid of holding one finger—only one finger!—in a little candle flame for five minutes and not afraid of burning all over in roasting hot furnaces for all eternity. "All eternity! Just think of that! A whole lifetime goes by and it's nothing, not even a drop in the ocean of your sufferings." The woman was really interesting about hell, but my attention was all fixed on the half-crown. At the end of the lesson she put it back in her purse. It was a great disappointment; a religious woman like that, you wouldn't think she'd bother about a thing like a half-crown.

Another day she said she knew a priest who woke one night to find a fellow he didn't recognize leaning over the end of his bed. The priest was a bit frightened—naturally enough—but he asked the fellow what he wanted, and the fellow said in a deep, husky voice that he wanted to go to confession. The priest said it was an awkward time and wouldn't it do in the morning, but the fellow said that last time he went to confession, there was one sin he kept back, being ashamed to mention it, and now it was always on his mind. Then the priest knew it was a bad case, because the fellow was after making a bad confession and committing a mortal sin. He got up to dress, and just then the cock crew in the yard outside, and—lo and behold!—when the priest looked round there was no sign of the fellow, only a smell of burning timber, and when the priest looked at his bed didn't he see the print of two hands burned in it? That was because the fellow had made a bad confession. This story made a shocking impression on me.

But the worst of all was when she showed us how to examine our conscience. Did we take the name of the Lord, our God, in vain? Did we honour our father and our mother? (I asked her did this include grandmothers and she said it did.) Did we love our neighbours as ourselves? Did we covet our neighbour's goods? (I thought of the way I felt about the penny that Nora got every Friday.) I decided that, between one thing and another, I must have broken the whole ten commandments, all on account of that old woman, and so far as I could see, so long as she remained in the house I had no hope of ever doing anything else.

I was scared to death of confession. The day the whole class went I let on to have a toothache, hoping my absence wouldn't be noticed; but at three o'clock, just as I was feeling safe, along comes a chap with a message from Mrs. Ryan that I was to go to confession myself on Saturday and be at the chapel for communion with the rest. To make it worse, Mother couldn't come with me and sent Nora instead.

Now, that girl had ways of tormenting me that Mother never knew of. She held my hand as we went down the hill, smiling sadly and saying how sorry she was for me, as if she were bringing me to the hospital for an operation.

"Oh, God help us!" she moaned. "Isn't it a terrible pity you weren't a good boy? Oh, Jackie, my heart bleeds for you! How will you ever think of all your sins? Don't forget you have to tell him about the time you kicked Gran on the shin."

"Lemme go!" I said, trying to drag myself free of her. "I don't want to go to confession at all."

"But sure, you'll have to go to confession, Jackie," she replied in the same regretful tone. "Sure, if you didn't, the parish priest would be up to the house, looking for you. 'Tisn't, God knows, that I'm not sorry for you. Do you remember the time you tried to kill me with the bread-knife under the table? And the language you used to me? I don't know what he'll do with you at all, Jackie. He might have to send you up to the bishop."

I remember thinking bitterly that she didn't know the half of what I had to tell— if I told it. I knew I couldn't tell it, and understood perfectly why the fellow in Mrs. Ryan's story made a bad confession; it seemed to me a great shame that people wouldn't stop criticizing him. I remember that steep hill down to the church, and the sunlit hillsides beyond the valley of the river, which I saw in the gaps between the houses like Adam's last glimpse of Paradise.

Then, when she had manœuvred me down the long flight of steps to the chapel yard, Nora suddenly changed her tone. She became the raging malicious devil she really was.

"There you are!" she said with a yelp of triumph, hurling me through the church door. "And I hope he'll give you the penitential psalms, you dirty little caffler."

I knew then I was lost, given up to eternal justice. The door with the coloured-glass panels swung shut behind me, the sunlight went out and gave place to deep shadow, and the wind whistled outside so that the silence within seemed to crackle like ice under my feet. Nora sat in front of me by the confession box. There were a couple of old woman ahead of her, and then a miserable-looking poor devil came and wedged me in at the other side, so that I couldn't escape even if I had the courage. He joined his hands and rolled his eyes in the direction of the roof, muttering aspirations in an anguished tone, and I wondered had he a grandmother too. Only a grandmother could account for a fellow behaving in that heartbroken way, but he was better off than I, for he at least could go and confess his sins; while I would make a bad confession and then die in the night and be continually coming back and burning people's furniture.

Nora's turn came, and I heard the sound of something slamming, and then her voice as if butter wouldn't melt in her mouth, and then another slam, and out she came. God, the hypocrisy of women! Her eyes were lowered, her head was bowed, and her hands were joined very low down on her stomach, and she walked up the aisle to the side altar looking like a saint. You never saw such an exhibition of devotion, and I remembered the devilish malice with which she had tormented me all the way from our door, and wondered were all religious people like that, really. It was my turn now. With the fear of damnation in my soul I went in, and the confessional door closed of itself behind me.

It was pitch-dark and I couldn't see priest or anything else. Then I really began to be frightened. In the darkness it was a matter between God and me, and He had all the odds. He knew what my intentions were before I even started; I had no chance. All I had ever been told about confession got mixed up in my mind, and I knelt to one wall and said: "Bless me, father, for I have sinned; this is my first confession." I waited for a few minutes, but nothing happened, so I tried it on the other wall. Nothing happened there either. He had me spotted all right.

It must have been then that I noticed the shelf at about one height with my head. It was really a place for grown-up people to rest their elbows, but in my distracted state I thought it was probably the place you were supposed to kneel. Of course, it was on the high side and not very deep, but I was always good at climbing and managed to get up all right. Staying up was the trouble. There was room only for my knees, and nothing you could get a grip on but a sort of wooden moulding a bit above it. I held on to the moulding and repeated the words a little louder, and this time something happened all right. A slide was slammed back; a little light entered the box, and a man's voice said: "Who's there?"

"'Tis me, father," I said for fear he mightn't see me and go away again. I couldn't see him at all. The place the voice came from was under the moulding, about level with my knees, so I took a good grip of the moulding and swung myself down till I saw the atonished face of a young priest looking up at me. He had to put his head on one side to see me, and I had to put mine on one side to see him, so we were more or less talking to one another upside-down. It struck me as a queer way of hearing confessions, but I didn't feel it my place to criticize.

"Bless me, father, for I have sinned; this is my first confession," I rattled off all in one breath, and swung myself down the least shade more to make it easier for him.

"What are you doing up there?" he shouted in an angry voice, and the strain the politeness was putting on my hold of the moulding, and the shock of being addressed in such an uncivil tone, were too much for me. I lost my grip, tumbled, and hit the door an unmerciful wallop before I found myself flat on my back in the middle of the aisle. The people who had been waiting stood up with their mouths open. The priest opened the door of the middle box and came out, pushing his biretta back from his forehead; he looked something terrible. Then Nora came scampering down the aisle.

"Oh, you dirty little caffler!" she said. "I might have known you'd do it. I might have known you'd disgrace me. I can't leave you out of my sight for one minute."

Before I could even get to my feet to defend myself she bent down and gave me a clip across the ear. This reminded me that I was so stunned I had even forgotten to cry, so that people might think I wasn't hurt at all, when in fact I was probably maimed for life. I gave a roar out of me.

"What's all this about?" the priest hissed, getting angrier than ever and pushing Nora off me. "How dare you hit the child like that, you little vixen?"

"But I can't do my penance with him, father," Nora cried, cocking an outraged eye up at him.

"Well, go and do it, or I'll give you some more to do," he said, giving me a hand up. "Was it coming to confession you were, my poor man?" he asked me.

"'Twas, father," said I with a sob.

"Oh," he said respectfully, "a big hefty fellow like you must have terrible sins. Is this your first?"

"'Tis, father," said I.

"Worse and worse," he said gloomily. "The crimes of a lifetime. I don't know will I get rid of you at all today. You'd better wait now till I'm finished with these old ones. You can see by the looks of them they haven't much to tell."

"I will, father," I said with something approaching joy.

The relief of it was really enormous. Nora stuck out her tongue at me from behind his back, but I couldn't even be bothered retorting. I knew from the very moment that man opened his mouth that he was intelligent above the ordinary. When I had time to think, I saw how right I was. It only stood to reason that a fellow confessing after seven years would have more to tell than people that went every week. The crimes of a lifetime, exactly as he said. It was only what he expected, and the rest was the cackle of old women and girls with their talk of hell, the bishop, and the penitential psalms. That was all they knew. I started to make my examination of conscience, and barring the one bad business of my grandmother it didn't seem so bad.

The next time, the priest steered me into the confession box himself and left the shutter back the way I could see him get in and sit down at the further side of the grille from me.

"Well, now," he said, "what do they call you?"

"Jackie, father," said I.

"And what's a-trouble to you, Jackie?"

"Father," I said, feeling I might as well get it over while I had him in good humour, "I had it all arranged to kill my grandmother."

He seemed a bit shaken by that, all right, because he said nothing for quite a while.

"My goodness," he said at last, "that'd be a shocking thing to do. What put that into your head?"

"Father," I said, feeling very sorry for myself, "she's an awful woman."

"Is she?" he asked. "What way is she awful?"

"She takes porter, father," I said, knowing well from the way Mother talked of it that this was a mortal sin, and hoping it would make the priest take a more favourable view of my case.

"Oh, my!" he said, and I could see he was impressed.

"And snuff, father," said I.

"That's a bad case, sure enough, Jackie," he said.

"And she goes round in her bare feet, father," I went on in a rush of self-pity, "and she knows I don't like her, and she gives pennies to Nora and none to me, and my da sides with her and flakes me, and one night I was so heart-scalded I made up my mind I'd have to kill her."

"And what would you do with the body?" he asked with great interest.

"I was thinking I could chop that up and carry it away in a barrow I have," I said.

"Begor, Jackie," he said, "do you know you're a terrible child?"

"I know, father," I said, for I was just thinking the same thing myself. "I tried to kill Nora too with a bread-knife under the table, only I missed her."

"Is that the little girl that was beating you just now?" he asked.

" 'Tis, father."

"Someone will go for her with a bread-knife one day, and he won't miss her," he said rather cryptically. "You must have great courage. Between ourselves, there's a lot of people I'd like to do the same to but I'd never have the nerve. Hanging is an awful death."

"Is it, father?" I asked with the deepest interest—I was always very keen on hanging. "Did you ever see a fellow hanged?"

"Dozens of them," he said solemnly. "And they all died roaring."

"Jay!" I said.

"Oh, a horrible death!" he said with great satisfaction. "Lots of the fellows I saw killed their grandmothers too, but they all said 'twas never worth it."

He had me there for a full ten minutes talking, and then walked out the chapel yard with me. I was genuinely sorry to part with him, because he was the most entertaining character I'd ever met in the religious line. Outside, after the shadow of the church, the sunlight was like the roaring of waves on a beach; it dazzled me; and when the frozen silence melted and I heard the screech of trams on the road my heart soared. I knew now I wouldn't die in the night and come back, leaving marks on my mother's furniture. It would be a great worry to her, and the poor soul had enough.

Nora was sitting on the railing, waiting for me, and she put on a very sour puss when she saw the priest with me. She was made jealous because a priest had never come out of the church with her.

"Well," she asked coldly, after he left me, "what did he give you?"

"Three Hail Marys," I said.

"Three Hail Marys," she repeated incredulously. "You mustn't have told him anything."

"I told him everything," I said confidently.

"About Gran and all?"

"About Gran and all."

(All she wanted was to be able to go home and say I'd made a bad confession.)

"Did you tell him you went for me with the bread-knife?" she asked with a frown.

"I did to be sure."

"And he only gave you three Hail Marys?"

"That's all."

She slowly got down from the railing with a baffled air. Clearly, this was beyond her. As we mounted the steps back to the main road she looked at me suspiciously.

"What are you sucking?" she asked.

"Bullseyes."

"Was it the priest gave them to you?"

"'Twas."

"Lord God," she wailed bitterly, "some people have all the luck! 'Tis no advantage to anybody trying to be good. I might just as well be a sinner like you."

## Langston Hughes (1902-1967)

# *Theme For English B*

| | |
|---|---:|
| The instructor said, | 1 |
| | |
| Go home and write | 2 |
| a page tonight. | 3 |
| And let that page come out of you— | 4 |
| Then, it will be true. | 5 |
| | |
| I wonder if it's that simple? | 6 |
| | |
| I am twenty-two, colored, born in Winston-Salem. | 7 |
| I went to school there, then Durham, then here | 8 |
| to this college on the hill above Harlem. | 9 |
| I am the only colored student in my class. | 10 |
| The steps from the hill lead down to Harlem, | 11 |
| through a park, then I cross St. Nicholas, | 12 |
| Eighth Avenue, Seventh, and I come to the Y, | 13 |
| the Harlem Branch Y, where I take the elevator | 14 |
| up to my room, sit down, and write this page: | 15 |
| | |
| It's not easy to know what is true for you or me | 16 |
| at twenty-two, my age. But I guess I'm what | 17 |
| I feel and see and hear. Harlem, I hear you: | 18 |
| hear you, hear me—we two—you, me talk on this page. | 19 |
| (I hear New York, too.) Me—who? | 20 |
| | |
| Well, I like to eat, sleep, drink, and be in love. | 21 |
| I like to work, read, learn, and understand life. | 22 |
| I like a pipe for a Christmas present, | 23 |
| or records—Bessie, bop, or Bach. | 24 |

| | |
|---|---:|
| I guess being colored doesn't make me not like | 25 |
| the same things other folks like who are other races. | 26 |
| So will my page be colored that I write? | 27 |
| Being me, it will not be white. | 28 |
| But it will be | 29 |
| a part of you, instructor. | 30 |
| You are white— | 31 |
| yet a part of me, as I am a part of you. | 32 |
| That's American. | 33 |
| Sometimes perhaps you don't want to be a part of me. | 34 |
| Nor do I often want to be a part of you. | 35 |
| But we are, that's true! | 36 |
| As I learn from you, | 37 |
| I guess you learn from me— | 38 |
| although you're older—and white— | 39 |
| and somewhat more free. | 40 |
| This is my page for English B. | 41 |

## Eudora Welty (1909–        )

# *A Worn Path*

It was December—a bright frozen day in the early morning. Far out in the country there was an old Negro woman with her head tied in a red rag, coming along a path through the pinewoods. Her name was Phoenix Jackson. She was very old and small and she walked slowly in the dark pine shadows, moving a little from side to side in her steps, with the balanced heaviness and lightness of a pendulum in a grandfather clock. She carried a thin, small cane made from an umbrella, and with this she kept tapping the frozen earth in front of her. This made a grave and persistent noise in the still air, that seemed meditative like the chirping of a solitary little bird.

She wore a dark striped dress reaching down to her shoe tops, and an equally long apron of bleached sugar sacks, with a full pocket: all neat and tidy, but every time she took a step she might have fallen over her shoelaces, which dragged from her unlaced shoes. She looked straight ahead. Her eyes were blue with age. Her skin had a pattern all its own of numberless branching wrinkles and as though a whole little tree stood in the middle of her forehead, but a golden color ran underneath, and the two knobs of her cheeks were illumined by a yellow burning under the dark. Under the rag her hair came down on her neck in the frailest of ringlets, still black, and with an odor like copper.

Now and then there was a quivering in the thicket. Old Phoenix said, "Out of my way, all you foxes, owls, beetles, jack rabbits, coons and wild animals! . . . Keep out from under these feet, little bob-whites. . . . Keep the big wild hogs out of my path. Don't let none of those come running my direction. I got a long way." Under her small black-freckled hand her cane, limber as a buggy whip, would switch at the brush as if to rouse up any hiding things.

On she went. The woods were deep and still. The sun made the pine needles almost too bright to look at, up where the wind rocked. The cones dropped as light as feathers. Down in the hollow was the mourning dove—it was not too late for him.

The path ran up a hill. "Seem like there is chains about my feet, time I get this far," she said, in the voice of argument old people keep to use with themselves. "Something always take a hold of me on this hill—pleads I should stay."

After she got to the top she turned and gave a full, severe look behind her where she had come. "Up through pines," she said at length. "Now down through oaks."

Her eyes opened their widest, and she started down gently. But before she got to the bottom of the hill a bush caught her dress.

Her fingers were busy and intent, but her skirts were full and long, so that before she could pull them free in one place they were caught in another. It was not possible to allow the dress to tear. "I in the thorny bush," she said. "Thorns, you doing your appointed work. Never want to let folks pass, no sir. Old eyes thought you was a pretty little *green* bush."

Finally, trembling all over, she stood free, and after a moment dared to stoop for her cane.

"Sun so high!" she cried, leaning back and looking, while the thick tears went over her eyes. "The time getting all gone here."

At the foot of this hill was a place where a log was laid across the creek.

"Now comes the trial," said Phoenix.

Putting her right foot out, she mounted the log and shut her eyes. Lifting her skirt, leveling her cane fiercely before her, like a festival figure in some parade, she began to march across. Then she opened her eyes and she was safe on the other side.

"I wasn't as old as I thought," she said.

But she sat down to rest. She spread her skirts on the bank around her and folded her hands over her knees. Up above her was a tree in a pearly cloud of mistletoe. She did not dare to close her eyes, and when a little boy brought her a plate with a slice of marble-cake on it she spoke to him. "That would be acceptable," she said. But when she went to take it there was just her own hand in the air.

So she left that tree, and had to go through a barbed-wire fence. There she had to creep and crawl, spreading her knees and stretching her fingers like a baby trying to climb the steps. But she talked loudly to herself: she could not let her dress be torn now, so late in the day, and she could not pay for having her arm or her leg sawed off if she got caught fast where she was.

At last she was safe through the fence and risen up out in the clearing. Big dead trees, like black men with one arm, were standing in the purple stalks of the withered cotton field. There sat a buzzard.

"Who you watching?"

In the furrow she made her way along.

"Glad this not the season for bulls," she said, looking sideways, "and the good Lord made his snakes to curl up and sleep in the winter. A pleasure I don't see no two-headed snake coming around that tree, where it come once. It took a while to get by him, back in the summer."

She passed through the old cotton and went into a field of dead corn. It whispered and shook and was taller than her head. "Through the maze now," she said, for there was no path.

Then there was something tall, black, and skinny there, moving before her.

At first she took it for a man. It could have been a man dancing in the field. But she stood still and listened, and it did not make a sound. It was as silent as a ghost.

"Ghost," she said sharply, "who be you the ghost of? For I have heard of nary death close by."

But there was no answer—only the ragged dancing in the wind.

She shut her eyes, reached out her hand, and touched a sleeve. She found a coat and inside that an emptiness, cold as ice.

"You scarecrow," she said. Her face lighted. "I ought to be shut up for good," she said with laughter. "My senses is gone. I too old. I the oldest people I ever know. Dance, old scarecrow," she said, "while I dancing with you."

She kicked her foot over the furrow, and with mouth drawn down, shook her head once or twice in a little strutting way. Some husks blew down and whirled in streamers about her skirts.

Then she went on, parting her way from side to side with the cane, through the whispering field. At last she came to the end, to a wagon track where the silver grass blew between the red ruts. The quail were walking around like pullets, seeming all dainty and unseen.

"Walk pretty," she said. "This is the easy place. This the easy going."

She followed the track, swaying through the quiet bare fields, through the little strings of trees silver in their dead leaves, past cabins silver from weather, with the doors and windows boarded shut, all like old women under a spell sitting there. "I walking in their sleep," she said, nodding her head vigorously.

In a ravine she went where a spring was silently flowing through a hollow log. Old Phoenix bent and drank. "Sweet-gum makes the water sweet," she said, and drank more. "Nobody know who made this well, for it was here when I was born."

The track crossed a swampy part where the moss hung as white as lace from every limb. "Sleep on, alligators, and blow your bubbles." Then the track went into the road.

Deep, deep the road went down between the high green-colored banks. Overhead the live-oaks met, and it was as dark as a cave.

A black dog with a lolling tongue came up out of the weeds by the ditch. She was meditating, and not ready, and when he came at her she only hit him a little with her cane. Over she went in the ditch, like a little puff of milkweed.

Down there, her senses drifted away. A dream visited her, and she reached her hand up, but nothing reached down and gave her a pull. So she lay there and presently went to talking. "Old woman," she said to herself, "that black dog come up out of the weeds to stall you off, and now there he sitting on his fine tail, smiling at you."

A white man finally came along and found her—a hunter, a young man, with his dog on a chain.

"Well, Granny!" he laughed. "What are you doing there?"

"Lying on my back like a June-bug waiting to be turned over, mister," she said, reaching up her hand.

He lifted her up, gave her a swing in the air, and set her down. "Anything broken, Granny?"

"No sir, them old dead weeds is springy enough," said Phoenix, when she had got her breath. "I thank you for your trouble."

"Where do you live, Granny?" he asked, while the two dogs were growling at each other.

"Away back yonder, sir, behind the ridge. You can't even see it from here."

"On your way home?"

"No sir, I going to town."

"Why, that's too far! That's as far as I walk when I come out myself, and I get something for my trouble." He patted the stuffed bag he carried, and there hung down a little closed claw. It was one of the bob-whites, with its beak hooked bitterly to show it was dead. "Now you go on home, Granny!"

"I bound to go to town, mister," said Phoenix. "The time come around."

He gave another laugh, filling the whole landscape. "I know you old colored people! Wouldn't miss going to town to see Santa Claus!"

But something held old Phoenix very still. The deep lines in her face went into a fierce and different radiation. Without warning, she had seen with her own eyes a flashing nickel fall out of the man's pocket onto the ground.

"How old are you, Granny?" he was saying.

"There is no telling, mister," she said, "no telling."

Then she gave a little cry and clapped her hands and said, "Git on away from here, dog! Look! Look at that dog!" She laughed as if in admiration. "He ain't scared of nobody. He a big black dog." She whispered, "Sic him!"

"Watch me get rid of that cur," said the man. "Sic him, Pete! Sic him!"

Phoenix heard the dogs fighting, and heard the man running and throwing sticks. She even heard a gunshot. But she was slowly bending forward by that time, further and further forward, the lids stretched down over her eyes, as if she were doing this in her sleep. Her chin was lowered almost to her knees. The yellow palm of her hand came out from the fold of her apron. Her fingers slid down and along the ground under the piece of money with the grace and care they would have in lifting an egg from under a setting hen. Then she slowly straightened up, she stood erect, and the nickel was in her apron pocket. A bird flew by. Her lips moved. "God watching me the whole time. I come to stealing."

The man came back, and his own dog panted about them. "Well, I scared him off that time," he said, and then he laughed and lifted his gun and pointed it at Phoenix.

She stood straight and faced him.

"Doesn't the gun scare you?" he said, still pointing it.

"No, sir, I seen plenty go off closer by, in my day, and for less than what I done," she said, holding utterly still.

He smiled, and shouldered the gun. "Well, Granny," he said, "you must be a hundred years old, and scared of nothing. I'd give you a dime if I had any money with me. But you take my advice and stay home, and nothing will happen to you."

"I bound to go on my way, mister," said Phoenix. She inclined her head in the red rag. Then they went in different directions, but she could hear the gun shooting again and again over the hill.

She walked on. The shadows hung from the oak trees to the road like curtains. Then she smelled wood-smoke, and smelled the river, and she saw a steeple and the cabins on their steep steps. Dozens of little black children whirled around her. There ahead was Natchez shining. Bells were ringing. She walked on.

In the paved city it was Christmas time. There were red and green electric lights strung and crisscrossed everywhere, and all turned on in the daytime. Old Phoenix would have been lost if she had not distrusted her eyesight and depended on her feet to know where to take her.

She paused quietly on the sidewalk where people were passing by. A lady came along in the crowd, carrying an armful of red-, green- and silver-wrapped presents; she gave off perfume like the red roses in hot summer, and Phoenix stopped her.

"Please, missy, will you lace up my shoe?" She held up her foot.

"What do you want, Grandma?"

"See my shoe," said Phoenix. "Do all right for out in the country, but wouldn't look right to go in a big building."

"Stand still then, Grandma," said the lady. She put her packages down on the sidewalk beside her and laced and tied both shoes tightly.

"Can't lace 'em with a cane," said Phoenix. "Thank you, missy. I doesn't mind asking a nice lady to tie up my shoe, when I gets out on the street."

Moving slowly and from side to side, she went into the big building, and into a tower of steps, where she walked up and around and around until her feet knew to stop.

She entered a door, and there she saw nailed up on the wall the document that had been stamped with the gold seal and framed in the gold frame, which matched the dream that was hung up in her head.

"Here I be," she said. There was a fixed and ceremonial stiffness over her body.

"A charity case, I suppose," said an attendant who sat at the desk before her.

But Phoenix only looked above her head. There was sweat on her face, the wrinkles in her skin shone like a bright net.

"Speak up, Grandma," the woman said. "What's your name? We must have your history, you know. Have you been here before? What seems to be the trouble with you?"

Old Phoenix only gave a twitch to her face as if a fly were bothering her.

"Are you deaf?" cried the attendant.

But then the nurse came in.

"Oh, that's just old Aunt Phoenix," she said. "She doesn't come for herself—she has a little grandson. She makes these trips just as regular as clockwork. She lives away back off the Old Natchez Trace." She bent down. "Well, Aunt Phoenix, why don't you just take a seat? We won't keep you standing after your long trip." She pointed.

The old woman sat down, bolt upright in the chair.

"Now, how is the boy?" asked the nurse.

Old Phoenix did not speak.

"I said, how is the boy?"

But Phoenix only waited and stared straight ahead, her face very solemn and withdrawn into rigidity.

"Is his throat any better?" asked the nurse. "Aunt Phoenix, don't you hear me? Is your grandson's throat any better since the last time you came for the medicine?"

With her hands on her knees, the old woman waited, silent, erect and motionless, just as if she were in armor.

"You mustn't take up our time this way, Aunt Phoenix," the nurse said. "Tell us quickly about your grandson, and get it over. He isn't dead, is he?"

At last there came a flicker and then a flame of comprehension across her face, and she spoke.

"My grandson. It was my memory had left me. There I sat and forgot why I made my long trip."

"Forgot?" The nurse frowned. "After you came so far?"

Then Phoenix was like an old woman begging a dignified forgiveness for waking up frightened in the night. "I never did go to school, I was too old at the Surrender," she said in a soft voice. "I'm an old woman without an education. It was my memory fail me. My little grandson, he is just the same, and I forgot it in the coming."

"Throat never heals, does it?" said the nurse, speaking in a loud, sure voice to old Phoenix. By now she had a card with something written on it, a little list. "Yes. Swallowed lye. When was it?—January—two, three years ago—"

Phoenix spoke unasked now. "No, missy, he not dead, he just the same. Every little while his throat begin to close up again, and he not able to swallow. He not get his breath. He not able to help himself. So the time come around, and I go on another trip for the soothing medicine."

"All right. The doctor said as long as you came to get it, you could have it," said the nurse. "But it's an obstinate case."

"My little grandson, he sit up there in the house all wrapped up, waiting by himself," Phoenix went on. "We is the only two left in the world. He suffer and it don't seem to put him back at all. He got a sweet look. He going to last. He wear a little patch quilt and peep out holding his mouth open like a little bird. I remembers so plain now. I not going to forget him again, no, the whole enduring time. I could tell him from all the others in creation."

"All right." The nurse was trying to hush her now. She brought her a bottle of medicine. "Charity," she said, making a check mark in a book.

Old Phoenix held the bottle close to her eyes, and then carefully put it into her pocket.

"I thank you," she said.

"It's Christmas time, Grandma," said the attendant. "Could I give you a few pennies out of my purse?"

"Five pennies is a nickel," said Phoenix stiffly.

"Here's a nickel," said the attendant.

Phoenix rose carefully and held out her hand. She received the nickel and then fished the other nickel out of her pocket and laid it beside the new one. She stared at her palm closely, with her head on one side.

Then she gave a tap with her cane on the floor.

"This is what come to me to do," she said. "I going to the store and buy my child a little windmill they sells, made out of paper. He going to find it hard to believe there such a thing in the world. I'll march myself back where he waiting, holding it straight up in this hand."

She lifted her free hand, gave a little nod, turned around, and walked out of the doctor's office. Then her slow step began on the stairs, going down.

# Index